THE NEW
PALGRAVE

GAME
THEORY

THE NEW PALGRAVE

GAME THEORY

EDITED BY

JOHN EATWELL · MURRAY MILGATE · PETER NEWMAN

W · W · NORTON

NEW YORK · LONDON

© The Macmillan Press Limited, 1987, 1989

First published in
The New Palgrave: A Dictionary of Economics
Edited by John Eatwell, Murray Milgate and Peter Newman
in four volumes, 1987

The New Palgrave is a trademark of
The Macmillan Press Limited

First American Edition, 1989
All rights reserved.

ISBN 0-393-02733-3

ISBN 0-393-95858-2   {PBK.}

W. W. Norton & Company, Inc.
500 Fifth Avenue
New York, NY 10110

W. W. Norton & Company, Ltd.
37 Great Russell Street
London WC1B 3NU

Printed in Hong Kong

1   2   3   4   5   6   7   8   9   0

Contents

Contents

Acknowledgements

The following contributors (articles shown in parentheses) acknowledge support from public bodies or permission to reprint copyright material:

John C. Harsanyi (Bargaining), financial support from the National Science Foundation through grant SES82-18938 administered by the Center for Research in Management, University of California, Berkeley.
Werner Hildenbrand (Cores), financial support by the Deutsche Forschungs-gemeinschaft, Sonderforschungsbereich 303 and MSRI University of California, Berkeley.

General Preface

The books in this series are the offspring of *The New Palgrave: A Dictionary of Economics*. Published in late 1987, the *Dictionary* has rapidly become a standard reference work in economics. However, its four heavy tomes containing over four million words on the whole range of economic thought is not a form convenient to every potential user. For many students and teachers it is simply too bulky, too comprehensive and too expensive for everyday use.

By developing the present series of compact volumes of reprints from the original work, we hope that some of the intellectual wealth of *The New Palgrave* will become accessible to much wider groups of readers. Each of the volumes is devoted to a particular branch of economics, such as econometrics or general equilibrium or money, with a scope corresponding roughly to a university course on that subject. Apart from correction of misprints, etc. the content of each of its reprinted articles is exactly the same as that of the original. In addition, a few brand new entries have been commissioned especially for the series, either to fill an apparent gap or more commonly to include topics that have risen to prominence since the dictionary was originally commissioned.

As *The New Palgrave* is the sole parent of the present series, it may be helpful to explain that it is the modern successor to the excellent *Dictionary of Political Economy* edited by R.H. Inglis Palgrave and published in three volumes in 1894, 1896 and 1899. A second and slightly modified version, edited by Henry Higgs, appeared during the mid-1920s. These two editions each contained almost 4,000 entries, but many of those were simply brief definitions and many of the others were devoted to peripheral topics such as foreign coinage, maritime commerce, and Scottish law. To make room for the spectacular growth in economics over the last 60 years while keeping still to a manageable length, *The New Palgrave* concentrated instead on economic theory, its originators, and its closely cognate disciplines. Its nearly 2,000 entries (commissioned from over 900 scholars) are all self-contained essays, sometimes brief but never mere definitions.

General Preface

Apart from its biographical entries, *The New Palgrave* is concerned chiefly with theory rather than fact, doctrine rather than data; and it is not at all clear how theory and doctrine, as distinct from facts and figures, *should* be treated in an encyclopaedia. One way is to treat everything from a particular point of view. Broadly speaking, that was the way of Diderot's classic *Encyclopédie raisonée* (1751–1772), as it was also of Léon Say's *Nouveau dictionnaire d'économie politique* (1891–2). Sometimes, as in articles by Quesnay and Turgot in the *Encyclopédie*, this approach has yielded entries of surpassing brilliance. Too often, however, both the range of subjects covered and the quality of the coverage itself are seriously reduced by such a self-limiting perspective. Thus the entry called '*Méthode*' in the first edition of Say's *Dictionnaire* asserted that the use of mathematics in economics 'will only ever be in the hands of a few', and the dictionary backed up that claim by choosing not to have any entry on Cournot.

Another approach is to have each entry take care to reflect within itself varying points of view. This may help the student temporarily, as when preparing for an examination. But in a subject like economics, the Olympian detachment which this approach requires often places a heavy burden on the author, asking for a scrupulous account of doctrines he or she believes to be at best wrong-headed. Even when an especially able author does produce a judicious survey article, it is surely too much to ask that it also convey just as much enthusiasm for those theories thought misguided as for those found congenial. Lacking an enthusiastic exposition, however, the disfavoured theories may then be studied less closely than they deserve.

The New Palgrave did not ask its authors to treat economic theory from any particular point of view, except in one respect to be discussed below. Nor did it call for surveys. Instead, each author was asked to make clear his or her own views of the subject under discussion, and for the rest to be as fair and accurate as possible, without striving to be 'judicious'. A balanced perspective on each topic was always the aim, the ideal. But it was to be sought not *internally*, within each article, but *externally*, between articles, with the reader rather than the writer handed the task of achieving a personal balance between differing views.

For a controversial topic, a set of several more or less synonymous headwords, matched by a broad diversity of contributors, was designed to produce enough variety of opinion to help form the reader's own synthesis; indeed, such diversity will be found in most of the individual volumes in this series.

This approach was not without its problems. Thus, the prevalence of uncertainty in the process of commissioning entries sometimes produced a less diverse outcome than we had planned. 'I can call spirits from the vasty deep,' said Owen Glendower. 'Why, so can I,' replied Hotspur, 'or so can any man;/ But will they come when you do call for them?' In our experience, not quite as often as we would have liked.

The one point of view we did urge upon every one of *Palgrave*'s authors was to write from an historical perspective. For each subject its contributor was asked to discuss not only present problems but also past growth and future prospects. This request was made in the belief that knowledge of the historical development of any theory enriches our present understanding of it, and so helps to construct better theories for the future. The authors' response to the request was generally so positive that, as the reader of any of these volumes will discover, the resulting contributions amply justified that belief.

John Eatwell
Murray Milgate
Peter Newman

Preface

Game Theory provides economists with a systematic way of analysing problems of *strategic behaviour* where one agent's actions depend essentially on what other agents may do. As early as 1838 Cournot had made clear that problems of economic optimization are greatly simplified when either no other agents are present, or there are unboundedly many. In the former case – Crusoe on his island – there are no external variables under human control; in the latter – Edgeworth's 'multeity of atoms' – there are so many that, in the limiting case of perfect competition, their influence is wholly and parametrically incorporated into market prices.

Matters are quite different when the number of agents is more than one but not large enough for each agent safely to ignore the identifiable influence that others' actions have on the outcomes of his decisions, and vice versa. For then strategic behaviour raises difficult and seemingly insoluble problems. 'I know that if I increase my output my rival will raise hers, but I don't know by how much; and she has the same problem with me; and she also knows that I know that if I increase my output she will raise hers, and that I don't know by how much; …' and so on.

Cournot understood this very well. His pioneering attempt to confront these problems produced a model of duopoly that, for all its difficulties, remains the point of departure for most non-game-theoretic analyses of oligopoly. With the advent of imperfect competition theory in the 1930s there appeared a profusion of oligopoly theories derived from a host of plausible assumptions, few of them readily testable by empirical evidence. It sometimes seemed as if every theorist aimed to produce a model of his own before breakfast each morning, limbering up with mental callisthenics.

No wonder that distinguished reviewers such as Leonid Hurwicz and Richard Stone eagerly welcomed the appearance in 1944 of von Neumann and Morgenstern's great work *The Theory of Games and Economic Behavior*. At last economists were properly equipped with powerful and elegant methods of tackling a subject that had become increasingly baroque, much as Newtonian methods of celestial mechanics had displaced the primitive and increasingly *ad hoc* models of the ancients.

Surprisingly and embarrassingly and for reasons hard to fathom, over the next twenty years game theory failed to live up to its early promise for economics. It may have been because the theory of two-person constant-sum games, the best-developed part of the work, appeared to be the least applicable to economics, whilst its approach to the more relevant *n* person games seemed tentative at best, despite (or perhaps because of) its length. The fact remains that, even though as early as 1950 Nash had developed an appealing concept of solution for non-cooperative games, economists still shied away from applying game theory to strategic economic behaviour, its natural home in our discipline.

There was, however, much progress in the mathematics of game theory, which Abraham Wald applied fruitfully to statistical inference. Rather paradoxically, some of this formal structure was used by Debreu and others to prove the existence of (perfectly) *competitive* equilibrium. Even more paradoxically, in those years the book's main direct influence on economics was its pioneering axiomation of expected utility theory, an application which the authors had considered so subsidiary to their main theme that it was confined to a mere appendix in the second (1947) edition.

Probably more important for economics was the work's programmatic impact. Its endorsement of formal methods, and its use of algebra and convexity theory rather than calculus, contributed significantly to both the rapid growth and the nature of economic theory during this very productive period. But none of this was relevant to the analysis of strategic behaviour.

That languished mightily until the mid-1960s, when important papers by Harsanyi and by Selten and others appeared. By the 1970s this trickle of articles had become a swiftly moving stream, and by the 1980s a roaring flood that threatened to engulf the rest of microeconomics, a sea-change that was effected with apparently no new fundamental mathematical theorems beyond those of von Neumann and Nash. Perhaps one reason is that, following the classical work of Arrow, Debreu, and McKenzie and many others, the theory of competitive systems had itself begun to encounter diminishing returns. Clever young theorists, allocating their resources efficiently, thus turned naturally to other topics such as the seductions of strategic behaviour. Now almost every week brings a new solution concept for non-cooperative games, a yet more subtle refinement of Nash equilibrium. Sometimes, it seems that we are back again at our early morning callisthenics, only this time using high-tech equipment.

The Editors

Game Theory

ROBERT J. AUMANN

INTRODUCTION

'Interactive Decision Theory' would perhaps be a more descriptive name for the discipline usually called Game Theory. This discipline concerns the behaviour of decision makers (*players*) whose decisions affect each other. As in non-interactive (one-person) decision theory, the analysis is from a rational, rather than a psychological or sociological viewpoint. The term 'Game Theory' stems from the formal resemblance of interactive decision problems (*games*) to parlour games such as chess, bridge, poker, monopoly, diplomacy or battleship. The term also underscores the rational, 'cold', calculating nature of the analysis.

The major applications of game theory are to economics, political science (on both the national and international levels), tactical and strategic military problems, evolutionary biology and, most recently, computer science. There are also important connections with accounting, statistics, the foundations of mathematics, social psychology and branches of philosophy such as epistemology and ethics. Game theory is a sort of umbrella or 'unified field' theory for the rational side of social science, where 'social' is interpreted broadly, to include human as well as non-human players (computers, animals, plants). Unlike other approaches to disciplines like economics or political science, game theory does not use different, ad-hoc constructs to deal with various specific issues, such as perfect competition, monopoly, oligopoly, international trade, taxation, voting, deterrence and so on. Rather, it develops methodologies that apply in principle to *all* interactive situations, then sees where these methodologies lead in each specific application. Often it turns out that there are close relations between results obtained from the general game-theoretic methods and from the more ad-hoc approaches. In other cases, the game-theoretic approach leads to new insights, not suggested by other approaches.

We use a historical framework for discussing some of the basic ideas of the theory, as well as a few selected applications. But the viewpoint will be modern; the older ideas will be presented from the perspective of where they have led. Needless to say, we do not even attempt a systematic historical survey.

1910–1930

During these earliest years, game theory was preoccupied with *strictly competitive* games, more commonly known as *two-person zero-sum* games. In these games, there is no point in cooperation or joint action of any kind: if one outcome is preferred to another by one player, then the preference is necessarily reversed for the other. This is the case for most two-person parlour games, such as chess or two-sided poker; but it seems inappropriate for most economic or political applications. Nevertheless, the study of the strictly competitive case has, over the years, turned out remarkably fruitful; many of the concepts and results generated in connection with this case are in fact much more widely applicable, and have become cornerstones of the more general theory. These include the following:

(i) The *extensive* (or *tree*) *form* of a game, consisting of a complete formal description of how the game is played, with a specification of the sequence in which the players move, what they know at the times they must move, how chance occurrences enter the picture, and the *payoff* to each player at the end of play. Introduced by von Neumann (1928), the extensive form was later generalized by Kuhn (1953), and has been enormously influential far beyond zero-sum theory.

(ii) The fundamental concept of *strategy* (or pure strategy) of a player, defined as a complete plan for that player to play the game, as a function of what he observes during the course of play, about the play of others and about chance occurrences affecting the game. Given a strategy for each player, the rules of the game determine a unique outcome of the game and hence a payoff for each player. In the case of two-person zero-sum games, the sum of the two payoffs is zero; this expresses the fact that the preferences of the players over the outcomes are precisely opposed.

(iii) The strategic (or matrix) form of a game. Given strategies $s^1, \ldots, s^n$ for each of the n players, the rules of the game determine a unique outcome, and hence a payoff $H^i(s^1, \ldots, s^n)$ for each player i. The *strategic* form is simply the function that associates to each profile $s := (s^1, \ldots, s^n)$ of strategies, the *payoff profile*

$$H(s) := (H^1(s), \ldots, H^n(s)).$$

For two-person games, the strategic form often appears as a matrix: the rows and columns represent pure strategies of Players 1 and 2 respectively, whereas the entries are the corresponding payoff profiles. For zero-sum games, of course, if suffices to give the payoff to Player 1. It has been said that the simple idea of thinking of a game in its matrix form is in itself one of the greatest contributions of game theory. In facing an interactive situation, there is a great temptation to think only in terms of 'what should I do?'. When one writes down the matrix, one is led to a different viewpoint, one that explicitly takes into account that the other players are also facing a decision problem.

(iv) The concept of *mixed* or *randomized* strategy, indicates that rational play is not in general describable by specifying a single pure strategy. Rather, it is often non-deterministic, with specified probabilities associated with each one of a specified set of pure strategies. When randomized strategies are used, payoff must be replaced by expected payoff. Justifying the use of expected payoff in this context is what led to expected utility theory, whose influence extends far beyond game theory (see *1930–1950*, viii).

(v) The concept of 'individual rationality'. The *security level* of Player i is the amount max min $H^i(s)$ that he can guarantee to himself, independent of what the other players do (here the max is over i's strategies, and the min is over $(n-1)$-tuples of strategies of the players other than i). An outcome is called *individually rational* if it yields each player at least his security level. In the game tic-tac-toe, for example, the only individually rational outcome is a draw; and indeed, it does not take a reasonably bright child very long to learn that 'correct' play in tic-tac-toe always leads to a draw.

Individual rationality may be thought of in terms of pure strategies or, as is

3

more usual, in terms of mixed strategies. In the latter case, what is being 'guaranteed' is not an actual payoff, but an expectation; the word 'guarantee' means that this level of payoff can be attained in the mean, regardless of what the other players do. This 'mixed' security level is always at least as high as the 'pure' one. In the case of tic-tac-toe, each player can guarantee a draw even in the stronger sense of pure strategies. Games like this – i.e. having only one individually rational payoff profile in the 'pure' sense – are called *strictly determined*.

Not all games are strictly determined, not even all two-person zero-sum games. One of the simplest imaginable games is the one that game theorists call 'matching pennies', and children call 'choosing up' ('odds and evens'). Each player privately turns a penny either heads up or tails up. If the choices match, 1 gives 2 his penny; otherwise, 2 gives 1 his penny. In the pure sense, neither player can guarantee more than -1, and hence the game is not strictly determined. But in expectation, each player can guarantee 0, simply by turning the coin heads up or tails up with $1/2-1/2$ probabilities. Thus $(0,0)$ is the only payoff profile that is individually rational in the mixed sense. Games like this – i.e. having only one individually rational payoff profile in the 'mixed' sense – are called *determined*. In a determined game, the (mixed) security level is called the *value*, strategies guaranteeing it *optimal*.

(vi) *Zermelo's theorem*. The very first theorem of game theory (Zermelo, 1913) asserts that chess is strictly determined. Interestingly, the proof does not construct 'correct' strategies explicitly; and indeed, it is not known to this day whether the 'correct' outcome of chess is a win for white, a win for black, or a draw. The theorem extends easily to a wide class of parlour games, including checkers, go, and chinese checkers, as well as less well-known games such as hex and gnim (Gale, 1979, 1974); the latter two are especially interesting in that one can use Zermelo's theorem to show that Player 1 can force a win, though the proof is non-constructive, and no winning strategy is in fact known. Zermelo's theorem does not extend to card games such as bridge and poker, nor to the variant of chess known as kriegsspiel, where the players cannot observe their opponents' moves directly. The precise condition for the proof to work is that the game be a two-person zero-sum game of *perfect information*. This means that there are no simultaneous moves, and that everything is open and 'above-board': at any given time, all relevant information known to one player is known to all players.

The domain of Zermelo's theorem – two-person zero-sum games of perfect information – seems at first rather limited; but the theorem has reverberated through the decades, creating one of the main strands of game theoretic thought. To explain some of the developments, we must anticipate the notion of *strategic equilibrium* (Nash, 1951; see *1950–1960*, i). To remove the two-person zero-sum restriction, H.W. Kuhn (1953) replaced the notion of 'correct', individually rational play by that of equilibrium. He then proved that *every n-person game of perfect information has an equilibrium in pure strategies*.

In proving this theorem, Kuhn used the notion of a *subgame* of a game;

this turned out crucial in later developments of strategic equilibrium theory, particularly in its economic applications. A subgame relates to the whole game like a subgroup to the whole group or a linear subspace to the whole space; while part of the larger game, it is self-contained, can be played in its own right. More precisely, if at any time all the players know everything that has happened in the game up to that time, then what happens from then on constitutes a subgame.

From Kuhn's proof it follows that every equilibrium (not necessarily pure) of a subgame can be extended to an equilibrium of the whole game. This, in turn, implies that every game has equilibria that remain equilibria when restricted to any subgame. R. Selten (1965) called such equilibria *subgame perfect*. In games of perfect information, the equilibria that the Zermelo–Kuhn proof yields are all subgame perfect.

But not all equilibria are subgame perfect, even in games of perfect information. Subgame perfection implies that when making choices, a player looks forward and assumes that the choices that will subsequently be made, by himself and by others, will be rational; i.e. in equilibrium. Threats which it would be irrational to carry through are ruled out. And it is precisely this kind of forward-looking rationality that is most suited to economic applications.

Interestingly, it turns out that subgame perfection is not enough to capture the idea of forward-looking rationality. More subtle concepts are needed. We return to this subject below, when we discuss the great flowering of strategic equilibrium theory that has taken place since 1975, and that coincides with an increased preoccupation with its economic applications. The point we wished to make here is that these developments have their roots in Zermelo's theorem.

A second circle of ideas to which Zermelo's theorem led has to do with the foundations of mathematics. The starting point is the idea of a game of perfect information with an infinite sequence of stages. Infinitely long games are important models for interactive situations with an indefinite time horizon – i.e. in which the players acts as if there will always be a tomorrow.

To fix ideas, let A be any subset of the unit interval (the set of real numbers between 0 and 1). Suppose two players move alternately, each choosing a digit between 1 and 9 at each stage. The resulting infinite sequence of digits is the decimal expansion of a number in the unit interval. Let G_A be the game in which 1 wins if this number is in A, and 2 wins otherwise. Using Set Theory's 'Axiom of Choice', Gale and Stewart (1953) showed that Zermelo's theorem is false in this situation. One can choose A so that G_A is not strictly determined; that is, against each pure strategy of 1, Player 2 has a winning pure strategy, and against each pure strategy of 2, Player 1 has a winning pure strategy. They also showed that if A is open or closed, then G_A *is* strictly determined.

Both of these results led to significant developments in foundational mathematics. The axiom of choice had long been suspect in the eyes of mathematicians; the extremely anti-intuitive nature of the Gale–Stewart non-determinateness example was an additional nail in its coffin, and led to an alternative axiom, which asserts that G_A is strictly determined for every set A. This axiom, which contradicts the

5

axiom of choice, has been used to provide an alternative axiomatization for set theory (Mycielski and Steinhaus, 1964), and this in turn has spawned a large literature (see Moschovakis, 1980, 1983). On the other hand, the positive result of Gale and Stewart was successively generalized to wider and wider families of sets A that are 'constructible' in the appropriate sense (Wolfe, 1955; Davis, 1964), culminating in the theorem of Martin (1975), according to which G_A is strictly determined whenever A is a Borel set.

Another kind of perfect information game with infinitely many stages is the *differential game.* Here time is continuous but usually of fine duration; a decision must be made at each instant, so to speak. Typical examples are games of pursuit. The theory of differential games was first developed during the 1950s by Rufus Isaacs at the Rand Corporation; his book on the subject was published in 1965, and since then the theory has proliferated greatly. A differential game need not necessarily be of perfect information, but very little is known about those that are not. Some economic examples may be found in Case (1979).

(vii) *The minimax theorem.* The minimax theorem of von Neumann (1928) asserts that every two-person zero-sum game with finitely many pure strategies for each player is determined; that is, when mixed strategies are admitted, it has precisely one individually rational payoff vector. This had previously been verified by E. Borel (e.g. 1924) for several special cases, but Borel was unable to obtain a general proof. The theorem lies a good deal deeper than Zermelo's, both conceptually and technically.

For many years, minimax was considered the elegant centrepiece of game theory. Books about game theory concentrated on two-person zero-sum games in strategic form, often paying only desultory attention to the non-zero sum theory. Outside references to game theory often gave the impression that non-zero sum games do not exist, or at least play no role in the theory.

The reaction eventually set in, as it was bound to. Game theory came under heavy fire for its allegedly exclusive concern with a special case that has little interest in the applications. Game theorists responded by belittling the importance of the minimax theorem. During the fall semester of 1964, the writer of these lines gave a beginning course in game theory at Yale University, without once even mentioning the minimax theorem.

All this is totally unjustified. Except for the period up to 1928 and a short period in the late Forties, game theory was never exclusively or even mainly concerned with the strictly competitive case. The forefront of research was always in n-person or non-zero sum games. The false impression given of the discipline was due to the strictly competitive theory being easier to present in books, more 'elegant' and complete. But for more than half a century, that is not where most of the action has been.

Nevertheless, it is a great mistake to belittle minimax. While not the centrepiece of game theory, it *is* a vital cornerstone. We have already seen how the most fundamental concepts of the general theory – extensive form, pure strategies, strategic form, randomization, utility theory – were spawned in connection with the minimax theorem. But its importance goes considerably beyond this.

The fundamental concept of non-cooperative n-person game theory – the strategic equilibrium of Nash (1951) – is an outgrowth of minimax, and the proof of its existence is modelled on a previously known proof the minimax theorem. In cooperative n-person theory, individual rationality is used to define the set of *imputations*, on which much of the cooperative theory is based. In the theory of repeated games, individual rationality also plays a fundamental role.

In many areas of interest – stochastic games, repeated games of incomplete information, continuous games (i.e. with a continuum of pure strategies), differential games, games played by automata, games with vector payoffs – the strictly competitive case already presents a good many of the conceptual and technical difficulties that are present in general. In these areas, the two-person zero-sum theory has become an indispensable spawning and proving ground, where ideas are developed and tested in a relatively familiar, 'friendly' environment. These theories could certainly not have developed as they did without minimax.

Finally, minimax has had considerable influence on several disciplines outside of game theory proper. Two of these are statistical decision theory and the design of distributed computing systems, where minimax is used for 'worst case' analysis. Another is mathematical programming; the minimax theorem is equivalent to the duality theorem of linear programming, which in turn is closely related to the idea of shadow pricing in economics. This circle of ideas has fed back into game theory proper; in its guise as a theorem about linear inequalities, the minimax theorem is used to establish the condition of Bondareva (1963) and Shapley (1967) for the non-emptiness of the core of an n-person game, and the Hart–Schmeidler (1988) elementary proof for the existence of correlated equilibria.

(viii) *Empirics*. The correspondence between theory and observation was discussed already by von Neumann (1928), who observed that the need to randomize arises endogenously out of the theory. Thus the phenomenon of bluffing in poker may be considered a confirmation of the theory. This kind of connection between theory and observation is typical of game theory and indeed of economic theory in general. The 'observations' are often qualitative rather than quantitative; in practice, we do observe bluffing, though not necessarily in the proportions predicted by theory.

As for experimentation, strictly competitive games constitute one of the few areas in game theory, and indeed in social science, where a fairly sharp, unique 'prediction' is made (though even this prediction is in general probabilistic). It thus invites experimental testing. Early experiments failed miserably to confirm the theory; even in strictly determined games, subjects consistently reached individually irrational outcomes. But experimentation in rational social science is subject to peculiar pitfalls, of which early experimenters appeared unaware, and which indeed mar many modern experiments as well. These have to do with the motivation of the subjects, and with their understanding of the situation. A determined effort to design an experimental test of minimax that would avoid these pitfalls was recently made by B. O'Neill (1987); in these experiments, the predictions of theory were confirmed to within less than one per cent.

1930–1950

The outstanding event of this period was the publication, in 1944, of the *Theory of Games and Economic Behavior* by John von Neumann and Oskar Morgenstern. Morgenstern was the first economist clearly and explicitly to recognize that economic agents must take the interactive nature of economics into account when making their decisions. He and von Neumann met at Princeton in the late Thirties, and started the collaboration that culminated in the *Theory of Games*. With the publication of this book, game theory came into its own as a scientific discipline.

In addition to expounding the strictly competitive theory described above, the book broke fundamental new ground in several directions. These include the notion of a cooperative game, its coalitional form, and its von Neumann–Morgenstern stable sets. Though axiomatic expected utility theory had been developed earlier by Ramsey (1931), the account of it given in this book is what made it 'catch on'. Perhaps most important, the book made the first extensive applications of game theory, many to economics.

To put these developments into their modern context, we discuss here certain additional ideas that actually did not emerge until later, such as the core, and the general idea of a solution concept. At the end of this section we also describe some developments of this period not directly related to the book, including games with a continuum of strategies, the computation of minimax strategies, and mathematical advances that were instrumental in later work.

(i) *Cooperative games.* A game is called *cooperative* if commitments – agreements, promises, threats – are fully binding and enforceable (Harsanyi 1966, p. 616). It is called *non-cooperative* if commitments are not enforceable, even if pre-play communication between the players is possible. (For motivation, see *1950–1960*, iv.)

Formally, cooperative games may be considered a special case of non-cooperative games, in the sense that one may build the negotiation and enforcement procedures explicitly into the extensive form of the game. Historically, however, this has not been the mainstream approach. Rather, cooperative theory starts out with a formalization of games (the coalitional form) that abstracts away altogether from procedures and from the question of how each player can best manipulate them for his own benefit; it concentrates, instead, on the possibilities for agreement. The emphasis in the non-cooperative theory is on the individual, on what strategy he should use. In the cooperative theory it is on the group: What coalitions will form? How will they divide the available payoff between their members?

There are several reasons that explain why cooperative games came to be treated separately. One is that when one does build negotiation and enforcement procedures explicitly into the model, then the results of a non-cooperative analysis depend very strongly on the precise form of the procedures, on the order of making offers and counter-offers and so on. This may be appropriate in voting situations in which precise rules of parliamentary order prevail, where a good strategist can indeed carry the day. But problems of negotiation are usually more amorphous; it is difficult to pin down just what the procedures are. More fundamentally, there is a feeling that procedures are not really all that relevant; that it is the possibilities for coalition forming, promising and threatening that are decisive, rather than whose turn it is to speak.

Another reason is that even when the procedures are specified, non-cooperative analyses of a cooperative game often lead to highly non-unique results, so that they are often quite inconclusive.

Finally, detail distracts attention from essentials. Some things are seen better from a distance; the Roman camps around Metzada are indiscernible when one is in them, but easily visible from the top of the mountain. The coalitional form of a game, by abstracting away from details, yields valuable perspective.

The idea of building non-cooperative models of cooperative games has come to be known as the *Nash program* since it was first proposed by John Nash (1951). In spite of the difficulties just outlined, the programme has had some recent successes (Harsanyi, 1982; Harsanyi and Selten, 1972; Rubinstein, 1982). For the time being, though, these are isolated; there is as yet nothing remotely approaching a general theory of cooperative games based on non-cooperative methodology.

(ii) A *game in coalitional form*, or simply *coalitional game*, is a function v associating a real number $v(S)$ with each subset S of a fixed finite set I, and satisfying $v(\varnothing) = 0$ ($\varnothing$ denotes the empty set). The members of I are called *players*, the subsets S of I *coalitions*, and $v(S)$ is the *worth* of S.

Some notation and terminology: the number of elements in a set S is denoted $|S|$. A *profile* (of strategies, numbers, etc.) is a function on I (whose values are strategies, numbers, etc.). If x is a profile of numbers and S a coalition, we write $x(S) := \Sigma_{i \in S} x^i$.

An example of a coalitional game is the *3-person voting game*; here $|I| = 3$, and $v(S) = 1$ or 0 according as to whether $|S| \geqslant 2$ or not. A coalition S is called *winning* if $v(S) = 1$, *losing* if $v(S) = 0$. More generally, if w is a profile of non-negative numbers (*weights*) and q (the *quota*) is positive, define the *weighted voting game* v by $v(S) = 1$ if $w(S) \geqslant q$, and $v(S) = 0$ otherwise. An example is a parliament with several parties. The players are the parties, rather than the individual members of parliament, w^i is the number of seats held by party i, and q is the number of votes necessary to form a government (usually a simple majority of the parliament). The weighted voting game with quota q and weights w^i is denoted $[q; w]$; e.g., the three-person voting game is $[2; 1, 1, 1]$.

Another example of a coalitional game is a *market game*. Suppose there are l natural resources, and a single consumer product, say 'bread', that may be manufactured from these resources. Let each player i have an endowment e^i of resources (an l-vector with non-negative coordinates), and a concave production function u^i that enables him to produce the amount $u^i(x)$ of bread given the vector $x = (x_1, \ldots, x_l)$ of resources. Let $v(S)$ be the maximum amount of bread that the coalition S can produce; it obtains this by redistributing its resources among its members in a manner that is most efficient for production, i.e.

$$v(S) = \max \left\{ \sum_{i \in S} u^i(x^i) : \sum_{i \in S} x^i = \sum_{i \in S} e^i \right\},$$

where the x^i are restricted to have non-negative coordinates.

These examples illustrate different interpretations of coalitional games. In one interpretation, the payoff is in terms of some single desirable physical commodity, such as bread; $v(S)$ represents the maximum total amount of this commodity that the coalition S can procure for its members, and it may be distributed among the members in any desired way. This is illustrated by the above description of the market game.

Underlying this interpretation are two assumptions. First, that of *transferable utility* (TU): that the payoff is in a form that is freely transferable among the players. Second, that of *fixed threats*: that S can obtain a maximum of $v(S)$ no matter what the players outside of S do.

Another interpretation is that $v(S)$ represents some appropriate index of S's strength (if it forms). This requires neither transferable utility nor fixed threats. In voting games, for example, it is natural to define $v(S) = 1$ if S is a winning coalition (e.g. can form a government or ensure passage of a bill), 0 if not. Of course, in most situations represented by voting games, utility is not transferable.

Another example is a market game in which the x^i are consumption goods rather than resources. Rather than bread, $\Sigma_{i \in S} u^i(x^i)$ may represent a social welfare function such as is often used in growth or taxation theory. While $v(S)$ cannot then be divided in an arbitrary way among the members of S, it still represents a reasonable index of S's strength. This is a situation with fixed threats but without TU.

Von Neumann and Morgenstern considered strategic games with transferable payoffs, which is a situation with TU but without fixed threats. If the profile s of strategies is played, the coalition S may divide the amount $\Sigma_{i \in S} H^i(s)$ among its members in any way it pleases. However, what S gets depends on what players outside S do. Von Neumann and Morgenstern defined $v(S)$ as the maxmin payoff of S in the two-person zero-sum game in which the players are S and $I \setminus S$, and the payoff to S is $\Sigma_{i \in S} H^i(s)$; i.e., as the expected payoff that S can assure itself (in mixed strategies), no matter what the others do. Again, this is a reasonable index of S's strength, but certainly not the only possible one.

We will use the term *TU coalitional game* when referring to coalitional games with the TU interpretation.

In summary, the coalitional form of a game associates with each coalition S a single number $v(S)$, which in some sense represents the total payoff that that coalition can get or may expect. In some contexts, $v(S)$ fully characterizes the possibilities open to S; in others, it is an index that is indicative of S's strength.

(iii) *Solution concepts.* Given a game, what outcome may be expected? Most of game theory is, in one way or another, directed at this question. In the case of two-person zero-sum games, a clear answer is provided: the unique individually rational outcome. But in almost all other cases, there is no unique answer. There are different criteria, approaches, points of view, and they yield different answers.

A *solution concept* is a function (or correspondence) that associates outcomes, or sets of outcomes, with games. Usually an 'outcome' may be identified with the profile of payoffs that outcome yields to the players, though sometimes we may wish to think of it as a strategy profile.

Of course a solution concept is not just any such function or correspondence, but one with a specific rationale; for example, the strategic equilibrium and its variants for strategic form games, and the core, the von Neumann–Morgenstern stable sets, the Shapley value and the nucleolus for coalitional games. Each represents a different approach or point of view.

What will 'really' happen? Which solution concept is 'right'? None of them; they are indicators, not predictions. Different solution concepts are like different indicators of an economy; different methods for calculating a price index; different maps (road, topo, political, geologic, etc., not to speak of scale, projection, etc.); different stock indices (Dow Jones, Standard and Poor's NYSE, etc., composite, industrials, utilities, etc.); different batting statistics (batting average, slugging average, RBI, hits, etc.); different kinds of information about rock climbs (arabic and roman difficulty ratings, route maps, verbal descriptions of the climb, etc.); accounts of the same event by different people or different media; different projections of the same three-dimensional object (as in architecture or engineering). They depict or illuminate the situation from different angles; each one stresses certain aspects at the expense of others.

Moreover, solution concepts necessarily leave out altogether some of the most vital information, namely that not entering the formal description of the game. When applied to a voting game, for example, no solution concept can take into account matters of custom, political ideology, or personal relations, since they don't enter the coalitional form. That does not make the solution useless. When planning a rock climb, you certainly want to take into account a whole lot of factors other than the physical characteristics of the rock, such as the season, the weather, your ability and condition, and with whom you are going. But you also do want to know about the ratings.

A good analogy is to distributions (probability, frequency, population, etc.). Like a game, a distribution contains a lot of information; one is overwhelmed by all the numbers. The median and the mean summarize the information in different ways; though other than by simply stating the definitions, it is not easy to say how. The definitions themselves do have a certain fairly clear intuitive content; more important, we gain a feeling for the relation between a distribution and its median and mean from experience, from working with various specific examples and classes of examples over the course of time.

The relationship of solution concepts to games is similar. Like the median and the mean, they in some sense summarize the large amount of information present in the formal description of a game. The definitions themselves have a certain fairly clear intuitive content, though they are not predictions of what will happen.

Finally, the relations between a game and its core, value, stable sets, nucleolus and so on is best revealed by seeing where these solution concepts lead in specific games and classes of games.

(iv) *Domination, the core and imputations.* Continuing to identify 'outcome' with 'payoff profile', we call an outcome y of a game *feasible* if the all-player set I can achieve it. An outcome x *dominates* y if there exists a coalition S that can achieve at least its part of x, and each of whose members prefers x to y; in that case we also say that S can *improve upon* y. The *core* of a game is the set of all feasible outcomes that are not dominated.

In a TU coalitional game v, feasibility of x means $x(I) \leqslant v(I)$, and x dominating y via S means that $x(S) \leqslant v(S)$ and $x^i > y^i$ for all i in S. The core of v is the set of all feasible y with $y(S) \geqslant v(S)$ for all S.

At first, the core sounds quite compelling; why should the players be satisfied with an outcome that some coalition can improve upon? It becomes rather less compelling when one realizes that many perfectly ordinary games have empty cores, i.e. every feasible outcome can be improved upon. Indeed, this is so even in as simple a game as the 3-person voting game.

For a coalition S to improve upon an outcome, players in S must trust each other; they must have faith that their comrades inside S will not desert them to make a coalition with other players outside S. In a TU 3-person voting game, $y := (1/3, 1/3, 1/3)$ is dominated via $\{1, 2\}$ by $x := (1/2, 1/2, 0)$. But 1 and 2 would be wise to view a suggested move from y to x with caution. What guarantee does 1 have that 2 will really stick with him and not accept offers from 3 to improve upon x with, say, $(0, 2/3, 1/3)$? For this he must depend on 2's good faith, and similarly 2 must depend on 1's.

There are two exceptions to this argument, two cases in which domination does not require mutual trust. One is when S consists of a single player. The other is when $S = I$, so that there is no one outside S to lure one's partners away.

The requirement that a feasible outcome y be undominated via one-person coalitions (*individual rationality*) and via the all-person coalition (*efficiency* or *Pareto optimality*) is thus quite compelling, much more so than that it be in the core. Such outcomes are called *imputations*. For TU coalitional games, individual rationality means that $y^i \geqslant v(i)$ for all i (we do not distinguish between i and $\{i\}$), and efficiency means that $y(I) = v(I)$. The outcomes associated with most cooperative solution concepts are imputations; the imputations constitute the stage on which most of cooperative game theory is played out.

The notion of core does not appear explicitly in von Neumann and Morgenstern, but it is implicit in some of the discussions of stable sets there. In specific economic contexts, it is implicit in the work of Edgeworth (1881) and Ransmeier (1942). As a general solution concept in its own right, it was developed by Shapley and Gillies in the early Fifties. Early references include Luce and Raiffa (1957) and Gillies (1959).

(v) *Stable sets.* The discomfort with the definition of core expressed above may be stated more sharply as follows. Suppose we think of an outcome in the core as 'stable'. Then we should not exclude an outcome y just because it is dominated by *some* other outcome x; we should demand that x itself be stable. If x is not itself stable, then the argument for excluding y is rather weak; proponents of y can argue with justice that replacing it with x would not lead to a more stable situation, so we may as well stay where we are. If the core were the set of all outcomes not dominated by any element of the core, there would be no difficulty; but this is not so.

Von Neumann and Morgenstern were thus led to the following definition: A set K of imputations is called *stable* if it is the set of all imputations not dominated by any element of K.

This definition guarantees neither existence nor uniqueness. On the face of it, a game may have many stable sets, or it may have none. Most games do, in fact, have many stable sets; but the problem of existence was open for many years. It was solved by Lucas (1969), who constructed a ten-person TU coalitional game without any stable set. Later, Lucas and Rabie (1982) constructed a fourteen-person TU coalitional game without any stable set and with an empty core to boot.

Much of the *Theory of Games* is devoted to exploring the stable sets of various classes of TU coalitional games, such as 3- and 4-person games, voting games, market games, compositions of games, and so on. (If v and w have disjoint player sets I and J, their *composition* u is given by $u(S) := v(S \cap I) + w(S \cap J)$.) During the 1950s many researchers carried forward with great vigour the work of investigating various classes of games and describing their stable sets. Since then work on stable sets has continued unabated, though it is no longer as much in the forefront of game-theoretic research as it was then. All in all, more than 200 articles have been published on stable sets, some 80 per cent of them since 1960. Much of the recent activity in this area has taken place in the Soviet Union.

It is impossible here even to begin to review this large and varied literature. But we do note one characteristic qualitative feature. By definition, a stable set is simply a set of imputations; there is nothing explicit in it about social structure. Yet the mathematical description of a given stable set can often best be understood in terms of an implicit social structure or form of organization of the players. Cartels, systematic discrimination, groups within groups, all kinds of subtle organizational forms spring to one's attention. These forms are endogenous, they are not imposed by definition, they emerge from the analysis. It is a mystery that just the stable set concept, and it only, is so closely allied with endogenous notions of social structure.

We adduce just one, comparatively simple example. The TU 3-person voting game has a stable set consisting of the three imputations $(1/2, 1/2, 0), (1/2, 0, 1/2), (0, 1/2, 1/2)$. The social structure implicit in this is that all three players will *not* compromise by dividing the payoff equally. Rather, one of the three 2-person coalitions will form and divide the payoff equally, with the remaining player being left 'in the cold'. Because any of these three coalitions can form, competition drives them to divide the payoff equally, so that no player will prefer any one coalition to any other.

Another stable set is the interval $\{(\alpha, 1 - \alpha, 0)\}$, where α ranges from 0 to 1. Here Player 3 is permanently excluded from all negotiations; he is 'discriminated against'. Players 1 and 2 divide the payoff in some arbitrary way, not necessarily equally; this is because a coalition with 3 is out of the question, and so competition no longer constraints 1 and 2 in bargaining with each other.

(vi) *Transferable utility.* Though it no longer enjoys the centrality that it did up to about 1960, the assumption of transferable utility has played and continues to play a major role in the development of cooperative game theory. Some economists have questioned the appropriateness of the TU assumption, especially in connection with market models; it has been castigated as excessively strong and unrealistic.

This situation is somewhat analogous to that of strictly competitive games, which as we pointed out above (*1930–1950*, vii), constitute a proving ground for developing and testing ideas that apply also to more general, non-strictly competitive games. The theory of NTU (non-transferable utility) coalitional games is now highly developed (see *1960–1970*, i), but it is an order of magnitude more complex than that of TU games. The TU theory is an excellent laboratory or model for working out ideas that are later applied to the more general NTU case.

Moreover, TU games are both conceptually and technically much closer to NTU games than strictly competitive games are to non-strictly competitive games. A very large part of the important issues arising in connection with non-strictly competitive games do not have any counterpart at all in strictly competitive games, and so simply cannot be addressed in that context. But by far the largest part of the issues and questions arising in the NTU theory do have counterparts in the TU theory; they can at least be addressed and dealt with there.

Almost every major advance in the NTU theory – and many a minor advance as well – has had its way paved by a corresponding advance in the TU theory. Stable sets, core, value and bargaining set were all defined first for TU games, then for NTU. The enormous literature on the core of a market and the equivalence between it and competitive equilibrium (c.e.) in large markets was started by Martin Shubik (1959a) in an article on TU markets. The relation between the value and c.e. in large markets was also explored first for the TU case (Shapley, 1964; Shapley and Shubik, 1969b; Aumann and Shapley, 1974; Hart, 1977a), then for NTU (Champsaur, 1975, but written and circulated circa 1970; Aumann, 1975; Mas-Colell, 1977; Hart, 1977b). The same holds for the bargaining set; first TU (Shapley, 1984); then NTU (Mas-Colell, 1988). The connection between balanced collections of coalitions and the non-emptiness of the core (*1960–1970*, viii) was studied first for TU (Bondareva, 1963; Shapley, 1967), then for NTU (Scarf, 1967; Billera, 1970b; Shapley, 1973a); this development led to the whole subject of Scarf's algorithm for finding points in the core, which he and others later extended to algorithms for finding market equilibria and fixed points of mappings in general. Games arising from markets were first abstractly characterized in the TU case (Shapley and Shubik, 1969a), then in the NTU case

(Billera and Bixby, 1973; Mas-Colell, 1975). Games with a continuum of players were conceived first in a TU application (Milnor and Shapley, 1978, but written and circulated in 1960), then NTU (Aumann, 1964). Strategic models of bargaining where time is of the essence were first treated for TU (Rubinstein, 1982), then NTU (Binmore, 1982). One could go on and on.

In each of these cases, the TU development led organically to the NTU development; it isn't just that the one came before the other. TU is to cooperative game theory what *Drosophila* is to genetics. Even if it had no direct economic interest at all, the study of TU coalitional games would be justified solely by their role as an outstandingly suggestive research tool.

(vii) *Single play.* Von Neumann and Morgenstern emphasize that their analysis refers to 'one-shot' games, games that are played just once, after which the players disperse, never to interact again. When this is not the case, one must view the whole situation – including expected future interactions of the same players – as a single larger game, and it, too, is to be played just once.

To some extent this doctrine appears unreasonable. If one were to take it literally, there would be only one game to analyse, namely the one whose players include all persons ever born and to be born. Every human being is linked to every other through some chain of interactions; no person or group is isolated from any other.

Savage (1954) has discussed this in the context of one-person decisions. In principle, he writes, one should 'envisage every conceivable policy for the government of his whole life in its most minute details, and decide here and now on one policy. This is utterly ridiculous...' (p. 16). He goes on to discuss the *small worlds* doctrine, 'the practical necessity of confining attention to, or isolating, relatively simple situations...' (p. 82).

To a large extent, this doctrine applies to interactive decisions too. But one must be careful, because here 'large worlds' have qualitative features totally absent from 'small words'. We return to this below (*1950–1960*, ii, iii).

(viii) *Expected utility.* When randomized strategies are used in a strategic game, payoff must be replaced by expected payoff (*1910–1930*, iv). Since the game is played only once, the law of large numbers does not apply, so it is not clear why a player would be interested specifically in the mathematical expectation of his payoff.

There is no problem when for each player there are just two possible outcomes, which we may call 'winning' and 'losing', and denominate 1 and 0 respectively. (This involves no zero-sum assumption; e.g. all players could win simultaneously.) In that case the expected payoff is simply the probability of winning. Of course each player wants to maximize this probability, so in that case use of the expectation is justified.

Suppose now that the values of i's payoff function H^i are numbers between 0 and 1, representing win probabilities. Thus, for the 'final' outcome there are still only two possibilities; each pure strategy profile s induces a random process that generates a win for i with probability $H^i(s)$. Then the payoff expectation when randomized strategies are used still represents i's overall win probability.

Now in any game, each player has a most preferred and a least preferred outcome, which we take as a win and a loss. For each payoff h, there is some probability p such that i would as soon get h with certainty as winning with probability p and losing with probability $1 - p$. If we replace all the h's by the corresponding p's in the payoff matrix, then we are in the case of the previous paragraph, so use of the expected payoff is justified.

The probability p is a function of h, denoted $u^i(h)$, and called i's von Neumann–Morgenstern *utility*. Thus, to justify the use of expectations, each player's payoff must be replaced by its utility.

The key property of the function u^i is that if h and g are random payoffs, then i prefers h to g iff $Eu^i(h) > Eu^i(g)$, where E denotes expectation. This property continues to hold when we replace u^i by a linear transform of the form $\alpha u^i + \beta$, where α and β are constants with $\alpha > 0$. All these transforms are also called utility functions for i, and any one of them may be used rather than u^i in the payoff matrix.

Recall that a strictly competitive game is defined as a two-person game in which, if one outcome is preferred to another by one player, the preference is reversed for the other. Since randomized strategies are admitted, this condition applies also to 'mixed outcomes' (probability mixtures of pure outcomes). From this it may be seen that a two-person game is strictly competitive if and only if, for an appropriate choice of utility functions, the utility payoffs of the players sum to zero in each square of the matrix.

The case of TU coalitional games deserves particular attention. There is no problem if we assume fixed threats and continue to denominate the payoff in bread (see ii). But without fixed threats, the total amount of bread obtainable by a coalition S is a random variable depending on what players outside S do; since this is not denominated in utility, there is no justification for replacing it by its expectation. But if we do denominate payoffs in utility terms, they they cannot be directly transferred. The only way out of this quandary is to assume that the utility of bread is linear in the amount of bread (Aumann, 1960). We stress again that no such assumption is required in the fixed threat case.

(ix) *Applications.* The very name of the book, *Theory of Games and Economic Behavior*, indicates its underlying preoccupation with the applications. Von Neumann had already mentioned *Homo Economicus* in his 1928 paper, but there were no specific economic applications there.

The method of von Neumann and Morgenstern has become the archetype of later applications of game theory. One takes an economic problem, formulates it as a game, finds the game-theoretic solution, then translates the solution back into economic terms. This is to be distinguished from the more usual methodology of economics and other social sciences, where the building of a formal model and a solution concept, and the application of the solution concept to the model, are all rolled into one.

Among the applications extensively treated in the book is voting. A qualitative feature that emerges is that many different weight-quota configurations have the same coalitional form; $[5; 2, 3, 4]$ is the same as $[2; 1, 1, 1]$. Though obvious to the sophisticated observer when pointed out, this is not widely recognized; most people think that the player with weight 4 is considerably stronger than the others (Vinacke and Arkoff, 1957). The Board of Supervisors of Nassau County operates by weighted voting; in 1964 there were six members, with weights of 31, 31, 28, 21, 2, 2, and a simple majority quota of 58 (Lucas, 1983, p. 188). Nobody realized that three members were totally without influence, that $[58; 31, 31, 28, 21, 2, 2] = [2; 1, 1, 1, 0, 0, 0]$.

In a voting game, a winning coalition with no proper winning subsets is called *minimal winning* (mw). The game $[q; w]$ is *homogeneous* if $w(S) = q$ for all minimal winning S; thus $[3; 2, 1, 1, 1]$ is homogeneous, but $[5; 2, 2, 2, 1, 1, 1]$ is not. A *decisive* voting game is one in which a coalition wins if and only if its complement loses; both the above games are decisive, but $[3; 1, 1, 1, 1]$ is not. TU decisive homogeneous voting games have a stable set in which some mw coalition forms and divides the payoff in proportion to the weights of its members, leaving nothing for those outside. This is reminiscent of some parliamentary democracies, where parties in a coalition government get cabinet seats roughly in proportion to the seats they hold in parliament. But this fails to take into account that the actual number of seats held by a party may well be quite disproportional to its weight in a homogeneous representation of the game (when there is such a representation).

The book also considers issues of monopoly (or monopsony) and oligopoly. We have already pointed out that stable set theory concerns the endogenous emergence of social structure. In a market with one buyer (monopsonist) and two sellers (duopolists) where supply exceeds demand, the theory predicts that the duopolists will form a cartel to bargain with the monopsonist. The core, on the other hand, predicts cut-throat competition; the duopolists end up by selling their goods for nothing, with the entire consumer surplus going to the buyer.

This is a good place to point out a fundamental difference between the game-theoretic and other approaches to social science. The more conventional approaches take institutions as given, and ask where they lead. The game-theoretic approach asks how the institutions came about, what led to them? Thus general equilibrium theory takes the idea of market prices for granted; it concerns itself with their existence and properties, calculating them, and so on. Game theory asks, *why* are there market prices? How did they come about? Under what conditions will all traders trade at given prices?

Conventional economic theory has several approaches to oligopoly, including competition and cartelization. Starting with any particular one of these, it calculates what is implied in specific applications. Game theory proceeds differently. It starts with the physical description of the situation only, making no institutional or doctrinal assumptions, then applies a solution concept and sees where it leads.

In a sense, of course, the doctrine is built into the solution concept; as we have seen, the core implies competition, the stable set cartelization. It is not that game theory makes no assumptions, but that the assumptions are of a more general, fundamental nature. The difference is like that between deriving the motion of the planets from Kepler's laws or from Newton's laws. Like Kepler's laws, which apply to the planets only, oligopoly theory applies to oligopolistic markets only. Newton's laws apply to the planets and also to apples falling from trees; stable sets apply to markets and also to voting.

To be sure, conventional economics is also concerned with the genesis of institutions, but on an information, verbal, ad-hoc level. In game theory, institutions like prices or cartels are outcomes of the formal analysis.

(x) Games with a *continuum of pure strategies* were first considered by Ville (1938), who proved the minimax theorem for them, using an appropriate continuity condition. To guarantee the minimax (security) level, one may need to use a continuum of pure strategies, each with probability zero. An example due to Kuhn (1952) shows that in general one cannot guarantee anything even close to minimax using strategies with finite support. Ville's theorem was extended in the Fifties to strategic equilibrium in non-strictly competitive games.

(xi) *Computing* security levels, and strategies that will guarantee them, is highly non-trivial. The problem is equivalent to that of linear programming, and thus succumbed to the simplex method of George Dantzig (1951a, 1951b).

(xii) The major advance in relevant mathematical methods during this period was *Kakutani's fixed point theorem* (1941). An abstract expression of the existence of equilibrium, it is the vital active ingredient of countless proofs in economics and game theory. Also instrumental in later work were Lyapounov's theorem on the range of a vector measure (1940) and von Neumann's selection theorem (1949).

1950–1960

The 1950s was a period of excitement in game theory. The discipline had broken out of its cocoon, and was testing its wings. Giants walked the earth. At Princeton, John Nash laid the goundwork for the general non-cooperative theory, and for cooperative bargaining theory; Lloyd Shapley defined the value for coalitional games, initiated the theory of stochastic games, co-invented the core with D.B. Gillies, and, together with John Milnor, developed the first game models with continua of players; Harold Kuhn worked on behaviour strategies and perfect recall; Al Tucker discovered the prisoner's dilemma; the Office of Naval Research was unstinting in its support. Three Game Theory conferences were held at Princeton, with the active participation of von Neumann and Morgenstern themselves. Princeton University Press published the four classic volumes of *Contributions to the Theory of Games*. The Rand Corporation, for many years to be a major centre of game theoretic research, had just opened its doors in Santa Monica. R. Luce and H. Raiffa (1957) published their enormously influential *Games and Decisions*. Near the end of the decade came the first studies of repeated games.

The major applications at the beginning of the decade were to tactical military problems: defence from missiles, Colonel Blotto, fighter-fighter duels, etc. Later the emphasis shifted to deterrence and cold-war strategy, with contributions by political scientists like Kahn, Kissinger, and Schelling. In 1954, Shapley and Shubik published their seminal paper on the value of a voting game as an index of power. And in 1959 came Shubik's spectacular rediscovery of the core of a market in the writings of F.Y. Edgeworth (1881). From that time on, economics has remained by far the largest area of application of game theory.

(i) An *equilibrium* (Nash, 1951) of a strategic game is a (pure or mixed) strategy profile in which each player's strategy maximizes his payoff given that the others are using their strategies. (See the entry on NASH EQUILIBRIUM.)

Strategic equilibrium is without doubt the single game-theoretic solution concept that is most frequently applied in economics. Economic applications include oligopoly, entry and exit, market equilibrium, search, location, bargaining, product quality, auctions, insurance, principal–agent, higher education, discrimination, public goods, what have you. On the political front, applications include voting, arms control and inspection, as well as most international political models (deterrence, etc.). Biological applications of game theory all deal with forms of strategic equilibrium; they suggest a simple interpretation of equilibrium quite different from the usual overt rationalism (see *1970–1986*, i). We cannot even begin to survey all this literature here.

(ii) *Stochastic and other dynamic games.* Games played in stages, with siome kind of stationary time structure, are called *dynamic*. They include stochastic games, repeated games with or without complete information, games of survival (Milnor and Shapley, 1957; Luce and Raiffa, 1957; Shubik, 1959b) or ruin (Rosenthal and Rubinstein, 1984), recursive games (Everett, 1957), games with varying opponents (Rosenthal, 1979) and similar models.

This kind of model addresses the concerns we expressed above (*1930–1950*, vii) about the single-play assumption. The present can only be understood in the context of the past and the future: 'Know whence you came and where you are going' (Ethics of the Fathers III:1). Physically, current actions affect not only current payoff but also opportunities and payoffs in the future. Psychologically, too, we learn: past experience affects our current expectations of what others will do, and therefore our own actions. We also teach: our current actions affect others' future expectations, and therefore their future actions.

Two dynamic models – stochastic and repeated games – have been especially 'successful'. *Stochastic* games address the physical point, that current actions affect future opportunities. A strategic game is played at each stage; the profile of strategies determines both the payoff at that stage and the game to be played at the next stage (or a probability distribution over such games). In the strictly competitive case, with future payoff discounted at a fixed rate, Shapley (1953a) showed that stochastic games are determined; also, that they have optimal strategies that are stationary, in the sense that they depend only on the game being played (not on the history or even on the date). Bewley and Kohlberg

(1976) showed that as the discount rate tends to 0 the value tends to a limit; this limit is the same as the limit, as $k \to \infty$, of the values of the k-stage games, in each of which the payoff is the mean payoff for the k stages. Mertens and Neyman (1981) showed that the value exists also in the undiscounted infinite stage game, when payoff is defined by the Cesaro limit (limit, as $k \to \infty$, of the average payoff in the first k stages). For an understanding of some of the intuitive issues in this work, see Blackwell and Ferguson (1968), which was extremely influential in the modern development of stochastic games.

The methods of Shapley, and of Bewley and Kohlberg, can be used to show that non-strictly competitive stochastic games with fixed discounts have equilibria in stationary strategies, and that when the discount tends to 0, these equilibria converge to a limit (Mertens, 1982). But unlike in the strictly competitive case, the payoff to this limit need not correspond to an equilibrium of the undiscounted game (Sorin, 1986b). It is not known whether undiscounted non-strictly competitive stochastic games need at all have strategic equilibria.

(iii) *Repeated games* model the psychological, informational side of ongoing relationships. Phenomena like cooperation, altruism, trust, punishment and revenge are predicted by the theory. These may be called 'subjective informational' phenomena, since what is at issue is information about the behaviour of the players. Repeated games of incomplete information (*1960–1970*, ii) also predict 'objective informational' phenomena such as secrecy, and signalling of substantive information. Both kinds of informational issue are quite different from the 'physical' issues addressed by stochastic games.

Given a strategic game G, consider the game G^∞, each play of which consists of an infinite sequence of repetitions of G. At each stage, all players know the actions taken by all players at all previous stages. The payoff in G^∞ is some kind of average of the stage payoffs; we will not worry about exact definitions here.

The reader is referred to the entry on REPEATED GAMES. Here we state only one basic result, known as the *Folk Theorem*. Call an outcome (payoff profile) x *feasible* in G if it is achievable by the all-player set when using a correlated randomizing device; i.e. is in the convex hull of the 'pure' outcomes. Call it *strongly individually rational* if no player i can be prevented from achieving x^i by the other players, when they are randomizing independently; i.e. if $x^i \geqslant$ min max $H^i(s)$, where the max is over i's strategies, and the min is over $(n-1)$-tuples of mixed strategies of the others. The Folk Theorem then says that the equilibrium outcomes in the repetition G^∞ *coincide with the feasible and strongly individually rational outcomes in the one-shot game* G.

The authorship of the Folk Theorem, which surfaced in the late Fifties, is obscure. Intuitively, the feasible and strongly individually rational outcomes are the outcomes that could arise in cooperative play. Thus the Folk Theorem points to a strong relationship between repeated and cooperative games. Repetition is a kind of enforcement mechanism; agreements are enforced by 'punishing' deviators in subsequent stages.

(iv) The *Prisoner's Dilemma* is a two-person non-zero sum strategic game with payoff matrix as depicted in Figure 1. Attributed to A. W. Tucker, it has deservedly attracted enormous attention; it is said that in the social psychology literature alone, over a thousand papers have been devoted to it.

One may think of the game as follows: Each player decides whether he will receive $1000 or the other will receive $3000. The decisions are simultaneous and independent, though the players may consult with each other before deciding.

The point is that ordinary rationality leads each player to choose the $1000 for himself, since he is thereby better off *no matter what the other player does*. But the two players thereby get only $1000 each, whereas they could have gotten $3000 each if both had been 'friendly' rather than 'greedy'.

The universal fascination with this game is due to its representing, in very stark and transparent form, the bitter fact that when individuals act for their own benefit, the result may well be disaster for all. This principle has dozens of applications, great and small, in everyday life. *People who fail to cooperate for their own mutual benefit are not necessarily foolish or irrational*; they may be acting perfectly rationally. The sooner we accept this, the sooner we can take steps to design the terms of social intercourse so as to encourage cooperation.

One such step, of very wide applicability, is to make available a mechanism for the enforcement of voluntary agreements. 'Pray for the welfare of government, without whose authority, man would swallow man alive' (Ethics of the Fathers III:2). The availability of the mechanism is itself sufficient; once it is there, the players are naturally motivated to use it. If they can make an *enforceable* agreement yielding $(3, 3)$, they would indeed be foolish to end up with $(1, 1)$. It is this that motivates the definition of a cooperative game (*1930–1950*, i).

The above discussion implies that (g, g) is the unique strategic equilibrium of the prisoner's dilemma. It may also be shown that in any finite repetition of the game, all strategic equilibria lead to a constant stream of 'greedy' choices by each player; but this is a subtler matter than the simple domination argument used for the one-shot case. In the infinite repetition, the Folk Theorem (iii) shows that $(3, 3)$ is an equilibrium outcome; and indeed, there are equilibria that lead

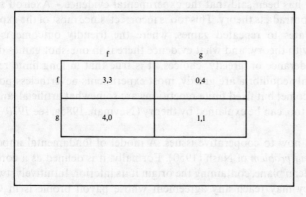

Figure 1

to a constant stream of 'friendly' choices by each player. The same holds if we discount future payoff in the repeated game, as long as the discount rate is not too large (Sorin, 1986a).

R. Axelrod (1984) has carried out an experimental study of the repeated prisoner's dilemma. Experts were asked to write computer programs for playing the game, which were matched against each other in a 'tournament'. At each stage, the game ended with a fixed (small) probability; this is like discounting. The most successful program in the tournament turned out to be a 'cooperative' one: Matched against itself, it yields a constant stream of 'friendly' choices; matched against others, it 'punishes' greedy choices. The results of this experiment thus fit in well with received theoretical doctrine.

The design of this experiment is noteworthy because it avoids the pitfalls so often found in game experiments: lack of sufficient motivation and understanding. The experts chosen by Axelrod understood the game as well as anybody. Motivation was provided by the investment of their time, which was much more considerable than that of the average subject, and by the glory of a possible win over distinguished colleagues. Using computer programs for strategies presaged important later developments (*1970–1986*, iv).

Much that is fallacious has been written on the one-shot prisoner's dilemma. It has been said that for the reasoning to work, pre-play communication between the players must be forbidden. This is incorrect. The players can communicate until they are blue in the face, and agree solemnly on (f, f); when faced with the actual decision, rational players will still choose g. It has been said that the argument depends on the notion of strategic equilibrium, which is open to discussion. This too is incorrect; the argument depends only on strong domination, i.e. on the simple proposition that people always prefer to get another $1000. 'Resolutions' of the 'paradox' have been put forward, suggesting that rational players will play f after all; that my choosing f has some kind of 'mirror' effect that makes you choose it also. Worse than just nonsense, this is actually vicious, since it suggests that the prisoner's dilemma does not represent a real social problem that must be dealt with.

Finally, it has been said that the experimental evidence – Axelrod's and that of others – contradicts theory. This too is incorrect, since most of the experimental evidence relates to repeated games, where the friendly outcome is perfectly consonant with theory; and what evidence there is in one-shot games does point to a preponderance of 'greedy' choices. It is true that in long finite repetitions, where the only equilibria are greedy, most experiments nevertheless point to the friendly outcome; but fixed finite repetitions are somewhat artificial, and besides, this finding, too, can be explained by theory (Neyman, 1985a, see *1970–1986*, iv).

(v) We turn now to cooperative issues. A model of fundamental importance is the *bargaining problem* of Nash (1950). Formally, it is defined as a convex set C in the Euclidean plane, containing the origin it its interior. Intuitively, two players bargain; they may reach any agreement whose payoff profile is in C; if they disagree, they get nothing. Nash listed four *axioms* – conditions that a reasonable compromise solution might be expected to satisfy – such as symmetry and efficiency. He then showed that there is one and only one solution satisfying them, namely the point x in the non-negative part of C that maximizes the product $x^1 x^2$. An appealing economic interpretation of this solution was given by Harsanyi (1956).

By varying the axioms, other authors have obtained different solutions to the bargaining problem, notably Kalai–Smorodinski (1975) and Maschler–Perles (1981). Like Nash's solution, each of these is characterized by a formula with an intuitively appealing interpretation.

Following work of A. Rubinstein (1982), K. Binmore (1982) constructed an explicit bargaining model which, when analysed as a non-cooperative strategic game, leads to Nash's solution of the bargaining problem. This is an instance of a successful application of the 'Nash program' (see *1930–1950*, vi). Similar constructions have been made for other solutions of the bargaining problem.

An interesting qualitative feature of the Nash solution is that it is very sensitive to risk aversion. A risk-loving or risk-neutral bargainer will get a better deal than a risk-averse one; this is so even when there are no overt elements of risk in the situation, nothing random. The very willingness to take risks confers an advantage, though in the end no risks are actually taken.

Suppose, for example, that two people may divide \$600 in any way they wish; if they fail to agree, neither gets anything. Let their utility functions be $u^1(\$x) = x$ and $u^2(\$x) = \sqrt{x}$, so that 1 is risk neutral, 2 risk averse. Denominating the payoffs in utilities rather than dollars, we find that the Nash solution corresponds to a dollar split of \$400–\$200 in favour of the risk neutral bargainer.

This corresponds well with our intuitions. A fearful, risk-averse person will not bargain well. Though there are no overt elements of risk, no random elements in the problem description, the bargaining itself constitutes a risk. A risk-averse person is willing to pay, in terms of a less favourable settlement, to avoid the risk of the other side's being adamant, walking away, and so on.

(vi) The *value* (Shapley, 1953b) is a solution concept that associates with each coalitional game v a unique outcome ϕv. Fully characterized by a set of axioms, it may be thought of as a reasonable compromise or arbitrated outcome, given the power of the players. Best, perhaps, is to think of it simply as an index of power, or what comes to the same thing, of social productivity (*see* SHAPLEY VALUE).

It may be shown that Player i's value is given by

$$\phi^i v = (1/n!) \sum v^i(S_R^i),$$

where Σ ranges over all $n!$ orders on the set I of all players, S_R^i is the set of players up to and including i in the order R, and $v^i(S)$ is the *contribution* $v(S) - v(S \setminus i)$ of i to the coalition S; note that this implies linearity of ϕv in v. In words, $\phi^i v$ is i's mean contribution when the players are ordered at random; this suggests the social productivity interpretation, an interpretation that is reinforced by the following remarkable theorem (Young, 1985): Let ψ be a mapping from games v to efficient outcomes ψv, that is symmetric among the players in the appropriate sense. Suppose $\psi^i v$ depends only on the 2^{n-1} contributions $v^i(S)$, and monotonically so. Then ψ must be the value ϕ. In brief, if it depends on the contributions only, it's got to be the value, even though we don't assume linearity to start with.

An intuitive feel for the value may be gained from examples. The value of the 3-person voting game is $(1/3, 1/3, 1/3)$, as is suggested by symmetry. This is not in the core, because $\{1, 2\}$ can improve upon it. But so can $\{1, 3\}$ and $\{2, 3\}$; starting from $(1/3, 1/3, 1/3)$, the players might be well advised to leave things as they are (see *1930–1950*, iv). Differently viewed, the symmetric stable set predicts one of the three outcomes $(1/2, 1/2, 0), (1/2, 0, 1/2), (0, 1/2, 1/2)$. Before the beginning of bargaining, each player may figure that his chances of getting into a ruling coalition are $2/3$, and conditional on this, his payoff is $1/2$. Thus his 'expected outcome' is the value, though in itself, this outcome has no stability.

In the homogeneous weighted voting game $[3; 2, 1, 1, 1]$, the value is $(1/2, 1/6, 1/6, 1/6)$; the large player gets a disproportionate share, which accords with intuition: 'l'union fait la force.'

Turning to games of economic interest, we model the market with two sellers and one buyer discussed above (*1930–1950*, ix) by the TU weighted voting game $[3; 2, 1, 1]$. The core consists of the unique point $(1, 0, 0)$, which means that the sellers must give their merchandise, for nothing, to the buyer. While this has clear economic meaning – cut-throat competition – it does not seem very reasonable as a compromise or an index of power. After all, the sellers do contribute something; without them, the buyer could get nothing. If one could be sure that the sellers will form a cartel to bargain with the buyer, a reasonable compromise would be $(1/2, 1/4, 1/4)$. In fact, the value is $(2/3, 1/6, 1/6)$, representing something between the cartel solution and the competitive one; a cartel is possible, but is not a certainty.

Consider next a market in two perfectly divisible and completely complementary goods, which we may call right and left gloves. There are four players; initially 1 and 2 hold one and two left gloves respectively, 3 and 4 hole one right glove each. In coalitional form, $v(1234) = v(234) = 2$, $v(ij) = v(12j) = v(134) = 1$, $v(S) = 0$ otherwise, where $i = 1$, 2, and $j = 3$, 4. The core consists of $(0, 0, 1, 1)$ only; that is, the owners of the left gloves must simply give away their merchandise, for nothing. This in itself seems strange enough. It becomes even stranger when one realizes that Player 2 could make the situation entirely symmetric (as between 1, 2 and 3, 4) simply by burning one glove, an action that he can take alone, without consulting anybody.

The value can never suffer from this kind of pathological breakdown in monotonicity. Here $\phi v = (1/4, 7/12, 7/12, 7/12)$, which nicely reflects the features of the situation. There *is* an oversupply of left gloves, and 3 and 4 do benefit from it. Also 2 benefits from it; he always has the option of nullifying it, but he can also use it (when he has an opportunity to strike a deal with both 3 and 4). The brunt of the oversupply is thus born by 1 who, unlike 2, cannot take measures to correct it.

Finally, consider a market with 2,000,001 players, 1,000,000 holding one right glove each, and 1,000,001 holding one left glove each. Again, the core stipulates that the holders of the left gloves must all give away their merchandise, for nothing. True, there *is* a slight oversupply of left gloves; but one would hardly have imagined so drastic an effect from one single glove out of millions. The value, too, takes the oversupply into account, but not in such an extreme form; altogether, the left-glove holders get about 499,557 pairs, the right about 500,443 (Shapley and Shubik, 1969b). This is much more reasonable, though the effect is still surprisingly large: The short side gains an advantage that amounts to almost a thousand pairs.

The value has many different characterizations, all of them intuitively meaningful and interesting. We have already mentioned Shapley's original axioms, the value formula and Young's characterization. To them must be added Harsanyi's (1959) dividend characterization, Owen's (1972) fuzzy coalition formula, Myerson's (1977) graph approach, Dubey's (1980) diagonal formula, the potential of Hart and Mas-Colell (1986), the reduced game axiomatization by the same authors, and Roth's (1977) formalization of Shapley's (1953b) idea that the value represents the utility to the players of playing a game. Moreover, because of its mathematical tractability, the value lends itself to a far greater range of applications than any other cooperative solution concept. And in terms of general theorems and characterizations for wide classes of games and economies, the value has a greater range than *any* other solution concept, bar none.

Previously (*1930–1950*, iii), we compared solution concepts of games to indicators of distributions, like mean and median. In fact the value is in many ways analogous to the mean, whereas the median corresponds to something like the core, or to core-like concepts such as the nucleolus (*1960–1970*, iv). Like the core, the median has an intuitively transparent and compelling definition (the point that cuts the distribution exactly in half), but lacks an algebraically neat formula; and like the value, the mean has a neat formula whose intuitive significance is not entirely transparent (though through much experience from childhood on, many people have acquired an intuitive feel for it). Like the value, the mean is linear in its data; the core, nucleolus and median are not. Both the mean and the value are very sensitive to their data: change one datum by a little, and the mean (or value) will respond in the appropriate direction; neither the median nor the core is sensitive in this way: one can change the data in wide ranges without affecting the median (or core) at all. On the other hand, the median can suddenly jump because of a moderate change in just one datum; thus the median of 1,000,001 zeros and 1,000,000 ones is 0, but jumps to 1 if we change just one datum from 0 to 1. We have already seen that the core may behave similarly, but the mean and the value cannot. Both the mean and the value are mathematically very tractable, resulting in a wide range of applications, both theoretical and practical; the median and core are less tractable, resulting in a narrower (though still considerable) range of applications.

The first extensive applications of the value were to various voting games

(Shapley and Shubik, 1954). The key observation in this seminal paper was that the value of a player equals his probability of *pivoting* – turning a coalition from losing to winning – when the players are ordered at random. From this there has grown a very large literature on voting games. Other important classes of applications are to market games (*1960–1970*, v) and political-economic games (e.g. Aumann and Kurz, 1977; Neyman, 1985b).

(vii) *Axiomatics*. The Shapley value and Nash's solution to the bargaining problem are examples of the axiomatic approach. Rather than defining a solution concept directly, one writes down a set of conditions for it to satisfy, then sees where they lead. In many contexts, even a relatively small set of fairly reasonable conditions turn out to be self-contradictory; there is no concept satisfying all of them. The most famous instance of this is Arrow's (1951) impossibility theorem for social welfare functions, which is one of the earliest applications of axiomatics in the social sciences.

It is not easy to pin down precisely what is meant by 'the axiomatic method'. Sometimes the term is used for any formal deductive system, with undefined terms, assumptions and conclusions. As understood today, all of game theory and mathematical economics fits that definition. More narrowly construed, an axiom system is a small set of individually transparent conditions, set in a fairly general and abstract framework, which when taken together have far-reaching implications. Examples are Euclid's axioms for geometry, the Zermelo–Fraenkel axioms for set theory, the conditions on multiplication that define a group, the conditions on open sets that define a topological space, and the conditions on preferences that define utility and/or subjective probability.

Game theoretic solution concepts often have both direct and axiomatic characterizations. The direct definition applies to each game separately, whereas most axioms deal with relationships between games. Thus the formula for the Shapley value ϕv enables one to calculate it without referring to any game other than v. But the axioms for ϕ concern relationships between games; they say that if the values of certain games are so and so, then the values of certain other, related games must be such and such. For example, the additivity axiom is $\phi(v + w) = \phi v + \phi w$. This is analogous to direct vs. axiomatic approaches to integration. Direct approaches such as limit of sum work on a single function; axiomatic approaches characterize the integral as a linear operator on a *space* of functions. (Harking back to the discussion at (vi), we note that the axioms for the value are quite similar to those for the integral, which in turn is closely related to the mean of a distribution.)

Shapley's value and the solutions to the bargaining problem due to Nash (1950), Kalai–Smorodinski (1975) and Maschler–Perles (1981) were originally conceived axiomatically, with the direct characterization coming afterwards. In other cases the process was reversed; for example, the nucleolus, NTU Shapley value and NTU Harsanyi value were all axiomatized only years after their original direct definition (see *1960–1970*). Recently the core, too, has been axiomatized (Peleg, 1985, 1986).

Since axiomatizations concern relations between different games, one may ask why the players of a given game should be concerned with other games, which they are not playing. This has several answers. Viewed as an indicator, a solution of a game doesn't tell us much unless it stands in some kind of coherent relationship to the solutions of other games. The ratings for a rock climb tell you something if you have climbed other rocks whose ratings you know; topographic maps enable you to take in a situation at a glance, if you have used them before, in different areas. If we view a solution as an arbitrated or imposed outcome, it is natural to expect some measure of consistency from an arbitrator or judge. Indeed, much of the law is based on precedent, which means relating the solution of the given 'game' to those of others with known solutions. Even when viewing a solution concept as a norm of actual behaviour, the very word 'norm' implies that we are thinking of a function on classes of games rather than of a single game; outcomes are largely based on mutual expectations, which are determined by previous experience with other games, by 'norms'.

Axiomatizations serve a number of useful purposes. First, like any other alternative characterization, they shed additional light on a concept, enable us to 'understand' it better. Second, they underscore and clarify important similarities between concepts, as well as differences between them. One example of this is the remarkable 'reduced game property' or 'consistency principle', which is associated in various different forms with just about every solution concept, and plays a key role in many of the axiomatizations (see *1970–1986*, vi). Another example consists of the axiomatizations of the Shapley and Harsanyi NTU values. Here the axioms are exact analogues, except that in the Shapley case they refer to payoff profiles, and in the Harsanyi case to 2^n-tuples of payoff profiles, one for each of the 2^n coalitions (Hart, 1985a). This underscores the basic difference in outlook between those two concepts: The Shapley value assumes that the all-player coalition eventually forms, the intermediate coalitions being important only for bargaining chips and threats, whereas the Harsanyi value takes into account a real possibility of the intermediate coalitions actually forming.

Last, an important function of axiomatics relates to 'counter-intuitive examples', in which a solution concept yields outcomes that seem bizarre; e.g. the cores of some of the games discussed above in (vi). Most axioms appearing in axiomatizations do seem reasonable on the face of it, and many of them are in fact quite compelling. The fact that a relatively small selection of such axioms is often categoric (determines a unique solution concept), and that different such selections yield different answers, implies that all together, these reasonable-sounding axioms are contradictory. This, in turn, implies that any one solution concept will necessarily violate at least some of the axioms that are associated with other solution concepts; thus if the axioms are meant to represent intuition, counter-intuitive examples are inevitable.

In brief, axiomatics underscores the fact that a 'perfect' solution concept is an unattainable goal, a *fata morgana*; there is something 'wrong', some quirk with every one. Any given kind of counterintuitive example can be eliminated by an appropriate choice of solution concept, but only at the cost of another quirk turning up. Different solution concepts can therefore be thought of as results of choosing not only which properties one likes, but also which examples one wishes to avoid.

1960–1970

The Sixties were a decade of growth. Extensions such as games of incomplete information and NTU coalitional games made the theory much more widely applicable. The fundamental underlying concept of common knowledge was formulated and clarified. Core theory was extensively developed and applied to market economies; the bargaining set and related concepts such as the nucleolus were defined and investigated; games with many players were studied in depth. The discipline expanded geographically, outgrowing the confines of Princeton and Rand; important centres of research were established in Israel, Germany, Belgium and the Soviet Union. Perhaps most important was the forging of a strong, lasting relationship with mathematical economics and economic theory.

(i) *NTU coalitional games and NTU value.* Properly interpreted, the coalitional form (*1930–1950*, ii) applies both to TU and to NTU games; nevertheless, for many NTU applications one would like to describe the opportunities available to each coalition more faithfully than can be done with a single number. Accordingly, define a game in *NTU coalitional form* as a function that associates with each coalition S a set V(S) of S-tuples of real numbers (functions from S to $\mathbb{R}$). Intuitively, V(S) represents the set of payoff S-tuples that S can achieve. For example, in an exchange economy, V(S) is the set of utility S-tuples that S can achieve when its members trade among themselves only, without recourse to agents outside of S. Another example of an NTU coalitional game is Nash's bargaining problem (*1950–1960*, iii), where one can take $V(\{1,2\}) = C$, $V(1) = \{0\}$, $V(2) = \{0\}$.

The definitions of stable set and core extend straightforwardly to NTU coalitional games, and these solution concepts were among the first to be investigated in that context (Aumann and Peleg, 1960; Peleg, 1963a; Aumann, 1961). The first definitions of NTU value were proposed by Harsanyi (1959, 1963), but they proved difficult to apply. Building on Harsanyi's work, Shapley (1969c) defined a value for NTU games that has proved widely applicable and intuitively appealing.

For each profile λ of non-negative numbers and each outcome x, define the *weighted outcome* λx by $(\lambda x)^i = \lambda^i x^i$. Let $v_\lambda(S)$ be the maximum total weight that the coalition S can achieve,

$$v_\lambda(S) := \max\left\{ \sum_{i \in S} \lambda^i x^i, x \in V(S) \right\}.$$

Call an outcome x an *NTU value* of V if $x \in V(N)$ and there exists a weight profile λ with $\lambda x = \phi v_\lambda$; in words, if x is feasible and corresponds to the value of one of the coalitional games v_λ.

Intuitively, $v_\lambda(S)$ is a numerical measure of S's total worth and hence $\phi^i v_\lambda$

measures i's social productivity. The weights λ^i are chosen so that the resulting value is feasible; an infeasible result would indicate that some people are overrated (or underrated), much like an imbalance between supply and demand indicates that some goods are overpriced (or underpriced).

The NTU value of a game need not be unique. This may at first sound strange, since unlike stability concepts such as the core, one might expect an 'index of social productivity' to be unique. But perhaps it is not so strange when one reflects that even a person's net worth depends on the prevailing (equilibrium) prices, which are not uniquely determined by the exogenous description of the economy.

The Shapley NTU value has been used in a very wide variety of economic and political-economic applications. To cite just one example, the Nash bargaining problem has a unique NTU value, which coincides with Nash's solution. For a partial bibliography of applications, see the references of Aumann (1985).

We have discussed the historical importance of TU as pointing the way for NTU results (*1930–1950*, vi). There is one piquant case in the reverse direction. Just as positive results are easier to obtain for TU, negative results are easier for NTU. Non-existence of stable sets was first discovered in NTU games (Stearns, 1965), and this eventually led to Lucas's famous example (1969) of non-existence for TU.

(ii) *Incomplete information.* In 1957, Luce and Raiffa wrote that a fundamental assumption of game theory is that 'each player... is fully aware of the rules of the game and the utility functions of each of the players... this is a serious idealization which only rarely is met in actual situations' (p. 49). To deal with this problem, John Harsanyi (1967–8) constructed the theory of games of incomplete information (sometimes called differential or asymmetric information). This major conceptual breakthrough laid the theoretical groundwork for the great blooming of information economics that got under way soon thereafter, and that has become one of the major themes of modern economics and game theory.

For simplicity, we confine attention to strategic form games in which each player has a fixed, known set of strategies, and the only uncertainty is about the utility functions of the other players; these assumptions are removable. Bayesian rationality in the tradition of Savage (1954) dictates that all uncertainty can be made explicit; in particular, each player has a personal probability distribution on the possible utility (payoff) functions of the other player. But these distributions are not sufficient to describe the situation. It is not enough to specify what each player thinks about the other's payoffs; one must also know what he thinks they think about his (and each others') payoffs, what he thinks they think he thinks about their payoffs, and so on. This complicated infinite regress would appear to make useful analysis very difficult.

To cut this Gordian knot, Harsanyi postulated that each player may be one of several *types*, where a type determines both a player's own utility function and his personal probability distribution on the types of the other players. Each

29

player is postulated to know his own type only. This enables him to calculate what he thinks the other players' types – and therefore their utilities – are. Moreover, his personal distribution on their types also enables him to calculate what he thinks they think about his type, and therefore about his utility. The reasoning extends indefinitely, and yields the infinite regress discussed above *as an outcome*.

Intuitively, one may think of a player's type as a possible state of mind, which would determine his utility as well as his distribution over others' states of mind. One need not assume that the number of states of mind (types) is finite; the theory works as well for, say, a continuum of types. But even with just two players and two types for each player, one gets a non-trivial infinite string of beliefs about utilities, beliefs about beliefs, and so on.

A model of this kind – with players, strategies, types, utilities and personal probability distributions – is called an *I-game* (incomplete information game). A *strategic equilibrium* in an I-game consists of a strategy for each *type* of each player, which maximizes that type's expected payoff given the strategies of the other players' types.

Harsanyi's formulation of I-games is primarily a device for thinking about incomplete information in an orderly fashion, bringing that wild, bucking infinite regress under conceptual control. An (incomplete) analogy is to the strategic form of a game, a conceptual simplification without which it is unlikely that game theory would have gotten very far. Practically speaking, the strategic form of a particular game such as chess is totally unmanageable, one can't even begin to write it down. The advantage of the strategic form is that it is a comparatively simple formulation, mathematically much simpler than the extensive form; it enables one to formulate and calculate examples, which suggest principles that can be formulated and proved as general theorems. All this would be much more difficult – probably unachievable – with the extensive form; one would be unable to see the forest for the trees. A similar relationship holds between Harsanyi's I-game formulation and direct formulations in terms of beliefs about beliefs. (Compare the discussion of perspective made in connection with the coalitional form (*1930–1950*, i).) That situation is somewhat different, though, since in going to the coalitional form, substantive information is lost. Harsanyi's formulation of I-games loses no information; it is a more abstract and simple – and hence transparent and workable – formulation of the same data as would be contained in an explicit description of the infinite regress.

Harsanyi called an I-game *consistent* if all the personal probability distributions of all the types are derivable as posteriors from a single prior distribution p on all n-tuples of types. Most applications of the theory have assumed consistency. A consistent I-game is closely related to the ordinary strategic game (C-*game*) obtained from it by allowing 'nature' to choose an n-tuple of types at random according to the distribution p, then informing each player of his type, and then playing the I-game as before. In particular, the strategic equilibria of a consistent I-game are essentially the same as the strategic equilibria of the related C-game. In the cooperative theory, however, an I-game is rather different from the related

C-game, since binding agreements can only be made after the players know their types. Bargaining and other cooperative models have been treated in the incomplete information context by Harsanyi and Selten (1972), Wilson (1978), Myerson (1979, 1984) and others.

In a repeated game of incomplete information, the same game is played again and again, but the players do not have full information about it; for example, they may not know the others' utility functions. The actions of the players may implicitly reveal private information, e.g. about preferences; this may or may not be advantageous for them. We have seen (*1950–1960*, iii) that repetition may be viewed as a paradigm for cooperation. Strategic equilibria of repeated games of incomplete information may be interpreted as a subtle bargaining process, in which the players gradually reach wider and wider agreement, developing trust for each other while slowly revealing more and more information (Hart, 1985b).

(iii) *Common knowledge*. Luce and Raiffa, in the statement quoted at the beginning of (ii), missed a subtle but important point. It is not enough that each player be fully aware of the rules of the game and the utility functions of the players. Each player must also be aware of this fact, i.e. of the awareness of all the players; moreover, each player must be aware that each player is aware that each player is aware, and so on ad infinitum. In brief, the awareness of the description of the game by all players must be a part of the description itself.

There is evidence that game theorists had been vaguely cognizant of the need for some such requirement ever since the late Fifties or early Sixties; but the first to give a clear, sharp formulation was the philosopher D.K. Lewis (1969). Lewis defined an event as *common knowledge* among a set of agents if all know it, all know that all know it, and so on ad infinitum.

The common knowledge assumption underlies all of game theory and much of economic theory. Whatever be the model under discussion, whether complete or incomplete information, consistent or inconsistent, repeated or one-shot, cooperative or non-cooperative, the model itself must be assumed common knowledge; otherwise the model is insufficiently specified, and the analysis incoherent.

(iv) *Bargaining set, kernel, nucleolus*. The core excludes the unique symmetric outcome $(1/3, 1/3, 1/3)$ of the three-person voting game, because any two-person coalition can improve upon it. Stable sets (*1930–1950*, v) may be seen as a way of expressing our intuitive discomfort with this exclusion. Another way is the bargaining set (Davis and Maschler, 1965). If, say, 1 suggests $(1/2, 1/2, 0)$ to replace $(1/3, 1/3, 1/3)$, then 3 can suggest to 2 that he is as good a partner as 1; indeed, 3 can even offer $2/3$ to 2, still leaving himself with the $1/3$ he was originally assigned. Formally, if we call $(1/2, 1/2, 0)$ an *objection* to $(1/3, 1/3, 1/3)$, then $(0, 2/3, 1/3)$ is a *counter objection*, since it yields to 3 at least as much as he was originally assigned, and yields to 3's partners in the counter-objection at least as much as they were assigned either originally or in the objection. In brief, the counter-objecting player tells the objecting one, 'I can maintain my level of payoff and that of my partners, while matching your offers to players we both need.'

An imputation is in the core iff there is no objection to it. It is in the *bargaining set* iff there is no *justified* objection to it, i.e. one that has no counter-objection.

Like the stable sets, the bargaining set includes the core (dominating and objecting are essentially the same). Unlike the core and the set of stable sets, the bargaining set is for TU games never empty (Peleg, 1967). For NTU it may be empty (Peleg, 1963b); but Asscher (1976) has defined a non-empty variant; see also Billera (1970a).

Crucial parameters in calculating whether an imputation x is in the bargaining set of v are the *excesses* $v(S) - x(S)$ of coalitions S w.r.t. x, which measure the ability of members of S to use x in an objection (or counter-objection). Not, as is often wrongly assumed, because the initiator of the objection can assign the excess to himself while keeping his partners at their original level, but for precisely the opposite reason: because he can parcel out the excess to his partners, which makes counterobjecting more difficult.

The excess is so ubiquitous in bargaining set calculations that it eventually took on intuitive significance of its own. This led to the formulation of two additional solution concepts: the *kernel* (Davis and Maschler, 1965), which is always included in the bargaining set but is often much smaller, and the *nucleolus* (Schmeidler, 1969), which always consists of a single point in the kernel.

To define the nucleolus, choose first all those imputations x whose maximum excess (among the 2^n excesses $v(S) - x(S)$) is minimum (among all imputations). Among the resulting imputations, choose next those whose second largest excess is minimum, and so on. Schmeidler's theorem asserts that by the time we have gone through this procedure 2^n times, there is just one imputation left.

We have seen that the excess is a measure of a coalition's 'manoeuvring ability'; in these terms the greatest measure of stability, as expressed by the nucleolus, is reached when all coalitions have manoeuvring ability as nearly alike as possible. An alternative interpretation of the excess is as a measure of S's total dissatisfaction with x, the volume of the cry that S might raise against x. In these terms, the nucleolus suggests that the final accommodation is determined by the loudest cry against it. Note that the *total* cry is determining, not the average cry; a large number of moderately unhappy citizens can be as potent a force for change as a moderate number of very unhappy ones. Variants of the nucleolus that use the average excess miss this point.

When the core is non-empty, the nucleolus is always in it. The nucleolus has been given several alternative characterizations, direct (Kohlberg, 1971, 1972) as well as axiomatic (Sobolev, 1975). The kernel was axiomatically characterized by Peleg (1986), and many interesting relationships have been found between the bargaining set, core, kernel and nucleolus (e.g. Maschler, Peleg and Shapley, 1979). There is a large body of applications, of which we here cite just one: In a decisive weighted voting game, the nucleolus constitutes a set of weights (Peleg, 1968). Thus the nucleolus may be thought of as a natural generalization of 'voting weights' to arbitrary games. (We have already seen that value and weights are quite different: see *1950–1960*, vi.)

(v) *The Equivalence Principle.* Perhaps the most remarkable single phenomenon in game and economic theory is the relationship between the price equilibria of a competitive market economy, and all but one of the major solution concepts for the corresponding game (the one exception is the stable set, about which more below). By a 'market economy' we here mean a pure exchange economy, or a production economy with constant returns.

We call an economy 'competitive' if it has many agents, each individual one of whom has too small an endowment to have a significant effect. This has been modelled by three approaches. In the *asymptotic approach*, one lets the number of agents tend to infinity, and shows that in an appropriate sense, the solution concept in question – core, value, bargaining set or strategic equilibrium – tends to the set of competitive allocations (those corresponding to price equilibria). In the *continuum approach*, the agents constitute a (non-atomic) continuum, and one shows that the solution concept in question actually equals the set of competitive allocations. In the *non-standard* approach, the agents constitute a non-standard model of the integers in the sense of Robinson (1966), and again one gets equality. Both the continuum and the non-standard approaches require extensions of the theory to games with infinitely many players; see vi.

Intuitively, the equivalence principle says that the institution of market prices arises naturally from the basic forces at work in a market, (almost) no matter what we assume about the way in which these forces work. (Compare *1930–1950*, ix.)

For simplicity in this section, unless otherwise indicated, the terms 'core', 'value', etc., refer to the limiting case. Thus 'core' means the limit of the cores of the finite economies, or the core of the continuum economy, or of the non-standard economy.

For the core, the asymptotic approach was pioneered by Edgeworth (1881), Shubik (1959a) and Debreu and Scarf (1963). Anderson (1986) is an excellent survey of the large literature that ensued. Early writers on the continuum approach included Aumann (1964) and Vind (1964); the non-standard approach was developed by Brown and Robinson (1975). Except for Shubik's, all these contributions were NTU. See the entry on CORES. After a twenty-year courtship, this was the honeymoon of game theory and mathematical economics, and it is difficult to convey the palpable excitement of those early years of intimacy between the two disciplines.

Some early references for the value equivalence principle, covering both the asymptotic and continuum approaches, were listed above (*1930–1950*, vi). For the non-standard approach, see Brown and Loeb (1976). Whereas the core of a competitive economy equals the set of *all* competitive allocations, this holds for the value only when preferences are smooth (Shapley, 1964; Aumann and Shapley, 1974; Aumann, 1975; Mas-Colell, 1977). Without smoothness, every value allocation is competitive, but not every competitive allocation need be a value allocation. When preferences are kinky (non-differentiable utilities), the core is often quite large, and then the value is usually a very small subset of the core; it gives much more information. In the TU case, for example, the value is always a single point, even when the core is very large. Moreover, it occupies a central position in the core (Hart, 1980; Tauman, 1981; Mertens, 1987); in particular, when the core has a centre of symmetry, the value is that centre of symmetry (Hart, 1977a).

For example, suppose that in a glove market (*1950–1960*, vi), the number (or measure) of left-glove holders equals that of right-glove holders. Then at a price equilibrium, the price ratio between left and right gloves may be anything between 0 and ∞ (inclusive!). Thus the left-glove holders may end up giving away their merchandise for nothing to the right-glove holders, or the other way round, or anything in between. The same, of course, holds for the core. But the value prescribes precisely equal prices for right and left gloves.

It should be noted that in a finite market, the core contains the competitive allocations, but usually also much more. As the number of agents increases, the core 'shrinks', in the limit leaving only the competitive allocations. This is not so for the value; in finite markets, the value allocations may be disjoint from the core, and a fortiori from the competitive allocations (*1950–1960*, vi).

We have seen (1930–1950, iv) that the core represents a very strong and indeed not quite reasonable notion of stability. It might therefore seem perhaps not so terribly surprising that it shrinks to the competitive allocations. What happens, one may ask, when one considers one of the more reasonable stability concepts that are based on domination, such as the bargaining set or the stable sets?

For the bargaining set of TU markets, an asymptotic equivalence theorem was established by Shapley and Shubik in the mid-Seventies, though it was not published until 1984. Extending this result to NTU, to the continuum, or to both seemed difficult. The problems were conceptual as well as mathematical; it was difficult to give a coherent formulation. In 1986, Shapley presented the TU proof at a conference on the equivalence principle that took place at Stony Brook. A. Mas-Colell, who was in the audience, recognized the relevance of several results that he had obtained in other connections; within a day or two he was able to formulate and prove the equivalence principle for the bargaining set in NTU continuum economies (Mas-Colell, 1988). In particular, this implies the core equivalence principle; but it is a much stronger and more satisfying result.

For the strategic equilibrium the situation had long been less satisfactory, though there were results (Shubik, 1973; Dubey and Shapley, 1980). The difficulty was in constructing a satisfactory strategic (or extensive) model of exchange. Very recently Douglas Gale (1986) provided such a model and used it to prove a remarkable equivalence theorem for strategic equilibria in the continuum mode.

The one notable exception to the equivalence principle is the case of stable sets, which predict the formation of cartels even in fully competitive economies (Hart, 1974). For example, suppose half the agents in a continuum initially hold 2 units of bread each, half initially hold 2 units of cheese, and the utility functions are concave, differentiable and symmetric (e.g., $u(x, y) = \sqrt{x} + \sqrt{y}$). There is then a unique price equilibrium, with equal prices for bread and cheese. Thus each agent ends up with one piece of bread and one piece of cheese; this is also the unique point in the core and in the bargaining set, and the unique NTU value. But stable set theory predicts that the cheese holders will form a cartel, the bread holders will form a cartel, and these two cartels will bargain with each other as if they were individuals. The upshot will depend on the bargaining, and may yield an outcome that is much better for one side than for the other. Thus at each point of the unique stable set with the full symmetry of the game, each agent on each side gets as much as each other agent on that side; but these two amounts depend on the bargaining, and may be quite different from each other.

In a sense, the failure of stable set theory to fall into line makes the other results even more impressive. It shows that there isn't some implicit tautology lurking in the background, that the equivalence principle makes a substantive assertion.

In the *Theory of Games*, von Neumann and Morgenstern (1944) wrote that

> when the number of participants becomes really great, some hope emerges that the influence of every particular participant will become negligible... These are, of course, the classical conditions of 'free competition'... The current assertions concerning free competition appear to be very valuable surmises and inspiring anticipations of results. But they are not results, and it is scientifically unsound to treat them as such.

One may take the theorems constituting the equivalence principle as embodying precisely this kind of 'result'. Yet it is interesting that Morgenstern himself, who died in 1977, never became convinced of the validity of the equivalence principle; he thought of it as mathematically correct but economically wrongheaded. It was his firm opinion that economic agents organize themselves into coalitions, that perfect competition is a fiction, and that stable sets explain it all. The greatness of the man is attested to by the fact that though scientifically opposed to the equivalence principle, he gave generous support, both financial and moral, to workers in this area.

(vi) *Many players*. The preface to *Contributions to the Theory of Games* I (Kuhn and Tucker, 1950) contains an agenda for future research that is remarkable in that so many of its items – computation of minimax, existence of stable sets, *n*-person value, NTU games, dynamic games – did in fact become central in subsequent work. Item 11 in this agenda reads, 'establish significant asymptotic properties of *n*-person games, for large *n*'. We have seen (v) how this was realized in the equivalence principle for large economies. But actually, political game models with many players are at least as old as economic ones, and may be older. During the early Sixties, L.S. Shapley, working alone and with various collaborators, wrote a series of seven memoranda at the Rand Corporation under the generic title 'Values of Large Games', several of which explored models of large elections, using the asymptotic and the continuum approaches. Among these were models which had both 'atoms' – players who are significant as individuals – and an 'ocean' of individually insignificant players. One example of this is a corporation with many small stockholders and a few large stockholders; see also Milnor and Shapley (1978). 'Mixed' models of this kind – i.e. with an ocean as well as atoms – have been explored in economic as well as political contexts using various solution notions, and a large literature has developed. The core of mixed markets has been studied by Drèze, Gabszewicz and Gepts (1969), Gabszewicz and Mertens (1971), Shitovitz (1973) and many others. For the nucleolus of 'mixed' voting games, see Galil (1974). Among the studies of values of mixed games are Hart (1973), Fogelman and Quinzii (1980) and Neyman (1987).

Large games in which *all* the players are individually insignificant – *non-atomic* games – have also been studied extensively. Among the early contributions to value theory in this connection are Kannai (1966), Riker and Shapley (1968) and Aumann and Shapley (1974). The subject has proliferated greatly, with well over a hundred contributions since 1974, including theoretical contributions as well as economic and political applications.

There are also games with infinitely many players in which *all* the players are atoms, namely games with a denumerable infinity of players. Again, values and voting games loom large in this literature. See, e.g., Shapley (1962), Artstein (1972) and Berbee (1981).

(vii) *Cores of finite games and markets.* Though the core was defined as an independent solution concept by Gillies and Shapley already in the early Fifties, it was not until the Sixties that a significant body of theory was developed around it. The major developments centre around conditions for the core to be non-empty; gradually it came to be realized that such conditions hold most naturally and fully when the game has an 'economic' rather than a 'political' flavour, when it may be thought of as arising from a market economy.

The landmark contributions in this area were the following: the Gale–Shapley 1962 paper on the core of a marriage market; the work of Bondareva (1963) and Shapley (1967) on the balancedness condition for the non-emptiness of the core of a TU game; Scarf's 1967 work on balancedness in NTU games; the work of Shapley and Shubik (1969a) characterizing TU market games in terms of non-emptiness of the core; and subsequent work, mainly associated with the names of Billera and Bixby (1973), that extended the Shapley–Shubik condition to NTU games. Each of these contributions was truly seminal, in that it inspired a large body of subsequent work.

Gale and Shapley (1962) asked whether it is possible to match *m* women with *m* men so that there is no pair consisting of an unmatched woman and man who prefer each other to the partners with whom they were matched. The corresponding question for homosexuals has a negative answer: the preferences of four homosexuals may be such that no matter how they are paired off, there is always an unmatched pair of people who prefer each other to the person with whom they were matched. This is so, for example, if the preferences of *a*, *b* and *c* are cyclic, whereas *d* is lowest in all the others' scales. But for the heterosexual problem, Gale and Shapley showed that the answer is positive.

This may be stated by saying that the appropriately defined NTU coalitional game has a non-empty core. Gale and Shapley proved not only the non-emptiness but also provided a simple algorithm for finding a point in it.

This work has spawned a large literature on the cores of discrete market games. One fairly general recent result is Kaneko and Wooders (1982), but there are many others. A fascinating application to the assignment of interns to hospitals has been documented by Roth (1984). It turns out that American hospitals, after fifty years of turmoil, finally developed in 1950 a method of assignment that is precisely a point in the core.

We come now to general conditions for the core to be non-empty. Call a TU game v superadditive at a coalition U if $v(U) \geqslant \Sigma_j v(S_j)$ for any partition of U into disjoint coalition S_j. This may be strengthened by allowing partitions of U into disjoint 'part-time' coalitions θS, interpreted as coalitions S operating during a proportion θ of the time ($0 \leqslant \theta \leqslant 1$). Such a partition is therefore a family $\{\theta_i S_j\}$, where the total amount of time that each player in U is employed is exactly 1; i.e., where $\Sigma_j \theta_j \chi_{S_j} = \chi_U$, where χ_S is the indicator function of S. If we think of $v(S)$ as the revenue that S can generate when operating full-time, then the part-time coalition θS generates $\theta v(S)$. Superadditivity at U for part-time coalitions thus means that

$$\sum_j \theta_j \chi_{S_j} = \chi_U \text{ implies } v(U) \geqslant \sum_j \theta_j v(S_j).$$

A TU game v obeying this condition for U = I is called *balanced*; for all U, *totally balanced*.

Intuitively, it is obvious that a game with a non-empty core must be superadditive at I; and once we have the notion of part-time coalitions, it is only slightly less obvious that it must be balanced,. The converse was established (independently) by Bondareva (1963) and Shapley (1967). Thus a *TU game has a non-empty core if and only if it is balanced*.

The connection between the core and balancedness (generalized superadditivity) led to several lines of research. Scarf (1967) extended the notion of balancedness to NTU games, then showed that every balanced NTU game has a non-empty core. Unlike the Bondareva–Shapley proof, which is based on linear programming methods, Scarf's proof was more closely related to fixed-point ideas. Eventually, Scarf realized that his methods could be used actually to prove Brouwer's fixed-point theorem, and moreover, to develop effective algorithms for approximating fixed points. This, in turn, led to the development of algorithms for approximating competitive equilibria of economies (Scarf, 1973), and to a whole area of numerical analysis dealing with the approximation of fixed points.

An extension of the Bondareva–Shapley result to the NTU case that is different from Scarf's was obtained by Billera (1970a).

Another line of research that grew out of balancedness deals with characterizing markets in purely game-theoretic terms. When can a given coalitional game v be expressed as a market game (*1930–1950*, ii)? The Bondareva–Shapley theorem implies that market games have non-empty cores, and this also follows from the fact that outcomes corresponding to competitive equilibria are always in the core. Since a subgame of a market game is itself a market game, it follows that *for v to be a market game, it is necessary that it and all its subgames have non-empty cores*, i.e., that the game be totally balanced. (A *subgame* of a coalitional game v is defined by restricting its domain to subcoalitions of a given coalition U.) Shapley and Shubik (1969a) showed that *this necessary condition is also sufficient.* Balancedness itself is not sufficient, since there exist games with non-empty cores having subgames with empty cores (e.g., $|I| = 4m$ $v(S) := 0$, 0, 1, 1, 2 when $|S| = 0$, 1, 2, 3, 4, respectively).

For the NTU case, characterization of market games have been obtained by Billera and Bixby (1973), Mas-Colell (1975), and others.

Though the subject of this section is finite markets, it is nevertheless worthwhile to relate the results to non-atomic games (where the players constitute a non-atomic continuum, an 'ocean'). The total balancedness conditon then takes on a particularly simple form. Suppose, for simplicity, that v is a function of finitely many measures, i.e., $v(S) = f(\mu(S))$, where $\mu(\mu_1, \ldots, \mu_n)$, and the μ_j are non-atomic measures. Then v is a market game iff f is concave and 1-homogeneous ($f(\theta x) = \theta(fx)$) when $\theta \geqslant 0$). This is equivalent to saying that v is superadditive (at all coalitions), and f is 1-homogeneous (Aumann and Shapley, 1974).

Perhaps the most remarkable expression of the connection between super-additivity and the core has been obtained by Wooders (1983). Consider coalitional games with a fixed finite number k of 'types' of players, the coalitional form being given by $v(S) = f(\mu(S))$, where $\mu(S)$ is the profile of type sizes in S, i.e. it is a vector whose ith coordinate represents the number of type i players in S. (To specify the game, $\mu(I)$ must also be specified.) Assume that f is superadditive, i.e. $f(x + y) \geqslant f(x) + f(y)$ for all x and y with non-negative integer coordinates; this assures the superadditivity of v. Moreover, assume that f obeys a 'Lipschitz' condition, namely that $|f(x) - f(y)/\|x - y\|$ is uniformly bounded for all $x \neq y$, where $\|x\| := \max_j |x_j|$. Then for each $\varepsilon > 0$, when the number of players is sufficiently large, the ε-core is non-empty. (The ε-core is defined as the set of all outcomes x such that $x(S) \geqslant v(S) - \varepsilon|S|$ for all S.) Roughly, the result says that the core is 'almost' non-empty for sufficiently large games that are superadditive and obey the Lipschitz condition. Intuitively, the superadditivity together with the Lipschitz condition yield 'approximate' 1-homogeneity, and in the presence of 1-homogeneity, superadditivity is equivalent to concavity. Thus f is approximately a 1-homogeneous concave function, so that we are back in a situation similar to that treated in the previous paragraph. What makes this result so remarkable is that other than the Lipschitz condition, the only substantive assumption is superadditivity.

Wooders (1983) also obtained a similar theorem for NTU; Wooders and Zame (1984) obtained a formulation that does away with the finite type assumption.

1970–1986

We do not yet have sufficient distance to see the developments of this period in proper perspective. Political and political economic models were studied in depth.

Non-cooperative game theory was applied to a large variety of particular economic models, and this led to the study of important variants on the refinements of the equilibrium concept. Great strides forward were made in almost all the areas that had been initiated in previous decades, such as repreated games (both of complete and of incomplete information), stochastic games, value, core, nucleolus, bargaining theory, games with many players and so on (many of these developments have been mentioned above). Game theory was applied to biology, computer science, moral philosophy, cost allocation. New light was shed on old concepts such as randomized strategies.

Sociologically, the discipline proliferated greatly. Some 16 or 17 people participated in the first international workshop on game theory held in Jerusalem in 1965; the fourth one, held in Cornell in 1978, attracted close to 100, and the discipline is now too large to make such workshops useful. An international workshop in the relatively restricted area of repeated games, held in Jerusalem in 1985, attracted over fifty participants. The *International Journal of Game Theory* was founded in 1972; *Mathematics of Operations Research*, founded in 1975, was organized into three major 'areas', one of them game theory. Economic theory journals, such as the *Journal of Mathematical Economics*, the *Journal of Economic Theory*, *Econometrica* and others devoted increasing proportions of their space to game theory. Important centres of research, in addition to the existing ones, sprang up in France, Holland, Japan, England and India, and at many Universities in the United States.

Gradually, game theory also became less personal, less the exclusive concern of a small 'in' group whose members all know each other. For years, it had been a tradition in game theory to publish only a fraction of what one had found, and then only after great delays, and not always what was most important. Many results were passed on by word of mouth, or remained hidden in ill-circulated research memoranda. The 'Folk Theorem' to which we alluded above (*1950–1960*, iii) is an example. This tradition had both beneficial and deleterious effects. On the one hand, people did not rush into print with trivia, and the slow cooking of results improved their flavour. As a result, phenomena were sometimes rediscovered several times, which is perhaps not entirely bad, since you understand something best when you discover it yourself. On the other hand, it was difficult for outsiders to break in; non-publication caused less interest to be generated than would otherwise have been, and significantly impeded progress.

Be that as it may, those days are over. There are now hundreds of practitioners, they do not all know each other, and sometimes have never even heard of one another. It is no longer possible to communicate in the old way, and as a result, people are publishing more quickly. As in other disciplines, it is becoming difficult to keep abreast of the important developments. Game theory has matured.

(i) *Applications to biology.* A development of outstanding importance, whose implications are not yet fully appreciated, is the application of game theory to evolutionary *biology*. The high priest of this subject is John Maynard Smith (1982), a biologist whose concept of *evolutionarily stable strategy*, a variant of strategic equilibrium, caught the imagination both of biologists and of game theorists. On the game theoretic side, the theme was taken up by Reinhard Selten (1980, 1983) and his school; a conference on 'Evolutionary theory in biology and economics', organized by Selten in Bielefeld in 1985, was enormously successful in bringing field biologists together with theorists of games to discuss these issues. A typical paper was tit for tat in the great tit (Regelmann and Curio, 1986); using actual field observations, complete with photographs, it describes how the celebrated 'tit for tat' strategy in the repeated prisoner's dilemma (Axelrod, 1984) accurately describes the behaviour of males and females of a rather common species of bird called the great tit, when protecting their young from predators.

It turns out that ordinary, utility maximizing rationality is much more easily observed in animals and even plants than it is in human beings. There are even situations where rats do significantly better than human beings. Consider, for example, the famous probability matching experiment, where the subject must predict the values of a sequence of i.i.d. random variables taking the values L and R with probabilities 3/4 and 1/4 respectively; each correct prediction is rewarded. It is of course optimal always to predict L; but human subjects tend to match the probabilities, i.e. to predict L about 3/4 of the time. On the other hand, while rats are not perfect (i.e. do not predict L *all* the time), they do predict L significantly more often than human beings.

Several explanations have been suggested. One is that in human experimentation, the subjects try subconsciously to 'guess right', i.e. to guess what the experimenter 'wants' them to do, rather than maximizing utility. Another is simply that the rats are more highly motivated. They are brought down to 80 per cent of their normal body weight, are literally starving; it is much more important for them to behave optimally than it is for human subjects.

Returning to theory, though the notion of strategic equilibrium seems on the face of it simple and natural enough, a careful examination of the definition leads to some doubts and questions as to why and under what conditions the players in a game might be expected to play a strategic equilibrium: see the essay on NASH EQUILIBRIUM. Evolutionary theory suggests a simple rationale for strategic equilibrium, in which there is no conscious or overt decision making at all. For definiteness, we confine attention to two-person games, though the same ideas apply to the general case. We think of each of the two players as a whole species rather than an individual; reproduction is assumed asexual. The set of pure strategies of each player is interpreted as the locus of some gene (examples of a locus are eye colour, degree of aggressiveness, etc.); individual pure strategies are interpreted as alleles (blue or green or brown eyes, aggressive or timid behaviour, etc.). A given individual of each species possesses just one allele at the given locus; he interacts with precisely one individual in the other species, who also has just one allele at the locus of interest. The result of the interaction is a definite increment or decrement in the fitness of each of the two individuals, i.e. the number (or expected number) of his offspring; thus the payoff in the game is denominated in terms of fitness.

In these terms, a mixed strategy is a distribution of alleles throughout the population of the species (e.g., 40% aggressive, 60% timid). If each individual of each species is just as likely to meet any one individual of the other species as any other one, then the probability distribution of alleles that each individual faces is precisely given by the original mixed strategy. It then follows that a given pair of mixed strategies is a strategic equilibrium if and only if it represents a population equilibrium, i.e. a pair of distributions of characteristics (alleles) that does not tend to change.

Unfortunately, sexual reproduction screws up this story, and indeed the entire Maynard Smith approach has been criticized for this reason. But to be useful, the story does not have to be taken entirely literally. For example, it applies to evolution that is cultural rather than biological. In this approach, a 'game' is interpreted as a *kind* of confrontational situation (like shopping for a car) rather than a specific instance of such a situation; a 'player' is a role ('buyer' or 'salesman'), not an individual human being; a pure strategy is a possible kind of behaviour in this role ('hard sell' or 'soft sell'). Up to now this is indeed not very different from traditional game theoretic usage. What is different in the evolutionary interpretation is that pure or mixed strategic equilibria do not represent conscious rational choices of the players, but rather a population equilibrium which evolves as the result of how successful certain behaviour is in certain roles.

(ii) *Randomization as ignorance.* In the traditional view of strategy randomization, the players use a randomizing device, such as a coin flip, to decide on their actions. This view has always had difficulties. Practically speaking, the idea that serious people would base important decisions on the flip of a coin is difficult to swallow. Conceptually, too, there are problems. The reason a player must randomize in equilibrium is only to keep others from deviating. For himself, randomizing is unnecessary; he will do as well by choosing any pure strategy that appears with positive probability in his equilibrium mixed strategy.

Of course, there is no problem if we adopt the evolutionary model described above in (i); mixed strategies appear as population distributions, and there is no explicit randomization at all. But what is one to make of randomization within the more usual paradigm of conscious, rational choice?

According to Savage (1954), randomness is not physical, but represents the ignorance of the decision maker. You associate a probability with every event about which you are ignorant, whether this event is a coin flip or a strategic choice by another player. The important thing in strategy randomization is that the *other* players be ignorant or what you are doing, and that they ascribe the appropriate probabilities to each of your pure strategies. It is not necessary for you actually to flip a coin.

The first to break away from the idea of explicit randomization was J. Harsanyi (1973). He showed that if the payoffs to each player i in a game are subjected to small independent random perturbations, known to i but not to the other players, then the resulting game of incomplete information has *pure* strategy equilibria that correspond to the mixed strategy equilibria of the original game. In plain words, nobody really randomizes. The appearance of randomization is due to the payoffs not being exactly known to all; each player, who does know his own payoff exactly, has a unique optimal action against his estimate of what the others will do.

This reasoning may be taken on step further. Even without perturbed payoffs, the players simply do not know which strategies will be chosen by the other players. At an equilibrium of 'matching pennies', each player knows very well what he himself will do, but ascribes $1/2-1/2$ probabilities to the other's actions; he also knows that the other ascribes those probabilities to his own actions, though it is admittedly not quite obvious that this is necessarily the case. In the case of a general n-person game, the situation is essentially similar; the mixed strategies of i can always be understood as describing the uncertainty of players other than i about what i will do (Aumann, 1987).

(iii) *Refinements of strategic equilibrium.* In analysing specific economic models using the strategic equilibrium – an activity carried forward with great vigour since about 1975 – it was found that Nash's definition does not provide adequately for rational choices given one's information at each stage of an extensive game. Very roughly, the reason is that Nash's definition ignores contingenices 'off the equilibrium path'. To remedy this, various 'refinements' of strategic equilibrium have been defined, starting with Selten's (1975) 'trembling hand' equilibrium. Please refer to our discussion of Zermelo's theorem (*1930–1950*, vi), and to Section IV of the entry on NASH EQUILIBRIUM.

The interesting aspect of these refinements is that they use *irrationality* to arrive at a strong form of rationality. In one way or another, all of them work by assuming that irrationality cannot be ruled out, that the players ascribe irrationality to each other with a small probability. True rationality requires 'noise'; it cannot grow in sterile ground, it cannot feed on itself only.

(iv) *Bounded rationality.* For a long time it has been felt that both game and economic theory assume too much rationality. For example, the hundred-times repeated prisoner's dilemma has some $2^{2^{100}}$ pure strategies; all the books in the world are not large enough to write this number even once in decimal notation. There is no practical way in which all these strategies can be considered truly available to the players. On the face of it, this would seem to render statements about the equilibrium points of such games (*1950–1960*, iv) less compelling, since it is quite possible that if the sets of strategies were suitably restricted, the equilibria would change drastically.

For many years, little on the formal level was done about these problems. Recently the theory of automata has been used for formulations of bounded rationality in repeated games. Neyman (1985a) assumes that only strategies that are programmable on an automaton of exogenously fixed size can be considered 'available' to the players. He then shows that even when the size is very large, one obtains results that are qualitatively different from those when all strategies are permitted. Thus in the n-times repeated prisoner's dilemma, only the greedy-greedy outcome can occur in equilibrium; but if one restricts the players to using automata with as many as $e^{o(n)}$ states, then for sufficiently large n, one can approximate in equilibrium any feasible individually rational outcome, and in particular the friendly-friendly outcome. For example, this is the case if the number of states is bounded by any fixed polynomial in n. In unpublished work, Neyman has generalized this result from the prisoner's dilemma to arbitrary games; specifically, he shows that a result similar to the Folk Theorem holds in any long finitely repeated game, when the automaton size is limited as above to subexponential.

Another approach has been used by Rubinstein (1986), with dramatically different results. In this work, the automaton itself is endogenous; all states of the automaton must actually be used on the equilibrium path. Applied to the prisoner's dilemma, this assumption leads to the conclusion that in equilibrium, one cannot get anywhere near the friendly-friendly outcome. Intuitively, the requirement that all states be used in equilibrium rules out strategies that punish deviations from equilibrium, and these are essential to the implicit enforcement mechanism that underlies the folk theorem. See the discussion at (*1950–1960*, iii) above.

(v) *Distributed computing.* In the previous subsection (iv) we discussed applications of computer science to game theory. There are also applications in the opposite direction; with the advent of distributed computing, game theory has become of interest in computer science. Different units of a distributed computing system are viewed as different players, who must communicate and coordinate. Breakdowns and failures of one unit are often modelled as malevolent, so as to get an idea as to how bad the worst case can be. From the point of view of computer tampering and crime, the model of the malevolent player is not merely a fiction; similar remarks hold for cryptography, where the system must be made proof against purposeful attempts to 'break in'. Finally, multi-user systems come close to being games in the ordinary sense of the word.

(vi) *Consistency* is a remarkable property which, in one form or another, is common to just about all game theoretic solution concepts. Let us be given a game, which for definiteness we denote v, though it may be NTU or even non-cooperative. Let x be an outcome that 'solves' the game in some sense, like the value or nucleolus or a point in the core. Suppose now that some coalition S wishes to view the situation as if the players outside S get their components of x so to speak exogenously, without participating in the play. That means that the players in S are playing the 'reduced game' v_x^S, whose all-player set is S. It is not always easy to say just how v_x^S should be defined, but let's leave that aside for the moment. Suppose we apply to v_x^S the same solution concept that when applied to v yields x. Then the consistency property is that $x|S$ (x restricted to S) is the resulting solution. For example, if x is the nucleolus of v, then for each v, the restriction of $x|S$ is the nucleolus of v_x^S.

Consistency implies that it is not too important how the player set is chosen.

One can confine attention to a 'small world', and the outcome for the denizens of this world will be the same as if we had looked at them in a 'big world'.

In a game theoretic context, consistency was first noticed by J. Harsanyi (1959) for the Nash solution to the n-person bargaining game. This is simply an NTU game V in which the only significant coalitions are the single players and the all-player coalition, and the single players are normalized to get 0. The Nash solution, axiomatized by Harsanyi (1959), is the outcome x that maximizes the product $x^1 x^2 \ldots x^n$. To explain the consistency condition, let us look at the case $n = 3$, in which case $V(\{1, 2, 3\})$ is a subset of 3-space. If we let $S = \{1, 2\}$, and if x_0 is the Nash solution, then 3 should get x_0^3. That means that 1 and 2 are confined to bargaining within that slice of $V\{(1, 2, 3)\}$ that is determined by the plane $x^3 = x_0^3$. According to the Nash solution for the two-person case, they should maximize $x^1 x^2$ over this slice; it is not difficult to see that this maximum is attained at (x_0^1, x_0^2), which is exactly what consistency requires.

Davis and Maschler (1965) proved that the kernel satisfies a consistency condition; so do the bargaining set, core, stable set and nucleolus, using the same definition of the reduced game v_x^S as for the kernel (Aumann and Drèze, 1974). Using a somewhat different definition of v_x^S, consistency can be established for the value (Hart and Mas-Colell, 1986). Note that strategic equilibria, too, are consistent; if the players outside S play their equilibrium strategies, an equilibrium of the resulting game on S is given by having the players in S play the same strategies that they were playing in the equilibrium of the large game.

Consistency often plays a key role in axiomatizations. Strategic equilibrium is axiomatized by consistency, together with the requirement that in one-person maximization problems, the maximum be chosen. A remarkable axiomatization of the Nash solution to the bargaining problem (including the 2-person case discussed at *1950–1960*, v), in which the key role is played by consistency, has been provided by T. Lensberg (1981). Axiomatizations in which consistency plays the key role have been provided for the nucleolus (Sobolev, 1975), core (Peleg, 1985, 1986), kernel (Peleg, 1986), and value (Hart and Mas-Colell, 1986). Consistency-like conditions have also been used in contexts that are not strictly game theoretic, e.g. by Balinski and Young (1982), W. Thomson, J. Roemer, H. Moulin, H.P. Young and others.

In law, the consistency criterion goes back at least to the 2000-year old Babylonian Talmud (Aumann and Maschler, 1985). Though it is indeed a very natural condition, its huge scope is still somewhat startling.

(vii) The fascination of *cost allocation* is that it retains the formal structure of cooperative game theory in a totally different interpretation. The question is how to allocate joint costs among users. For example, the cost of a water supply or sewage disposal system serving several municipalities (e.g. Bogardi and Szidarovsky, 1976); the cost of telephone calls in an organization such as a university or corporation (Billera, Heath and Raanan, 1978); or the cost of an airport (Littlechild and Owen, 1973; Littlechild, 1976). In the airport case, for example, each 'player' is one landing of one airplane, and $v(S)$ is the cost of building and running an airport large enough to accommodate the set S of landings. Note that $v(S)$ depends not only on the number of landings in S but also on its composition; one would not charge the same for a landing of a 747 as for a Piper, for example because the 747 requires a longer runway. The allocation of cost would depend on the solution concept; for example, if we are using the Shapley value ϕ, then the fee for each landing i would be $\phi^i v$.

The axiomatic method is particularly attractive here, since in this application the axioms often have rather transparent meaning. Most frequently used has been the Shapley value, whose axiomatic characterization (*see* SHAPLEY VALUE) is particularly transparent (Billera and Heath, 1982).

The literature on the game theoretic approach to cost allocation is quite large, probably several hundred items, many of them in the accounting literature (e.g. Roth and Verrecchia, 1979).

CONCLUDING REMARKS

(i) *Ethics*. While game theory does have intellectual ties to ethics, it is important to realize that in itself, it has no moral content, makes no moral recommendations, is ethically neutral. Strategic equilibrium does not tell us to maximize utility, it explores what happens when we do. The Shapley values does not recommend dividing payoff according to power, it simply measures the power. Game theory is a tool for telling us where incentives will lead. History and experience teach us that if we want to achieve certain goals, including moral and ethical ones, we had better see to the incentive effects of what we are doing; and if we do not want people to usurp power for themselves, we had better build institutions that spread power as thinly and evenly as possible. Blaming game theory – or, for that matter, economic theory – for selfishness is like blaming bacteriology for disease. Game theory studies selfishness. It does not recommend it.

(ii) *Mathematical methods*. We have had very little to say about mathematical methods in the foregoing, because we wished to stress the conceptual side. Worth nothing, though, is that mathematically, game theoretic results developed in one context often have important implications in completely different contexts. We have already mentioned the implications of two-person zero-sum theory for the theory of the core and for correlated equilibria (*1910–1930*, vii). The first proofs of the existence of competitive equilibrium (Arrow and Debreu, 1954) used the existence of strategic equilibrium in a generalized game (Debreu, 1952). Blackwell's 1956 theory of two-person zero-sum games with vector payoffs is of fundamental importance for n-person repeated games of complete information (Aumann, 1961) and for repeated games of incomplete information (e.g. Mertens, 1982; Hart, 1985b). The Lemke–Howson algorithm (1962) for finding equilibria of 2-person non-zero sum non-cooperative games was seminal in the development of the algorithms of Scarf (1967, 1973) for finding points in the core and finding economic equilibria.

(iii) *Terminology*. Game theory has sometimes been plagued by haphazard, inappropriate terminology. Some workers, notably L.S. Shapley (1973b), have tried to introduce more appropriate terminology, and we have here followed their lead. What follows is a brief glossary to aid the reader in making the proper associations.

Used here	Older term
Strategic form	Normal form
Strategic equilibrium	Nash equilibrium
Coalitional form	Characteristic function
Transferable utility	Side payment
Decisive voting game	Strong voting game
Improve upon	Block
Worth	Characteristic function value
Profile	n-tuple
1-homogeneous	Homogeneous of degree 1

BIBLIOGRAPHY

Anderson, R.M. 1986. Notions of core convergence. In Hildenbrand and Mas-Colell (1986), 25–46.

Arrow, K.J. 1951. *Social Choice and Individual Values*. New York: John Wiley.

Arrow, K.J. and Debreu, G. 1954. Existence of an equilibrium for a competitive economy. *Econometrica* 22, 265–90.

Artstein, Z. 1972. Values of games with denumerably many players. *International Journal of Game Theory* 3, 129–40.

Asscher, N. 1976. An ordinal bargaining set for games without side payments. *Mathematics of Operations Research* 1, 381–9.

Aumann, R.J. 1960. Linearity of unrestrictedly transferable utilities. *Naval Research Logistics Quarterly* 7, 281–4.

Aumann, R.J. 1961. The core of a cooperative game without side payments. *Transactions of the American Mathematical Society* 98, 539–52.

Aumann, R.J. 1964. Markets with a continuum of traders. *Econometrica* 32, 39–50.

Aumann, R.J. 1975. Values of markets with a continuum of traders. *Econometrica* 43, 611–46.

Aumann, R.J. 1985. On the non-transferable utility value: a comment on the Roth–Shafer examples. *Econometrica* 53, 667–77.

Aumann, R.J. 1987. Correlated equilibrium as an expression of Bayesian rationality. *Econometrica* 55, 1–18.

Aumann, R.J. and Drèze, J.H. 1974. Cooperative games with coalition structures. *International Journal of Game Theory* 3, 217–38.

Aumann, R.J. and Kurz, M. 1977. Power and taxes. *Econometrica* 45, 1137–61.

Aumann, R.J. and Maschler, M. 1985. Game theoretic analysis of a bankruptcy problem from the Talmud. *Journal of Economic Theory* 36, 195–213.

Aumann, R.J. and Peleg, B. 1960. Von Neumann–Morgenstern solutions to cooperative games without side payments. *Bulletin of the American Mathematical Society* 66, 173–9.

Aumann, R.J. and Shapley, L.S. 1974. *Values of Non-Atomic Games*. Princeton: Princeton University Press.

Axelrod, R. 1984. *The Evolution of Cooperation*. New York: Basic Books.

Balinski, M.L. and Young, H.P. 1982. *Fair Representation*. New Haven: Yale University Press.

Berbee, H. 1981. On covering single points by randomly ordered intervals. *Annals of Probability* 9, 520–28.

Bewley, T. and Kohlberg, E. 1976. The asymptotic theory of stochastic games. *Mathematics of Operations Research* 1, 197–208.

Billera, L.J. 1970a. Existence of general bargaining sets for cooperative games without side payments. *Bulletin of the American Mathematical Society* 76, 375–9.

Billera, L.J. 1970b. Some theorems on the core of an n-person game without side payments. *SIAM Journal of Applied Mathematics* 18, 567–79.

Billera, L.J. and Bixby, R. 1973. A characterization of polyhedral market games. *International Journal of Game Theory* 2, 253–61.

Billera, L.J. and Heath, D.C. 1982. Allocation of shared costs: a set of axioms yielding a unique procedure. *Mathematics of Operations Research* 7, 32–9.

Billera, L.J., Heath, D.C. and Raanan, J. 1978. Internal telephone billing rates – a novel application of non-atomic game theory. *Operations Research* 26, 956–65.

Binmore, K. 1982. Perfect equilibria in bargaining models. *ICERD Discussion Paper* No. 58, London School of Economics.

Blackwell, D. 1956. An analogue of the minimax theorem for vector payoffs. *Pacific Journal of Mathematics* 6, 1–8.

Blackwell, D. and Ferguson, T.S. 1968. The big match. *Annals of Mathematical Statistics* 39, 159–63.

Bogardi, I. and Szidarovsky, F. 1976. Application of game theory in water management. *Applied Mathematical Modelling* 1, 11–20.

Bondareva, O.N. 1963. Some applications of linear programming methods to the theory of cooperative games (in Russian). *Problemy kibernetiki* 10, 119–39.

Borel, E. 1924. Sur les jeux où interviennent l'hasard et l'habilité des joueurs. In *Eléments de la théorie des probabilités*, ed. J. Hermann, Paris; Librairie Scientifique, 204–24.

Braithwaite, R.B. (ed.) 1950. F.P. Ramsey, *The Foundations of Mathematics and Other Logical Essays*. New York: Humanities Press.

Brams, S.J., Lucas, W.F. and Straffin, P.D., Jr. (eds) 1983. *Political and Related Models*. New York: Springer.

Brown, D.J. and Loeb, P. 1976. The values of non-standard exchange economies. *Israel Journal of Mathematics* 25, 71–86.

Brown, D.J. and Robinson, A. 1975. Non-standard exchange economies. *Econometrica* 43, 41–55.

Case, J.H. 1979. *Economics and the Competitive Process*. New York: New York University Press.

Champsaur, P. 1975. Cooperation vs. competition. *Journal of Economic Theory* 11, 394–417.

Dantzig, G.B. 1951a. A proof of the equivalence of the programming problem and the game problem. In Koopmans (1951), 330–38.

Dantzig, G.B. 1951b. Maximization of a linear function of variables subject to linear inequalities. In Koopmans (1951), 339–47.

Davis, M. 1964. Infinite games with perfect information. In Dresher, Shapley and Tucker (1964), 85–101.

Davis, M. 1967. Existence of stable payoff configurations for cooperative games. In Shubik (1967), 39–62.

Davis, M. and Maschler, M. 1965. The kernel of a cooperative game. *Naval Research Logistics Quarterly* 12, 223–59.

Debreu, G. 1952. A social equilibrium existence theorem. *Proceedings of the National*

Academy of Sciences of the United States 38, 886–93.

Debreu, G. and Scarf, H. 1963. A limit theorem on the core of an economy. *International Economic Review* 4, 236–46.

Dresher, M.A., Shapley, L.S. and Tucker, A.W. (eds) 1964. *Advances in Game Theory*. Annals of Mathematics Studies Series 52, Princeton: Princeton University Press.

Dresher, M.A., Tucker, A.W. and Wolfe, P. (eds) 1957. *Contributions to the Theory of Games III*. Annals of Mathematics Studies Series 39, Princeton: Princeton University Press.

Drèze, J.H., Gabszewicz, J. and Gepts, S. 1969. On cores and competitive equilibria. In Guilbaud (1969), 91–114.

Dubey, P. 1980. Asymptotic semivalues and a short proof of Kannai's theorem. *Mathematics of Operations Research* 5, 267–70.

Dubey, P. and Shapley, L.S. 1980. Non cooperative exchange with a continuum of traders: two models. *Technical Report of the Institute for Advanced Studies*, Hebrew University of Jerusalem.

Edgeworth, F.Y. 1881. *Mathematical Psychics*. London: Kegan Paul; New York: A.M. Kelley, 1967.

Everett, H. 1957. Recursive games. In Dresher, Tucker and Wolfe (1957), 47–78.

Fogelman, F. and Quinzii, M. 1980. Asymptotic values of mixed games. *Mathematics of Operations Research* 5, 86–93.

Gabszewicz, J.J. and Mertens, J.F. 1971. An equivalence theorem for the core of an economy whose atoms are not 'too' big. *Econometrica* 39, 713–21.

Gale, D. 1974. A curious nim-type game. *American Mathematical Monthly* 81, 876–79.

Gale, D. 1979. The game of hex and the Brouwer fixed-point theorem. *American Mathematical Monthly* 86, 818–27.

Gale, D. 1986. Bargaining and competition, Part I: Characterization; Part II: Existence. *Econometrica* 54, 785–806; 807–18.

Gale, D. and Shapley, L.S. 1962. College admissions and the stability of marriage. *American Mathematical Monthly* 69, 9–15.

Gale, D. and Stewart, F.H. 1953. Infinite games with perfect information. In Kuhn and Tucker (1953), 245–66.

Galil, Z. 1974. The nucleolus in games with major and minor players. *International Journal of Game Theory* 3, 129–40.

Gillies, D.B. 1959. Solutions to general non-zero-sum games. In Luce and Tucker (1959), 47–85.

Guilbaud, G.T. (ed.) 1969. *La décision: aggrégation et dynamique des ordres de préférence*. Paris: Editions du CNRS.

Harsanyi, J.C. 1956. Approaches to the bargaining problem before and after the theory of games: a critical discussion of Zeuthen's, Hicks' and Nash's theories. *Econometrica* 24, 144–57.

Harsanyi, J.C. 1959. A bargaining model for the cooperative n-person game. In Tucker and Luce (1959), 325–56.

Harsanyi, J.C. 1963. A simplified bargaining model for the n-person cooperative game. *International Economic Review* 4, 194–220.

Harsanyi, J.C. 1966. A general theory of rational behavior in game situations. *Econometrica* 34, 613–34.

Harsanyi, J.C. 1967–8. Games with incomplete information played by 'Bayesian' players, parts I, II and III. *Management Science* 14, 159–82, 320–34, 486–502.

Harsanyi, J.C. 1973. Games with randomly disturbed payoffs: a new rationale for mixed strategy equilibrium points. *International Journal of Game Theory* 2, 1–23.

Harsanyi, J.C. 1982. Solutions for some bargaining games under the Harsanyi–Selten solution theory I: Theoretical preliminaries; II: Analysis of specific games. *Mathematical Social Sciences* 3, 179–91; 259–79.

Harsanyi, J.C. and Selten, R. 1972. A generalized Nash solution for two-person bargaining games with incomplete information. *Management Science* 18, 80–106.

Harsanyi, J.C. and Selten, R. 1988. *A General Theory of Equilibrium Selection in Games.* Cambridge, Mass.: MIT Press.

Hart, S. 1973. Values of mixed games. *International Journal of Game Theory* 2, 69–86.

Hart, S. 1974. Formation of cartels in large markets. *Journal of Economic Theory* 7, 453–66.

Hart, S. 1977a. Asymptotic values of games with a continuum of players. *Journal of Mathematical Economics* 4, 57–80.

Hart, S. 1977b. Values of non-differentiable markets with a continuum of traders. *Journal of Mathematical Economics* 4, 103–16.

Hart, S. 1980. Measure-based values of market games. *Mathematics of Operations Research* 5, 197–228.

Hart, S. 1985a. An axiomatization of Harsanyi's nontransferable utility solution. *Econometrica* 53, 1295–314.

Hart, S. 1985b. Non zero-sum two-person repeated games with incomplete information. *Mathematics of Operations Research* 10, 117–53.

Hart, S. and Mas-Colell, A. 1986. The potential: a new approach to the value in multi-person allocation problems. Harvard University Discussion Paper 1157.

Hart, S. and Schmeidler, D. 1988. Correlated equilibria: an elementary existence proof. *Mathematics of Operations Research.*

Hildenbrand, W. (ed.) 1982. *Advances in Economic Theory.* Cambridge: Cambridge University Press.

Hildenbrand, W. and Mas-Colell, A. 1986. *Contributions to Mathematical Economics in Honor of G. Debreu.* Amsterdam: North-Holland.

Hu, T.C. and Robinson, S.M. (eds) 1973. *Mathematical Programming.* New York: Academic Press.

Isaacs, R. 1965. *Differential Games: A Mathematical Theory with Applications to Warfare and Pursuit, Control and Optimization* New York: John Wiley.

Kakutani, S. 1941. A generalization of Brouwer's fixed point theorem. *Duke Mathematical Journal* 8, 457–9.

Kalai, E. and Smorodinsky, M. 1975. Other solutions to Nash's bargaining problem. *Econometrica* 43, 513–18.

Kaneko, M. and Wooders, M. 1982. Cores of partitioning games. *Mathematical Social Sciences* 3, 313–27.

Kannai, Y. 1966. Values of games with a continuum of players. *Israel Journal of Mathematics* 4, 54–8.

Kohlberg, E. 1971. On the nucleolus of a characteristic function game. *SIAM Journal of Applied Mathematics* 20, 62–6.

Kohlberg, E. 1972. The nucleolus as a solution to a minimization problem. *SIAM Journal of Applied Mathematics* 23, 34–49.

Koopmans, T.C. (ed.) 1951. *Activity Analysis of Production and Allocation.* New York: Wiley.

Kuhn, H.W. 1952. *Lectures on the Theory of Games.* Issued as a report of the Logistics Research Project, Office of Naval Research, Princeton University.

Kuhn, H.W. 1953. Extensive games and the problem of information. In Kuhn and Tucker

(1953), 193–216.

Kuhn, H.W. and Tucker, A.W. (eds) 1950. *Contributions to the Theory of Games I*. Annals of Mathematics Studies Series 24, Princeton: Princeton University Press.

Kuhn, H.W. and Tucker, A.W. (eds) 1953. *Contributions to the Theory of Games II*. Annals of Mathematics Studies Series 28, Princeton: Princeton University Press.

Lemke, L.E. and Howson, J.T. 1962. Equilibrium points of bimatrix games. *SIAM Journal of Applied Mathematics* 12, 413–23.

Lensberg, T. 1981. The stability of the Nash solution. Unpublished.

Lewis, D.K. 1969. *Convention*. Cambridge, Mass.: Harvard University Press.

Littlechild, S.C. 1976. A further note on the nucleolus of the 'airport game'. *International Journal of Game Theory* 5, 91–5.

Littlechild, S.C. and Owen, G. 1973. A simple expression for the Shapley value in a special case. *Management Science* 20, 370–72.

Lucas, W.F. 1969. The proof that a game may not have a solution. *Transactions of the American Mathematical Society* 137, 219–29.

Lucas, W.F. 1983. Measuring power in weighted voting systems. In Brams, Lucas and Straffin (1983), ch. 9.

Lucas, W.F. and Rabie, M. 1982. Games with no solutions and empty core. *Mathematics of Operations Research* 7, 491–500.

Luce, R.D. and Raiffa, H. 1957. *Games and Decisions, Introduction and Critical Survey*. New York: John Wiley.

Luce, R.D. and Tucker, A.W. (eds) 1959. *Contributions to the Theory of Games IV*. Annals of Mathematics Studies Series 40, Princeton: Princeton University Press.

Lyapounov, A.A. 1940. On completely additive vector-functions (in Russian, abstract in French). *Akademiia Nauk USSR Izvestiia Seriia Mathematicheskaia* 4, 465–78.

Martin, D.A. 1975. Borel determinacy. *Annals of Mathematics* 102, 363–71.

Maschler, M. (ed.) 1962. *Recent Advances in Game Theory*. Proceedings of a Conference, privately printed for members of the conference, Princeton: Princeton University Conferences.

Maschler, M., Peleg, B. and Shapley, L.S. 1979. Geometric properties of the kernel, nucleolus, and related solution concepts. *Mathematics of Operations Research* 4, 303–38.

Maschler, M. and Perles, M. 1981. The superadditive solution for the Nash bargaining game. *International Journal of Game Theory* 10, 163–93.

Mas-Colell, A. 1975. A further result on the representation of games by markets. *Journal of Economic Theory* 10, 117–22.

Mas-Colell, A. 1977. Competitive and value allocations of large exchange economies. *Journal of Economic Theory* 14, 419–38.

Mas-Colell, A. 1988. An equivalence theorem for a bargaining set. *Journal of Mathematical Economics*.

Maynard Smith, J. 1982. *Evolution and the Theory of Games*. Cambridge: Cambridge University Press.

Mertens, J.F. 1982. Repeated games: an overview of the zero-sum case. In Hildenbrand (1982), 175–82.

Mertens, J.F. 1987. The Shapley value in the non-differentiable case. *International Journal of Game Theory*.

Mertens, J.F. and Neyman, A. 1981. Stochastic games. *International Journal of Game Theory* 10, 53–66.

Milnor, J.W. and Shapley, L.S. 1957. On games of survival. In Dresher, Tucker and Wolfe (1957), 15–45.

Milnor, J.W. and Shapley, L.S. 1978. Values of large games II: Oceanic games. *Mathematics of Operations Research* 3, 290–307.

Moschovakis, Y.N. 1980. *Descriptive Set Theory*. New York: North-Holland.

Moschovakis, Y.N. (ed.) 1983. *Cabal Seminar 79–81: Proceedings, Caltech–UCLA Logic Seminar 1979–81*. Lecture Notes in Mathematics 1019, New York: Springer-Verlag.

Mycielski, J. and Steinhaus, H. 1964. On the axiom of determinateness. *Fundamenta Mathematicae* 53, 205–24.

Myerson, R.B. 1977. Graphs and cooperation in games. *Mathematics of Operations Research* 2, 225–9.

Myerson, R.B. 1979. Incentive compatibility and the bargaining problem. *Econometrica* 47, 61–74.

Myerson, R.B. 1984. Cooperative games with incomplete information. *International Journal of Game Theory* 13, 69–96.

Nash, J.F., Jr. 1950. The bargaining problem. *Econometrica* 18, 155–62.

Nash, J.F., Jr. 1951. Non-cooperative games. *Annals of Mathematics* 54, 289–95.

Neyman, A. 1985a. Bounded complexity justifies cooperation in the finitely repeated prisoner's dilemma. *Economics Letters* 19, 227–30.

Neyman, A. 1985b. Semivalues of political economic games. *Mathematics of Operations Research* 10, 390–402.

Neyman, A. 1987. Weighted majority games have an asymptotic value. *Mathematics of Operations Research.*

O'Neill, B. 1987. Non-metric test of the minimax theory of two-person zero-sum games. *Proceedings of the National Academy of Sciences of the United States* 84, 2106–9.

Owen, G. 1972. Multilinear extensions of games. *Management Science* 18, 64–79.

Peleg, B. 1963a. Solutions to cooperative games without side payments. *Transactions of the American Mathematical Society* 106, 280–92.

Peleg, B. 1963b. Bargaining sets of cooperative games without side payments. *Israel Journal of Mathematics* 1, 197–200.

Peleg, B. 1967. Existence theorem for the bargaining set $M_1^{(i)}$. In Shubik (1967), 53–6.

Peleg, B. 1968. On weights of constant-sum majority games. *SIAM Journal of Applied Mathematics* 16, 527–32.

Peleg, B. 1985. An axiomatization of the core of cooperative games without side payments. *Journal of Mathematical Economics* 14, 203–14.

Peleg, B. 1986. On the reduced game property and its converse. *International Journal of Game Theory* 15, 187–200.

Pennock, J.R. and Chapman, J.W. (eds) 1968. *Representation*. New York: Atherton.

Ramsey, F.P. 1931. Truth and probability. In Braithwaite (1950).

Ransmeier, J.S. 1942. *The Tennessee Valley Authority: A Case Study in the Economics of Multiple Purpose Stream Planning*, Nashville: Vanderbilt University Press.

Regelmann, K. and Curio, E. 1986. How do great tit (Parus Major) pair mates cooperate in broad defence? *Behavior* 97, 10–36.

Riker, W.H. and Shapley, L.S. 1968. Weighted voting: a mathematical analysis for instrumental judgements. In Pennock and Chapman (1968), 199–216.

Robinson, A. 1966. *Non-Standard Analysis*. Amsterdam: North-Holland.

Rosenthal, R.W. 1979. Sequences of games with varying opponents. *Econometrica* 47, 1353–66.

Rosenthal, R.W. and Rubinstein, A. 1984. Repeated two player games with ruin. *International Journal of Game Theory* 13, 155–77.

Roth, A.E. 1977. The Shapley value as a von Neumann–Morgenstern utility. *Econometrica*

45, 657–64.

Roth, A.E. 1984. The evolution of the labor market for medical interns and residents: a case study in game theory. *Journal of Political Economy* 92, 991–1016.

Roth, A.E. and Verrecchia, R.E. 1979. The Shapley value as applied to cost allocation: a reinterpretation. *Journal of Accounting Research* 17, 295–303.

Rubinstein, A. 1982. Perfect equilibrium in a bargaining model. *Econometrica* 50, 97–109.

Rubinstein, A. 1986. Finite automata play the repeated prisoner's dilemma. *Journal of Economic Theory* 39, 83–96.

Savage, L.J. 1954. *The Foundations of Statistics.* New York: John Wiley.

Scarf, H.E. 1967. The core of an n-person game. *Econometrica* 35, 50–69.

Scarf, H.E. 1973. *The Computation of Economic Equilibria.* New Haven: Yale University Press.

Schelling, T.C. 1960. *The Strategy of Conflict.* Cambridge, Mass.: Harvard University Press.

Schmeidler, D. 1969. The nucleolus of a characteristic function game. *SIAM Journal of Applied Mathematics* 17, 1163–70.

Selten, R.C. 1965. Spieltheoretische Behandlung eines Oligopolmodells mit Nachfrageträgheit. *Zeitschrift für die gesammte Staatswissenschaft* 121, 301–24; 667–89.

Selten, R.C. 1975. Reexamination of the perfectness concept for equilibrium points in extensive games. *International Journal of Game Theory* 4, 25–55.

Selten, R.C. 1980. A note on evolutionary stable strategies in asymmetric animal conflicts. *Journal of Theoretical Biology* 84, 101.

Selten, R.C. 1983. Evolutionary stability in extensive two-part games. *Mathematical Social Sciences* 5, 269–363.

Shapley, L.S. 1953a. Stochastic games. *Proceedings of the National Academy of Sciences of the United States* 39, 1095–100.

Shapley, L.S. 1953b. A value for n-person games. In Kuhn and Tucker (1953), 305–17.

Shapley, L.S. 1962. Values of games with infinitely many players. In Maschler (1962), 113–18.

Shapley, L.S. 1964. Values of large games, VII: a general exchange economy with money. *RAND Publication* RM–4248, Santa Monica, California.

Shapley, L.S. 1967. On balanced sets and cores. *Naval Research Logistics Quarterly* 14, 453–60.

Shapley, L.S. 1969c. Utility comparison and the theory of games. In Guilbaud (1969), 251–63.

Shapley, L.S. 1973a. On balanced games without side payments. In Hu and Robinson (1973), 261–90.

Shapley, L.S. 1973b. Let's block 'block'. *Econometrica* 41, 1201–2.

Shapley, L.S. 1984. Convergence of the bargaining set for differentiable market games. Appendix B in Shubik (1984), 683–92.

Shapley, L.S. and Shubik, M. 1954. A method for evaluating the distribution of power in a committee system. *American Political Science Review* 48, 787–92.

Shapley, L.S. and Shubik, M. 1969a. On market games. *Journal of Economic Theory* 1, 9–25.

Shapley, L.S. and Shubik, M. 1969b. Pure competition, coalitional power and fair division. *International Economic Review* 10, 337–62.

Shitovitz, B. 1973. Oligopoly in markets with a continuum of traders. *Econometrica* 41, 467–501.

Shubik, M. 1959a. Edgeworth market games. In Luce and Tucker (1959), 267–78.

Shubik, M. 1959b. *Strategy and Market Structure.* New York: John Wiley.

Shubik, M. (ed.) 1967. *Essays in Mathematical Economics in Honor of Oskar Morgenstern.*

Princeton: Princeton University Press.

Shubik, M. 1973. Commodity, money, oligopoly, credit and bankruptcy in a general equilibrium model. *Western Economic Journal* 11, 24–36.

Shubik, M. 1982. *Game Theory in the Social Sciences, Concepts and Solutions*. Cambridge, Mass.: MIT Press.

Shubik, M. 1984. *A Game Theoretic Approach to Political Economy*. Cambridge, Mass.: MIT Press.

Sobolev, A.I. 1975. Characterization of the principle of optimality for cooperative games through functional equations (in Russian). In Vorobiev (1975), 94–151.

Sorin, S. 1986a. On repeated games of complete information. *Mathematics of Operations Research* 11, 147–60.

Sorin, S. 1986b. An asymptotic property of non-zero sum stochastic games. *International Journal of Game Theory* 15(2), 101–7.

Stearns, R.E. 1965. A game without side payments that has no solution. Report of the Fifth Conference on Game Theory, Princeton.

Tauman, Y. 1981. Value on a class of non-differentiable market games. *International Journal of Game Theory* 10, 155–62.

Ville, J.A. 1938. Sur le théorie générale des jeux où intervient l'habilité des joueurs. In *Traité du calcul des probabilités et de ses applications*, Vol. 4, ed. E. Borel, Paris: Gauthier-Villars, 105–13.

Vinacke, W.E. and Arkoff, A. 1957. An experimental study of coalitions in the triad. *American Sociological Review* 22, 406–15.

Vind, K. 1964. A theorem on the core of an economy. *Review of Economic Studies* 32, 47–8.

von Neumann, J. 1928. Zur Theorie der Gesellschaftsspiele. *Mathematische Annalen* 100, 295–320.

von Neumann, J. 1949. On rings of operators. Reduction theory. *Annals of Mathematics* 50, 401–85.

von Neumann, J. and Morgenstern, O. 1944. *Theory of Games and Economic Behavior*. Princeton: Princeton University Press.

Vorobiev, N.N. (ed.) 1975. *Mathematical Methods in Social Science* (in Russian). Vipusk 6, Vilnius.

Wilson, R. 1978. Information, efficiency, and the core of an economy. *Econometrica* 46, 807–16.

Wolfe, P. 1955. The strict determinateness of certain infinite games. *Pacific Journal of Mathematics* 5, 841–7.

Wooders, M.H. 1983. The epsilon core of a large replica game. *Journal of Mathematical Economics* 11, 277–300.

Wooders, M.H. and Zame, W.R. 1984. Approximate cores of large games. *Econometrica* 52, 1327–50.

Young, H.P. 1985. Monotonic solutions of cooperative games. *International Journal of Game Theory* 14, 65–72.

Zermelo, E. 1913. Über eine Anwendung der Mengenlehre auf die theorie des Schachspiels. *Proceedings of the Fifth International Congress of Mathematicians* 2, 501–4.

Bargaining

JOHN C. HARSANYI

By bargaining we mean negotiations between two or more parties about the terms of possible cooperation, which may involve trade, employment (collective bargaining), a joint business venture, etc. For lack of space we will only discuss bargaining between two parties, and will restrict ourselves to the case of complete information. (For n-person bargaining, see Harsanyi, 1977, chs 10 to 13; for the case of incomplete information, see Harsanyi, 1982, and Harsanyi and Selten, 1987).

The outcome of bargaining is either an *agreement* about the terms of mutual cooperation, or it is a *conflict* in case no agreement can be reached.

For the purposes of economic analysis, any possible outcome can be identified with a vector $x = (x_1, x_2)$, where x_1 and x_2 are the commodity bundles (commodity vectors) that this outcome would yield to parties 1 and 2, respectively. (A simple special case of this is when x_1 and x_2 are not vectors but rather are scalars representing the two sides' money payoffs.) An alternative approach is to identify each outcome with a utility vector $u = (u_1, u_2)$, where $u_1 = U_1(x_1)$ and $u_2 = U_2(x_2)$ are the two sides' utility payoffs, i.e., the utilities they would derive from the commodity payoffs or the money payoffs x_1 and x_2 in accordance with their utility functions U_1 and U_2. For convenience, the vectors $x = (x_1, x_2)$ defined in terms of commodities or in terms of money will be called *physical outcomes* whereas the corresponding vectors $u = (u_1, u_2)$ will be called *utility outcomes*.

In terms of the physical outcomes, a bargaining situation can be characterized by its *physical feasible set* F^*, defined as the set of all its possible physical outcomes x, and by its *physical conflict point* $c^* = (c_1^*, c_2^*)$, whose two components are the commodity payoffs or the money payoffs c_1^* and c_2^* the two sides would receive if they were unable to reach an agreement. Of course always

$$c^* \in F^* \tag{1}$$

because c^* is one of the possible physical outcomes.

On the other hand, in terms of the utility outcomes, a bargaining situation can be characterized by its (utilistic) *feasible set F*, defined as the set of all its possible utility outcomes u, and by its (utilistic) *conflict point* $c = (c_1, c_2)$, specifying the two sides' utility payoffs c_1 and c_2 in the absence of an agreement, to be called the two sides' *conflict payoffs*. Obviously, we have

$$c_1 = U_1(c_1^*), \qquad c_2 = U_2(c_2^*), \tag{2}$$

and

$$F = \{(u_1, u_2) | u_1 = U_1(x_1), u_2 = U_2(x_2) \text{ and } (x_1, x_2) \in F^*\}. \tag{3}$$

Moreover, in view of (1)

$$c \in F. \tag{4}$$

Most of the economic literature on bargaining is based on the assumption of:

Sufficiency of utility outcomes. No essential information is lost by basing the economic analysis of a bargaining situation solely on its possible utility outcomes as defined by its feasible set F and by its conflict point $c = (c_1, c_2)$.

This assumption is motivated by the fact that the two bargainers will be interested only in the *utility outcome* of their bargaining process, in the sense that they will be indifferent between two physical outcomes x and x' if both of them yield the same utility outcome u. (This follows from the very definition of the two sides' utility functions; cf. Roemer, 1985.)

BARGAINING IN CLASSICAL ECONOMIC THEORY

Prior to the advent of game theory, what economic theory had to say about two-person bargaining situations amounted to two rationality postulates:

1. Individual rationality. A rational bargainer will not agree to a utility payoff smaller than his conflict payoff so that

$$u_1 \geqslant c_1 \qquad \text{and} \qquad u_2 \geqslant c_2; \tag{5}$$

and:

2. Joint rationality. Two rational bargainers will not agree on a utility outcome $u = (u_1, u_2)$ if in the feasible set F there is another utility outcome $u' = (u_1', u_2')$ yielding higher payoffs $u_1' > u_1$ and $u_2' > u_2$ for both of them. (In other words, the outcome to be agreed upon will be a *Pareto optimal* – at least a weakly Pareto optimal – point of the feasible set F. See Figure 1.)

In Figure 1, the area F is the feasible set whereas the point c is the conflict point. The triangular area bcd is the set of all points satisfying the individual-rationality requirement. The upper-right boundary $abde$ of F is the set of all Pareto optimal points, which satisfy the joint-rationality requirement. The intersection of the area bcd and of the boundary line $abde$ is the arc bd: it is the set of all points satisfying *both* rationality requirements. Edgeworth (1881) called

55

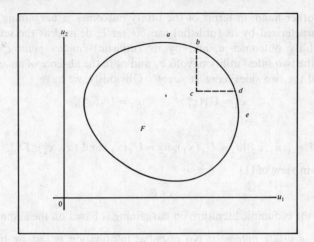

Figure 1

all points of *bd* possible *final settlements*. Pigou (1905) called *bd* itself the *range of practicable bargains*. Luce and Raiffa (1957) called it the *negotiation set*. We will follow this latter terminology. But we need also terms to describe the two end points of this set: We will call *b* party 1's *concession limit* because it is the least favourable outcome party 1 can rationally accept. By the same token, *d* will be called party 2's *concession limit*.

Neoclassical economics offers only what may be called a *weak* bargaining theory because it tells us no more than that the *agreement point* of two rational bargainers (i.e. the utility vector they will agree on) will lie somewhere within the negotiation set *bd*. But it does not tell us anything about *where* it will actually lie between the two sides' concession limits *b* and *d*, or about the economic forces that may move it closer to either limit.

THE NASH SOLUTION

It was the Danish economist Zeuthen (1930) who first realized the need for a *strong* bargaining theory predicting a *unique* agreement point, and who first understood that such a theory must be based on the two sides' attitudes toward *risk taking* and, more specifically, on the extent to which each side is willing to risk a conflict rather than accept unfavourable terms. But his path-breaking analysis of bargaining was seriously impaired by being done prior to von Neumann and Morgenstern's *Theory of Games and Economic Behavior* (1944), when neither the value of the axiomatic method in economic analysis nor the difference between expected-utility maximization and expected-money-income maximization was clearly understood.

Yet, even though von Neumann and Morgenstern's theory of games was an essential step toward a *strong* bargaining theory, their own analysis of two-person bargaining games did not go significantly beyond the *weak* bargaining theory of neoclassical economics. But they did provide the conceptual tools needed for a strong theory by introducing the concepts of moves, strategies, payoff functions, as well as games in extensive form, in normal form and in characteristic-function form, etc. What is particularly important, they introduced the concept of von Neumann–Morgenstern utility functions, which offered a rigorous and convenient mathematical representation for the various players' attitudes toward risk taking – an essential prerequisite for a *strong* bargaining theory. Accordingly, the assumption of *sufficiency of utility outcomes* has to be restated as follows:

Necessity of von Neumann–Morgenstern utilities. A *strong* bargaining theory must be based on the feasible set F and on the conflict point $c = (c_1, c_2)$ defined in terms of the two sides' von Neumann–Morgenstern utilities. (But a *weak* bargaining theory can be based on defining F and c in terms of the two sides' *ordinal* utilities.)

The first author to use the analytical tools of game theory to propose a *strong* bargaining theory, was John Nash (1950, 1953), a brilliant student of von Neumann's. He assumed that the feasible set F, defined in terms of von Neumann–Morgenstern utilities, is a *compact* and *convex* set. (It will be convex because if u and u' are two feasible outcomes, then any probability mixture $pu + (1 - p)u'$ of the two will be likewise a feasible outcome.)

Nash postulates that the agreement point $\bar{u} = (\bar{u}_1, \bar{u}_2)$ of the game – commonly known as the *Nash solution* – will satisfy the following four axioms:

1. Efficiency. This is just the joint-rationality postulate of the last section.

A given game G is called *symmetrical* if interchanging the two players will not change the game. Geometrically this means that the feasible set F must be symmetrical with respect to the line λ defined by the equation $u_1 = u_2$, that is, with respect to the $+45°$ line going through the origin; and that the conflict point $c = (c_1, c_2)$ must lie on this line λ itself so that $c_1 = c_2$ (see Figure 2).

2. Symmetry. A symmetric game will have a symmetric agreement point $\bar{u} = (\bar{u}_1, \bar{u}_{2'})$ with $\bar{u}_1 = \bar{u}_2$. (In a symmetric game the two players have exactly the same strategic possibilities and have exactly the same bargaining power. Therefore, neither player will have any reason to accept an agreement yielding him a lower payoff than his opponent's.)

Axioms 1 and 2 already uniquely define the agreement point $\bar{u}$ of a symmetrical game: in such a game, $\bar{u}$ must be the intersection of line λ and of the upper-right boundary bd of the feasible set F (see Figure 2). The remaining two axioms are needed to extend the theory to nonsymmetrical games.

It is well known that two von Neumann–Morgenstern utility functions are behaviourally equivalent if one can be obtained from the other by an order-preserving linear transformation (i.e., by shifting the zero point of the utility scale and/or by changing the utility unit). This fact motivates axiom 3.

3. Linear invariance. Suppose that game G' can be obtained from game G by subjecting (say) player 1's utilities to an order-preserving linear transformation

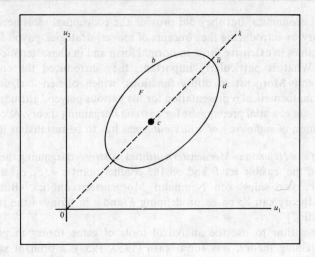

Figure 2

while keeping the other player's utilities unchanged so that, for any physical outcome $x = (x_1, x_2)$, the corresponding utility outcome $u = (u_1, u_2)$ is replaced by the transformed utility outcome $u' = (u'_1, u'_2)$ where

$$u'_1 = au_1 + b \quad \text{with} \quad a > 0 \quad \text{and} \quad u'_1 = u'_2. \tag{6}$$

Suppose also that in the old game G the players would have agreed on the physical outcome $\bar{x} = (\bar{x}_1, \bar{x}_2)$ corresponding to the utility outcome $\bar{u} = (\bar{u}_1, \bar{u}_2)$. Then, in the new game G', the players will agree on the *same* physical outcome $\bar{x}$, now corresponding to the utility outcome $\bar{u}' = (\bar{u}'_1, \bar{u}'_2)$ with

$$\bar{u}'_1 = a\bar{u}_1 + b \quad \text{and} \quad \bar{u}'_2 = \bar{u}_2. \tag{7}$$

(In other words, the physical outcome $\bar{x}$ will not change if we choose to change the way we measure one player's von Neumann–Morgenstern utilities – even though, of course, the utility coordinates of $\bar{x}$ will change in accordance with the newly adopted method of measurement.)

Note that axiom 3 ensures that the outcome of bargaining will be independent of *interpersonal comparisons* of the two players' utilities. For by permitting transformation of one player's utilities without any transformation of the other player's it destroys the possibility that the outcome should depend on interpersonal utility comparisons. Note also that in ethical contexts we cannot avoid making, or at least attempting, interpersonal utility comparisons. For instance, if I have to choose between giving my apple to Peter or to Paul, I may decide that Peter has a stronger moral claim to the apple because he would probably derive a *higher utility* from it (say, because he has not eaten for two days). In contrast, typically the outcome of bargaining is *not* decided by moral considerations. When one side makes a concession to the other he will do so out of *self-interest*, that is because he thinks it is unlikely that he can reach an agreement with the other side without making this concession. To be sure, sometimes people are guided by a mixture of pure bargaining considerations and of moral considerations. But in our theoretical analysis we must keep these two things apart. Unfortunately, many authors (including Luce and Raiffa, 1957) did not do so (see Harsanyi, 1977, pp. 13–15).

4. Independence of irrelevant alternatives. Let G be a bargaining game with conflict point c, with feasible set F, and with agreement point $\bar{u}$; and let G' be a game obtained from G by restricting the feasible set to a smaller set $F' \subset F$ in such a way that c and $\bar{u}$ remain within the new feasible set F', c remaining the conflict point also for G'. Then, $\bar{u}$ will be the agreement point also for this new game G'.

First, to explain the term 'irrelevant alternatives': by an 'alternative' we mean simply a feasible outcome. By an 'irrelevant' alternative we mean a feasible outcome *not* chosen by the players as their agreement point. Game G' is obtained from game G by excluding some of these irrelevant alternatives from the original feasible set F, without excluding the original agreement point $\bar{u}$ itself. What axiom 4 asserts is that by excluding such irrelevant alternatives from F we do not change the agreement point $\bar{u}$ of the game.

The upper-right boundary of the feasible set F will be called δF. The mathematical effect of axiom 4 is to make the agreement point $\bar{u}$ depend only on the shape of δF in the *neighbourhood* of $\bar{u}$, and to make the latter independent of the more distant parts of δF. The axiom is motivated by the way bargaining actually proceeds: It is a process of voluntary mutual concessions, which gradually *decreases* the set of possible outcomes under serious consideration from the entire boundary set δF to smaller and smaller subsets of δF around the eventual agreement point $\bar{u}$, and in the end to the one point $\bar{u}$ itself. What axiom 4 asserts is that this winnowing process does not change this agreement point $\bar{u}$ – which is a natural enough assumption since $\bar{u}$ is actually *chosen* by the winnowing process.

Yet even though axiom 4, it seems to me, has considerable intuitive appeal, it is no doubt the most controversial of Nash's axioms.

Nash has shown that these axioms imply the following theorem.

Theorem 1. The agreement point of the game is the unique utility vector $\bar{u} = (\bar{u}_1, \bar{u}_2)$ that maximizes the product

$$\pi = (u_1 - c_1)(u_2 - c_2), \tag{8}$$

called the *Nash product*, subject to

$$(u_1, u_2) \in F \tag{9}$$

and to

$$u_1 \geqslant c_1 \quad \text{and} \quad u_2 \geqslant c_2. \tag{10}$$

For a proof of this theorem, see Nash (1950, p. 59) of Harsanyi (1977, pp. 147–8).

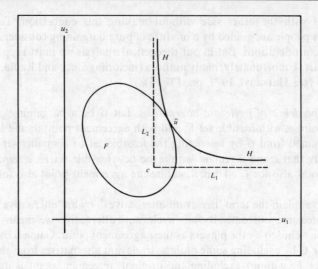

Figure 3

Geometrically, the agreement point $\bar{u}$ can be characterized as follows: Let L_1 and L_2 be the horizontal and the vertical line going through the conflict point $c = (c_1, c_2)$. Then, $\bar{u}$ will be that particular point of the boundary set δF that lies on the highest rectangular hyperbola HH asymptotic to lines L_1 and L_2 and having a point in common with the feasible set F (see Figure 3).

ZEUTHEN'S BARGAINING MODEL

Even though Zeuthen's analysis is technically much inferior to Nash's it does usefully supplement the latter because it makes the dependence of bargaining on the two sides' attitudes toward *risk taking* more explicit.

Suppose that, at a given stage of the bargaining process, player 1's last offer corresponded to the utility vector $v = (v_1, v_2)$ whereas player 2's last offer corresponded to the utility vector $w = (w_1, w_2)$ such that v and $w \in \delta F$, with $v_1 > w_1$ but $v_2 < w_2$. Which player will have to make the next concession? Zeuthen tries to answer this question as follows:

If player 1 accepts his opponent's last offer w, then he will obtain the utility payoff w_1, with certainty. On the other hand, if he insists on his own last offer v, then he will obtain *either* payoff v_1 (if his opponent accepts this offer v) *or* will obtain the conflict payoff c_1 (if his opponent refuses to accept v). Suppose player 1 assigns the subjective probability p to the latter possibility and assigns the complementary probability $(1 - p)$ to the former possibility. Then, he must conclude that by insisting on his last offer u and by making no further concession he will obtain the expected payoff $(1 - p)v_1 + pc_1$, whereas by being conciliatory and accepting player 2's last offer w he will obtain payoff w_1.

Therefore, player 1 can rationally stick to his last offer only if

$$(1 - p)v_1 + pc_1 \geqslant w_1, \tag{11}$$

i.e., if

$$p \leqslant \frac{v_1 - w_1}{v_1 - c_1} = r_1. \tag{12}$$

By similar reasoning, if player 2 assigns probability q to the hypothesis that player 1 will stick to his last offer v, then he himself can rationally stick to his own last offer w only if

$$(1-q)w_2 + qc_2 \geqslant v_2, \tag{13}$$

i.e., if

$$q \leqslant \frac{w_2 - v_2}{w_2 - c_2} = r_2. \tag{14}$$

Thus, the quantities r_1 and r_2 defined by (12) and by (14) can be interpreted as the *highest probability of a conflict* that player 1 and player 2, respectively, would face rather than accept the last offer of the other player. We will call r_1 and r_2 the two players' *risk limits*. Note that each player's risk limit is a ratio of two utility differences. The first one of these (such as the difference $v_1 - w_1$ in the case of player 1) measures the cost of *accepting the opponent's last offer* whereas the second (such as the difference $v_1 - c_1$ in the case of player 1) measures the cost of *provoking a conflict*.

Zeuthen suggests that the *next concession* must always come from the player with a *smaller* risk limit (except that if the two players' risk limits are equal then both of them must make concessions to avoid a conflict). We will call this suggestion *Zeuthen's principle*. This principle turns out to be closely related to the Nash solution.

Theorem 2. If the two players follow Zeuthen's principle then the next concession will always be made by the player whose last offer is associated with a higher Nash product (unless both are associated with equal Nash products, in which case both of them have to make concessions).

Proof. We have to show that $r_1 \geqslant r_2$ if and only if $(v_1 - c_1)(v_2 - c_2) \geqslant (w_1 - c_1)(w_2 - c_2)$, and then that if the first inequality is reversed then so is the second. But this follows from (12) and (14).

Corollary. If the two players act in accordance with Zeuthen's principle then they will tend to reach the Nash solution as their agreement point.

Proof. By Theorem 2, at each stage of the bargaining the offer point with the smaller Nash product will be replaced by a new offer point with a higher Nash product. The process will end at the utility vector with the highest possible Nash product, which is the Nash solution.

This statement, however, is subject to two qualifications.

61

1. If the two players make continually decreasing concessions to each other then the bargaining process may not converge to any agreement point at all. This can be prevented by requiring that all concessions should have a uniform lower bound (say, 1¢).

2. The process may 'overshoot' the Nash solution if either player makes unreasonably large concessions. But this can happen only if the players do not realize that they can always reach an agreement without accepting a payoff lower than the Nash solution would give them.

SELTEN'S AXIOMS FOR THE NASH SOLUTION

The Zeuthen–Nash theory in its original form postulates a feasible set F consisting of infinitely many feasible points. But it is worth considering a simpler bargaining situation where the players can choose only between *two* possible agreement points $v(v_1, v_2)$ and $w = (w_1, w_2)$. If they agree on which one to choose then this will be the outcome. But if they disagree then they will obtain only the conflict payoffs c_1 and c_2. Without loss of generality, we can choose the two players' utility functions in such a way that $c_1 = c_2 = 0$. The resulting 2×2 game can be represented by the payoff matrix shown in Game 1.

We will assume that outcome v is better for player 1 whereas outcome w is better for player 2 so that

$$v_1 > w_1 \quad \text{but} \quad v_2 < w_2. \tag{15}$$

Selten has shown that a game of this simple form can be fully analysed by using only two axioms (cf. Harsanyi and Selten, 1987, ch. 3).

One is the *linear-invariance* axiom (which is the same as Nash's axiom 3). The other is a *monotonicity* axiom (see below).

Definition. A 2×2 game like Game 1 will be called *symmetrical* if $v_1 = w_2 = a$ and $v_2 = w_1 = b$. Thus, a symmetrical game will have the form as in Game 2.

Clearly, in a symmetrical game there can be no mathematical criterion which selects *either* one of the two equilibrium points $\bar{V}$ and $\bar{W}$ as the solution in preference to the other equilibrium point.

Monotonicity axiom. Suppose that game G is symmetrical (like Game 2), and that game G^* can be obtained from G by *increasing* one or both payoffs associated with equilibrium point $\bar{V}$ (or $\bar{W}$). Then $\bar{V}$ (or $\bar{W}$) will be the solution of G^*. (In game G the two equilibrium points are equally attractive. But we can make $\bar{V}$ more attractive than $\bar{W}$ as a possible solution by increasing the payoff(s) associated with $\bar{V}$, and conversely.)

The linear-invariance and the monotonicity axioms imply:

Theorem 3. Game 1 will have $\bar{V}$ or $\bar{W}$ as its solution depending on whether $\pi(\bar{V}) > \pi(\bar{W})$ or $\pi(\bar{W}) > \pi(\bar{V})$, where $\pi(\bar{V}) = v_1 v_2$ and $\pi(\bar{W}) = w_1 w_2$ are the Nash products associated with $\bar{V}$ and with $\bar{W}$, respectively.

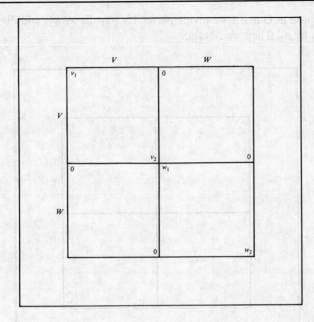

Game 1

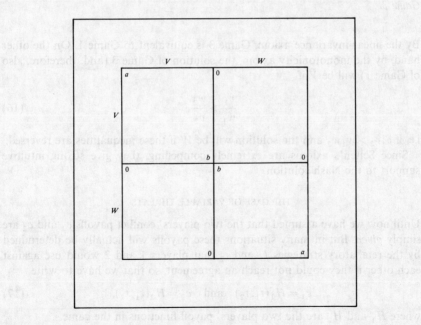

Game 2

63

Proof. Suppose in Game 1 we divide player 1's payoffs by w_1, and divide player 2's payoffs by v_2. Then we obtain:

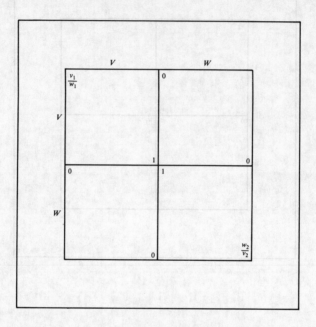

Game 3

By the linear-invariance axiom, Game 3 is equivalent to Game 1. On the other hand, by the monotonicity axiom, the solution of Game 3 (and, therefore, also of Game 1) will be $\bar{V}$ if

$$\frac{v_1}{w_1} > \frac{w_2}{v_2}, \tag{16}$$

i.e. if $v_1 v_2 > w_1 w_2$ and the solution will be $\bar{W}$ if these inequalities are reversed.

Since Selten's axioms are extremely compelling, they give strong intuitive support to the Nash solution.

THE CASE OF VARIABLE THREATS

Until now we have assumed that the two players' conflict payoffs c_1 and c_2 are simply *given*. But in many situations these payoffs will actually be determined by the retaliatory strategies t_1 and t_2 that players 1 and 2 would use against each other if they could not reach an agreement, so that we have to write

$$c_1 = H_1(t_1, t_2) \quad \text{and} \quad c_2 = H_2(t_1, t_2), \tag{17}$$

where H_1 and H_2 are the two players' payoff functions in the game.

To extend his theory to this kind of situation, Nash proposed the following model. The game is played in two stages. At stage 1, the two players announce their *threat strategies* t_1 and t_2, that is, the retaliatory strategies they would use in case of disagreement; and they will be *required* to implement these strategies if in fact no agreement is reached. (Implementation is assumed to be compulsory to exclude bluffing). These threat strategies t_1 and t_2 then define the players' conflict payoffs c_1 and c_2 in accordance with (17).

Then, at stage 2 the two players will choose an agreement point $\bar{u} = (\bar{u}_1, \bar{u}_2)$ in accordance with Theorem 3 above, now regarding their conflict payoffs c_1 and c_2 as *given*.

In the bargaining model of Theorem 3 each player had only *one* possible threat, that of simple noncooperation. In contrast, in the model just described, each player may have a *choice* among various alternative threat strategies. The former is called the Nash model with *fixed threats*. The latter is called the Nash model with *variable threats*.

In this latter model, at stage 1 each player i must obviously choose his threat strategy t_i so as to maximize his final payoff $\bar{u}_i$. Maximization of his conflict payoff c_i would *not* be a rational objective because he expects $\bar{u}_i$ rather than c_i to be his actual payoff. (Prior to Nash, this was not properly understood. Even such distinguished economists as Hicks (1932) got it quite wrong (see Harsanyi, 1977, pp. 189–91)). The problem of how to choose an optimal threat strategy can be elucidated by the following theorem.

Theorem 4. Suppose that player 2's threat strategy t_2 is given. Then player 1 must choose his own threat strategy t_1 in such a way as to *maximize* the ratio

$$R = \frac{u_2 - c_2}{u_1 - c_1} = \frac{u_2 - H_2(t_1, t_2)}{u_1 - H_1(t_1, t_2)}. \tag{18}$$

On the other hand, given player 1's threat strategy t_1, player 2 must choose his own threat strategy t_2 so as to *minimize* this ratio R. (For a proof of the theorem, see Harsanyi, 1977, pp. 176–7).

Note. When it comes to choosing threat strategies then the quantities $(u_2 - c_2)$ and $(u_1 - c_1)$ are to be interpreted as player 2's and player 1's *conflict costs* so that R itself becomes the *ratio* of these two costs.

CONCLUSION

Nash's theory of two-person bargaining is what we have called a *strong* theory: it defines a unique utility vector $\bar{u} = (\bar{u}_1, \bar{u}_2)$ as the agreement point to be chosen by two rational bargainers. For each player $i(i = 1, 2)$, this agreement point will yield a higher payoff $\bar{u}_i$:

(1) The greater his own willingness, and the less his opponent's willingness, to risk a conflict rather than accept unfavourable terms – as determined by his and his opponent's von Neumann–Morgenstern utility functions.

(2) The smaller the utility gain he could confer on his opponent at a given utility cost to himself if he made a further concession to him. (Thus, if the boundary curve δF were replaced by a *flatter* curve $\delta F'$ intersecting δF at agreement point $\bar{u}$ then this agreement point would move to the *right*, increasing player 1's payoff and decreasing player 2's.)

(3) The higher his own conflict payoff c_i and the lower his opponent's conflict payoff c_j would be if no agreement could be reached.

In case a player i has a choice among alternative threat strategies, he will maximize his final payoff u_i by maximizing the quantity $R = (u_i - c_i)/(u_j - c_j)$, that is, the ratio of his own conflict costs to his opponent's conflict costs, both measured in terms of von Neumann–Morgenstern utilities.

Finally, let me add the following qualification. Nash's theory is an attempt to predict how two rational bargainers will interact. But these predictions are based on the assumption that both sides' expectations about each other's behaviour are *endogenous*, that is, are based on the intrinsic parameters of the bargaining situation (game situation) as such. But in many cases this may not be true. For example, the two parties may live in a society where it is customary for an older person to receive twice the payoff his younger opponent will receive. If each player *expects* the other player to follow this role, it will become rational for him to follow it too. (For an experiment based on imparting exogenous expectations, see Roth and Schoumaker, 1983. For an excellent discussion of alternative axioms and of alternative solution concepts as well as for a very good bibliography, the reader is referred to Roth, 1979.)

BIBLIOGRAPHY

Edgeworth, F.Y. 1881. *Mathematical Psychics*. London: Kegan Paul; New York: A.M. Kelley, 1967.

Harsanyi, J.C. 1956. Approaches to the bargaining problem before and after the theory of games: a critical discussion of Zeuthen's, Hicks', and Nash's theories. *Econometrica* 24, 144–57.

Harsanyi, J.C. 1977. *Rational Behavior and Bargaining Equilibrium*. Cambridge and New York: Cambridge University Press.

Harsanyi, J.C. 1982. Solutions for some bargaining games under the Harsanyi–Selten solution theory, I-II. *Mathematical Social Sciences* 3, 179–91 and 259–79.

Harsanyi, J.C. and Selten, R. 1987. *A General Theory of Equilibrium Selection in Games*. Cambridge, Mass.: MIT Press.

Hicks, J.R. 1932. *The Theory of Wages*. London: Macmillan; New York: St. Martin's Press, 1963.

Luce, R.D. and Raiffa, H. 1957. *Games and Decisions*. New York: Wiley.

Nash, J.F. 1950. The bargaining problem. *Econometrica* 18, 155–62.

Nash, J.F. 1953. Two-person cooperative games. *Econometrica* 21, 128–40.

Neumann, J. von and Morgenstern, O. 1944. *Theory of Games and Economic Behavior*. Princeton: Princeton University Press.

Pigou, A.C. 1905. *Principles and Methods of Industrial Peace*. London and New York: Macmillan.

Roemer, J.E. 1985. Axiomatic bargaining theory of economic environments. University of California, Davis, Working Papers Series No. 264.

Roth, A.E. 1979. *Axiomatic Models of Bargaining*. Berlin: Springer-Verlag.

Roth, A.E. and Schoumaker, F. 1983. Subjective probability and the theory of games: some further comments. *Management Science* 29, 1337–40.

Zeuthen, F. 1930. *Problems of Monopoly and Economic Warfare*. London: Routledge & Kegan Paul; New York: A.M. Kelley, 1968.

Joseph Louis François Bertrand

MARTIN SHUBIK

Bertrand was born in Paris in 1822 and died there in 1900. He was an eminent but not great mathematician, graduate and professor of mathematics at the Ecole Polytechnique and from 1862 to 1900 a member of the Collège de France. His relevance to economic thought comes in his criticism of 'pseudo-mathematicians' in the *Journal des Savants* (1883) where he reviewed *Théorie mathématique de la richesse sociale* of Walras and *Recherches sur les principes mathématiques de la théorie des richesses* of Cournot. It is doubtful if Bertrand considered the problems of formal economic modelling more than casually, viewing the two works through the eyes of a mathematician with little substantive interest of understanding. His comments on Cournot were not only somewhat harsh, but as the subsequent developments in oligopoly theory and the theory of games have shown, both Cournot's model of duopoly and Bertrand's remodelling of duopoly with price rather than quantity as a strategic variable are worth investigation. Cournot's model has been (until recently) more generally treated than Bertrand's model. It remained for Edgeworth to point out the limitations of Bertrand's model (see Shubik, 1959). Bertrand also raised objections to the reference and realism of the process description of Walras of 'tâtonnement'.

It has been suggested (Blaug and Sturges, 1983) that Bertrand's critical review was used by opponents of mathematical economics as the basis for their position. Although explicit proof of this is hard to establish the tone and force of Bertrand's critique makes this highly probable.

SELECTED WORKS

1883. (Review of) *Théorie mathématique de la richesse sociale* par Léon Walras: *Recherches sur les principes mathématiques de la théorie des richesses* par Augustin Cournot. *Journal des Savants*, September, 499–508.

BIBLIOGRAPHY

Blaug, M. and Sturges, P. (eds) 1983. *Who's Who in Economics*. Brighton, England: Wheatsheaf Books; Cambridge, Mass.: MIT Press.

Byron, G.H. 1899–1900. Joseph Bertrand. *Nature* 1591 (61), 614–16.

Shubik, M. 1959. *Strategy and Market Structure*. New York: Wiley.

Storick, D.L. 1970. Joseph Louis François Bertrand. *Dictionary of Scientific Biography*, Vol. 2, New York: Scribners.

Bilateral Monopoly

JAMES W. FRIEDMAN

A bilateral monopoly is a market that is characterized by one firm or individual, a monopolist, on the supply side and one firm or individual, a monopsonist, on the demand side. The input markets of the monopolist and the output market of the monopsonist can be of any form. The essential ingredient is the single seller–single buyer situation. Because a buyer and a seller of a product, perforce, do business with each other, they are clearly able to make legally binding agreements. This contrasts with firms in the same industry, which do not sell to one another, and which are often precluded by anti-collusion laws from making legally enforceable contracts. Of course, it is also possible to view bilateral monopoly noncooperatively.

The following coverage is chronological, starting first with the cooperative treatment due to Edgeworth (1881) and Marshall (1890). The noncooperative formulations, due to Wicksell (1925) and Bowley (1928) are considered next, along with Bowley's reformulation of the Marshallian cooperative contribution. Finally, bilateral monopoly is viewed in game-theoretic terms as a two-player cooperative game, principally in the manner of Nash (1950).

Bilateral monopoly is a special instance of two-person trade; therefore, the natural starting point is Edgeworth's (1881, pp. 20–30) well known analysis. Suppose the two agents, A and B, have utility functions $u^A(x, y)$ and $u^B(X - x, Y - y)$, where x and y are quantities of two goods consumed by A. The totals available to the pair are X and Y, respectively; hence, the consumption of B is $(X - x, Y - y)$. Edgeworth proposed that the two persons would trade to a Pareto optimal outcome that left each at least as well off as he would be in the absence of trade.

Marshall (1890, Appendix F and Mathematical Note XII) noted that, if both persons' marginal utilities are constant for one of the goods (say y), then any Pareto optimal trade will involve a fixed quantity of the other good (x). This is

70

easily seen by recalling that a Pareto optimal (interior) trade requires equality of the two traders' marginal rates of substitution,

$$\frac{u_x^A(x, y)}{u_y^A(x, y)} = \frac{u_x^B(X - x, Y - y)}{u_y^B(X - x, Y - y)}$$

and then invoking Marshall's condition, which is

$$u^A(x, y) = v^A(x) + ay$$

and

$$u^B(X - x, Y - y) = v^B(X - x) + b(Y - y).$$

Note that Marshall's condition is actually that the two traders each have utility functions that are separable and linear with respect to one good. Equality of the marginal rates of substitution is given by

$$\frac{v_x^A(x)}{a} = \frac{v_x^B(X - x)}{b}$$

which is independent of y.

Bowley (1928) put Marshall's result in the following standard bilateral monopoly model: suppose the seller has the profit function $\pi^A = rx - C(x)$, where r is the firm's selling price, x is the amount sold, and $C(x)$ is the firm's total cost function; the buyer's profit function is $\pi^B = f(x) - rx$, where x is the buyer's only input, and $f(x)$ is its total revenue as a function of the sole input x. (That is, $f(x) = d[h(x)] \cdot h(x)$, where h is the production function and d is the inverse demand function for the firm.) The decision variables are x and r, and the Pareto optimality condition is

$$\frac{\partial \pi^A / \partial x}{\partial \pi^A / \partial r} = \frac{\partial \pi^B / \partial x}{\partial \pi^B / \partial r} \quad \text{or} \quad \frac{r - C'(x)}{x} = \frac{f'(x) - r}{-x}.$$

The latter condition is independent of r and is equivalent to $f'(x) = C'(x)$, which states that the marginal revenue of the buying firm should equal the marginal cost of the selling firm – the condition for joint profit maximization. The way that the joint profit is split depends upon r, the transfer price between the two firms.

An equilibrium in a noncooperative vein was suggested by Wicksell (1925, pp. 223–5) and developed by Bowley (1928). Wicksell's equilibrium features a price announcement by the seller, followed by a quantity selection by the buyer. The seller is committed to deliver whatever amount the buyer wishes at the named price. Thus, the seller is a Stackelberg (1934) leader that knows the buyer will maximize $f(x) - rx$ with respect to x, and with r assumed constant. This allows the seller to solve $f'(x) = r$ for x as a function of r [denote this $x = \phi(r)$] and use this in its own profit function, $r\phi(r) - C[\phi(r)]$, which it then maximizes with respect to r to find the best price to announce.

In addition to working out the details of the foregoing model, Bowley suggested an alternative in which the roles of the two firms are exactly reversed: the buyer announces a price at which it will buy any quantity the seller cares to deliver, and the seller then chooses an amount to transact. The buyer can calculate the optimal choice of x for the seller as a function of r and then use this information to determine its most profitable price.

These noncooperative outcomes are not in general Pareto optimal; therefore, they are implausible in a setting such as this where there are only two agents who can discuss a transaction with one another and who are quite able to make binding agreements that do give them Pareto optimal outcomes.

Another way to visualize the possible outcomes in a bilateral monopoly is in the profit (or utility) space of the agents. In the Marshall–Bowley model the payoff possibility frontier is a straight line of slope $-b/a$. Were the two players a firm and a labour union, then, depending on the utility function assigned to the union, the payoff possibility frontier need not be a straight line. The union's utility function might well depend on the wage rate, the number of workers employed, and the average hours worked per employee. The representation of the model in profit, or utility, space is useful in approaching the model as a game-theoretic bargaining problem.

Perhaps the most famous two-person cooperative game solution is that due to Nash (1950), in which there is a *threat outcome* that would prevail in the absence of agreement between the two players, with the bargained outcome being on the payoff possibility frontier at that point where the product of the players' gains from cooperation is maximized. Though this product maximization rule seems arbitrary on the surface, it is implied by several axioms that are plausible. For the bilateral monopoly model the threat of each firm is to refuse to trade with the other. This threat would force zero profit onto the buyer and $-C(0)$ onto the seller.

Nash's approach can be enriched in several ways. First, the threat of no trade need not leave the firms at profits of 0 and $-C(0)$. Perhaps the seller could enter the buyer's line of business. Similarly, the buyer may have other options open: there may be substitutes for the input supplied by the seller that are more expensive or less effective. If both possibilities hold at once, then 'no trade' does not completely specify the threat situation. The firms could become duopolists in a vertically integrated industry, and carry out threats in terms of the output levels that they decide to produce. This leads to a *variable threat* game, analysed by Nash (1953).

Neither of the Nash models appears to deal with the process of bargaining. Interestingly, the Nash outcome coincides with the outcome of a bargaining process proposed by Zeuthen (1930). On this, see Harsanyi (1956) who also shows the relationship between the Nash model and a suggestion of Hicks (1932).

Observation of labour–management bargaining indicates that agreements often are more costly than theory suggests. Strikes occur which impose costs on both sides even though both sides could have been better off by accepting the very same contract prior to a strike. Several directions are suggested in the literature in this regard. First, there are two-person cooperative game models in which offers and counter-offers are made until a settlement is reached. During this process, real time is assumed to elapse, and the total size of the players' joint gain is supposed to shrink. Cross (1965) has such a model and, in an elegant paper, Rubinstein (1982) models the bargaining process in a way that turns the bargaining game into a noncooperative game having the Nash (1950) solution as its outcome. Second, it can be assumed, following Harsanyi and Selten (1972), that each player is ignorant of the payoff function of the other player. Each player makes a *demand*; however, if the two demands taken together lie beyond the payoff possibility frontier of the game, then no agreement is made. A third line of investigation, not formally applied to bilateral monopoly, is that of *repeated games* or *supergames*. Under this approach, one instance of bargaining between two players is seen as one episode in a larger game. For example, in labour–management negotiations, a contract is reached for a specific interval, say three years, and both firm and union are concerned with the effect that the current contract will have on later contract negotiations. This situation is easily seen as a game of many players, if it is added that the union may deal with more than one firm, and that the various contracts are inter-connected. This latter consideration embeds a bilateral monopoly in a larger context, hence may be thought to go beyond the present topic. Additional discussion of bargainning models can be found in Roth (1979) and Friedman (1986).

BIBLIOGRAPHY

Bowley, A. 1928. Bilateral monopoly. *Economic Journal* 38, 651–9.

Cross, J. 1965. A theory of the bargaining process. *American Economic Review* 54, 67–94.

Edgeworth, F. 1881. *Mathematical Psychics*. London: Kegan Paul; New York: A.M. Kelley, 1967.

Fellner, W. 1949. *Competition Among the Few*. New York: Knopf.

Friedman, J. 1986. *Game Theory with Applications to Economics*. New York: Oxford University Press.

Harsanyi, J. 1956. Approaches to the bargaining problem before and after the theory of games. *Econometrica* 24, 144–56.

Harsanyi, J. and Selten, R. 1972. A generalized Nash solution for two-person bargaining games with incomplete information. *Management Science* 18, 80–106.

Hicks, J. 1932. *The Theory of Wages*. London: Macmillan; New York: St. Martin's Press, 1963.

Marshall, A. 1890. *Principles of Economics*. 9th (variorum) edn, with annotations by C.W. Guillebaud, London and New York: Macmillan, 1961.

Nash, J. 1950. The bargaining problem. *Econometrica* 18, 155–62.

Nash, J. 1953. Two person cooperative games. *Econometrica* 21, 128–40.

Roth, A. 1979. *Axiomatic Models in Bargaining*. Berlin: Springer.

Rubinstein, A. 1982. Perfect equilibrium in a bargaining model. *Econometrica* 50, 97–109.

Stackelberg, H. von 1934. *Marktform und Gleichgewicht*. Vienna: Julius Springer.

Wicksell, K. 1925. Mathematical economics. In K. Wicksell, *Selected Papers on Economic Theory*, ed. E. Lindahl, Cambridge, Mass.: Harvard University Press, 1958.

Zeuthen, F. 1930. *Problems of Monopoly and Economic Warfare*. London: Routledge & Kegan Paul; New York: A.M. Kelley, 1968.

Common Knowledge

SÉRGIO RIBEIRO DA COSTA WERLANG

The concept of *knowledge* is central to economics as well as to many other sciences whose object is the study of man, such as psychology, linguistics and artificial intelligence. Rational expectations models, for example, assume not only that economic agents form their expectations according to the model, but also that they all know the model. In the same way, game theorists always assume that the game is known to all the players, at least to some extent. The famous Lucas critique of the application of econometric models to policy assumes that the public knows the models that are being used by the policy maker. In all these examples the message is clear: the extent to which knowledge is shared is fundamental in economics.

In what follows we will suppose that the reader understands what it means both to know a fact and to know the truth-value of a proposition. A closely related but distinct concept is that of *belief*. That a person believes a fact to be true does not of itself imply the truth of that fact. Thus in this discussion people may well hold false beliefs but cannot, by definition, have false knowledge.

That a person knows a fact is itself a fact. So we may further consider the knowledge that one individual, say i, has about the knowledge of another individual, say j, concerning a particular fact. This process may be repeated as many times as we wish. Hence, if there are several agents, we may say that a fact is *known up to level m* by these agents if: '(everyone knows that)$^{m-1}$ everyone knows that the fact is true', i.e. the phrase 'everyone knows that' appears side by side in $(m-1)$ repetitions before the words 'everyone knows the fact is true'.

In this way we define a fact to be *common knowledge* among a group of persons if that fact is known up to level m for every $m > 0$. In other words, a fact is common knowledge if everyone knows it, everyone knows that everyone knows it, everyone knows that everyone knows it, ..., and so on *ad infinitum*.

The concept of knowledge has of course long been discussed by philosophers, incorporated as it is into the very name of the discipline. However, the ideas of *common* knowledge and of the importance of higher levels of knowledge are quite recent, being introduced in 1966 by David Lewis in his philosophical study *Convention*. Independently, the game theorist John Harsanyi in his triptych of papers (1967–68) on games with incomplete information, where the payoff functions of the players depend upon an unknown (possibly multidimensional) parameter, noticed the importance of iterated guesses about that parameter. Roughly, he argued that, because in a game of incomplete information the action chosen by any player will depend on his (or her) beliefs about the values of the unknown parameter, he (or she) will attribute the same understanding to the other players. Since, further, the action of any player influences the payoffs of all the other players, each should try to guess what the other players believe about the unknown parameter, and guess what the other players are guessing about the beliefs of the other players, and so on.

The definition of higher levels of knowledge prompts us to wonder what use there can be in any level higher than the first. In order to see why they can be important we consider a well-known puzzle, told in story-book form. Once upon a time an evil King decided to grant sadistic amnesty to a large group of male prisoners, who were each kept incommunicado in the royal dungeons. Summoning the prisoners to his presence and commanding them under penalty of death not to look upward, the King had a hat placed upon the head of each one; two of these hats were red, the rest white. Thus each prisoner could see the hat of every one of his fellow prisoners, but not his own.

The King spoke thus: 'As you will have noticed, most of you prisoners are wearing white hats. *But at least one of you is wearing a red one.* Every day from now on you will be brought to this chamber from your solitary confinement in the cells. The day that you guess correctly the colour of the hat that you are wearing is the day you will go free. If you guess incorrectly, however, you will be instantly beheaded.'

How many days would it take the two red-hatted prisoners to infer, rationally, the colour of their hats? Let us reason day by day. On the first day, that of the King's speech, each prisoner with a white hat sees two red hats and each with a red hat sees only one. Since all they know is what the King has told them, none can conclude anything about the colour of his own hat.

Thus on the second day everyone, barring accidents, will be back in the King's chamber. Once again all the white-hatted prisoners will see two red hats and both the red-hatted wretches, named Smith and Jones, say, will see only one. But now there is more information, albeit of a perculiar kind. For one day has passed and neither Smith nor Jones has left, either one way or the other. Because they were both present at the King's speech, Smith knows that Jones knows that there is at least one red hat, so he reasons that on the first day Jones must have seen a red hat. For if he had not, Jones would have seen only white hats and thus would have correctly inferred that the only possible red hat was perched atop his own head. So, Smith reasons, since the only red hat that *I* can now see is on Jones's head, that which Jones saw on the first day must have been on mine.

Jones, having the same information set and abilities as Smith, will arrive at the same conclusion. Both will correctly guess – more properly, infer – their hats to be red, and both will go free on the second day. The story does not say what happens to the unfortunate white-hatted prisoners.

How would the rest of the story change if the King had, instead, arranged for three red hats rather than two? A similar though more complicated argument would apply, with Smith requiring three appearances in the chamber rather than two before he could conclude anything from the behaviour of the other red-hatted prisoners Jones and Brown; and similarly for them. Obviously, this reasoning could go on for any number of red hats that is no greater than the number of white hats.

The puzzle shows clearly that different levels of knowledge of a particular fact are connected with quite distinct situations. Thus take the single proposition 'everyone sees at least one red hat'. In the story of two red hats, on the first day Smith sees Jones's red hat (and vice versa), but does not know whether Jones also sees one (and vice versa). Thus, on the first day the proposition is actually true but not everyone knows that it is true; it takes another appearance in the chamber, another 'round' so to say, for everyone to be able to infer its truth. In the story of three red hats, on the other hand, on the first day Smith sees two red hats and so knows that everyone must see at least one; and similarly for Jones and Brown. So in this case at the first round everyone already knows that everyone knows a fact – 'everyone sees at least one red hat' – which in the two red hat case is not apparent to everybody until the second. But of course this further information does not suffice to solve the more complicated case of three red hats.

We could go on to show inductively that each higher level of knowledge of the fact 'everyone sees at least one red hat' is attained for versions of the puzzle with increasing numbers of red hats. As these various puzzles are quite distinct problems (in particular, their solutions are different), we can see the importance of different levels of knowledge of a fact.

THE FORMALIZATION OF COMMON KNOWLEDGE

The formalization of common knowledge is not obvious. To begin with, it is necessary to define what are the objects of knowledge. The first formalization was due to Robert Aumann in 1976. In his model, knowledge refers to events which are subsets of a set of states of the world. Call it Ω. Aumann represents the agents by information partitions, $\Pi_1, \ldots, \Pi_n$. These partitions work in the following way: if a state $\omega \in \Omega$ occurs, then agent i observes the occurrence of the cell of his partition which contains ω. We denote it by $\Pi_i(\omega)$. The description of the set of states of the world and of the information structure above, has to be taken to be common knowledge in a primitive sense. Then, one agent knows an event A at the state ω if the cell $\Pi_i(\omega)$ is contained in A. The iterations of the word 'know' are a little more subtle. They depend entirely on the primitive common knowledge of the information structure. In the picture below, we can see an example with two agents. The set Ω is an interval, the partitions of the agents are Π_1 and Π_2, and the event is A. For convenience, we draw the set Ω twice. In the first we see the information partition of the first agent, and in the second we see the information partition of the second agent.

We will verify the knowledge of the event A in its various layers, by both of the agents, when the state of the world that has occurred is ω, as displayed.

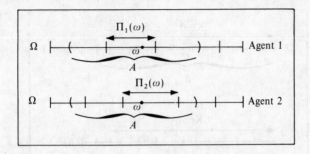

Figure 1

Because agent 1 has the information partition Π_1, she 'sees' the event $\Pi_1(\omega)$. As $\Pi_1(\omega)$ is contained in A, agent 1 knows that the event A occurred. Similarly, for agent 2, as $\Pi_2(\omega)$ is contained in A, agent 2 knows A. As agent 1 sees $\Pi_1(\omega)$, and she knows agent 2 has the partition Π_2, she knows that agent 2 has observed the occurrence of $\Pi_2(\omega')$ for some $\omega' \in \Pi_1(\omega)$. So, she knows that agent 2 has seen the occurrence of the union of the cells $\Pi_2(\omega')$ for ω' in $\Pi_1(\omega)$. As this set is contained in A (see Figure 2), agent 1 knows that agent 2 knows A.

On the other hand, the same cannot be said about agent 2. In fact, as agent 2 sees $\Pi_2(\omega)$, it turns out that the state $\bar{\omega}$ shown in Figure 2 could be the real state of the world. As he knows agent 1 has partition Π_1, he knows agent 1 could be observing $\Pi_1(\bar{\omega})$, and hence she would be uncertain about the occurrence of the event A. It follows that agent 2 does not know whether agent 1 knows A.

Suppose now that we are considering the knowledge of the event B, drawn in Figure 3. The set $CK(\omega)$ is observed by both agents. Furthermore, as the information partitions Π_1 and Π_2 are common knowledge to begin with, both agents know each other see $CK(\omega)$, know they know $CK(\omega)$, and so on. This set has a sort of fixed point property: $CK(\omega)$ belongs at the same time to the set of events that agent 1 observes in her information structure and the set of events that agent 2 observes in his information structure. That is to say, $CK(\omega)$ belongs to the meet of the two partitions, i.e., the finest common coarsening of the partitions, denoted by $\Pi_1 \wedge \Pi_2$. As the set B contains $CK(\omega)$, and it is common knowledge that the set $CK(\omega)$ is observed by both, B is common knowledge.

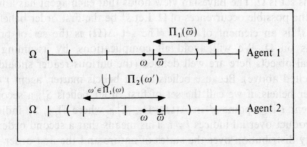

Figure 2

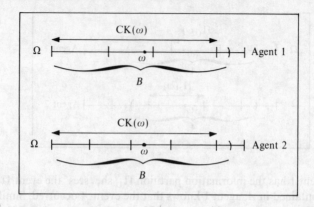

Figure 3

Based on the intuition above, Aumann defines an event B to be common knowledge at ω, if there is an element of $\Pi_1 \wedge \Pi_2$ which contains ω and is contained in B. Aumann's definition is elegant, and can be readily generalized to n agents. A further, and more complicated, step allows for richer information structures, generated by σ-algebras. On this refer to Nielsen (1984) and Brandenburger and Dekel (1987).

The problem with his definition is the difficulty with its application. Imagine that we tried to formalize the following statement: 'the model is common knowledge among the agents'. The first thing we would have to do, would be to embed 'the model' as an event in a large space of states of the world. Also it would be necessary to figure out what were the information structures which represented the agents in this world. Not only this, but this representation should be intuitively common knowledge a priori.

Aiming at avoiding these problems, and at applying knowledge and common knowledge to games, an alternative formalization was developed by Tan and Werlang (1985) (see also Brandenburger and Dekel, 1985; Tan and Werlang, 1984, 1988, 1988b; and Werlang, 1986). The idea behind it is the direct modelling of layers of knowledge (to be precise, this is a model of belief with probability one). Suppose there are n agents, and each of the n agents is uncertain about some basic set of states of the world. To be consistent with the discussion up to now, say this set is Ω. The Bayesian view holds that each agent has a first order belief over the possible occurrences of Ω. Let s_i^1 be the first order belief of agent i. That is, s_i^1 is an element of $\Delta(\Omega)$. The set $\Delta(\Omega)$ is the set of probability distributions on Ω. We will avoid all complications, by assuming that all mathematical objects here are well defined (the curious reader should refer to the papers cited above). Because beliefs about beliefs matter, agent i will have second order beliefs: if we call the set of first order beliefs S_i^1, a second order belief of agent i is a point s_i^2 in $\Delta(\Omega \times \Pi_{j \neq i} S_j^1)$, where $\Pi_{j \neq i} S_j^1$ indicates the cartesian product over all indices $j \neq i$. This means that a second order belief is a probability distribution over the states of nature and the first order beliefs of all other agents. Call the set of second order beliefs of agent i, S_i^2. Inductively an

mth order belief, s_i^m, is a belief on $\Omega \times \Pi_{j \neq i} S_j^{m-1}$, where S_j^{m-1} is the set of $(m-1)$th order beliefs of agent j. Formally one has: s_i^m belongs to $\Delta(\Omega \times \Pi_{j \neq i} S_j^{m-1})$. The 'psychology' (or 'type') of agent i is summarized by his infinite hierarchy of beliefs: $(s_i^1, s_i^2, \ldots) \in \Pi_{m \geq 1} S_i^m$.

This set is, however, too large. It allows the existence of extremely inconsistent beliefs. We impose a minimum consistency requirement: whenever there is an event whose probability can be evaluated by the mth order belief, as well as by the pth order belief, then the probability assessment given by both orders of beliefs must coincide. For example, this implies that the first order belief must be the marginal of the second order belief on Ω: $s_i^1 = \text{marg}_\Omega(s_i^2)$. Recall that the marginal distributions, or simply the marginals of a probability measure P which is defined on a product space $U \times V$, are defined by $\text{marg}_U(A) = P(A \times V)$, and similarly $\text{marg}_V(B) = P(B \times U)$ for any event A in U and any event B in V. Hence, agent i is characterized by a point s_i in the set $S_i = \{(s_i^1, s_i^2, \ldots): \text{the beliefs satisfy the minimum consistency requirement}\}$. By a theorem first proved by Böge (1974) (and later by Armbruster and Böge, 1979; Böge and Eisele, 1979; Mertens and Zamir, 1985; and Brandenburger and Dekel, 1985), a point in this set of psychologies has a very important property: any s_i in S_i can be viewed as a joint probability distribution (belief) on the occurrence of nature and on the other agents' psychologies. In formal terms, there is an homeomorphism $\phi_i : S_i \to \Delta(\Omega \times \Pi_{j \neq i} S_j)$. Moreover, this homeomorphism has the property that the mth order belief of agent i, s_i^m, is the marginal of $\phi_i(s_i)$ on the set $\Omega \times \Pi_{j \neq i} S_j^{m-1}$, that is: $s_i^m = \text{marg}_{\Omega \times \Pi_{j \neq i} S_j^{m-1}}[\phi_i(s_i)]$.

The interpretation given to the support of the marginal distribution of $\phi_i(s_i)$ on S_j, denoted by supp $\text{marg}_{S_j}[\phi_i(s_i)]$ lies at the heart of the definition of knowledge. Recall that the support of a probability measure is the smallest closed set with probability one. We interpret supp $\text{marg}_{S_j}[\phi_i(s_i)]$ as the set of psychologies of the jth agent that agent i considers possible. In other words, it is the set of jth agents which are possible in the eyes of agent i.

Let R_j be a subset of S_j, $j = 1, \ldots, n$. Suppose one wants to formalize: 'agent i knows that agent j is in R_j'. Making use of the interpretation given to $\phi_i(s_i)$, one has to say: every s_j which, in the eyes of agent i, could possibly be true must satisfy $s_j \in R_j$. Formally this means: for any $j \neq i$, for any $s_j \in$ supp $\text{marg}_{S_j}[\phi_i(s_i)]$, one has $s_j \in R_j$. By extending this idea further, we can formalize longer sentences where the verb 'know' appears many times. Given s_i and $R_1, \ldots, R_n$ as above, we define that the sets $R_1, \ldots, R_n$ are known up to level k, in the eyes of agent i, if: $s_i \in \bigcap_{m=1}^k R_i^m$, where $R_i^1 = R_i$ and if $m \geq 2$, $R_i^m = \{s_i \in R_i^{m-1}: \text{for all } j \neq i, \text{supp } \text{marg}_{S_j}[\phi_i(s_i)] \subset R_j^{m-1}\}$. It is easy to see that by taking $k = \infty$ we obtain the definition of common knowledge (in the eyes of agent i).

This framework is more complex than Aumann's from the mathematical point of view. However, it allows the direct formalization of higher levels of knowledge. For example, an event $A \subset \Omega$ may be common knowledge without any reference to the information partitions Π_{i1} or the true state of the world $\omega \in \Omega$. In fact, let

$$A_i = \{s_i \in S_i: \text{supp } \text{marg}_\Omega[\phi_i(s_i)] \subset A\} \text{ for all } i.$$

The set A_i represents the psychologies of agent i for which the first order beliefs are concentrated in a subset of A. This means that A is known for sure. We can apply the iterative procedure above to define that A is common knowledge (in the eyes of agent i) if $s_i \in \bigcap_{m \geq 1} A_i^m$, where $A_i^1 = A_i$, and for $m \geq 2$

$$A_i^m = \{ s_i \in A_i^{m-1}: \text{for all } j \neq i, \text{ supp marg}_{s_j}[\phi_i(s_i)] \subset A_j^{m-1} \}.$$

We may also define common knowledge of the partitions, which was implicitly assumed by Aumann. Given the partitions $\Pi_1, \ldots, \Pi_n$, we say that agent i knows that agent j uses Π_j, if $s_i \in P_i$, where the set $P_i = \{ s_i \in S_i: \text{for } j \neq i, (\omega, s_j) \in \text{supp marg}_{\Omega \times S_j}[\phi_i(s_i)] \Rightarrow \text{supp marg}_\Omega[\phi_j(s_j)] = \Pi_j(\omega) \}$. Again, the interpretation is straightforward. If a state of the world ω is thought possible to occur jointly with a psychology s_j, it must be the case that s_j has a belief over Ω whose support coincides with the set of states of nature that agent j observes. As we have seen before, this set is $\Pi_j(\omega)$, the element of the partition Π_j which contains ω. Inductively, we can define that the information partitions are common knowledge (in the eyes of agent i) if $s_i \in \bigcap_{m \geq 1} P_i^m$, where $P_i^1 = P_i$ above, and for $m \geq 2$,

$$P_i = \{ s_i \in P_i^{m-1}: \text{for all } j \neq i, \text{ supp marg}_{s_j}[\phi_i(s_i)] \subset P_j^{m-1} \}.$$

To compare this framework with Aumann's, we still need to formalize the fact that the state ω has occurred in the eyes of agent i. Clearly this is the same as supp marg$_\Omega[\phi_i(s_i)] = \Pi_i(\omega)$. Tan and Werlang (1985) prove the following theorem:

Theorem. Assume that in the eyes of agent i the information partitions $\Pi_1, \ldots, \Pi_m$ are common knowledge and that state ω occurred. Then an event A is common knowledge at ω in the sense of Aumann if, and only if, in the eyes of agent i A is common knowledge.

Observe that we always mention that the knowledge or common knowledge occurs in the eyes of agent i. The reason for that was seen before. We formalized a belief with probability one. As a matter of fact, agent i could be completely wrong in his beliefs. This would not invalidate any of the results above.

The infinite hierarchies of beliefs allowed us to state precisely the notions of knowledge and common knowledge of rationality in a game (see Tan and Werlang, 1984, 1988b; and Werlang, 1986).

There is a third way to model common knowledge: through the logic-theoretic framework. This consists basically of an iterative formalization as above, but with a less rich mathematical structure. The main source for that is Fagin, Halpern and Vardi (1984). We will not discuss it in further detail, mainly because of the difficulty with its applicability. Since the mathematical structure behind it is not rich enough, it turns out to be very hard to formalize even simple statements like 'rationality'.

APPLICATIONS OF COMMON KNOWLEDGE

There are several applications of the concepts of knowledge and common knowledge in economics. Among them are the Bayesian foundations of solution concepts of games, no-trade results for speculative markets, rational expectations models, games with incomplete information, the mechanism of acquiring knowledge through information transmission, and the study of games whose payoffs depend on knowledge about the outcomes. Outside the realm of economics, we can name some other applications: the theory of social conventions, the theory of communication and language, and the theory of information sharing in parallel processing. All the topics mentioned here are covered in the list of references. We will review only two of the most important consequences in economic theory.

Foundations of Solution Concepts of Games. There is a plethora of notions of equilibrium in games. The theory of knowledge and common knowledge applied to games helps one to understand the implicit assumptions on the players which underlie some of these solution concepts. We will concentrate on the study of normal form noncooperative games. The interested reader should refer to Tan and Werlang (1984, 1988, 1988b). The programme of this literature is simply stated: given a solution concept, find the implicit assumptions about the knowledge and the common knowledge of the players which will lead to this solution concept. One should be aware of another trend to investigate the foundations of solution concepts, the evolutionary view (see Samuelson, 1988; and Maynard Smith, 1982). Also, there are some developments on the Bayesian foundations in extensive form. On this see Reny (1988), Binmore (1988) and Bicchieri (1988).

The following solution concepts have been studied in the normal form: iterative elimination of strictly dominated strategies, rationalizable strategic behavior (defined by Bernheim, 1984, and Pearce, 1984), correlated equilibrium (defined by Aumann, 1974), Nash equilibrium, perfect equilibrium (defined by Selten, 1975) and proper equilibrium (defined by Myerson, 1978). We will analyse two of them, namely iterative elimination of strictly dominant strategies and Nash equilibrium. We say that a player is Bayesian rational (or simply rational) when this player chooses an action which maximizes her expected utility given the beliefs she has about the actions of the other players. Thus, in the game of Figure 4, player II has a strictly dominant strategy, which is l. Hence, whatever player II thinks player I will do (i.e. given any belief about player I's actions), player II will always play l, if she is rational. If player I knows that player II is rational, then player I, being himself rational, will play u. This example shows us the links between layers of knowledge of rationality and interactions in the elimination of strictly dominated strategies. It is possible to show as in Tan and Werlang (1988b) that if Bayesian rationality is known up to level m, then the players will play strategies which survive $m + 1$ iterations of elimination of strictly dominated strategies. Carrying this argument to the limit, if it is common knowledge that players are Bayesian rational, then the outcome of the game has to survive iterative elimination of strictly dominated strategies. Converses of the results above are also true: in a game with n players, any n-tuple which survives $m + 1$ rounds of elimination of strictly dominated strategies is played by some n-tuple of players (represented by their 'psychologies' or 'types') for whom Bayesian

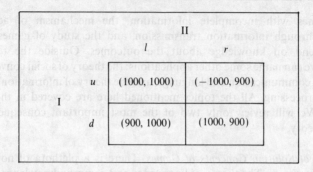

	II	
	l	*r*
I *u*	(1000, 1000)	(−1000, 900)
I *d*	(900, 1000)	(1000, 900)

Figure 4

rationality is known up to level *m*. The same goes for $m = \infty$ (i.e., common knowledge).

When we come to Nash equilibrium, matters are not so nice. There are several ways to derive Nash behavior from the Bayesian point of view, none of them entirely satisfactory. In the case of two players as in Armbruster and Böge (1979), we could require common knowledge of rationality as well as knowledge of each other's beliefs. Or as in Werlang (1986), Tan and Werlang (1988b) and Bacharach (1987), it is possible to show that if one requires a solution concept to be single valued, then the only solution concept which is consistent with common knowledge of rationality and of itself is a Nash equilibrium. This last explanation for Nash behavior shows the strong coordination requirements behind this solution concept. Not only rationality has to be common knowledge, but also the actions taken, before they are taken.

No-Trade Results for Speculative Markets. It has been known for a long time that in any economy with no asymmetry of information, there is no reason for the existence of speculative markets. In fact, consider the case of the stock market. A stock is a claim on the future random profits of a firm. Since everyone knows the same probability distribution of the future profits (because there is no asymmetry of information), the only reason to trade stocks would be differences in risk aversion. But then the role of the stock exchanges could be taken by insurance companies.

Milgrom and Stokey (1982) prove a much stronger result. They consider trade of a risky asset in an economy with three periods: today, tomorrow and the day after tomorrow. Today, the state of the world is not realized yet, and we can trade the risky asset. Tomorrow, the state of the world occurs, and each trader has access to his own private information. The value of the asset is not yet disclosed, so the traders are allowed one more round of exchange. The day after tomorrow, the value of the risky asset becomes common knowledge, and more trade makes no sense. This is an economy with asymmetric information, where trade can occur before and after part of the information is revealed to the agents.

Their main result is thus: Suppose that tomorrow (after the state of the world is realized, but only partially revealed to the agents through their information structure) it is common knowledge that the agents want to trade. Then the only trade possible has to be indifferent to no-trade for every agent. The idea of the proof is simple: if it is common knowledge ex-post that the agents benefit from trade, then ex-ante there would be a feasible contract which could be written and would leave everyone better off, so that there would have been trade ex-ante. Here, the assumption of common knowledge is central. They give examples where everyone wants to trade ex-post, but the fact they want to trade is not common knowledge.

Their result is a problem for the theory of speculative markets: asymmetric information alone cannot be responsible for the existence of large stock exchanges. A very important research project in the finance literature is to find where Milgrom–Stokey's model departs from reality. It is a point which is crucial for the understanding of the very complex speculative markets we see nowadays.

The present essay does not pretend to be exhaustive. For surveys of the area which contain more diverse material, see Binmore and Brandenburger (1988), Tan and Werlang (1988) and Brandenburger (1987).

REFERENCES

Armbruster, W. and Böge, W. 1979. Bayesian game theory. In *Game Theory and Related Topics*, ed. O. Moeschlin and D. Pallaschke, Amsterdam: North-Holland.

Aumann, R. 1974. Subjectivity and correlation in randomized strategies. *Journal of Mathematical Economics* 1, 67–96.

Aumann, R. 1976. Agreeing to disagree. *Annals of Statistics* 4, 1236–9.

Aumann, R. 1987. Correlated equilibrium as an expression of Bayesian rationality. *Econometrica* 55, 1–18.

Bacharach, M. 1985. Some extensions to a claim of Aumann in an axiomatic model of knowledge. *Journal of Economic Theory* 37, 167–90.

Bacharach, M. 1987. A theory of rational decision in games *Erkenntnis* 27, 17–55.

Barwise, J. 1981. Scenes and other situations. *Journal of Philosophy* 78, 369–97.

Barwise, J. 1988. Three views of common knowledge. In Vardi (1988).

Basu, K. 1985. Strategic irrationality in extensive games. Institute for Advanced Studies, Princeton, Mimeo.

Bernheim, B.D. 1984. Rationalizable strategic behavior. *Econometrica* 52, 1007–28.

Bernheim, B.D. 1987. Axiomatic characterizations of rational choice in strategic environments. *Scandinavian Journal of Economics* 88, 473–88.

Bicchieri, C. 1988. Common knowledge and backward induction: a solution to the paradox. In Vardi (1988).

Binmore, K. 1988. Modelling rational players I and II. *Journal of Economics and Philosophy*, forthcoming.

Binmore, K. and Brandenburger, A. 1988. Common knowledge and game theory. London School of Economics, Mimeo.

Blume, L. 1986. Lexicographic refinements of Nash equilibrium. Department of Economics, University of Michigan, Mimeo.

Böge, W. 1974. Gedanken über die Angewandte Mathematik. In *Mathematiker über die Mathematik*, ed. M. Otte, Heidelberg: Springer.

Böge, W. and Eisele, T. 1979. On solutions of Bayesian games. *International Journal of Game Theory* 8, 193–215.

Brandenburger, A. 1987. The role of common knowledge assumptions in game theory. In

The Economics of Information, Games, and Missing Markets, ed. F. Hahn, forthcoming.

Brandenburger, A. and Dekel, E. 1985. Hierarchies of beliefs and common knowledge. Research Paper No. 841, Graduate School of Business, Stanford University.

Brandenburger, A. 1986. On an axiomatic approach to refinements of Nash equilibrium. Department of Economics, University of California at Berkeley, Mimeo.

Brandenburger, A. 1987. Common knowledge with probability 1. *Journal of Mathematical Economics* 16, 237–45.

Brandenburger, A. and Dekel, E. 1987. Rationalizability and correlated equilibria. *Econometrica* 55, 1391–402.

Cave, J. 1983. Learning to agree. *Economic Letters* 12, 147–52.

Fagin, R., Halpern, J.Y. and Vardi, M. 1984. A model-theoretic analysis of knowledge: preliminary report. *Proc. 25th IEEE Symposium on Foundations of Computer Science*, West Palm Beach, Florida.

Geanakoplos, J.D. and Polemarchakis, H.M. 1982. We can't disagree forever. *Journal of Economic Theory* 28, 192–200.

Gilbert, M. 1981. Game theory and conventions. *Synthèse* 46, 41–93.

Gilbert, M. 1983. Agreements, conventions and language. *Synthèse* 54, 375–404.

Gilboa, I. 1988. Information and meta-information. In Vardi (1988).

Gilboa, I. and Schmeidler, D. 1988. Information-dependent games: can common sense be common knowledge? In Vardi (1988).

Halpern, J.Y. 1986. *Proceedings of the 1986 Conference on Theoretical of Reasoning About Knowledge*. Asilomar, CA: Morgan Kaufman.

Halpern, J.Y. and Fagin, R. 1985. A formal model of knowledge, action and communication in distributed systems: preliminary report. *Proc. ACM Symposium on Principles of Distributed Computation*.

Halpern, J.Y. and Moses, Y. 1986. Knowledge and common knowledge in a distributed environment. IBM Research Report RJ 4421, January.

Harsanyi, J. 1967–8. Games with incomplete information played by 'Bayesian' players. *Management Science* 14, 159–82, 320–34, 486–502.

Kaneko, M. 1987. Structural common knowledge and factual common knowledge. RUEE Working Paper No. 87-27, Hitotsubashi University.

Kaneko, M. and Nagashima, T. 1988. Player's deductions and deductive knowledge and common knowledge on theorems. Working Paper No. E88-02-01, Department of Economics, Virginia Polytechnic Institute and State University.

Kripke, S. 1963. Semantical analysis of modal logic. *Zeitschrift für Mathematische Logik und Grundlagen der Mathematik* 9, 67–96.

Lewis, D. 1966. *Convention: A Philosophical Study*. Cambridge, Massachusetts: Harvard University Press.

Maynard Smith, J. 1982. *Evolution and the Theory of Games*. Cambridge: Cambridge University Press.

McKelvey, R. and Page, T. 1986. Common knowledge, consensus, and aggregate information. *Econometrica* 54, 109–27.

Mertens, J.F. and Zamir, S. 1985. Formulation of Bayesian analysis for games with incomplete information. *International Journal of Game Theory* 14, 1–29.

Milgrom, P. 1981. An axiomatic characterization of common knowledge. *Econometrica* 49, 219–22.

Milgrom, P. and Stokey, N. 1982. Information, trade and common knowledge. *Journal of Economic Theory* 26, 17–29.

Moses, Y., Doley, D. and Halpern, J.Y. 1986. Cheating husbands and other stories: a case study of knowledge, action, and communication. *Distributed Computing* 1, 167–76.

Myerson, R. 1978. Refinements of the Nash equilibrium concepts. *International Journal of Game Theory* 7, 73–80.

Myerson, R. 1985. Bayesian equilibrium and incentive-compatibility an introduction. In *Social Goals and Social Organization*: *Essays in Memory of Elisha Pazner*, ed. Hurwicz, L., Schmiedler, D. and Sonnenschein, H. Cambridge: Cambridge University Press.

Newman, P. 1988. Common knowledge and the game of red hats. Working Papers in Economics #210, Johns Hopkins University.

Nielsen, L. 1984. Common knowledge, communication, and convergence of beliefs, *Mathematical Social Sciences* 8, 1–14.

Parikh, P. 1988. Language and strategic inference. PhD Dissertation, Stanford University.

Parikh, R. and Krasucki, P. 1987. Communication, consensus and knowledge. Department of Mathematics, CUNY Graduate Center, New York, NY, Mimeo.

Pearce, D. 1984. Rationalizable strategic behavior and the problem of perfection. *Econometrica* 52, 1029–50.

Reny, P. 1988. Rationality, common knowledge and the theory of games. PhD Thesis, Princeton University, Chapter 1.

Rubinstein, A. 1988. A game with almost common knowledge: an example. London School of Economics, Mimeo.

Samet, D. 1987. Ignoring ignorance and agreeing to disagree. MEDS Discussion Paper, Northwestern University.

Samuelson, L. 1988. Evolutionary foundations of solution concepts for finite, two players, normal-form games. In Vardi (1988).

Savage, L. 1954. *The Foundations of Statistics.* New York: Wiley.

Sebenius, J.K. and Geanakoplos, J.D. 1983. Don't bet on it: contingent agreements with asymmetric information. *Journal of the American Statistical Association* 78, 424–6.

Selten, R. 1975. Reexamination of the perfectness concept for equilibrium points in extensive games. *International Journal of Game Theory* 4, 25–55.

Shin, H.S. 1987. Logical structure of common knowledge, I and II, Nuffield College, Mimeo.

Tan, T.C.-C. and Werlang, S.R. da C. 1984. The Bayesian foundations of rationalisable strategic behaviour and Nash equilibrium behaviour. Princeton University, Mimeo.

Tan, T.C.-C. and Werlang, S.R. da C. 1985. On Aumann's notion of common knowledge: an alternative approach. Princeton University, Mimeo.

Tan, T.C.-C. and Werlang, S.R. da C. 1988. On Aumann's notion of common knowledge: an alternative approach. Extensively Revised Version, CARESS Working Paper, University of Pennsylvania.

Tan, T.C.-C. and Werlang, S.R. da C. 1988a. A guide to knowledge and games. In Vardi (1988).

Tan, T.C.-C. and Werland, S.R. da C. 1988b. The Bayesian foundations of solution concepts of games. *Journal of Economic Theory* 45, 370–91.

Vardi, M. (ed.) 1988. *Proceedings of the Second Conference on Theoretical Aspects of Reasoning About Knowledge.* Asilomar, CA: Morgan Kaufman.

Werlang, S.R. da C. 1986. Common knowledge and game theory. PhD thesis, Princeton University.

Conflict and Settlement

JACK HIRSHLEIFER

All living beings are competitors for the means of existence. Competition takes the more intense form we call *conflict* when contenders seek to disable or destroy opponents, or even convert them into a supply of resources. Conflict need not always be violent; we speak, for example, of industrial conflicts (strikes and lockouts) and legal conflicts (law suits). But physical struggle is a relevant metaphor for these ordinarily non-violent contests.

THE STATICS OF CONFLICT

Involved in a rational decision to engage in conflict, economic reasoning suggests, will be the deicision-maker's *preferences*, *opportunities* and *perceptions*. These three elements correspond to traditional issues debated by historians and political scientists about the 'causes of war': Is war mainly due to hatred and ingrained pugnacity (hostile preferences)? Or to the opportunities for material gain at the expense of weaker victims? Or is war mainly due to mistaken perceptions, on one or both sides, of the other's motives or capacities?

Of course it is quite a leap from the choices of individuals to the war-making decisions of collectivities like tribes or states. Group choice-making processes notoriously fail to satisfy the canons of rationality, most fundamentally owing to disparities among the interests of the individual members. Thus the internal decision-making structures of the interacting groups may also be implicated among the causes of war.

Setting aside this last complication, Figures 1 and 2 are alternative illustrations of how preferences, opportunities and perceptions might come together in a simple dyadic interaction. In each diagram the curve QQ bounds the 'settlement opportunity set' – what the parties can jointly attain by peaceful agreement or compromise – drawn on axes representing Blue's income I_B and Red's income I_R. The points P_B and P_R, in contrast, indicate the parties' separate *perceptions*

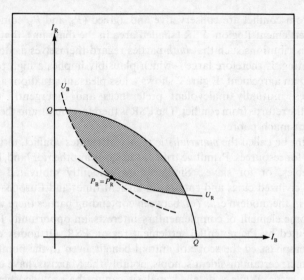

Figure 1. Statics of conflict – large potential settlement region.

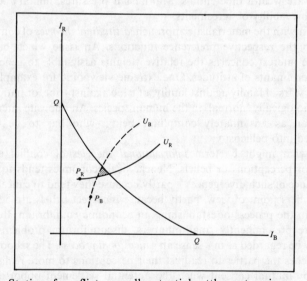

Figure 2. Statics of conflict – small potential settlement region.

of the income distribution resulting from conflict. The families of curves labelled U_B and U_R are the familiar utility indifference contours of the two agents.

Figure 1 shows a relatively benign situation: settlement opportunities are complementary, so there is a considerable mutual gain from avoiding conflict; the respective preferences display benevolence on each side; and the perceptions of returns from conflict are conservative and agreed (P_B and P_R coincide). The 'Potential Settlement Region' PSR (shaded area in the diagram), that is, the set of income distributions such that *both* parties regard themselves as doing better than by fighting, is therefore large – which plausibly implies a high probability of coming to an agreement. Figure 2 shows a less pleasant situation: antithetical opportunities, mutually malevolent preferences and divergently optimistic estimates of the returns from conflict. The PSR is therefore small, and the prospects for settlement much poorer.

What might be called the *materialistic theory* attributes conflict, ultimately, to competition for resources. Primitive tribes attack one another for land, for hoards of consumables, or for slaves. Similar aims evidently motivated barbarian invasions of civilized cities and empires in ancient times and European colonial imperialism in the modern era. Yet, between contending parties there will almost always be some element of complementary interests, an opportunity for mutual gain represented by the potential settlement region PSR. Orthodox economics has always emphasized the scope of mutual benefit, even to the point of losing sight of conflict; certain dissident schools, notably the Marxists, have committed the opposite error. While a detailed analysis cannot be provided here, among the factors underlying the relative material profitability of fighting versus negotiating are wealth differentials, Malthusian pressures, military technology and the enforceability of agreements.

In contrast with the materialistic approach, *attitudinal theories* of conflict direct attention to the respective preference functions. An issue which has excited considerable interest concerns the relative weights assignable to genetic versus cultural determinants of attitudes. One extreme viewpoint, for example, regards xenophobic wars of family against family, of tribe against tribe, or nation against nation, as biologically 'normal' in the human species. An opposite interpretation pictures man as an innately compliant being, who has to be culturally indoctrinated into bellicosity.

Finally, what might be term *informational theories* of conflict emphasize differences or perceptions or beliefs. Neoclassical economics tends to minimize the importance of such divergences – partly because they tend to cancel out from a large-numbers point of view, partly because incorrect beliefs are adjusted by experience in the process of establishing an economic equilibrium. But conflict and war are pre-eminently small-numbers, disequilibrium problems. Indeed, conflict may be regarded as in a sense an *educational process*. The school of actual struggle teaches the parties to readjust their perceptions to more realistic levels. Wars end by mutual consent when the potential settlement opportunities are seen as more attractive than continued fighting.

THE DYNAMICS OF CONFLICT

Static and dynamic elements are both importantly involved in conflict or settlement processes. In game theory terms, the *payoff environment*, represented by the familiar normal-form matrix, is the static element. The dynamic element may be called the *protocol of play*; as pictured in the game tree, the protocol specifies the allowable step-by-step moves in the light of the players' information at each stage.

A few very simple payoff environments are shown in Matrices 1 to 4. The numbers in each cell indicate ordinally ranked payoffs for each player, 1 being the poorest outcome in each case. In Matrix 1, 'Land or Sea', the environment is characterized by completely antithetical (constant-sum) payoffs. The other three matrices – 'Chicken', 'Reciprocity' and 'Prisoner's Dilemma' – represent several of the many different possible mixed-motive situations combining an element of opposition of interests with an opportunity for mutual gain.

Matrix 1
LAND OR SEA

	Defend by land	Defend by sea
Attack by land	1,2	2,1
Attack by sea	2,1	1,2

Matrix 2
CHICKEN

	Soft	Tough
Soft	3,3	2,4
Tough	4,2	1,1

Matrix 3
RECIPROCITY

	Soft	Tough
Soft	4,4	1,3
Tough	3,1	2,2

Matrix 4
PRISONERS' DILEMMA

	Co-operate	Defect
Co-operate	3,3	1,4
Defect	4,1	2,2

The simplest protocol to analyse is *one-round sequential play*: first Row selects one of his options, then Column makes his move in the light of Row's choice, and the game ends. In a sequential-play protocol it is always possible to find a 'rational' solution. If Column can be relied to choose his best final move then Row, knowing this, can calculate his best first move accordingly. (This process results in what is called a 'perfect equilibrium'.) In contrast, where the protocol dictates that players in a single-round game choose *simultaneously* – or, equivalently, where each chooses in ignorance of the other's move – solution concepts are harder to justify. The most commonly employed is called the 'Nash equilibrium' (or 'equilibrium point'), a pair of strategies from which neither player would want to diverge unilaterally.

In the 'Land or Sea' payoff environment, under the one-round *sequential-move* protocol, it is the second-mover or defender who has the advantage. If Row moves first, for example, Column can always successfully counter; e.g. if Row attacks by land, Column will defend by land. Hence the (1, 2) payoff-pair is the outcome regardless of Row's initial move. In military terms the defence has an intrinsic advantage whenever the attacker must visibly commit his forces to one or another line of attack. And, of course, where the defence has such an advantage neither party is motivated to initiate warfare through aggression. But if 'Land or Sea' is played under the *simultaneous-move* protocol, both parties are groping in the dark and little can be said with confidence. (Here the Nash equilibrium would have each side choosing its move at random, in effect tossing a coin.)

In the payoff environment of 'Chicken' (Matrix 2), while the opportunities remain highly antithetical there is now a mutual interest in avoiding the disastrous (1, 1) outcome that comes about when both play Tough. In contrast with 'Land or Sea', in the 'Chicken' payoff environment the advantage lies with the *first-mover*. Specifically, Row should rationally play Tough, knowing that Column then has to respond with Soft. For, Column must accept the bad (payoff of 2) to avoid the worst (payoff of 1). If the protocol dictates simultaneous moves, however, once again the players are groping in the dark. Under the Nash equilibrium concept they choose probabilistically, which implies that the disastrous (1, 1) outcome will indeed occur a percentage of the time. There is a suggestive application of this model to industrial conflict. If union (or management) becomes committed to play Soft, it will be at a disadvantage in negotiations – the other side will then surely play Tough. But if both play Tough, there is no hope for peaceful settlement. Hence each side should rationally adopt a 'mixed' strategy, with the consequence that strikes and lockouts will occur in a certain fraction of the dealings.

The 'Reciprocity' payoff environment (Matrix 3) is more rewarding to cooperative behaviour. The idea is that each player would answer Soft with Soft – leading to the mutually preferred (4, 4) payoffs – but failing this, would respond to Tough with Tough. If the *sequential-move* protocol applies, the first-mover would then always rationally choose Soft, and so the ideal (4, 4) payoff-pair should be achieved. But under the *simultaneous-move* protocol, with each party in the dark about the other's move, again the outcome is quite unclear. In fact there are three Nash equilibria: pure-strategy solutions at (4, 4) and (2, 2), and a mixed-strategy solution as well.

Finally, in the famous 'Prisoner's Dilemma' payoff environment (Matrix 4) the parties are likely to find themselves in the Defect–Defect 'trap' with (2, 2) payoffs, even though (3, 3) could be achieved were each to play Cooperate. Here the 'trap' takes hold under both sequential-move and simultaneous-move protocols.

The preceding discussion could only be suggestive, limited as it was to 2-player single-round games, within that category to only a few 2-strategy symmetrical payoff environments and finally to the very simplest protocols – excluding, for example, all negotiations and communications between the parties. Space limitations permit comment upon only a few additional points:

Perceptions. Standard game models assume that players know not only their own payoffs but also their opponents'. Unintentional error on this score, or else deliberate deception, may play a crucial role. Suppose two parties in the 'Reciprocity' payoff environment of Matrix 3 find themselves initially playing Tough–Tough with outcome (2, 2). Imagine now they are given a chance to shift strategies under a *sequential-move* protocol. As first-mover, Row would be happy to change from Tough to Soft if only he could rely upon Column to respond in kind. But Row may, mistakenly, believe that Column's payoffs are as in 'Chicken', from which he infers that Column would stand pat with Tough. Row would therefore not shift from Tough, hence Column in his turn would not change either. (Some authors have gone so far as to attribute all or almost all of human conflict to such mistaken 'self-fulfilling beliefs' about the hostility of opponents, but of course this pattern is only one of many possibilities.)

Commitment and deterrence. In some circumstances the second-mover in point of time (Column) may be able to *commit* himself to a given response strategy before Row makes his first move. While Column thereby surrenders freedom of choice, doing so may be advantageous. Consider threats and promises. A *threat* is a commitment to undertake a second-move punishment strategy even where execution thereof is costly. A *promise* similarly involves commitment to a costly reward strategy. Matrices 5 and 6 illustrate how a threat works. Row's choices

	Matrix 5 DETERRENCE WITH- OUT COMMITMENT			*Matrix 6* DETERRENCE REQUIRING COMMITMENT	
	Fold	Retaliate		Fold	Retaliate
Refrain	2,3	2,3	Refrain	2,3	2,3
Attack	3,1	1,2	Attack	3,2	1,1

are Attack or Refrain, while Column's only options are to Retaliate or Fold if Row attacks. Column's problem, of course, is to deter Row's attack. In Matrix 5 Column prefers to Retaliate if attacked, a fact that – given Row's preferences – suffices for deterrence. Commitment is not required. (Since Column prefers to Retaliate, there is no need to *commit* himself to do so.) In Matrix 6 the Column player prefers to turn the other cheek; if attacked, he would rather Fold than Retaliate. Unfortunately, this guarantees he will be attacked! (Note that here it is not excessive hostility, but the reverse, that brings on conflict.) But if Column could *commit* himself to Retaliate, for example by computerizing the associated machinery beyond the possibility of his later reneging, then deterrence succeeds. In short, if a pacific player can reliably *threaten* to do what he does not really want to do, he won't have to do it! (Needless to say, so dangerous an arrangement is not to be casually recommended.)

THE TECHNOLOGY OF STRUGGLE

Conflict is a kind of 'industry' in which different 'firms' compete by attempting to disable opponents. Just as the economist, without being a manager or engineer, can apply certain broad principles to the processes of industrial production, so, without claiming to replace the military commander, he can say something about the principles governing how desired results are 'produced' through violence.

Battles typically proceed to a definitive outcome – victory or defeat. *Wars* on the whole tend to be less conclusive, often ending in a compromise settlement. These historical generalizations reflect the working of increasing versus decreasing returns applied to the production of violence:

(1) Within a sufficiently small geographical region such as a battlefield, there

is a critical range of increasing returns to military strength – a small increment of force can make the difference between victory and defeat.

(2) But there are decreasing returns in projecting military power away from one's base area, so that it is difficult to achieve superiority over an enemy's entire national territory. The increasing-returns aspect explains why there is a 'natural monopoly' of military force *within* the nation-state. The diminishing-returns aspect explains why a multiplicity of nation-states have remained militarily viable to this date. (However, there is some reason to believe, the technology of attack through long-range weapons has now so come to prevail over the defence that a single world-state is indeed impending.)

Going into the basis for increasing returns, at any moment the stronger in battle can inflict a more-than-proportionate loss upon his opponent, thus becoming progressively stronger still. Important special cases of this process are modelled via Lanchester's equations. In combat, in the ideal case where all the military units distribute their fire equally over the enemy's line, the process equations are:

$$dB/dt = -k_R R$$

$$dR/dt = -k_B B.$$

Here B and R are the given force sizes for Blue and Red, and the per-unit military efficiencies are given by the k_B and k_R coefficients. It follows that military strengths are equal when:

$$k_B B^2 = k_R R^2.$$

But even where military strength varies less sensitively than as the square of force size, it remains quite generally the case that in the combat process the strong become stronger and the weak weaker, leading to ultimate annihilation unless flight or surrender intervene. (Of course, a skilful commander finding himself with an adverse force balance will attempt to change the tactical situation – by timely withdrawal, deception or other manoeuvre.)

One implication of increasing returns may be called the 'last-push principle'. In the course of a conflict each side will typically not be fully aware of the force size and strength that the opponent is ultimately able and willing to put in the field. Hence the incentive to stand fast, even at high cost, lest a potentially won battle be lost. (Foch: 'A battle won is a battle in which one will not confess oneself beaten.') This valid point unfortunately tends to lead to battlefield carnage beyond all reasonable prior calculations, as experienced for example at Verdun.

On the other hand, an effective substitute for force size is superior *organization*. An integrated military unit is far more powerful than an equally numerous conglomeration of individual fighters, however brave. Organizational superiority, far more than superiority in weapons, explains why small European expeditionary contingents in early modern times were able even to defeat vast indigenous forces in America, Africa and Asia. Battles are thus often a contest of organizational forms; the army whose command structure first cracks under pressure is the loser.

As for diminishing returns, in the simplest case an equilibrium is achieved at a geographical boundary such that:

$$M_B - s_B x_B = M_R - s_R x_R.$$

Here M_B and M_R are military strengths at the respective home bases, s_B and s_R are decay gradients, and x_B and x_R are the respective distances from base. The condition of equality determines the allocation of territory.

The 'social physics' of struggle is of course far more complex than these simplistic initial models suggest. There are more or less distinct offence and defence technologies, first-strike capability is not the same as retaliatory strength, countering insurgency is a different problem from central land battle, etc.

CONFLICT, SOCIETY AND ECONOMY

Conflict theory can help explain not only the size and shape of nations, but the outcomes of competition in all aspects of life: contests among social classes, among political factions and ideologies, between management and labour, among contenders for licences and privileges ('rent-seeking'), between plaintiffs and defendants in law suits, among members of cartels like OPEC, between husband and wife and sibling and sibling within the family, and so on. Whenever resources can be seized by aggression, invasion attempts can be expected to occur. Invasive and counter-invasive efforts absorb a very substantial fraction of society's resources in every possible social structure, whether egalitarian or hierarchical, liberal or totalitarian, centralized or decentralized. Furthermore, every form of human social organization, whatever else can be said for or against it, must ultimately meet the survival test of internal and external conflict.

Notes on the literature of conflict (of special relevance for economists). Classical military thought from Machiavelli to Clausewitz to Liddle Hart, though rarely analytical in the economist's sense, remains well worth study. An excellent survey is Edward Mead Earle (1941). Modern work in this classical genre understandably concentrates upon the overwhelming fact of nuclear weaponry and the problem of deterrence; the contributions of Herman Kahn (1960, 1962) are notable. There is of course a huge historical literature on conflict and war. An interesting economics-oriented interpretive history of modern warfare is Geoffrey Blainey (1973). William H. McNeill (1982) examines the course of military organization and technology from antiquity to the present, emphasizing the social and economic context. On a smaller scale John Keegan (1976) provides a valuable picture of how men, weapons and tactics compete with and one another on the battlefield. There is also a substantial body of statistical work attempting in a variety of ways to summarize and classify the sources and outcomes of wars; the best known is Lewis F. Richardson (1960b). Mathematical analysis of military activity, that is, quantifiable modelling of the clash of contending forces, is surprisingly sparse. The classic work is Frederick William Lanchester (1916 [1956]).

The modern analysis of conflict, typically combining the theory of games with the rational-decision economics of choice, is represented by three important books by economists: Thomas C. Schelling (1960), Kenneth E. Boulding (1962) and Gordon Tullock (1974). Works by non-economists that are similar in spirit include Glenn H. Snyder and Paul Diesing (1977) and Bruce Bueno de Mesquita (1981). A tangentially related literature, making use of the rather mechanical psychologistic approach of Richardson (1960a), includes a very readable book by Anatol Rapoport (1960).

BIBLIOGRAPHY

Blainey, G. 1973. *The Causes of War*. New York: The Free Press.

Boulding, K.E. 1962. *Conflict and Defense: A General Theory*. New York: Harper & Brothers.

Bueno de Mesquita, B. 1981. *The War Trap*. New Haven and London: Yale University Press.

Earle, E.M. (ed.) 1941. *Makers of Modern Strategy: Military Thought from Machiavelli to Hitler*. Princeton, NJ: Princeton University Press.

Kahn, H. 1960. *On Thermonuclear War*. Princeton, NJ: Princeton University Press.

Kahn, H. 1962. *Thinking About the Unthinkable*. New York: Avon Books.

Keegan, J. 1976. *The Face of Battle*. New York: Viking Press.

Lanchester, F.W. 1916. *Aircraft in Warfare: The Dawn of the Fourth Arm*. London: Constable. Extract reprinted in *The World of Mathematics*, ed. James R. Newman, vol. 4, New York: Simon & Schuster, 1956, 2138–57.

McNeill, W.H. 1982. *The Pursuit of Power: Technology, Armed Force, and Society since AD 1000*. Chicago: University of Chicago Press.

Rapoport, A. 1960. *Fights, Games, and Debates*. Ann Arbor: University of Michigan Press.

Richardson, L.F. 1960a. *Arms and Insecurity: A Mathematical Study of the Causes and Origins of War*. Pittsburgh: Boxwood; Chicago: Quadrangle.

Richardson, L.F. 1960b. *Statistics of Deadly Quarrels*. Pittsburgh: Boxwood; Chicago: Quadrangle.

Schelling, T.C. 1960. *The Strategy of Conflict*. Cambridge, Mass.: Harvard University Press.

Snyder, G.H. and Diesing, P. 1977. *Conflict Among Nations: Bargaining, Decision Making, and System Structure in International Crises*. Princeton, NJ: Princeton University Press.

Tullock, G. 1974. *The Social Dilemma: The Economics of War and Revolution*. Blacksburg, Virginia: University Publications.

Cooperative Equilibrium

A. MAS-COLELL

I. INTRODUCTION

The term 'cooperative equilibria' has been imported into economics from game theory. It refers to the equilibria of economic situations modelled by means of cooperative games and solved by appealing to an appropriate cooperative solution concept. The influence is not entirely one way, however. Many game theoretic notions (e.g. Cournot–Nash equilibrium, the Core) are formalizations of pre-existing ideas in economics.

The distinguishing feature of the cooperative approach in game theory and economics is that it does not attempt to model how a group of economic agents (say a buyer and a seller) may communicate among themselves. The typical starting point is the hypothesis that, in principle, any subgroup of economic agents (or perhaps some distinguished subgroups) has a clear picture of the possibilities of joint action and that its members can communicate freely before the formal play starts. Obviously, what is left out of cooperative theory is very substantial. The justification, or so one hopes, is that the drastic simplification brings to centre stage the implications of actual or potential coalition formation. In their classic book, von Neumann and Morgenstern (1944) already emphasized that the possibility of strategic coalition formation was the key aspect setting apart two from three or more players' games.

The previous remarks emphasize free preplay communication as the essential distinguishing characteristic of cooperative theory. There is a second feature common to most of the literature but which nonetheless may not be intrinsic to the theory (this the future will determine). We refer to the assumed extensive ability of coalitions' players to commit to a course of action once an agreement has been reached.

The remaining exposition is divided in three sections. Sections II and IV discuss the two main approaches to cooperative theory (domination and valuation, respectively). Section III contains qualifications to the domination approach.

An excellent reference for the topic of this entry is Shubik (1983).

II. THE DOMINANCE APPROACH

Suppose we have N economic agents. Every agent has a strategy set S_i. Denote $S = S_1 \times \ldots \times S_N$ with generic element $s = (s_1, \ldots, s_N)$. Given s and a coalition $C \subset N$, the expression s_C denotes the strategies corresponding to members of C. Letting C' be the complement of C, the expression $(s_C, s_{C'})$ defines s in the obvious way. For every i there is a utility function $u_i(s)$. If $u = (u_1, \ldots, u_N)$ is an N-list of utilities, expressions such as u_C or $(u_C, u_{C'})$ have the obvious meaning.

Example 1 (Exchange economies): There are N consumers and l desirable goods. Each consumer has a utility function $u_i(x_i)$ and initial endowments ω_i. A strategy of consumer i is an N non-negative vector $\mathbf{s}_i = (s_{i1}, \ldots, s_{iN})$ such that $\Sigma_{j=1}^N s_{ij} \leqslant \omega_i$, i.e. s_i is an allocation of the initial endowments of i among the N consumers. Of course, $u_j(s) = u_j(\Sigma_i s_{ij})$.

Example 2 (Public goods): Suppose that to the model of Example 1 we add a public good y with production function $y = F(v)$. Utility functions have the form $u_j(x_j, y)$. A strategy for i is now an $(N+1)l$ vector $\mathbf{s}_i = (s_{i1}, \ldots, s_{i,N+1})$ where $s_{i,N+1}$ is allocated as input to production. We have $u_j(s) = u_j[\Sigma_i s_{ij}, F(\Sigma_i s_{i,N+1})]$.

Example 3 (Exchange with private bads): This is as the first example, except that there is no free disposal, i.e. $\Sigma_{j=1}^N s_{ij} = \omega_i$ for every i. Some of the goods may actually be bads. To be concrete, suppose that $l = 2$, one of the goods is a desirable numéraire and the other is garbage. All consumers are identical and each owns one unit of numéraire and one of garbage (see Shapley and Shubik, 1969).

For a strategy profile s to be called a *cooperative equilibrium* we require that there is no coalition C that *dominates* the utility vector $u(s) = (u_1(s), \ldots, u_N(s))$, i.e. that can 'make effective' for its members utility levels u_i, $i \in C$, such that $u_i > u_i(s)$ for all $i \in C$. Denote by $V(C)$ the utility levels that C can 'make effective' for its members. The precise content of the equilibrium concept depends, of course, on the definition of $V(C)$. I proceed to discuss several possibilities (Aumann, 1959, is a key reference for all this).

(A) In line with the idea of Cournot–Nash equilibrium, we could define $V_s(C) = \{u_C : u_C \leqslant u_C(s'_C, s_{C'})$ for some $s'_C \in S_C\}$, that is, the agents in C take the strategies of C' as fixed. They do not anticipate, so to speak, any retaliatory move. The cooperative solution concept that uses $V_s(C)$ is called *strong Cournot–Nash equilibrium*. It is very strong indeed. So strong, that it rarely exists. Obviously, this limits the usefulness of the concept. It is immediately obvious that it does not exist for any of the three examples above.

Note that $V_s(C)$ depends on the reference point s. We now go to the other extreme and consider definitions where when a coalition contemplates deviating, it readies itself for retaliatory behaviour on the part of the complementary coalition; that is, the deviation erases the initial position and is carried out if and only if better levels of utility can be reached, no matter what the agents outside the coalition do. On defining $V(C)$, however, there is an important subtlety. The set $V(C)$ can be defined as either what the members of C cannot be prevented from getting (i.e. the members of C move second) or, more strictly, as what the members of C can guarantee themselves (i.e. they move first). More precisely:

(B) For every C, define:

$$V_\beta(C) = [u_C: \text{for any } s_{C'} \text{ there is an } s_C \text{ such that } u_C \leqslant u(s_C, s_{C'})].$$

This is what C cannot be prevented from getting. The set of corresponding cooperative equilibria is called the β-core of the game or economy. For any s we have $V_\beta(C) \subset V_s(C)$, and so there is more of a chance for a β-core equilibrium to exist than for a strong Cournot–Nash equilibrium. But there is no general existence theorem. As we shall see, the β-core is non-empty in examples 1 and 2. It is instructive to verify that it is empty in example 3. By symmetry, it is enough to check that the strategies where each agent consumes its own endowment is not an equilibrium. Take the coalition formed by two of the three (identical) agents. As a retaliatory move, the third agent would, at worst, be dumping its unit of garbage on one of the members of the coalition (or perhaps splitting it among them), but the coalition can still be better off than at the initial endowment point by dumping its two units on the third member *and* transferring some money from the nonreceptor to the receptor of outside garbage.

(C) For every C define:

$$V_\alpha(C) = [u_C: \text{there is } s_C \text{ such that } u_C \leqslant u_C(s_C, s_{C'}) \text{ for any } s_{C'}].$$

This is what C can guarantee itself of getting. It represents the most pessimistic appraisal of the possibilities of C. The set of corresponding equilibria is called the α-core of the game or economy. For any s we have $V_\alpha(C) \subset V_\beta(C)$ and so there is more of a chance for an α-core equilibrium to exist than for a β-core equilibrium. For the α-core there is a general existence theorem:

Theorem (Scarf, 1971): If S is convex, compact and every $u_i(s)$ is continuous and quasiconcave, then the α-core is non-empty.

The conditions of the above theorem are restrictive. Note that the quasiconcavity of u_i is required for the entire s and not only (as for Cournot–Nash equilibrium) for the vector s_i of own strategies. Nonetheless, it is a useful result. It tells us, for instance, that under the standard quasiconcavity hypothesis on utility functions, the α-core is non-empty in each of the three examples above. It will be instructive to very why the initial endowment allocation is an equilibrium in example 3. In contrast to the β-core situation, a coalition of two members cannot now improve over the initial endowments because they have to move first and therefore cannot know who of the two will receive the outside member's garbage and will need, as a consequence, some extra amount of money.

If, as in examples 1 and 2, there are no bads, the distinction between V_α and V_β disappears. There is a unique way for the members of C' to hurt C, namely withholding its own resources. So in both the α and β senses the set $V(C)$ represents the utility combinations that can be attained by the members of C using only its own resources. This, incidentally, shows that the β-core is non-empty in examples 1 and 2 (since it is equal to the α-core!) There is another approach to existence in the no-bads case. Indeed, a Walrasian equilibrium (in the case of example 2 this takes the guise of a Lindahl equilibrium) is always in this core with no need of α or β qualification. In the context of example 1, the Core was first defined and exploited by Edgeworth (1881) (*see* CORES).

Underlying both the α- and the β-core there is a quite pessimistic appraisal on what C' may do if C deviates. The next two remarks discuss, very informally, other, less extreme, possibilities.

(D) In the context of exchange economies (such as example 1) it seems sensible to suppose that a coalition of buyers and sellers in one market may neglect retaliation possibilities in unrelated markets. As it stands in subsections (B) and (C), it is very difficult for a group of traders to improve, since, so to speak, they have to set up a separate economy covering all markets. See Mas-Colell (1982) for further discussion of this point.

(E) For transferable utility situations (and for purposes more related to the valuation theory to be discussed in section IV), Harsanyi (1959), taking inspiration in Nash (1953), proposed that the total utility of the coalition C be defined as $\Sigma_{i \in C} u_i(\bar{s}_C, \bar{s}_{C'})$ where $(\bar{s}_C, \bar{s}_{C'})$ are the minimax strategies of the zero sum game between C and C' obtained by letting the payoff of C be $\Sigma_{i \in C} u_i(s_C, s_{C'}) - \Sigma_{i \in C'} u_i(s_C, s_{C'})$. Note: if the minimax strategies are not unique, a further qualification is required.

III. CONSISTENCY QUALIFICATIONS

In this section, several solution concepts are reviewed. Loosely, their common theme is that coalitions look beyond the one-step deviation possibilities.

A. The von Neumann–Morgenstern stable set solutions. Suppose that the game is described to us by the sets $V(C)$ that the members of coalitions of C can make effective for themselves. These sets do not depend on any reference combination of strategies. They are constructed from the underlying situation in some of the ways described in section II. One says that the N-tuple of utilities $u \in V(N)$ dominates the N-tuple $v \in V(N)$ via coalition C, denoted $u \succ_C v$, if $u_C \in V(C)$. We write $u \succ v$ if $\bar{u}$ dominates $\bar{v}$ via some coalition. A *core utility computation* is then any maximal element of $\succ$, i.e. any $u \in V(N)$ which is not dominated by any other imputation.

The following paradoxical situation may easily arise. An imputation u is not in the core. Nonetheless, all the members of any coalition that dominates u are treated, at any core imputation, worse than at u (consider, for example, the predicament of a Bertrand duopolist at the joint monopoly outcome). If $\succ$ was transitive, then this could not happen, since (continuity complications aside) for any u there would be a core imputation directly dominating u. But $\succ$ is very far from transitive. The approach of von Neumann and Morgenstern consists in focusing on *sets* of imputations K, called *stable sets*, having the properties: (i) if $u \in K$ then there is no $v \in K$ that dominates u (internal stability) and (ii) if $u \in K$

then $v \succ u$ for some $v \in K$ (external stability). Note that these are the properties that the set of maximal elements of $\succ$ would have if $\succ$ was transitive. The interpretation of K is as a standard of behaviour. If for any reason the imputations in K are regarded as acceptable, then there is an inner consistency to this: drop all the imputations dominated by an acceptable imputation and what you have left is precisely the set of acceptable imputations.

Important as the von Neumann–Morgenstern solution is, its impact in economics has been limited. There is an existence problem, but the main difficulty is that the sets are very hard to analyse.

B. The bargaining set. This solution was proposed by Aumann and Maschler (1964) and is available in several versions. Describing one of them will give the flavour of what is involved. For an imputation u to be disqualified, it will be necessary, but not sufficient, that it be dominated (in the terminology of bargaining set theory: objected to) via some coalition C^*. The objection will not 'stick', i.e. throw u out of the negotiation table as a tentative equilibrium, unless it is found justified. The justifiability criterion is the following: there is no other coalition C^* having a $v_C^* \in V(C^*)$ with the property that $v_i \geq u_i$ for every i and which gives to every common member of C and C^* at least as much as they get at the objection. In other words, an objection can be countered if one of the members left out of the objecting coalition can protect themselves in a credible manner (credible in the sense that they can give to any member of C they need, as much as C gives them).

The bargaining set contains the core and, while it is conceptually quite different from a von Neumann–Morgenstern stable set solution, it still does avoid the most myopic features of the core. It is also much easier to analyse than the stable sets, although it is by no means a straightforward tool. But, again, its impact in economics has so far been limited.

A common aspect of stable set and bargaining set theory is that, implicitly or explicitly, a deviating coalition takes into consideration a subsequent, induced move by other coalitions. This is still true for the next two concepts, with one crucial qualification: a deviating coalition only takes into account subsequent moves of its own subcoalitions.

C. Coalition-proof Cournot–Nash equilibrium. This solution concept has been proposed recently by Bernheim, Peleg and Whinston (1987). It can be viewed as a self-consistent enlargement of the set of strong Cournot–Nash equilibria. Consider the simplest case, a three-player game. Given a strategy profile $\bar{s}$, which deviations are possible for two players coalitions? If anything, then we are led to strong Cournot–Nash equilibria. But, there is something inconsistent about this. If the strategy profile $\bar{s}$ is not immune to deviations (i.e. there is no commitment at $\bar{s}$), why should the deviation be so? That is, why should it be possible to commit oneself to a deviation? This suggests that the deviation should be required to be immune to further deviations, that is, they should be Cournot–Nash equilibria of the induced two person game (the third player remains put at $\bar{s}$). Obviously, deviating becomes more difficult and the equilibrium set has more of a chance of being non-empty. Unfortunately, there is no general existence theorem. For three-person games, this is precisely the Coalition-Proof Cournot–Nash equilibrium. By recursion, one obtains a definition for any number of players.

D. The core. It may be surprising to list the core in a section on concepts that attempts to be less myopic than the core. But, in fact, the core as a set can be made consistent against further deviations by *subcoalitions* of the deviating coalition. Simply make sure always to deviate via coalitions of smallest possible cardinality.

IV. THE VALUATION APPROACH

The aim of the valuation approach to games and conflict situations (of which the Shapley value is the central concept) is to associate to every game a reasonable outcome taking into account and compromising among all the conflicting claims. In games, those are expressed by sets $V(C)$ of utility vectors for which C is effective. The criteria of reasonableness are expressed axiomatically. Thus the valuation approach has to be thought of more as input for an arbitrator than as a descriptive theory of equilibrium. Except perhaps for the bargaining set, this point of view is strikingly different to anything discussed so far.

Sometimes the term 'fair' is used in connection with the valuation approach. There are at least two reasons to avoid this usage. The first is that the initial position (embodied in the sets $V(C)$) is taken as given. The second is that the fairness of a solution to a game can hardly be judged in isolation, i.e. independently of the position of the players in the overall socioeconomic game.

The valuation of a game will depend on the claims, i.e. on how the sets $V(C)$ are constructed. We saw in Section II that there was nothing straightforward about this. We will not repeat it here. It may be worthwhile to observe informally, however, that the valuation approach is altogether less strategic than the dominance one and that a useful way to think of $V(C)$ is as the utility levels the members of C could get if the members of C' did not exist, rather than as what the members of C could get if they go it alone (in defining $V(C)$ this point of view can make a difference).

Consider first games with transferable utilities (N, v) where N is a set of players and $v: 2^N \to R$ is a real valued function satisfying $v(\phi) = 0$. The restriction of v to a $C \in N$ is denoted (C, v). The *Shapley value* is a certain rule that associates to every game (N, v) an imputation $Sh(N, v)$, i.e. $\Sigma_{i \in N} Sh^i(N, v) = v(N)$.

The *Shapley value* was characterized by Shapley (1953) by four axioms that can be informally described as: (i) efficiency, i.e. $Sh(N, v)$ is an imputation, (ii) symmetry, i.e. the particular names of the players do not matter, (iii) linearity over games and (iv) dummy, i.e. a player that contributes nothing to any coalition receives nothing.

There is a simple way to compute the Shapley value. Put $P(\phi, v) = 0$ and, recursively, associate to every game (N, v) a number $P(N, v)$ such that

$$\sum_{i \in N} [P(N, v) - P(N/(i), v)] = v(N).$$

That is, the sum of marginal increments of P equals $v(N)$. This function is called the *potential* and it turns out that the marginal increments of P constitute precisely the Shapley valuations, i.e. $Sh^i(N, v) = P(N, v) - P[N/(i), v]$ for all (N, v) and $i \in N$. This is discussed in Hart and Mas-Colell (1985).

The Shapley value for transferable utility games admits several generalizations to the nontransferable utility case (with convex sets $V(C)$). See Harsanyi (1959), Shapley (1969), Aumann (1985). Perhaps the most natural, although not necessarily the simplest to work with, was proposed by Harsanyi (1959) and has recently been axiomatized by Hart (1985). For a given game, an Harsanyi value imputation is obtained by rescaling individual utilities so as to guarantee the existence of an N-tuple $u \in V(N)$ satisfying, simultaneously:
(i) the convex set $V(N)$ is supported at u by a hyperplane with normal $q = (1, \ldots, 1)$,
(ii) if a potential P on the set of all games is defined by formula (1) (but replacing '$= v(N)$' by '$\in Bdry. V(N)$') then, as before, $u_i = P(N, V) - P(N/(i), V)$ for all $i \in N$.

One of the most striking features of the applications of Shapley value theory to economics is that, in economies with many traders, it has turned out to be intimately related to the notion of Walrasian equilibrium. Interestingly, this is in common with the dominance approach. Aumann (1975) is a representative paper of the very extensive literature on the topic.

BIBLIOGRAPHY

Aumann, R. 1959. Acceptable points in general cooperative n-person games. *Annals of Mathematics Studies Series* 40, 287–324.
Aumann, R. 1975. Values of markets with a continuum of traders. *Econometrica* 43, 611–46.
Aumann, R. 1985. An axiomatization of the non-transferable utility value. *Econometrica* 53, 599–612.
Aumann, R. and Maschler, M. 1964. The bargaining set for cooperative games. In *Advances in Game Theory*, ed. M. Dresher, L. Shapley and A.W. Tucker, Princeton: Princeton University Press, 443–7.
Bernheim, B.D., Peleg, B. and Whinston, M. 1987. Coalition-proof Nash equilibria I. Concepts. *Journal of Economic Theory* 42, 1–29.
Edgeworth, F. 1881. *Mathematical Psychics*. London: Kegan Paul; New York: A.M. Kelley, 1967.
Harsanyi, J. 1959. A bargaining model for the cooperative n-person game. In *Contributions to the Theory of Games*, Vol. 4, ed. A.W. Tucker and R.D. Luce, Princeton: Princeton University Press, 324–56.
Hart, S. 1985. An axiomatization of Harsanyi nontransferable utility solution. *Econometrica* 53, 1295–314.
Hart, S. and Mas-Colell, A. 1985. The potential: a new approach to the value in multiperson allocation problems. Harvard Discussion Paper 1157.

Mas-Colell, A. 1982. Perfect competition and the core. *Review of Economic Studies* 49, 15–30.

Nash, J. 1953. Two-person cooperative games. *Econometrica* 21, 128–40.

Neumann, J. von and Morgenstern, O. 1944. *Theory of Games and Economic Behavior.* Princeton: Princeton University Press.

Scarf, H. 1971. On the existence of a cooperative solution for a general class of n-person games. *Journal of Economic Theory* 3, 169–81.

Shapley, L. 1953. A value for n-person games. In *Contributions to the Theory of Games*, Vol. 2, ed. H. Kuhn and A.W. Tucker, Princeton: Princeton University Press, 307–17.

Shapley, L. 1969. Utility comparison and the theory of games. In *La Décision*, Paris: Editions du CNRS, 251–63.

Shapley, L. and Shubik, M. 1969. On the core of an economic system with externalities. *American Economic Review* 59, 678–84.

Shubik, M. 1983. *Game Theory in the Social Sciences.* Cambridge Mass.: MIT Press.

Cooperative Games

MARTIN SHUBIK

The title 'cooperative games' would be better termed games in coalitional form. The theory of games originally developed different conceptual forms, together with their associated solution concepts, namely, games in extensive form, in strategic form and in coalitional form (von Neumann and Morgenstern, 1944). The game in strategic form is sometimes referred to as the game in normal form, while that in coalitional form is also referred to as the game in characteristic form.

The game in extensive form provides a process account of the detail of individual moves and information structure; the tree structure often employed in its description enables the researcher to keep track of the full history of any play of the game. This is useful for the analysis of reasonably well-structured formal process models where the beginning, end and sequencing of moves is well-defined, but is generally not so useful to describe complex, loosely structured social interaction.

A simple example shows the connections among the three representations of a game. Consider a game with two players where the rules prescribe that Player A moves first. He must decide between two moves. After he has selected a move, Player B is informed and in turn selects between two moves. After B has selected a move the game ends and depending upon the history of the game each player obtains a payoff. Figure 1(a) shows this game in extensive form. The vertex labelled 0 indicates the starting point of the game. It is also circled to indicate the information structure. Figure 2(a) shows a game whose only difference from the game in Figure 1(a) is that in the latter Player B when called upon to select a move does not know to which of the choice points in his information set the game has progressed. In the game in Figure 1(a), when Player B makes his choice he knows precisely if Player A has selected move 1 or 2. Each vertex of the game is a choice point except the terminal vertices. Several vertices may be enclosed in the same information set. The player who 'owns' a particular information set is unable to distinguish among the choice points in a set. An arc (or branch of a tree) connecting a choice point with another choice point or a terminal point is a move. The moves emanating from any choice point are indexed so that they can be identified.

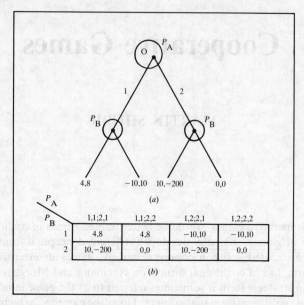

Figure 1

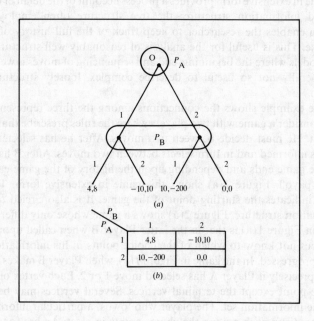

Figure 2

The final nodes at the bottom of the tree are not choice points but points of termination of the game and the numbers displayed indicate the value of the outcome to each player. The first number is the payoff to Player A and the second to Player B.

The extensive form may be reduced to the strategic form by means of strategies. A strategy is plan covering all contingencies. Figure 1(b) shows that the moves and strategies for P_A are the same, choose 1 or 2. But P_B has four strategies as he can plan for the contingency that P_B selects 1 or 2. A sample strategy 1, 1; 2, 1 may be read as: 'If P_A selects 1, select 1; if P_A selects 2, select 1'.

The progression from extensive form to strategic form entails loss of fine structure. Details of information are no longer available. There are many extensive forms other than Figure 1(a) which are consistent with Figure 1(b).

A further compression of the game representation beyond the strategic form may be called for. At the level of bargaining or diplomacy details of strategy may be of little importance. Instead emphasis is laid upon the value of cooperation. The cooperative or coalitional form represents the game in terms of the jointly optimal outcomes obtainable by every set of players. If payoffs are comparable and side-payments are possible the gain from cooperation can be represented by a single number. If not then the optimal outcomes attainable by a set S of players will be a Pareto optimal surface in $s = |S|$ dimensions (where $|S|$ is the number of elements in S).

A game in cooperative form with side-payments can be represented by a characteristic function which is a superadditive set function. We use the symbol $\Gamma(N, v)$ to stand for a game in coalitional form with a set N of players and a characteristic function v defined on all of the 2^n subsets of N (where $n = |N|$). The condition of superadditivity is a reasonable economic assumption in a transactions cost-free world. $v(S) + v(T) \leqslant v(S \cup T)$ where $S \cap T = \theta$ states that the amounts obtained by two independent coalitions S and T will be less than or at most equal to the amount that they could obtain by cooperatin and acting together.

Returning to Figures 1(b) and 2(b) we can reduce them to coalitional form by specifying how to calculate $v(\theta)$, $v(\bar{1})$, $v(\bar{2})$ and $v(\overline{1,2})$. The notation '$\overline{1,2}$' reads as the set consisting of the players whose names are 1 and 2.

Let $\bar{S} = N - S$ be the complement to S. The worst that could happen to S is that $\bar{S}$ acts as a unit to minimize the joint payoff to S. Applying this highly pessimistic view to the games in Figures 1(b) and 2(b), letting $P_A = 1$ and $P_B = 2$, we obtain the following:

$v(\theta) = 0$, the coalition of no one obtains nothing, by convention.

$v(\bar{1}) = 0$, $v(\bar{2}) = 0$

$v(\overline{1,2}) = 12$.

Although the extensive and strategic forms of these games differ, they coincide in this coalitional form. More detail has been lost. The coalitional form is symmetric but the underlying games do not appear to be symmetric. The pessimistic way of calculating $v(S)$ may easily overlook the possibility that it is highly costly for $\bar{S}$ to minimize the payoff to S. Thus it is possible that $v(S)$ does not reflect the threat structure in the underlying game. Prior to carrying out further game theoretic analysis on a game in characteristic function form, the modeller must decide if the characteristic function is an adequate representation of the game. Harsanyi and Selten have suggested a way to evaluate threats (see Shubik, 1982).

APPLICATIONS. Depending upon the application, the extensive, strategic or coalitional forms may be the starting point for analysis. Thus in economic applications involving oligopoly theory one might go from economic data to the strategic form in order to study Cournot-type duopoly. Yet to study the relationship of the Edgeworth contract curve to the price system one can model the coalitional form directly from the economic data without being able even to describe an extensive or strategic form.

In any application, the description of the game in coalitional form is a major step in the specification of the problem. After the coalitional form has been specified a solution is applied to it. There are many solution concepts which have been suggested for games in coalitional form. Among the better known are the core, the value, the nucleolus, the kernel, the bargaining set and the stable set solutions. Only the core and value are noted here (for an exposition of the others see Shubik, 1982).

The core of an n-person game in characteristic function form was originally investigated by Gillies and adopted by Shapley as a solution. The value was developed by Shapley (1951) and has been considered in several modifications to account for the presence or absence of threats and side-payments.

We define $\alpha = (\alpha_1, \alpha_2, \ldots, \alpha_n)$ where $\alpha_i \geqslant 0$ for all $i \in N$, and $\Sigma_{i \in N} \alpha_i = v(N)$ to be an imputation for the game $\Gamma(N, v)$. It is an individually rational division of the proceeds from total cooperation. The core is the set of imputations such that $\Sigma_{i \in S} \alpha_i \geqslant v(S)$ for all $S \subset N$. It is, in some sense, the set of imputations impervious to countervailing power. No subset of players can effectively claim that they could obtain more by acting by themselves. The core may be empty. An exchange economy with the usual Arrow–Debreu assumptions modelled as a game in coalitional form always has a core, and the imputation (or imputations) selected by the competitive equilibria of an exchange economy are always in the core of the associated market game.

The Shapley value is intuitively the average of all marginal contributions that an individual i can make to all coalitions. He developed the explicit formula to calculate the value imputation for any game in coalitional form with side-payments. It is

$$\phi_i = \sum_{i \in S} \sum_{S \subset N} \frac{(n-s)!(s-l)!}{n!} [v(S) - v(S/i)].$$

The term $v(S) - v(S/i)$ measures the marginal contribution of i to the coalition

S. The remaining terms provide the count of all of the ways the various coalitions involving *i* can be built up. For exchange economies with many traders a relationship between the competitive equilibria and the value can be established (for further discussion, see Shubik, 1984).

Many situations involving voting can be modelled as a game in coalitional form where the characteristic function takes only two values, 0 and 1. Such games are called simple games (Shapley, 1962). Shapley and Shubik (1954) suggested the use of the value to provide a power index for committee voting. The basic observation is that the power of a player increases in a nonlinear manner as the number of votes he controls increases. The value applied to a simple game provides an index of this power.

Cooperative games provide a way to carry out an analysis of many problems of interest to the social sciences without concern for the detail of the structure of process. Von Neumann and Morgenstern aptly noted that the difficulties to be encountered in the development of theories of dynamics in the social sciences were so large that the development of a primarily static theory of games in cooperative form was called for as a first step, bearing in mind that the eventual form of a theory of dynamics might have little resemblance to the statics. Some forty years after their seminal work much still remains to be done in the development of games in coalitional form.

BIBLIOGRAPHY

Shapley, L.S. 1951. The value of an n-person game. Rand Publication RM-670.
Shapley, L.S. 1962. Simple games: an outline of the descriptive theory. *Behavioral Science* 7, 59–66.
Shapley, L.S. and Shubik, M. 1954. A method for evaluating the distribution of power in a committee system. *The American Political Science Review* 48(3), 787–92.
Shubik, M. 1982. *Game Theory in the Social Sciences*, Vol. I. Cambridge, Mass.: Harvard University Press.
Shubik, M. 1984. *Game Theory in the Social Sciences*, Vol. II. Cambridge, Mass.: MIT Press.
Von Neumann, J. and Morgenstern, O. 1944. *Theory of Games and Economic Behavior*. Princeton: Princeton University Press.

Cores

WERNER HILDENBRAND

The *core* of an economy consists of those states of the economy which no group of agents can 'improve upon'. A group of agents can improve upon a state of the economy if, by using the means available to that group, each member can be made better off. Nothing is said in this definition of how a state in the core actually is reached. The actual process of economic transactions is not considered explicitly.

To keep the presentation as simple as possible, we shall consider only the core for exchange economies with an arbitrary number l of commodities, even though the core concept applies to more general situations.

Consider a finite set A of economic agents; each agent a in A is described by his *preference relation* $\precsim_a$ (defined on the positive orthant R^l_+) and his *initial endowments* e_a (a vector in R^l_+). The outcome of any exchange, that is to say, a state (x_a) of the exchange economy $\mathscr{E} = \{\precsim_a, e_a\}_{a \in A}$, is a *redistribution* of the total endowments, i.e.

$$\sum_{a \in A} x_a = \sum_{a \in A} e_a.$$

A *coalition* of agents, say $S \subset A$, can *improve upon* a redistribution (x_a), if that coalition S, by using the endowments available to it, can make each member of that coalition better off, that is to say, there is a redistribution, say $(y_a)_{a \in S}$, such that

$$y_a \succ_a x_a \text{ for every } a \in S \qquad \text{and} \qquad \sum_{a \in S} y_a = \sum_{a \in S} e_a.$$

The set of redistributions for the exchange economy $\mathscr{E}$ that no coalition can improve upon is called the *core* of the economy $\mathscr{E}$, and is denoted by $C(\mathscr{E})$.

The core is, however, a rather theoretical fundamental equilibrium concept. Indeed, the core provides a theoretical foundation of a more operational equilibrium concept, the *competitive equilibrium* which, in fact, is a very different notion of equilibrium. The allocation process is organized through markets; there is a price for every commodity. All economic agents take the price system as given and make their decisions independently of each other. The equilibrium price system coordinates these independent decisions in such a way that all markets are simultaneously balanced.

More formally, an allocation (x_a^*) for the exchange economy $\mathscr{E} = \{ \precsim_a, e_a \}_{a \in A}$ is a *competitive equilibrium* (or a *Walras allocation*) if there exists a price vector $p^* \in R_+^l$ such that for every $a \in A$, $x_a^* \in \phi_a(p^*)$ and

$$\sum_{a \in A} x_a^* = \sum_{a \in A} e_a.$$

Here $\phi_a(p^*)$, or more explicitly, $\phi(p^*, e_a, \precsim_a)$ denotes the demand of agent a with preferences $\precsim_a$ and endowment e_a, i.e. the set of most desired commodity vectors (with respect to $\precsim_a$) in the budget-set $\{ x \in R_+^l \,|\, p^* \cdot x \leqslant p^* \cdot e_a \}$.

The set of all competitive equilibria for the economy $\mathscr{E}$ is denoted by $W(\mathscr{E})$.

The core and the set of competitive equilibria for an economy with two agents and two commodities can be represented geometrically by the well-known Edgeworth–Box (see figure 1). The size of the box is determined by the total endowments $e_1 + e_2$. Every point P in the box represents a redistribution; the first agent receives $x_1 = P$ and the second receives $x_2 = (e_1 + e_2) - P$.

It is easy to show that for every exchange economy $\mathscr{E}$ a competitive equilibrium belongs to the core,

$$W(\mathscr{E}) \subset C(\mathscr{E}).$$

Thus, a state of the economy $\mathscr{E}$ which is decentralized by a price system cannot be improved upon by cooperation. This proposition strengthens a well-known result of Welfare Economics – every competitive equilibrium is Pareto-efficient.

The inclusion $W(\mathscr{E}) \subset C(\mathscr{E})$ is typically strict. Indeed, if the initial allocation of endowments is not Pareto-efficient, which is the typical case, then, if there are any allocations in the core at all, there are core-allocations which are not competitive equilibria.

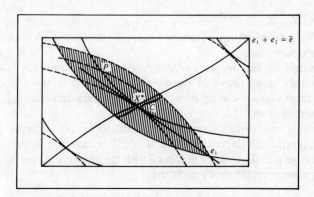

Figure 1

This leads us to the *basic problem* in the theory of the core:

For which kind of economies is the 'difference' between the core and the set of competitive equilibria small? Or in other words, under which circumstances do cooperative barter and competition through decentralized markets lead essentially to the same result?

Naturally, the answer depends on the way one measures the 'difference' between the two equilibrium concepts. However this is done one expects that the economy must have a large number of participants.

In answering the basic question we try to be comprehensible (for example by avoiding the use of measure-theoretic concepts) but not comprehensive. Therefore, if we refer in the remainder of this entry to an economy $\mathscr{E} = \{ \precsim_a, e_a \}_{a \in A}$ we shall always assume that preference relations are continuous, complete, transitive, monotone and strictly convex. The total endowments $\Sigma_{a \in A} e_a$ of an economy are always assumed to be strictly positive. We shall not repeat these assumptions. Furthermore, if we call an economy smooth, then we assume in addition that preferences are smooth (hence representable by sufficiently differentiable utility functions) and individual endowments are strictly positive.

These assumptions simplify the presentation tremendously. For generalizations we refer to the extensive literature.

We remark that under the above assumptions there always exists a competitive equilibrium, and hence, the core is not empty.

LARGE ECONOMIES

The simplest and most stringent measure of difference between the two equilibrium sets, $C(\mathscr{E})$ and $W(\mathscr{E})$, which we shall denote by $\delta(\mathscr{E})$, can be defined as follows.

Let $\delta(\mathscr{E})$ be the smallest number δ with the property: for every allocation $(x_a) \in C(\mathscr{E})$ there exists an allocation $(x_a^*) \in W(\mathscr{E})$ such that

$$|x_a - x_a^*| \leqslant \delta$$

for every agent a in the economy $\mathscr{E}$.

Thus, if $\delta(\mathscr{E})$ is small, then from every agent's view a core allocation is like a competitive equilibrium.

Unfortunately for this measure of difference, it is not true that $\delta(\mathscr{E})$ can be made arbitrarily small provided the number of agents in the economy $\mathscr{E}$ is sufficiently large (even if one restricts the agents' characteristics ($\precsim_a, e_a$) to an *a priori* given finite set).

Consequently one considers also weaker measures for the 'difference' between the two equilibrium concepts $C(\mathscr{E})$ and $W(\mathscr{E})$. For example, define $\delta_1(\mathscr{E})$ and $\delta_2(\mathscr{E})$, respectively, as the smallest number δ with the property: for every $(x_a) \in C(\mathscr{E})$ there exists a price vector $p \in R_+^i$ such that

(δ_1) $\qquad\qquad |x_a - \phi_a(p)| \leqslant \delta$ $\qquad$ for every agent a in $\mathscr{E}$

or

$$(\delta_2) \qquad\qquad \frac{1}{\# A} \sum_{a \in A} |x_a - \phi_a(p)| \leq \delta.$$

Clearly, the measures δ_1 and δ_2 are weaker than δ since the price vector p is not required to be an equilibrium price vector for the economy $\mathscr{E}$. The number $\delta_1(\mathscr{E})$ (and, *a fortiori*, $\delta_2(\mathscr{E})$) does not measure the distance between the sets $C(\mathscr{E})$ and $W(\mathscr{E})$ but the degree by which an allocation in the core can be decentralized via a price system. Obviously one has $\delta_2(\mathscr{E}) \leq \delta_1(\mathscr{E}) \leq \delta(\mathscr{E})$.

One can show that $\delta_2(\mathscr{E})$ becomes arbitrarily small for sufficiently large economies. More precisely,

THEOREM 1.   Let T be a finite set of agents' characteristics $(\precsim, e)$ and let b be a strictly positive vector in R^l. Then for every $\varepsilon > 0$ there exists an integer N such that for every economy $\mathscr{E} = \{\precsim_a, e_a\}_{a \in A}$ with $\# A \geq N$,

$$\frac{1}{\# A} \sum_{a \in A} e_a \geq b$$

and $(\precsim_a, e_a) \in T$ one has

$$\delta_2(\mathscr{E}) \leq \varepsilon.$$

(The finite set T in Theorem 1 can be replaced by a compact set with respect to a suitably chosen topology: see Hildenbrand, 1974.) We emphasize that this result does not imply that in large economies core-allocations are near to competitive equilibria. In fact, Theorem 1 does not hold if δ_2 is replaced by the measure of difference δ or even δ_1. Theorem 1 does imply, however, that for sufficiently large economies one can associate to every core-allocation a price vector which 'approximately decentralizes' the core-allocation. Some readers might consider this conclusion as a perfectly satisfactory answer to our basic problem. If one holds this view, then the rest of the paper is a superfluous intellectual pastime. We would like to emphasize, however, that the meaning of 'approximate decentralization' is not very strong. First, the demand $\phi_a(p)$ is not necessarily near to x_a for every agent a in the economy; only the mean deviation

$$\frac{1}{\# A} \sum_{a \in A} |x_a - \phi_a(p)|$$

becomes small. Second, total demand is not equal to total supply; only the mean excess demand

$$\frac{1}{\# A} \sum_{a \in A} [\phi_a(p) - e_a]$$

becomes small.

There are alternative proofs in the literature, e.g. Bewley (1973), Hildenbrand (1974), Anderson (1981) or Hildenbrand (1982). These proofs are based either on a result by Vind (1965) or Anderson (1978).

Sharper conclusions than the one in Theorem 1 will be stated in the following sections. There we consider a sequence $(\mathscr{E}_n)_{n=1,\dots}$ of economies and then study the asymptotic behaviour of $\delta(\mathscr{E}_n)$.

Before we present these limit theorems we should mention another approach of analysing the inclusion $W(\mathscr{E}) \subset C(\mathscr{E})$. Instead of analysing the asymptotic behaviour of the difference $\delta(\mathscr{E}_n)$ for a sequence of finite economies one can define a large economy where every agent has strictly no influence on collective actions. This leads to a *measure space without atoms* of economic agents (also called a *continuum of agents*). For such economies the two equilibrium concepts coincide. See Aumann (1964).

REPLICA ECONOMIES

Let $\mathscr{E} = \{\precsim_i, e_i\}$ be an exchange economy with m agents. For every integer n we define the n-fold *replica economy* $\mathscr{E}_n$ of $\mathscr{E}$ as an economy with $n \cdot m$ agents; there are exactly n agents with characteristics $(\precsim_i, e_i)$ for every $i = 1, \dots, m$.

More formally,

$$\mathscr{E}_n = \{\precsim_{(i,j)}, e_{(i,j)}\}_{\substack{1 \leqslant i \leqslant m \\ 1 \leqslant j \leqslant n}}$$

where $\precsim_{(i,j)} = \precsim_i$ and $e_{(i,j)} = e_i$, $1 \leqslant i \leqslant m$ and $1 \leqslant j \leqslant n$. Thus, an agent a in the economy $\mathscr{E}_n$ is denoted by a double index $a = (i,j)$. We shall refer to agent (i,j) sometimes as the jth agent of type i.

Replica economies were first analysed by F. Edgeworth (1881) who proved a limit theorem for such sequences in the case of two commodities and two types of agents. A precise formulation of Edgeworth's analysis and the generalization to an arbitrary finite number of commodities and types of agents is due to Debreu and Scarf (1963).

Here is the basic result for replica economies.

THEOREM 2. For every sequence $(\mathscr{E}_n)$ of replica economies the difference between the core and the set of competitive equilibria tends to zero, i.e.,

$$\lim_{n \to \infty} \delta(\mathscr{E}_n) = 0.$$

Furthermore, if $\mathscr{E}$ is a smooth and regular economy than $\delta(\mathscr{E}_n)$ converges to zero at least as fast as the inverse of the number of participants, i.e., there is a constant K such that

$$\delta(\mathscr{E}_n) \leqslant \frac{K}{n}.$$

The proof of this remarkably neat result is based on the fact that a core–allocation (x_{ij}) assigns to every agent of the same type the same commodity bundle, i.e., $x_{ij} = x_{ik}$. This 'equal treatment' property simplifies the analysis of $\delta(\mathscr{E}_n)$ tremendously. Indeed, an allocation (x_{ij}) in $C(\mathscr{E}_n)$, which can be considered as a vector in $R^{l \cdot m \cdot n}$, is completely described by the commodity bundle of one agent in each type, thus by a vector $(x_{11}, x_{21}, \ldots, x_{m1})$ in $R^{l \cdot m}$, a space whose dimension is independent of n.

Thus, let

$$C_n = \{(x_{11}, x_{21}, \ldots, x_{m1}) \in R^{l \cdot m} | (x_{ij}) \in C(\mathscr{E}_n)\}.$$

One easily shows that $C_{n+1} \subset C_n$. It is not hard to see that Theorem 1 follows if

$$\cap_{n=1}^{\infty} C_n = W(\mathscr{E}_1).$$

But this is the well-known theorem of Debreu and Scarf (1963). The essential arguments in the proof go as follows. Let $(x_1, \ldots, x_m) \in \cap_{n=1}^{\infty} C_n$. One has to show that there is a price vector p^* such that $x \succ_i x_i$ implies $p^* \cdot x > p^* \cdot e_i$. For this it suffices to show that there is a p^* such that

$$p^* \cdot z \geqslant 0 \text{ for every } z \in \cup_{i=1}^{m} (\{x \in R_+^l | x \succ_i x_i\} - e_i) = Z,$$

i.e., there is a hyperplane (whose normal is p^*) which supports the set z. One shows that the assumption $(x_1, \ldots, x_m) \in \cap_{n=1}^{\infty} C_n$ implies that 0 does not belong to the convex hull of z. Minkowski's Separation Theorem for convex sets then implies the existence of the desired vector p^*.

The second part of the conclusion of Theorem 2 is due to Debreu (1975).

TYPE ECONOMIES

The limit theorem on the core for replica economies is not fully satisfactory since replication is a very rigid way of enlarging an economy. The conclusion '$\delta(\mathscr{E}_n) \to 0$' in Theorem 2, to be of general relevance, should be robust to small deviations from the strict replication procedure.

Consider a sequence $(\mathscr{E}_n)$ of economies where the characteristics of every agent belong to a given finite set of types $T = \{(\precsim_1, e_1), \ldots, (\precsim_m, e_m)\}$. We do not consider this as a restrictive assumption (considered as an approximation, one can always group agents' characteristics into a finite set of types). Let the economy $\mathscr{E}_n$ have N_n agents; $N_n(1)$ agents of the first type, $N_n(i)$ agents of type i. Of course the idea is that N_n tends to ∞ with increasing n. Consider the fraction $v_n(i)$ of agents in the economy $\mathscr{E}_n$ which are of type i, i.e.,

$$v_n(i) = \frac{N_n(i)}{N_n}.$$

The sequence $(\mathscr{E}_n)$ is a replica sequence of an economy $\mathscr{E}$ (not necessarily of $\mathscr{E}_1$) if and only if the fractions $v_n(i)$ are all independent of n. It is this rigidity which we want to weaken now.

A sequence $(\mathscr{E}_n)$ of economies with characteristics in a finite set T is called a *sequence of type economies* (over T) if

(i) the number N_n of agents in $\mathscr{E}_n$ tends to infinity

113

and

(ii) $v_n(i) = \dfrac{N_n(i)}{N_n} \xrightarrow[(n \to \infty)]{} v(i) > 0.$

EXAMPLE (random sampling of agents' characteristics):

Let π be a probability distribution over the finite set T. Define the economy $\mathscr{E}_n$ as a random sample of size n from this distribution $\pi(\cdot)$. The law of large numbers then implies property (ii): $v_n(i) \to \pi(i)$.

The step from replica economies to type economies – as small as it might appear to the reader – is conceptually very important. Yet with this 'small' generalization the analysis of the limit behaviour of $\delta(\mathscr{E}_n)$ or $\delta_1(\mathscr{E}_n)$ is made more difficult. Even worse, it is no longer true that for *every* sequence $(\mathscr{E}_n)$ of type economies one obtains $\delta(\mathscr{E}_n) \to 0$ – even if the preferences of all types are assumed to be very nice, say smooth. There are some 'exceptional cases' where the conclusion $\delta(\mathscr{E}_n) \to 0$ does not hold. But these are 'exceptional' cases and the whole difficulty in the remainder of this section is to explain in which precise sense these cases are 'exceptional' and can therefore be ignored. We shall first exhibit the 'cases' where the conclusion fails to hold. Then we shall show that these cases are exceptional.

We denote by $\Pi(\mathscr{E})$ the set of normalized *equilibrium price vectors* for the economy $\mathscr{E} = \{\precsim_a, e_a\}_{a \in A}$. Thus, for $p^* \in \Pi(\mathscr{E})$ the excess demand is zero, i.e.,

$$\sum_{a \in A} [\phi_a(p^*) - e_a] = 0.$$

To every sequence $(\mathscr{E}_n)$ of type economies we associate a '*limit economy*' $\mathscr{E}_\infty$. This economy has an 'indefinitely large' number of agents of every type; the fraction of agents of type i is given by $v(i)$. The mean (per capita) excess demand of that limit economy $\mathscr{E}_\infty$ is defined by

$$z_v(p) = \sum_{i=1}^m v(i) [\phi(p, e_i, \precsim_i) - e_i].$$

An equilibrium price vector p^* of the limit economy $\mathscr{E}_\infty$ is defined by $z_v(p^*) = 0$. Let $\Pi(v)$ denote the set of normalized equilibrium price vectors for $\mathscr{E}_\infty$. Obviously for a replica sequence $(\mathscr{E}_n)$ we have $\Pi(\mathscr{E}_n) = \Pi(v)$ for all n. However, for a sequence of type economies the set $\Pi(\mathscr{E}_n)$ of equilibrium prices of the economy $\mathscr{E}_n$ depends on n, and it might happen that the set $\Pi(v)$ is not similar to $\Pi(\mathscr{E}_n)$ even for arbitrarily large n. To fix ideas, it might happen that $\Pi(\mathscr{E}_n) = \{p_n\}$ and $\Pi(v)$ contains not only $p = \lim p_n$ but also another equilibrium price vector. Such a situation has to be excluded.

We call a sequence of type economies *sleek* if $\Pi(\mathscr{E}_n)$ converges (in the Hausdorff-distance) to $\Pi(v)$.

It is known (Hildenbrand, 1974) that the sequence $(\Pi(\mathscr{E}_n))$ converges to $\Pi(v)$ if $\Pi(v)$ is a singleton (i.e., the limit economy has a unique equilibrium) or, in general, if (and only if) for every open set O in R^l with $O \cap \Pi(v) \neq \varnothing$ it follows that $O \cap \Pi(\mathscr{E}_n) \neq \varnothing$ for all n sufficiently large.

We now have exhibited the cases where a limit theorem on the core holds true.

THEOREM 3.   For every sleek sequence $(\mathscr{E}_n)$ of type economies

$$\lim_{n \to \infty} \delta(\mathscr{E}_n) = 0.$$

Unfortunately there seems to be no short and easy proof. The main difficulty arises from the fact that for allocations in the core of a type economy the 'equal treatment' property, which made the replica case so manageable is no longer true. For a proof see Hildenbrand and Kirman (1976) or Hildenbrand (1982) and the references given there. The main step in the proof is based on a result of Bewley (1973).

It remains to show that non-sleek sequences of type economies are 'exceptional cases'.

The strongest form of 'exceptional' is, of course, 'never'. We mentioned already that a sequence $(\mathscr{E}_n)$ is sleek if its limit economy has a unique equilibrium. Unfortunately, however, only under very restrictive assumptions on the set T of agents' characteristics does uniqueness prevail; for example,

(1) if every preference relation leads to a demand function which satisfies gross-substitution (Cobb–Douglas utility functions are typical examples),
(2) if every preference relation is homothetic and the endowment vectors $e_i (i = 1, \ldots, m)$ are collinear.

Since there is no reasonable justification for restricting the set T to such special types of agents we have to formulate a model in which we allow non–sleek sequences to occur provided, of course, this can be shown to be 'exceptional cases'. Let S^{m-1} denote the open simplex in R^m, i.e.

$$S^{m-1} = \left\{ x \in R^m \mid x_i > 0, \sum_{i=1}^m x_i = 1 \right\}.$$

The limit distribution $v(i)$ of a sequence of type economies with m types is a point in S^{m-1}.

A cloud subset C in S^{m-1} which has $(m-1$ dimensional Lebesgue) measure zero is called *negligible*. Thus, if a distribution v is not in C then a sufficiently small change will not lead to C. Furthermore, given any arbitrary small positive number $\mathscr{E}$ one can find a countable collection of balls in S^{m-1} such that their union covers C, and that the sum of the diameters of these balls is smaller than $\mathscr{E}$. Thus, in particular, if $v \in C$ then one can approximate v by points which do not belong to C. Clearly, a negligible set is a small set in S^{m-1}.

THEOREM 4.   Given a finite set T of m smooth types of agents, there exists a negligible subset C in S^{m-1} and a constant K such that for every sequence $(\mathscr{E}_n)$ of type economies over T whose limit distribution v does not belong to C one has $\delta(\mathscr{E}_n) \leqslant K / \# A_n$, thus in particular, $\lim_{n \to \infty} \delta(\mathscr{E}_n) = 0$.

The convergence of $\delta(\mathscr{E}_n)$ follows from Theorem 3 and Theorem 5.4.3 and 5.8.15 in Mas-Colell (1985). For the rate of convergence see Grodal (1975).

BIBLIOGRAPHY

There is an extensive literature on limit theorems on the core which contains important generalizations of the results given here. For a general reference we refer to Hildenbrand (1974) or (1982), Mas-Colell (1985), Anderson (1985) and the references given there.

Anderson, R.M. 1978. An elementary core equivalence theorem. *Econometrica* 46, 1483–7.

Anderson, R.M. 1981. Core theory with strongly convex preferences. *Econometrica* 49, 1457–68.

Aumann, R.J. 1964. Markets with a continuum of traders. *Econometrica* 32, 39–50.

Bewley, T.F. 1973. Edgeworth's conjecture. *Econometrica* 41, 425–54.

Debreu, G. 1975. The rate of convergence of the core of an economy. *Journal of Mathematical Economics* 2, 1–8.

Debreu, G. and Scarf, H. 1963. A limit theorem on the core of an economy. *International Economic Review* 4, 235–46.

Edgeworth, F.Y. 1881. *Mathematical Psychics*. London: Kegan Paul. Reprinted New York: A.M. Kelley, 1967.

Grodal, B. 1975. The rate of convergence of the core for a purely competitive sequence of economies. *Journal of Mathematical Economics* 2, 171–86.

Hildenbrand, W. 1974. *Core and Equilibria of a Large Economy*. Princeton: Princeton University Press.

Hildenbrand, W. 1982. Core of an economy. In *Handbook of Mathematical Economics*, ed. K.J. Arrow and M.D. Intriligator, Vol. II, Amsterdam: North-Holland.

Hildenbrand, W. and Kirman, A.P. 1976. *Introduction to Equilibrium Analysis*. Amsterdam: North-Holland.

Mas-Colell, A. 1985. *The Theory of General Economic Equilibrium, A Differentiable Approach*. Cambridge: Cambridge University Press.

Vind, K. 1965. A theorem on the core of an economy. *Review of Economic Studies* 32, 47–8.

Antoine Augustin Cournot

MARTIN SHUBIK

Cournot was born at Gray (Haute-Saône) on 28 August 1801 and died in Paris on 30 March 1877. Until the age of fifteen his education was at Gray. After studying at Besançon he was admitted to the Ecole Normale Supérieure in Paris in 1821. In 1823 he obtained his licentiate in sciences and in October of that year was employed by Marshal Gouvion-Saint-Cyr as literary adviser to the Marshal and tutor to his son. In 1829 he obtained his doctorate in science with a main thesis in mechanics and a secondary one in astronomy. Through the sponsorship of Poisson in 1834 he obtained the professorship in analysis and mechanics at Lyon.

After a year of teaching he became primarily involved in university administration. In 1835 he became rector of the Académie de Grenoble and subsequently became inspector general of education and from 1854 to 1862 was rector of the Académie de Dijon. He became a Knight of the Legion of Honour in 1838 and an Officer in 1845. He was afflicted with failing eyesight and in the last part of his life was nearly blind. In 1862 he retired from public life but continued his own researches in Paris until his death.

Cournot was a prolific writer. His writings can be broadly divided into three categories: (1) mathematics; (2) economics; and (3) the philosophy of science and philosophy of history.

In considering Cournot as an economist it is necessary to place his major economic work, *Recherches sur les principes mathématiques de la théorie des richesses* (1838) in the context not only of *Principes de la théorie des richesses* (1863), which can be regarded as a literary version of his work of a quarter of a century earlier; and his *Revue sommaire des doctrines économiques* (1877) which appeared in the last year of his life; but also of his writings on probability and the philosophy of science, in particular *Exposition de la théorie des chances et des probabilités* (1843) and *Matérialisme, vitalisme, rationalisme: Etudes des données de la science en philosophie* (1875).

It is possible to weave a broad cloth of interpretation taking into account not

117

merely Cournot's other works, but what appears to be known of his personality and the considerable social and political flux in France during the times in which he lived. Guitton (1968) has suggested that Cournot had a rather melancholic and solitary temperament and 'did nothing to make his books attractive'. He notes that: 'Cournot was a pioneer. He did nothing to court his contemporaries, and they, in turn, not only failed to appreciate him but ignored him'. Palomba ([1981], 1984) provides a sketch of the historical background of his time, noting the growth of socialist ideas in Europe, the political actions and reactions to the French Revolution and the challenges to the concept of ownership. Rather than challenge or repeat the broad contextual interpretation of Cournot provided by Palomba, this essay is confined primarily to the direct interpretation of his works in economics and supporting texts, in the light of many of the developments in economics which are consistent with and may be indebted to his original ideas.

The texts followed here include the French given in the complete works of Cournot (1973) and the Nathaniel T. Bacon translation (1899) entitled 'Researches into the Mathematical Principles of the Theory of Wealth' which also contains an essay by Irving Fisher on Cournot and Mathematical Economics as well as a bibliography on Mathematical Economics from 1711 to 1897. The 1929 reprint of the 1899 edition was used.

The preface sets forth with great clarity Cournot's fundamental approach to Political Economy. He states:

> But the title of this work sets forth not only theoretical researches; it shows also that I intend to apply to them the forms and symbols of mathematical analysis. Most authors who have devoted themselves to political economy seem also to have had a wrong idea of the nature of the applications of mathematical analysis to the theory of wealth.
>
> But those skilled in mathematical analysis know that its object is not simply to calculate numbers, but that it is also employed to find the relations between magnitudes which cannot be expressed in numbers and between *functions* whose law is not capable of algebraic expression. Thus the theory of probabilities furnishes a demonstration of very important propositions, although without the help of experience it is impossible to give numerical values for contingent events, except in questions of mere curiosity, such as arise from certain games of chance (p. 3).

Cournot continues in the preface to note that only the first principles of differential and integral calculus are required for his treatise. Professional mathematicians could be interested in it for the questions raised rather than the level of mathematics presented. He ends the preface with the caveat:

> I am far from having thought of writing in support of any system, and from joining the banners of any party; I believe that there is an immense step in passing from theory to governmental applications; I believe that theory loses none of its value in thus remaining preserved from contact with impassioned polemics; and I believe, if this essay is of any practical value, it will be chiefly

in making clear how far we are from being able to solve, with full knowledge of the case, a multitude of questions which are boldly decided every day (p. 5).

The first chapter, 'of value in exchange or of wealth in general', provides insight into the breadth of Cournot's concern for the social and historical context of wealth.

Property, power, the distinctions between masters, servants and slaves, abundance, and poverty, rights and privileges, all these are found among the most savage tribes, and seem to flow necessarily from the natural laws which preside over aggregations of individuals and of families; but such an idea of wealth as we draw from our advanced state of civilization, and such as is necessary to give rise to a theory, can only be slowly developed as a consequence of the progress of commercial relations, and of the gradual reaction of those relations on civil institutions (pp. 7–8).

He notes that: 'it is a long step to the abstract idea of *value in exchange* which supposes that the objects to which such value is attributed *are in commercial circulation.*'

In order to illustrate the distinction between the word *wealth* in ordinary speech and value in exchange, he presents an example of a publisher who destroys two thirds of his stock expecting to derive more profit from the remainder than the entire edition. The economics of elasticity is developed more formally in chapter 4 on demand, but the concept is clear.

Chapter 2, 'on changes in value, absolute and relative', begins by noting that 'we can only assign value to a commodity by reference to other commodities'. This leads to a discussion of the use of a corrected money which would serve as 'the equivalent of the mean sun of the astronomers'.

Chapter 3, 'of the exchanges', is the first in which formal mathematical manipulation is employed. He considers a silver standard in which all currencies are fixed in ratio to a gram of fine silver. He observes that the ratios of exchange for the same weight of fine silver cannot differ by more than transportation and smuggling costs. Given the volume of trade measured in silver he considers the arbitrage conditions for the $m(m-1)/2$ ratios among m centres. Fisher (1892) notes however that Cournot did not appear to be acquainted with determinants as he did not attempt a general solution of the exchange equations he proposed, but limited his calculations to three centres of exchange.

It is in chapter 4, 'on the law of demand', that the modernity of his approach stands out. He is interested in demand as it is revealed in sales at a given price. He represents the relationship between sales and price by the continuous function $D = F(p)$ and observes that this function generally increases in size with a fall in price and that the empirical problem is to determine the form of $F(p)$. He indicates an appreciation of the concept of elasticity of demand although he did not develop the formal measure.

Chapters 5 and 6 deal with monopoly without and with taxation; chapter 7 is on the competition of producers and chapter 8 on unlimited competition. The

119

ninth chapter is on the mutual relations of producers and the tenth on the communication of markets. The final two chapters are somewhat macroeconomic in scope. Chapter 11 is entitled 'of the social income' and 12 'of variations in the social income, resulting from the communication of markets'.

As our commentary is primarily on chapters 5–8, the order is reversed and 11 and 12 are dealt with first. Cournot explicitly avoids setting up the whole closed microeconomic system.

It seems, therefore, as if, for a complete and rigorous solution of the problems relative to some parts of the economic system, it were indispensable to take the entire system into consideration. But this would surpass the powers of mathematical analysis and of our practical methods of calculation, even if the values of all the constants could be assigned to them numerically. The object of this chapter and of the following one is to show how far it is possible to avoid this difficulty, while maintaining a certain kind of approximation, and to carry on, by the aid of mathematical symbols, a useful analysis of the most general questions which this subject brings up.

We will denote by *social income* the sum, not only of incomes properly so called, which belong to members of society in their quality of real estate owners or capitalists, but also the wages and annual profits which come to them in their capacity of workers and industrial agents. We will also include in it the annual amount of the stipends by means of which individuals or the state sustained those classes of men which economic writers have characterized as unproductive, because the product of their labour is not anything material or saleable (pp. 127–8).

But, using a first order approximation, he studies the effect of a change in price and consumption of a good on social income as a whole under competition, under monopoly and when a new product is introduced.

Finally, although we make continuous and almost exclusive use of the word *commodity*, it must not be lost sight of (Article 8) that in this work we assimilate to commodities the rendering of services which have for their object the satisfaction of wants or the procuring of enjoyment. Thus when we say that funds are diverted from the demand for commodity A to be applied to the demand for commodity B, it may be meant by this expression that the funds diverted from the demand for a commodity properly so called, are employed to pay for services or vice versa. When the population of a great city loses its taste for taverns and takes up that for theatrical representations, the funds which were used in the demand for alcoholic beverages go to pay actors, authors, and musicians, whose annual income, according to our definition, appears on the balance sheet of the social income, as well as the rent of the vineyard owner, the vine-dresser's wages, and the tavern-keeper's profits (p. 149).

The last chapter considers international trade and national income and uses a first order approximation rather than a closed equilibrium system to study the benefits of opening up trade.

Moreover (and this is the favourite argument of writers of the school of Adam Smith), it should be inferred from the asserted advantage assigned to the exporting market, and the asserted disadvantage suffered by the importing market, that a nation should so arrange as always to export and never to import, which is evidently absurd, as it can only export on condition of importing, and even the sum of the values exported, calculated at the moment of leaving the national market, must necessarily be equal to the sum of the values imported, calculated at the moment of arrival on the national market (p. 161).

Cournot also notes the problem of analysing a tariff war:

The question would no longer be the same if establishment of a barrier for the benefit of A producers might provoke, by way of retaliation, the establishment of another barrier for the benefit of B producers, against whom the first barrier was raised. The government of A would then have to weigh the advantage resulting from the first measure to the citizens of A against the drawbacks caused by the retaliation. The two markets A and B would thus again be placed in symmetrical conditions, and each should be considered as acting the double part of an exporting and importing market (p. 164).

He closes his comments with:

We have just laid a finger on the question which is at the bottom of all discussions on measures which prohibit or restrict freedom of trade. It is not enough to accurately analyse the influence of such measures on the national income; their tendency as to the distribution of the wealth of society should also be looked into. We have no intention of taking up here this delicate question, which would carry us too far away from the purely abstract discussions with which this essay has to do. If we have tried to overthrow the doctrine of Smith's school as to barriers, it was only from theoretical considerations, and not in the least to make ourselves the advocates of prohibitory and restrictive laws. Moreover, it must be recognized that such questions as that of commercial liberty are not settled either by the arguments of scientific men or even by the wisdom of statesmen (p. 171).

He closes his work with the observation about theory that:

By giving more light on a debated point, it soothes the passions which are aroused. Systems have their fanatics, but the science which succeeds to systems never has them. Finally, even if theories relating to social organization do not guide the doings of the day, they at least throw light on the history of accomplished facts (p. 171).

Although the contribution of these last chapters is not as great as those to which we now turn, the spirit and style is that of a major theorist concerned deeply and objectively with application to practical affairs.

In chapters 5–9 Cournot develops his theory of monopoly, oligopoly and unlimited competition. This can be contrasted with Ricardo (1817) before and Walras (1874) after, who concentrated on unlimited competition with no aim at producing a unified theory involving numbers.

In chapter 5 Cournot deals with monopoly, considering increasing, decreasing and constant returns and in chapter 6 the influence of taxation on a monopoly is considered. He notes direct taxes and indirect taxes as well as bounties and their influences on both producers and consumers; and closes with an examination of two variations of taxation in kind.

Chapter 7 provides a smooth transformation from single person maximization to noncooperative optimization where agents who mutually influence each other act without explicit cooperation.

> We say *each independently*, and this restriction is very important, as will soon appear; for if they should come to an agreement so as to obtain for each the greatest possible income, the results would be entirely different, and would not differ, so far as consumers are concerned, from those obtained in treating of a monopoly.
>
> Instead of adopting $D = F(p)$ as before, in this case it will be convenient to adopt the inverse notation $p = f(D)$; and then the profits of proprietors (1) and (2) will be respectively expressed by
>
> $$D_1 f(D_1 + D_2), \quad \text{and} \quad D_2 f(D_1 + D_2),$$
>
> i.e. by functions into each of which enter two variables, D_1 and D_2 (p. 80).

It is at this point that Cournot switches from price to quantity of a homogeneous product at the strategic variable used by the competitors. His words and the mathematics do not quite match. He says, 'This he will be able to accomplish by properly adjusting his price.' The first order condition for the existence of a noncooperative equilibrium with quantity as the strategic variable is given. A diagram showing a stable equilibrium and another with a nonstable equilibrium are presented. The analysis is generalized to n producers including the possibility of an extra group of producers beyond n, all of whom produce at capacity. He obtains n symmetric equations for the firms with interior production levels and sets the others at capacity.

When he introduces n different general cost functions for the n firms he handles the situation with all having an equilibrium defined by the simultaneous satisfaction of the equations arising from the first order conditions. But he does not deal with the possibility that costs could be such that different subsets of firms could be active in different equilibria.

The criticism levelled by Bertrand (1883) in his review written well after Cournot's death concerns the modelling rather than the mathematics. As Cournot considered competition without entry among firms selling an identical product it was fairly natural to avoid the discontinuity in the payoff function caused by selecting price as an independent variable. But the observation of Bertrand matters for markets with a finite number of firms. The choice of strategic variable causes not only mathematical difficulties but raises questions concerning economic realism and relevance. Quantity, price, quality, product differentiation and scope can all be considered as playing dominant roles in different markets. But the general explanation of price and quantity as strategic variables was and is critical to the development of economic theory. Cournot provided the foundations for the understanding of quantity. Bertrand, whose review of the books of Cournot and Walras was somewhat tangential to his professional interests, offered only an example rather than a developed theory of price competition. It remained for Edgeworth (1925, pp. 111–42) to explore the underlying difficulties with the payoff functions for duopoly with increasing marginal costs; and it has only been in the last thirty years with the advent of the theory of games that there has been an adequate study of the properties of noncooperative equilibria in games with price and quantity as strategic variables, without or with product differentiation.

The thesis of Nash (1951) on the existence of noncooperative equilibria for a class of games in strategic form provided a broad general underpinning for the concept of noncooperative equilibrium. It was then immediately observable that although Cournot's work with equilibria of games with a continuum of strategies was not strictly covered by Nash's work, conceptually Cournot's solution could be viewed as an application of noncooperative equilibrium theory to oligopoly (see Mayberry, Nash and Shubik, 1953). The broader investigation of the price model and the interpretation of the instability of the Edgeworth cycle in terms of mixed strategy equilibria has only taken place recently. This also includes a growing literature on how to embed both the Cournot and Bertrand–Edgeworth models into a closed economic system or Walrasian framework. A summary of much of this work is presented by Shubik (1984).

It is important to appreciate that the developments in the theory of monopolistic competition such as those of Hotelling (1929) and Chamberlin (1933) and J. Robinson (1933) were based upon the Cournot noncooperative game model. Although it may be argued that Chamberlin's and Mrs Robinson's works possibly contained broader and richer models of competition among the few than that of Cournot, they represented a step backwards in their lack of mathematical sophistication and analysis. The Chamberlin discussion of large group equilibrium does have price as the strategic variable along with product differentiation and entry, but the solution concept is the noncooperative equilibrium à la Cournot, with the *caveat* that an attempt to produce a strict formal mathematical model of Chamberlin's large group equilibrium leads one to conclude that the game having price as a strategic variable is closer to Edgeworth's analysis than that of Cournot and a price strategy noncooperative equilibrium may not exist.

In chapter 8 Cournot shows his basic grasp of the important strategic difference between pure competition and oligopolistic competition. Using his own words, he states:

The effects of competition have reached their limit, when each of the partial productions D_2 is *inappreciable*, not only with reference to the total production $D = F(p)$, but also with reference to the derivative $F'(p)$, so that the partial production D_k could be subtracted from D without any appreciable variation resulting in the price of the commodity. This hypothesis is the one which is realized, in social economy, for a multitude of products, and, among them, for the most important products. It introduces a great simplification into the calculations, and this chapter is meant to develop the consequences of it (p. 90).

In modern mathematical economics, in the linking of competition among the few and the Walrasian system into a logically consistent whole, two approaches to the study of large numbers have been adopted. The first is replication and has its roots in Cournot and, more formally, Edgeworth (1881). Following Edgeworth this method was used in cooperative core theory by Shubik (1959). The second involves considering a continuum of economic agents where each agent can be regarded as a set of measure zero. Cournot clearly saw the need to consider a market in which each individual firm is too small to influence price. But it remained for Aumann (1964) to fully formalize the concept of an economic game with a continuum of agents.

After twenty-five years during which his seminal work in mathematical economics was essentially ignored, Cournot demonstrated his concern for his ideas by publishing *Principes de la théorie des richesses* (1863), where he offered a nonmathematical rendition of his early work. This book is of considerably greater length than its predecessor and is divided into four books: Book 1, Les Richesses (eight chapters); Book 2, Les Monnaies (seven chapters); Book 3, Le Systeme économique (ten chapters) and Book 4, L'Optimisme économique (seven chapters).

This book met with no more immediate success than his original work and is not as deep. For example the chapters on money, although they contain discursive and historical material of interest, have little material of analytic depth.

In spite of the indifference of the environment to his writings in economics, Cournot regarded his contribution as sufficiently important that some fourteen years later, in the year of his death, he published his *Revue sommaire des doctrines économiques* (1877). This book was also longer, non-mathematical and of less significance than the work of almost forty years earlier. But Cournot's own sense of having been at least partially vindicated after forty-odd years is indicated in his *avant-propos*:

It was at that point in 1863, when I had the desire to find out whether I had sinned in the substance of ideas or only in their form. To that end, I went back to my work of 1838, expanding it where needed, and, most of all, removing entirely the algebraic apparatus which intimidates so much in these subjects. Whence the book entitled: 'Principes de la theorie des richesses'. 'Since it took me,' I said in the preface, 'twenty-five years to lodge an appeal of the first sentence, it goes without saying that I do not intend, whatever happens, to resort to any other means. If I lose my case a second time, I will be left only with the consolation which never abandons disgraced authors: that of thinking that the sentence that condemns them will one day be quashed in the interest of the law, that is of the truth.'

When I took this engagement in 1863, I did not think that I would live long enough to see my 1838 case reviewed as a matter of course. Nevertheless, more than thirty years later, another generation of economists, to put it like Mr. the commander Boccardo, discovered that I opened up back then, though too timidly and too partially, a good path to be followed, on which I was even somewhat preceded by a man of merit, the doctor Whewell. While another Englishman, Mr. Jevons, was undertaking to enlarge this path, a young Frenchman, Mr. Leon Walras, professor of Political Economy at Lausanne, dared to maintain right in the Institute that it was wrong to pay so little attention to my method and my algorithm, which he used rightfully to expose a new theory, more amply developed.

Now, look at my bad luck. If I won a little late, without any involvement, my 1838 case, I lost my 1863 case. If one wanted in retrospective to make a case for my algebra, my prose (I am ashamed of saying it) did not get better success from the publisher. The *Journal des Economistes* (August 1864) criticized me mainly 'for not having moved on from Ricardo,' for not having taken into account the discoveries that so many men of merit have made in twenty-five years in the field of political economy; thus the poor author that no one of the official world of French economists wanted to quote incurred the reproach of not having quoted others enough.

Cournot was central to the founding of modern mathematical economics. The average reader tends not to be aware that the textbook presentations of the 'marginal cost equals marginals revenue' optimizing condition for monopoly and 'marginal cost equals price' for the firm in pure competition come directly from the work of Cournot (including an investigation of the second order conditions).

He had to wait many years for recognition, but when it came in the works of Jevons, Marshall, Edgeworth, Walras and others, it moved the course of economic theory. Marshall notes (*Memorials of Alfred Marshall*, pp. 412–13, letter 2, July 1900) 'I fancy I read Cournot in 1868', this was when Marshall was twenty-six, some thirty years after the book appeared. He acknowledges him both as a great master and as his source 'as regards the form of thought' for Marshall's theory of distribution. Jevons, in his preface to the second edition of *The Theory of Political Economy* records 'I procured a copy of the work as far back as 1872' and that it 'contains a wonderful analysis of the laws of supply and demand, and of the relations of prices, production, consumption, expenses and profits'. He excuses himself for his lateness in coming to Cournot observing: 'English economists can hardly be blamed for their ignorance of Cournot's economic works when we find French writers equally bad.' Walras in the preface to the fourth edition of *Elements of Pure Economics* (Jaffé translation, p. 37) acknowledges his 'father Auguste Walras, for the fundamental principles of my economic doctrine'; and 'Augustin Cournot for the idea of using the calculus of functions in the elaboration of this doctrine'. His liberal references to Cournot include his discussion of monopoly and the description of supply and demand.

The art of formal modelling is different from but related to the use of mathematical analysis in economics. The clarity and parsimony of Cournot's modelling stand out and have served as beacons guiding the development of mathematical economics.

An important feature missing from Cournot's seminal work is the discussion of the role of chance and uncertainty in the economy. He stressed the importance of chance in both his book *Exposition de la théorie des chances et des probabilités* (1843) and in *Matérialisme, vitalisme, rationalisme* (1875).

Although economics was the only social science he attempted to mathematize, he was well aware of the simplifications being made in cutting economic analysis from the context of history and society.

> The economist considers the body social in a state of division and so to say of extreme pulverization, where all the particularities of organization and of individual life offset each other and vanish. The laws that he discovers or believes to discover are those of a mechanism, not those of a living organism. For him, it is no longer a question of social physiology, but of what is rightfully called social physics (p. 56). We mention that these cases of regression, which imply abstractions of the same kind, if not of the same type and of the same value, reappear in various stages of scientific construction.

Cournot's work on chance and probability does not appear to have provided any new mathematical analysis, but he made three distinctions concerning the nature of probability. His book of 1843 was a text with the dual purpose of teaching the non-mathematician the rules of the calculus of probability and of dissipating the obscurities on the delicate subject of probability. He stressed the distinction between objective and subjective probability. His opening chapters provide a discussion of the appropriate combinatorics and frequency of occurrence interpretation of probability.

Cournot stressed the distinction between objective probability where frequencies are known and subjective probability. He noted:

> We could, since then, relying on the theorem of Jacques Bernoulli, who was already aware of their meaning and scope, pass immediately to the applications those theorems had in the sciences of facts and observations. However, a principle, first stated by the Englishman Bayes, and on which Condorcet, Laplace and their successors wanted to build the doctrine of 'a posteriori' probabilities, became the source of much ambiguity which must first be clarified, of serious mistakes which must be corrected and which are corrected as soon as one has in mind the fundamental distinction between probabilities which have an objective existence, which give a measure of the possibility of things, and subjective probabilities, relating partly to one's knowledge, partly to one's ignorance, depending on one's intelligence level and on the available data (p. 155).

Subjective probability rests on the consideration of events which our ignorance calls for us to treat as equiprobable due to insufficient cause.

He added a third category which he entitled 'philosophical probability', 'where probabilities are not reducible to an enumeration of chances' but 'which depend mainly on the idea that we have of the simplicity of the laws of nature' (chapter 17, p. 440).

Cournot's views on probability appear to be intimately related to his concern for social statistics and economic modelling. Although he did not establish formal links between his mathematical economics models and chance, he regarded history and the development of institutions as dependent on chance and economics as set in the context of institutions.

Cournot was at best an indifferent mathematician. Bertrand clearly dominated him in that profession. But from his own writings it is clear that Cournot was well aware of both his purpose in applying mathematics to economics and his limitations as a mathematician. At the age of 58 he wrote his *Souvenirs* which he finished in Dijon in October 1859. They were published many years later with an introduction by Botinelli (1913). In these writings Cournot provides his self assessment as a mathematician.

> I was starting to be a little known in the academic world through a fairly large number of scientific articles. This was the basis of my fortune. Some of these articles ended up with Mr. Poisson, who was then the leader in Mathematics at the Institute, and mainly at the University, and he liked them particularly. He found in them philosophical insight, which I think was not all that wrong. Furthermore, he foresaw that I would go a long way in the field of pure mathematical speculation, which was (I always thought it and never hesitated to say it) one of his mistakes.

The general tenor of his *Souvenirs* is of a moderately conservative, quietly humourous, self-effacing man with considerable understanding of his environment and a broad belief in science and its value to society.

Regarding his work as a whole, his dedication and power as the founder of mathematical economics and the promoter of empirical numerical investigations emerges. He strove for around forty years to have his ideas accepted. He did so with persistence and humour (referring to his major work as 'mon opuscule'). He understood the need to wait for a generation to die. And before his death with the work and words of Jevons and Walras he saw the vindication of his approach.

SELECTED WORKS

1838. *Researches into the Mathematical Principles of the Theory of Wealth*. Trans. N.T. Bacon, New York: Macmillan, 1899, reprinted 1929.

1841. *Traité élémentaire de la théorie des fonctions et du calcul infinitésimal*. 2nd edn, Paris: Hachette, 1857.

1843. *Exposition de la théorie des chances et des probabilités*. Paris: Hachette.

1861. *Traité de l'enchaînement des idées fondamentales dans les sciences et dans l'histoire*. New edn, Paris: Hachette, 1911.

1863. *Principes de la théorie des richesses*. Paris: Hachette.

1872. *Considérations sur la marche des idées et des évènements dans les temps modernes*. 2 vols, Paris: Boivin, 1934.

1875. *Matérialisme, vitalisme, rationalisme: Études des données de la science en philosophie.* Paris: Hachette, 1923.

1877. *Revue sommaire des doctrines économiques.* Paris: Hachette.

1913. *Souvenirs* (1760–1860). With an introduction by E.P. Botinelli. Paris: Hachette. Published posthumously.

1973. *A.A. Cournot Oeuvres Complètes.* 5 vols, ed. André Robinet, Paris: Librairie Philosophique J. Vrin.

BIBLIOGRAPHY

Aumann, R.J. 1964. Markets with a continuum of traders. *Econometrica* 32, 39–50.

Bertrand, J.L.F. 1883. (Reviews of) *Théories mathematique de la richesse sociale* par Leon Walras; *Recherches sur les principes mathématiques de la théorie de la richesse* par Augustin Cournot. *Journal des Savants*, 499–508.

Chamberlin, E.H. 1933. *The Theory of Monopolistic Competition.* Cambridge, Mass.: Harvard University Press.

Edgeworth, F.Y. 1881. *Mathematical Psychics.* London: Kegan Paul; New York: A.M. Kelley, 1967.

Edgeworth, F.Y. 1925. *Papers Relating to Political Economy*, I. London: Macmillan; New York: B. Franklin, 1963.

Fisher, I. 1892. *Mathematical Investigations in the Theory of Value and Prices.* New Haven: Connecticut Academy of Arts and Sciences. Reprinted New York: Augustus M. Kelley, 1961.

Guillebaud, C.W. (ed.) 1961. *Marshall's Principles of Economics.* Vol. II, *Notes.* London and New York: Macmillan.

Guitton, H. 1968. Antoine Augustin Cournot. In *The International Encyclopedia of the Social Sciences*, Vol. 3, New York: Macmillan and Free Press.

Hotelling, H. 1929. Stability in competition. *Economic Journal* 34, 41–57.

Jevons, W.S. 1911. *The Theory of Political Economy.* 4th edn, London: Macmillan, 1931; 5th edn, New York, Kelley & Millman, 1957.

Mayberry, J., Nash, J.F. and Shubik, M. 1953. A comparison of treatments of a duopoly situation. *Econometrica* 21, 141–55.

Nash, J.F., Jr. 1951. Noncooperative games. *Annals of Mathematics* 54, 289–95.

Palomba, G. 1984. Introduction à l'oeuvre de Cournot. *Economie Appliquée* 37, 7–97. Trans. from Italian, extracted from *Cournot Opere*, Turin: UTET (1981).

Ricardo, D. 1817. *The Principles of Political Economy and Taxation.* Homewood, Ill.: R.D. Irwin, 1963. London: J.M. Dent, 1965.

Robinson, J. 1933. *The Economics of Imperfect Competition.* London: Macmillan; New York: St. Martin's Press, 1954.

Shubik, M. 1959. Edgeworth market games. In *Contributions to the Theory of Games IV*, ed. A.W. Tucker and R.D. Luce, Princeton, NJ: Princeton University Press.

Shubik, M. 1984. *A Game Theoretic Approach to Political Economy.* Cambridge, Mass: MIT Press.

Walras, L. 1874–7. *Elements of Pure Economics.* Trans. W. Jaffé, London: George Allen & Unwin, 1954; Homewood, Ill.: R.D. Irwin, 1954.

Differential Games

SIMONE CLEMHOUT AND HENRY Y. WAN, JR.

A differential game studies system dynamics determined by the interactions of agents with divergent purposes. As a limit form of multi-stage games, its noncooperative solution is subgame perfect; thus it may facilitate the study of credible threats and repeated play. Reducing each stage to a single point in continuous time, differential game applies control theoretic tools (including phase diagrams) to yield results more general and more detailed than other methods. Its applications range from common-property resource utilization to macro-economic stabilization.

MODEL. A differential game has four components: (a) a *state space*, X, where x in X embodies all relevant data at a particular stage, (b) a *time horizon*, T: a closed interval with a final instant equal to infinity or decided by some termination rule, (c) a *set of players*, $\bar{N} = \{1, \ldots, i, \ldots, N\}$, with each player distinguished by four aspects: (1) a *space for possible moves* (or 'controls', K_i; (2) a *point-to-set correspondence for allowable moves*, $C_i: X \times T \overset{\rightarrow}{\rightarrow} K_i, (x, t) \mapsto C_i(x, t)$, which vary with (x, t); (3) a *space for admissible 'strategies'* (or 'policies'), $R_i = \{r_i r_i: X \times T \to \cup_{X \times T} C_i(x, t)$ and r_i satisfies *additional conditions*\}, where each r_i assigns an allowable move at every (x, t); and (4) the *instantaneous payoff* $u_i: X \times T \times \Pi_j K_j \to R, ((x, t), (c_j)) \mapsto u_i((x, t), (c_j))$. The additional conditions include (i) any restrictions on the information used for decisions, (ii) regularity conditions (e.g., being step-wise continuous) needed for a well defined model. (d) A *state equation* for state transition, $F: X \times T \times \Pi_j K_j \to X, ((x, t), (c_j)) \mapsto \dot{x}, X$ and $K_1, \ldots, K_n$ are all subsets of Euclidean spaces.

Players select *strategies* at the outset, not piecemeal *moves*. Strategies are defined here as state-and-time dependent or 'feedback' strategies including the subclass which are 'open-loop' or time-dependent (only).

AN EXAMPLE WITH TWO VARIATIONS. Two users share a natural resource, which may be a petroleum reserve or fishery, under common-property tenure. The state space X is the set of all non-negative resource levels and the time horizon is

$T = [0, t_f]$ where $t_f = +\infty$ or the instant when all the resource is used up. For all (x, t), $i = 1, 2$, and the 'allowable moves' form a set $C_i(x, t) = K_i = R_+$, the set of all non-negative rates of use. Specimens of strategies include $r_i = kx$ for some $k \geqslant 0$, or $r_i = g(t)$ for some non-negative-valued function. The instantaneous payoffs of both players are assumed to be: $u_i = \exp(-at) \log c_i$ for some $a > 0$. The 'state equation' is: $dx/dt = f(x) - c_1 - c_2$ where: $f(x) = 0$ for the case of petroleum reserves, and $f(x) = x(b - \log x)$ for the fishery. The latter form agrees with the Gompertz recruitment function.

SOLUTION CONCEPTS. How players choose strategies under various scenarios is summarized as three *solution concepts*, i.e. (1) *The noncooperative equilibrium* (Cournot–Nash): each player's choice is his 'best reply' to the choices of all other players. This choice must be 'best' for all initial (x, t); (2) *The cooperative equilibrium* (Pareto): all players make choices such that no modification can benefit any player without harming another. This property holds for all initial (x, t); (3) *The hierarchical equilibrium* (Stackelberg): the 'leader' selects a committed choice to elicit the followers' 'best replies' so that the leader's payoff is maximized.

An equilibrium is a vector of strategies, one for each player, which is not liable to change. In differential games, players may change strategies in midgame, unless prevented by prior commitment (as in (3)), or by requiring the choices to be appropriate, once *and* forever (as in (1) and (2)). Significantly, the Cournot–Nash solution is thus subgame perfect à la Selten.

The Cournot–Nash solution is most frequently used. In particular, it depicts externalities under laissez-faire. For any problem it can be compared to Pareto solutions which assess any extra gains resulting from cooperation.

If an acknowledged leader (e.g. the *government* in a macroeconomy) can offer credible commitments, he prefers to play Stackelberg (with a higher payoff for himself) rather than Cournot–Nash, since all followers' best replies are now under his influence rather than given independently.

The differential game sheds light on two additional features: (i) the *credibility* of the leader's professed strategy which is at issue, since he has both (a) the opportunity to renege on promises made and honoured at different times, and (b) the incentive to renege (his choice is subgame imperfect); (ii) 'Reputation' (rather than 'enforcement') is often the reason why commitments are kept, and may be modelled as a state variable as suggested in Clemhout and Wan (1979). Hence credibility is established from a balance of the gains of reneging with the damage from reputation lost. This suggests a synergistic approach between Cournot–Nash and Stackelberg.

ALTERNATIVE FORMULATIONS OF COURNOT–NASH MODELS OVER TIME. To characterize the Cournot–Nash differential game in feedback strategy, one contrasts it with alternative versions of differing assumptions, 'what information players use' and 'the modelling of time'. Examples show that:

(a) To explain *reality* and provide *policy relevance*, 'feedback' strategies are preferable to 'open-loop' strategies for two reasons; (1) in noncooperative games, the subgame-perfect equilibrium is the image of reality, and (2) in models of common-property resources, policy relevance hinges on identifying the source of inefficiency. Our petroleum example (cf. Clemhout and Wan, 1985a) is a noncooperative model of common-property utilization, and thus should have an *inefficient* but *subgame-perfect* equilibrium. This is the case when strategies are 'feedbacks'. The opposite is true if strategies are modelled as 'open-loop' in which all equilibria are then *efficient* and *subgame-imperfect* and each is compatible only with one initial resource stock.

(b) For *reasonableness* and *convenience*, 'history-dependent state variables' are preferable to 'history-dependent strategies'. While history matters in contexts such as performance contracts, history-dependent strategies tend to require an infinite amount of information at every move. The use of history-dependent state variables (Smale, 1980, cf. Clemhout and Wan, 1979) is a reasonable alternative for players with bounded rationality. It also conforms to the finite-dimensional state space in differential games.

(c) For *game-theoretic* and *analytic* reasons 'continuous time' is preferable to 'discrete time'. Our fishery example (Clemhout and Wan, 1985a) illustrates two points. First, only in continuous time is the model a game, according to Ichiishi (1983). To ensure non-negativity of the resource level, discrete-time models require the allowability of one player's move to depend upon the moves of all others at the same time, thus they become 'pseudo-games' by losing playability. The second point is that only in continuous time are the dual variables (which are analytically important) derivable from the conditions necessary for optimality whether the recruitment function is concave or not. This is because the adjoint system, in differential equation form, involves the slope of the recruitment function alone and not its curvature.

STRENGTHS OF DIFFERENTIAL GAMES. Differential games can obtain precise results either independently of particular functional forms, or by using empirically validated formulations. In our fishery example these include characterization of the resource level: (a) does it reach a sustained level? (b) does it approach extinction asymptotically, if so, how rapidly? (c) is it heading for extinction in finite time? (d) what difference do risks of random perturbation or extinction make? (e) what if several harvested species form pre-predator chains? and (f) do tax-incentives improve allocation efficiency? (Clemhout and Wan, 1985a,b,c).

In contrast with differential games, intuitive reasoning or simple examples (in two or three periods) can suggest certain outcomes, but cannot rule out the opposite outcome occurring in plausible situations. Simulation models can start from any assumptions but cannot assure equilibrium.

In macro-economics, the linear-quadratic-Gaussian differential game can further quantitatively analyse real-life data. The estimation and interpretation of the parameters in such models is still subject to ongoing research. The same model also yields deep economic insights in their micro-economic applications.

131

CONCLUDING REMARKS. Pioneered by Isaacs and generalized by Case, the theory of differential games is now covered by excellent texts (e.g., Basar and Olsder, 1982), with reference to contributions by Blaquiere, Berkovitz, Cruz, Fleming, Friedman, Haurie, Ho and Leitmann, among others. Further progress in its economic applications now hinges on the development of 'techniques of analysis', akin to phase diagrams in control theory. Using these techniques one can deduce implications crucial to economists working with particular classes of models. This is often accomplished by utilizing structural properties common to entire families of models. The explicit solutions are neither required nor derived. Such feats are clearly attainable for differential games, as they have been for control models: the phase diagram itself has been recently applied to some models (Clemhout and Wan, 1985b) and contraction mappings in others (Stokey, 1985). Given the state of the art in this field, additional advances in theory (e.g., generalizing the model, proposing new solution concepts, etc.) are certainly most welcome, but no longer crucial for economic applications.

BIBLIOGRAPHY

Basar, T. and Olsder, G.J. 1982. *Dynamic Noncooperative Game Theory*. New York: Academic Press.

Clemhout, S. and Wan, H., Jr. 1979. Interactive economic dynamics and differential games. *Journal of Optimization, Theory and Applications* 27(1), 7–30.

Clemhout, S. and Wan, H., Jr. 1985a. Resource exploitation and ecological degradations as differential games. *Journal of Optimization, Theory and Applications*, August.

Clemhout, S. and Wan, H., Jr. 1985b. Cartelization conserves endangered species? In *Optimal Control Theory and Economic Analysis 2*, ed. G. Feichtinger, Amsterdam: North-Holland.

Clemhout, S. and Wan, H., Jr. 1985c. Common-property exploitations under risks of resource extinctions. In *Dynamic Games and Applications in Economics*, ed. T. Basar. New York: Springer-Verlag.

Ichiishi, T. 1983. *Game Theory for Economic Analysis*. New York: Academic Press.

Smale, S. 1980. The Prisoner's Dilemma and dynamical systems associated to non-cooperative games. *Econometrica* 48(7), November, 1917–34.

Stokey, N. 1985. The dynamics of industry-wide learning. In *Essays in Honour of Kenneth J. Arrow*, ed. W.P. Heller, R.M. Starr and D.A. Starrett, Cambridge: Cambridge University Press.

Duopoly

JAMES W. FRIEDMAN

A duopoly is a market in which two firms sell a product to a large number of consumers. Each consumer is too small to affect the market price for the product: that is, on the buyers' side, the market is competitive. Therefore, in its essence duopoly is a two-player variable-sum game. Each of the two duopolists is a rational decision-maker whose actions will affect both himself and his rival. Although the interests of the duopolists are intertwined, they are not wholly coincident nor wholly in conflict. In contrast to the agents in competitive markets, the duopolists must each concern themselves with what the other duopolist is likely to do.

The situation facing the duopolists is noncooperative in the sense that they are barred from making binding agreements with one another. The relevance of this depends crucially on whether the model is a static market (i.e. a one-time-only, or one-shot market) or a market consisting of many time periods.

The first study of duopoly is the great contribution of Cournot (1838) in which the decision problem of the firms is posed for a homogeneous products market in a static setting. The equilibrium concept proposed by Cournot, variously called the *Cournot equilibrium* or the *Cournot–Nash equilibrium*, has become a cornerstone of noncooperative game theory. To sketch his model let x and y be the output levels of firms A and B, let $f(x + y)$ be the inverse demand function for the market, let $C(x)$ and $\Gamma(y)$ be the two firms' total cost functions, and let their respective profit functions be $\pi^A = xf(x + y) - C(x)$ and $\pi^B = yf(x + y) - \Gamma(y)$.

Cournot proposed as an equilibrium a pair of output levels (x, y) such that neither firm could have obtained higher profit by having chosen some other output. Thus π^A is maximized with respect to x (with y given), while, simultaneously, π^B is maximized with respect to y (with x given). If $x^c > 0$ and $y^c > 0$ the Cournot equilibrium is a solution to the simultaneous equations

$$\frac{\partial \pi^A}{\partial x} = f(x + y) + xf'(x + y) - C'(x) = 0$$

133

$$\frac{\partial \pi^B}{\partial y} = f(x + y) + y f'(x + y) - \Gamma'(x) = 0.$$

The Cournot equilibrium defines consistency conditions. If firm A contemplates (x^c, y^c) as an outcome, and believes firm B is contemplating the same output pair, then firm A will see (a) that it cannot do better than to choose x^c (given the expectation that firm B will choose y^c) and (b) that, should firm B go through the same thought process, it will reach a parallel conclusion.

To translate this model into the language of game theory, player A chooses a *strategy* x from the set of all allowed output levels, say all $x \geqslant 0$. This set, $(0, \infty)$, is called the *strategy space* or *strategy set* of the player. Similarly for player B. The players' *payoff functions* are their respective profit functions. Thus the payoff function of a player gives his payoff as a function of the strategies of all players in the game. At a noncooperative equilibrium (see Nash, 1951; Owen, 1968, or Friedman, 1986) no player could obtain a higher payoff through the use of a different strategy, given the strategies of the other players. Note, finally, that the actual behaviour of one duopolist cannot affect the actual behaviour of the other in this static setting, because they choose their output levels simultaneously. They do take one another into account in making decisions by analysing the game using *both* payoff functions.

Cournot's contribution went largely unnoticed for nearly half a century, after which it was scathingly reviewed by Bertrand (1883). Bertrand berates Cournot on two grounds. First he says that the firms will collude to achieve monopoly-like profits. This possibility is acknowledged by Cournot who made a conscious choice to explore behaviour in the absence of collusion. Bertrand's point was echoed later by Chamberlin (1933), although neither of them showed how the duopolists could be expected to maintain a collusive agreement nor did they solve the problem of the distribution of profits between the firms. These issues are addressed below in connection with recent developments.

Bertrand's second criticism is that price, not output, should be the firm's decision variable. Then, using Cournot's *mineral spring* example in which $C(x) = \Gamma(y) = 0$, he sketches the Bertrand equilibrium, arguing that consumers will buy from the firm charging the lower price, and showing that the only prices that can be in equilibrium are zero for both firms. Bertrand's equilibrium concept is precisely that of Cournot, transferred to the price choosing variant of Cournot's model. Bertrand's analysis was taken up, elaborated and extended by Edgeworth (1897). He supposed that the firms have production capacity limits, each of which is less than the market demand at zero price. Consequently no pair of prices is an equilibrium.

While the logic of Bertrand and Edgeworth is correct, the economic relevance is dubious. Real world firms choose both prices and output levels; however, the discontinuity of one firm's scales with respect to another firm's decision variable is *not* an obvious feature of economic life. Consequently, the Cournot formulation seems preferable. A way to reconcile price choosing firms with an absence of demand discontinuities is via differentiated products models.

Edgeworth and many of his contemporaries though there was no worthwhile content in Cournot's duopoly theory. Edgeworth (1925, p. 111), writing forty years after Bertrand, said 'Now the demolition of Cournot's theory is generally accepted, Professor Amoroso is singular in his fidelity to Cournot'. Amoroso's good judgement was shared by Wicksell (1925). It is now generally accepted that Cournot was the first to perceive clearly and enunciate the game theoretic concept of *noncooperative equilibrium*, which received a general statement from Nash (1951) and is the cornerstone of one of the main parts of game theory.

The next influential innovation is due to Bowley (1924) who invented the conjectural variation (which later received this name from Frisch, 1933). He wrote the two firms' first order conditions for equilibrium as $\partial \pi^A / \partial x + (\partial \pi^A / \partial y)(\partial y / \partial x) = 0$ for firm A and $\partial \pi^B / \partial y + (\partial \pi^B / \partial x)(\partial x / \partial y) = 0$ for firm B. The $\partial y / \partial x$ in firm A's condition indicates the way that A thinks B's output choice will vary according to the way that A varies his own output choice. A parallel meaning attaches to $\partial x / \partial y$ in B's first order condition. The presence of these conjectural variation terms is indefensible in a static model, but it shows the underlying concern that writers had with dynamic models, while, at the same time, limiting their formal analysis to static models. Given that the model is static with the two firms simultaneously selecting outputs, *and doing so only once*, there can be no conjectural variation. B's output choice will depend on what B expects A to do, but that expectation will not vary as A changes his mind about what output to select. B's expectation depends on B's thought processes and the information B has about the structure of the model, and does not depend on A's actual thought processes.

Dynamic elements of reaction of one firm to the choice of another go back to Cournot who performed a 'stability' analysis. He solved $\partial \pi^A / \partial x = 0$ to obtain $x = v(y)$ and $\partial \pi^B / \partial y = 0$ to obtain $y = w(x)$. He looked for conditions under which, starting from an arbitrary x^0, the sequence (x_n, y^{n+1}) for $n = 0, 2, 4, \ldots$ would converge to (x^c, y^c), the Cournot equilibrium. Bertrand and Edgeworth also wrote of actions and reactions, and Bowley introduces a new reactive element with his conjectural variation terms. Later Stackelberg (1934) posed the leader–follower duopoly in which one firm, say A, chooses x and, after that choice is communicated to B, y is chosen. B will always choose y according to $y = w(x)$ and this is known to A who maximizes $\pi^A = xf[x + w(x)] - C(x)$ with respect to x. Note that a conjectural variation term for A makes a legitimate appearance because B's decision is, in fact, a function of A's choice. Wicksell (1925) and Bowley (1928) anticipate Stackelberg's leader–follower equilibrium in their discussions of bilateral monopoly. All of these treatments strongly suggest an explicitly multiperiod formulation under which each firm maximizes a discounted profit stream and behaves according to a *reaction function* under which a firm's output choice in time t is selected as a function of the other firm's output choice in time $t - 1$. The last twenty years have seen such analysis, beginning with Friedman (1968).

The next major step in duopoly was the recognition that, in many industries, the firms sell very similar, non-identical products. In such a market, it is equally easy to represent the firms as price choosers or as quantity choosers. In either case, equilibrium can readily involve the firms selling at different prices. The pioneers here are Hotelling (1929) and Chamberlin (1933). To sketch a differentiated products duopoly, let the firm's prices be p and r, and let their demand functions be $x = \phi(p, r)$ and $y = \psi(p, r)$, respectively. The two firms are assumed to produce gross (but imperfect) substitutes, so $\phi_r(p, r) > 0$ and $\psi_p(p, r) > 0$, but the own-price derivatives (ϕ_p and ψ_r) are negative and both firms' total revenues are bounded. Profit functions are $\pi^A = p\phi(p, r) - C[\phi(p, r)]$ and $\pi^B = r\psi(p, r) - \Gamma[\psi(p, r)]$. A noncooperative (Cournot–Nash) equilibrium occurs at a price pair (p^c, r^c) for which π^A is maximized with respect to p (given $r = r^c$) and π^B is maximized with respect to r (given $p = p^c$).

Many writers have maintained that the Cournot equilibrium should not be expected to occur in practice because it does not lie on the firm's profit possibility frontier. In addition to Bertrand and Chamberlin there is a famous passage in Smith (1776) maintaining that people in the same line of business will attempt to collude whenever they get together. In response to such observations several points can be made. Smith's passage is a comment in passing that is not made within an analytical framework, so it cannot be closely judged. Bertrand and Chamberlin are discussing specific models within which their remarks do not hold up well, because the consistency condition embodied in the Cournot equilibrium is quite compelling and would be violated by collusive behaviour. Any agreement between the two firms – in a static setting where binding agreements cannot be made – will break down because at least one firm will note that, given the agreed decision for the rival, it can do better by violating its agreement. But both firms can perceive the incentives of either one of them, thus the only acceptable agreement in such circumstances is for a price pair (or output pair, if the firms are output choosers) such that, given the price of its rival, neither firm can gain by deviating from its agreement. Such a *self-enforcing agreement* is merely a noncooperative equilibrium. We are back at Cournot.

However, this is far from the last word on collusion in the absence of legally binding agreements. Bertrand and Chamberlin, and others who have made, or agreed with, their assertion probably are motivated by a belief that voluntary collusion sometimes occurs in actual markets. They may be correct in their empirical observation; however, it remains true that voluntary collusion is not convincing in the traditional one-shot models. Therefore, the clear suggestion is that one-shot models are simply inadequate for analysing voluntary collusion. Suppose, then, that the model is changed to have an infinite horizon with each firm having a discount parameter of α. Then, letting t denote time, player A seeks to maximize

$$\sum_{t=0}^{\infty} \alpha^t \pi^A = \sum_{t=0}^{\infty} \alpha^t [p_t \phi(p_t, r_t) - C[\phi(p_t, r_t)]],$$

and the objective function of player B is

$$\sum_{t=0}^{\infty} \alpha^t \pi^B = \sum_{t=0}^{\infty} \alpha^t [r_t \psi(p_t, r_t) - \Gamma[\psi(p_t, r_t)]].$$

Strategy becomes much more complex than in the static model, because there will be an infinite succession of price choices by each firm and, prior to making a price choice any time after $t = 0$, the firm will know what past prices have been selected by its rival. For each t, a firm can choose its price according to a function (i.e. a rule) that depends on *all* past price choices of both of them. The rule for one period can be different from the rule for another. A strategy for a firm is a collection of such rules, one for each period t.

In this model it may be possible to find a noncooperative equilibrium that yields an outcome on the profit possibility frontier. Such an equilibrium is based on three critical prices for each firm. First there is (p^c, r^c), the Cournot price pair. Second there is (p^*, r^*), chosen so that profits at (p^*, r^*) are on the profit possibility frontier and are higher for each firm than at (p^c, r^c). Third define p' as the price for A that maximizes $\pi^A = p\phi(p, r^*) - C[\phi(p, r^*)]$, and define r' in a parallel way for B. Now consider the following strategy for firm A: $p_0 = p^*$, $p_t = p^*$ for $t > 0$ if $(p_k, r_k) = (p^*, r^*)$ for $k = 0, \ldots, t - 1$, and $p_t = p^c$ otherwise. Imagine a parallel strategy for B. These strategies amount to a firm saying 'I will begin by cooperating and will continue to cooperate as long as we both have cooperated in the past. If ever a lapse from cooperation occurs, I will revert to static Cournot behaviour'.

Whether this pair of strategies is a noncooperative equilibrium depends on the sizes of α and the profits at (p^*, r^*), (p', r^*), (p^*, r') and (p^c, r^c). A's choice boils down to comparing (i) receiving the profit associated with (p^*, r^*) in all periods or (ii) obtaining the larger profit associated with (p', r^*) for just one period and the reduced profit associated with (p^c, r^c) in all subsequent periods. If α is near enough to one, both firms will prefer alternative (i). Thus both firms can be better off following the 'cooperative' strategy. Note, however, that this cooperative outcome is the result of following noncooperative equilibrium strategies. The strategy pair is chosen so that no single firm can increase its payoff by altering its strategy, given the strategy of the of the other firm. The strategies are designed so that deviating from cooperative behaviour is followed by punishment, and the punishment is carefully crafted so that it will be in the interests of all players to carry it out when the strategies call for it. This latter property, that the threats of punishment are credible because they are incentive compatible, is called *subgame perfection*. On the concept of subgame perfect noncooperative equilibria, see Selten (1975) or Friedman (1986).

The work of Hotelling and Chamberlin raises an important issue that has received some recent attention: firms not only choose prices (or output levels), they decide on the design of their products. In deciding on how to design a product, the firm needs to known how design is related to cost of production and how it is related to consumers' tastes. The latter has been modelled by Lancaster (1979) in terms of inherent characteristics. The underlying notion is that consumers value certain attributes of goods that are analogous to the nutrients in foods. A particular product (e.g. a chair of a given design) is a specific bundle of characteristics. The product of a rival seller is a somewhat different bundle of characteristics. A difficulty with this approach in the most general form that Lancaster discusses is that it is difficult to define these characteristics. Less abstract versions are used in oligopoly models where, following Hotelling, physical location is used as the only characteristic chosen by firms. Any single measurable attribute, such as sweetness of a bottled drink, can also be used.

Other topics treated in the duopoly theory literature include capital stock decisions, advertising and entry. They can be found in Friedman (1983), along with a fuller account of the topics sketched above.

BIBLIOGRAPHY

Bertrand, J. 1883. Review of Cournot (1838). *Journal des Savants*, 499–508.

Bowley, A. 1924. *The Mathematical Groundwork of Economics.* New York: Kelley, 1965.

Bowley, A. 1928. Bilateral monopoly. *Economic Journal* 38, 651–9.

Chamberlin, E. 1933. *The Theory of Monopolistic Competition*, 7th edn, Cambridge: Harvard, 1956.

Cournot, A. 1838. *Recherches sur les principes mathématiques de la théorie des richesses.* Trans. N.T.Bacon, New York: Macmillan, 1927.

Edgeworth, F. 1897. The pure theory of monopoly. *Papers Relating to Political Economy*, vol. I, 111–42.

Edgeworth, F. 1925. *Papers Relating to Political Economy.* New York: Burt Franklin, 1970.

Friedman, J. 1968. Reaction functions and the theory of duopoly. *Review of Economic Studies* 35, 257–72.

Friedman, J. 1983. *Oligopoly Theory.* Cambridge: Cambridge University Press.

Friedman, J. 1986. *Game Theory with Applications to Economics.* New York: Oxford University Press.

Frisch, R. 1933. Monopole – polypole – la notion de force dans l'économie. *Festschrift til Harald Westergaard.* Supplement to *Nationalekonomisk Tidsskrift.*

Hotelling, H. 1929. Stability in competition. *Economic Journal* 39, 41–57.

Lancaster, K. 1979. *Variety, Equity, and Efficiency.* New York: Columbia University Press.

Nash, J. 1951. Noncooperative games. *Annals of Mathematics* 45, 286–95.

Owen, G. 1968. *Game Theory.* 2nd edn, New York: Academic Press, 1982.

Selten, R. 1975. Reexamination of the perfectness concept for equilibrium points in extensive games. *International Journal of Game Theory* 4, 25–55.

Smith, A. 1776. *An Inquiry into the Nature and Causes of the Wealth of Nations.* Ed. R.H. Campbell, A.S. Skinner and W.M. Todd, Oxford: Clarendon Press, 1976.

Stackelberg, H. von. 1934. *Marktform und Gleichgewicht.* Vienna: Julius Springer.

Wicksell, K. 1925. Mathematical economics. In K. Wicksell, *Selected Papers on Economic Theory*, ed. Erik Lindahl, Cambridge, Mass.: Harvard University Press, 1958.

Extensive Form Games

ERIC VAN DAMME

The most general model used to describe conflict situations is the extensive form model, which specifies in detail the dynamic evolution of each situation and thus provides an exact description of 'who knows what when' and 'what is the consequence of which'. The model should contain all relevant aspects of the situation; in particular, any possibility of (pre)commitment should be explicitly included. This implies that the game should be analysed by solution concepts from noncooperative game theory, that is, refinements of Nash equilibria. The term extensive form game was coined in von Neumann and Morgenstern (1944) in which a set theoretic approach was used. We will describe the graph theoretical representation proposed in Kuhn (1953) that has become the standard model. For convenience, attention will be restricted to finite games.

The basic element in the Kuhn representation of an n-person extensive form grame is a rooted tree, that is, a directed acyclic graph with a distinguished vertex. The game starts at the root of the tree. The tree's terminal nodes correspond to the endpoints of the game and associated with each of these there is an n-vector of real numbers specifying the payoff to each player (in von Neumann–Morgenstern utilities) that results from that play. The nonterminal nodes represent the decision points in the game. Each such point is labelled with an index i ($i \in \{0, 1, \ldots, n\}$) indicating which player has to move at that point. Player O is the chance player who performs the moves of nature. A maximal set of decision points that a player cannot distinguish between is called an information set. A choice at an information set associates a unique successor to every decision point in this set, hence, a choice consists of a set of edges, exactly one edge emanating from each point in the set. Information sets of the chance player are singletons and the probability of each choice of chance is specified. Formally then, an extensive form game is a sixtuple $\Gamma = (K, P, U, C, p, h)$ which respectively specify the underlying tree, the player labelling, the information sets, the choices, the probabilities of chance choices and the payoffs.

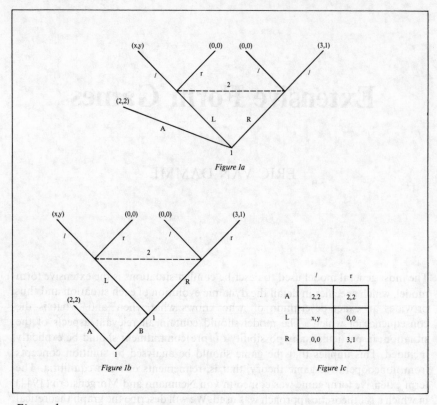

Figure 1

As an example, consider the 2-person game of Figure 1a. First player 1 has to move. If he chooses *A*, the game terminates with both players receiving 2. If he chooses *L* or *R*, player 2 has to move and, when he is called to move, this player does not know whether *L* or *R* has been chosen. Hence, the 2 decision points of player 2 constitute an information set and this is indicated by a dashed line connecting the points. If the choices *L* and *ℓ* are taken, then player 1 receives *x*, while player 2 gets *y*. The payoff vectors at the other endpoints are listed similarly, that is, with player 1's payoff first. The game of Figure 1b differs from that in Figure 1a only in the fact that now player 1 has to choose between *L* and *R* only after he has decided not to choose *A*. In this case, the game admits a proper subgame starting at the second decision point of player 1. This subgame can also be interpreted as the players making their choices simultaneously.

A strategy is a complete specification of how a player intends to play in every contingency that might arise. It can be planned in advance and can be given to an agent (or a computing machine) who can then play on behalf of the player. A pure strategy specifies a single choice at each information set, a behaviour strategy prescribes local randomization among choices at information sets and a mixed strategy requires a player to randomize several pure strategies at the beginning of the game. The normal form of an extensive game is a table listing all pure strategy combinations and the payoff vectors resulting from them. Figure 1c displays the normal form of Figure 1a, and, up to inessential details, this also represents the game of Figure 1b. The normal form suppresses the dynamic structure of the extensive game and condenses all decision-making into one stage. This normalization offers a major conceptual simplification, at the expense of computational complexity: the set of strategies may be so large that normalization is not practical. Below we return to the question of whether essential information is destroyed when a game is normalized.

A game is said to be of perfect recall if each player always remembers what he has previously known or done, that is, if information is increasing over time. A game may fail to have perfect recall when a player is in a team such as in bridge and in this case behaviour strategies may be inferior to mixed strategies since the latter allow for complete correlation between different agents of the team. However, by modelling different agents as different players with the same payoff function one can restore perfect recall, hence, in the literature attention is usually restricted to this class of games. In Kuhn (1953) and Aumann (1964) it has been shown that, if there is perfect recall, the restriction to behaviour strategies is justified.

A game is said to be of perfect information if all information sets are singletons, that is, if there are no simultaneous moves and if each player always is perfectly informed about anything that happened in the past. In this case, there is no need to randomize and the game can be solved by working backwards from the end (as already observed in Zermelo, 1913). For generic games, this procedure yields a unique solution which is also the solution obtained by iterative elimination of dominated strategies in the normal form. The assumption of the model that there are no external commitment possibilities implies that only this dynamic programming solution is viable; however, this generally is not the unique Nash equilibrium. In the game of Figure 2, the roll-back procedure yields (R, r) but a

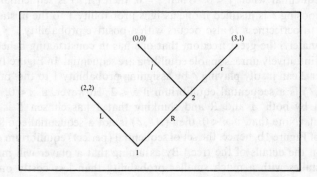

Figure 2

second equilibrium is (L, ℓ). The latter is a Nash equilibrium since player 2 does not have to execute the threat when it is believed. However, the threat is not credible: player 2 has to move only when 1 has chosen R and facing the *fait accompli* that R has been chosen, player 2 is better off choosing r. Note that it is essential that 2 cannot commit himself: If he could we would have a different game of which the outcome could perfectly well be $(2, 2)$.

A major part of noncooperative game theory is concerned with how to extend the backwards induction principle to games with imperfect information, that is how to exclude intuitively unreasonable Nash equilibria in general. This research originates with Selten (1965) in which the concept of subgame perfect equilibria was introduced, that is, of strategies that constitute an equilibrium in every subgame. If $y < 0$, then the unique equilibrium of the subgame in Figure 1b is (R, r) and, consequently, (BR, r) is the unique subgame perfect equilibrium in that case. If $x < 2$, however, then (AL, ℓ) is an equilibrium that is not subgame perfect. The game of Figure 1a does not admit any proper subgames; hence, any equilibrium is subgame perfect, in particular (A, ℓ) is subgame perfect if $x > 2$. This shows that the set of subgame perfect equilibria depends on the details of the tree and that the criterion of subgame perfection does not eliminate all intuitively unreasonable equilibria.

To remedy the latter drawback, the concept of (trembling hand) perfectness was introduced in Selten (1975). The idea behind this concept is that with a small probability players make mistakes, so that each choice is taken with an infinitesimal probability and, hence, each information set can be reached. If $y \leqslant 0$, then the unique perfect equilibrium outcome in Figure 1a and 1b is $(1, 3)$: player 2 is forced to choose r since L and R occur with positive probability.

The perfectness concept is closely related to the sequential equilibrium concept proposed in Kreps and Wilson (1982). The latter is based on the idea of 'Bayesian' players who construct subjective beliefs about where they are in the tree when an information set is reached unexpectedly and who maximize expected payoffs associated with such beliefs. The requirements that beliefs be shared by players and that they be consistent with the strategies being played (Bayesian updating) imply that the difference from perfection is only marginal. In Figure 1a, only (R, r) is sequential when $y < 0$. When $y = 0$, then (A, ℓ) is sequential, but not perfect: choosing ℓ is justified if one assigns probability 1 to the mistake L, but according to perfectness R also occurs with a positive probability.

Unfortunately, the great freedom that one has in constructing beliefs implies that many intuitively unreasonable equilibria are sequential. In Figure 1a, if $y > 0$, then player 2 can justify playing ℓ by assigning probability 1 to the 'mistake' L, hence, (A, ℓ) is a sequential equilibrium if $x \leqslant 2$. However, if $x < 0$, then L is dominated by both A and R and thinking that 1 has chosen L is certainly nonsensical. (Note that, if $x < 0$, then (AL, ℓ) is not a sequential equilibrium of the game of Figure 1b, hence, the set of sequential (perfect) equilibrium outcomes depends on the details of the tree.) By assuming that a player will make more costly mistakes with a much smaller probability than less costly ones (as in Myerson's (1978) concept of proper equilibria) one can eliminate the equilibrium

(A, ℓ) when $x \leqslant 0$ (since then L is dominated by R), but this does not work if $x > 0$. Still, the equilibrium (A, ℓ) is nonsensical if $x < 2$; If player 2 is reached, he should conclude that player 1 has passed off a payoff of 2 and, hence, that he aims for the payoff of 3 and has chosen R. Consequently, player 2 should respond by r: only the equilibrium (R, r) is viable.

What distinguished the equilibrium (R, r) in Figure 1 is that this is the only one that is stable against all small perturbations of the equilibrium strategies, and the above discussion suggests that such equilibria might be the proper objects to study. An investigation of these stable equilibria has been performed in Kohlberg and Mertens (1984) and they have shown that whether an equilibrium outcome is stable or not can already be detected in the normal form. This brings us back to the question of whether an extensive form is adequately represented by its normal form, that is, whether two extensive games with the same normal form are equivalent. One answer is that this depends on the solution concept employed: it is affirmative for Nash equilibria, for proper equilibria (van Damme, 1983, 1984) and for stable equilibria, i.e. for the strongest and the weakest concepts, but it is negative for the intermediate concepts of (subgame) perfect and sequential equilibria. A more satisfactory answer is provided by a theorem of Thompson (1952) (see Kohlberg and Mertens, 1984) that completely characterizes the class of transformations that can be applied to an extensive form game without changing its (reduced) normal form: The normal form is an adequate representation if and only if these transformations are inessential. Nevertheless, the normal form should be used with care, especially in games with incomplete information (cf. Harsanyi, 1967–8; Aumann and Maschler, 1972), or when communication is possible (cf. Myerson, 1986).

BIBLIOGRAPHY

Aumann, R.J. 1964. Mixed and behavior strategies in infinite extensive games. In *Advances in Game Theory*, ed. M. Dresher, L.S. Shapley and A.W. Tucker, Princeton: Princeton University Press.

Aumann, R.J. and Maschler, M. 1972. Some thoughts on the minimax principle. *Management Science* 18(5), January 54–63.

Harsanyi, J.C. 1967–8. Games with incomplete information played by 'Bayesian' players. *Management Science* 14; Pt I (3), November 1967, 159–82; Pt II (5), January 1968, 320–34; Pt III (7), March 1968, 486–502.

Kohlberg, E. and Mertens, J.-F. 1984. On the strategic stability of equilibria. Mimeo, Harvard Graduate School of Business Administration. Reprinted, *Econometrica* 53, 1985, 1375–85.

Kreps, D.M. and Wilson, R. 1982. Sequential equilibria. *Econometrica* 50(4), July, 863–94.

Kuhn, H.W. 1953. Extensive games and the problem of information. *Annals of Mathematics Studies* 28, 193–216.

Myerson, R.B. 1978. Refinements of the Nash Equilibrium concept. *International Journal of Game Theory* 7(2), 73–80.

Myerson, R.B. 1986. Multistage games with communication. *Econometrica* 54(2), March, 323–58.

Selten, R. 1965. Spieltheoretische Behandlung eines Oligopolmodells mit Nachfrageträgheit. *Zeitschrift für die gesamte Staatswissenschaft* 121, 301–24; 667–89.

Selten, R. 1975. Reexamination of the perfectness concept for equilibrium points in extensive games. *International Journal of Game Theory* 4(1), 25–55.

Thompson, F.B. 1952. Equivalence of games in extensive form. RAND Publication RM-769.

Van Damme, E.E.C. 1983. *Refinements of the Nash equilibrium concept*. Lecture Notes in Economics and Mathematical Systems, No. 219, Berlin: Springer-Verlag.

Van Damme, E.E.C. 1984. A relation between perfect equilibria in extensive form games and proper equilibria in normal form games. *International Journal of Game Theory* 13(1), 1–13.

Von Neumann, J. and Morgenstern, O. 1944. *Theory of Games and Economic Behavior*. Princeton: Princeton University Press.

Zermelo, E. 1913. Über eine Anwendung der Mengenlehre auf die Theorie des Schachspiels. *Proceedings, Fifth International Congress of Mathematicians* 2, 501–4.

Fair Division

VINCENT P. CRAWFORD

The theory of fair division is concerned with the design of procedures for allocating a bundle of goods among n persons who are perceived to have equal rights to the goods. Both equity (according to criteria discussed below) and efficiency are sought. The theory is of interest primarily because its approach to allocation problems enjoys some important advantages over the alternative approach suggested by neoclassical welfare economics, and because studying the sense in which procedures actually in use are equitable is a good way to learn about popular notions of equity.

The modern theory of fair division has its origins in papers by Steinhaus (1948) and Dubins and Spanier (1961), who described methods (attributed by Steinhaus in part to S. Banach and K. Knaster) for sharing a perfectly divisible 'cake' among n people. In the method described by Steinhaus, the people are ordered (randomly, if desired) and the first person cuts a slice from the cake. Then each other person, in turn, may diminish the slice if he wishes. The last person to diminish the slice must take it as his share, with the slice reverting to the first person if no one chooses to diminish it. The process then continues, sharing the remainder of the cake in the same way among those people who have not yet received a share.

In the closely related method described by Dubins and Spanier, one person passes a knife continuously over the cake, at each instant determing a well-defined slice, which grows over time. The first other person to indicate his willingness to accept the slice then determined by the knife's location receives it as his share. The process then continues as before.

These n-person fair-division schemes are in the spirit of the classical two-person method of divide and choose, in which one person divides the cake into two portions and the other then chooses between them. Neither n-person scheme, however, is a true generalization of the two-person method. Steinhaus (1950) proposed a three-person scheme (formalized and generalized to n persons by

Kuhn, 1967) that is a true generalization. In this scheme, one person divides the cake into n portions and the others announce which of the portions are acceptable to them. Then, if it is possible to give each of the others a share acceptable to him, this is done. Otherwise, it is possible to assign a share to the divider in such a way that it is still feasible to give each other person $1/n$th of the cake in his own estimation. This share is assigned, and the process then continues as before.

Each of these schemes is fair in the sense that, under reasonably general conditions (see Kuhn, 1967), it allows each person to ensure, independent of the others' behaviour, that he will obtain at least $1/n$th of the total value of the cake in his estimation. In the Steinhaus (1948) method, if a person is called upon to cut, he takes a slice with $1/n$th the value of the original cake; and a person given an opportunity to diminish a slice reduces it to $1/n$th value, if possible, or does nothing if it already has value $1/n$th or less. In the method described by Dubins and Spanier, each person indicates his willingness to accept any slice whose value reaches $1/n$th of the total value of the cake. Finally, in the method of Steinhaus (1950), the divider divides the cake into n portions, each acceptable to him, and the others declare acceptable all portions they deem to have at least $1/n$th of the value of the entire cake.

These results are of considerable interest, but are incomplete in several ways. First, they ignore the question of efficiency, which is central to the problem of designing allocation mechanisms.

Second, although it does not involve interpersonal comparisons, the notion of fairness employed is inherently cardinal, and therefore difficult to make operational. This obscures a major advantage of the fair-division approach over that of neoclassical welfare economics.

Finally, when operationally meaningful notions of fairness are employed in an environment with nontrivial efficiency issues, the fact that each person has a strategy that ensures him at least his share of the cake does not guarantee that allocations resulting from strategic behaviour are fair: a person might give up the social desideratum of fairness to get more of the goods he desires.

The modern theory of fair division answers these criticisms by studying the implications of rational behaviour and employing a different concept of equity. A fair procedure is defined as one that always yields a fair allocation, in the sense formalized by Foley (1967): an allocation is *fair* if and only if no person prefers any other person's share to his own.

Kolm (1972) and Crawford (1977) (see also Luce and Raiffa, 1957, and Crawford and Heller, 1979) use this notion to formalize the sense in which the two-person method of divide and choose is fair. They characterize the perfect-equilibrium strategies when the divider (D) knows the preferences of the chooser (C) and show that in equilibrium, D divides so that he is indifferent about C's choice and C then chooses as D would prefer. The resulting allocation is fair, in Foley's sense, but not generally efficient unless D and C have identical preferences. The allocation is, however, efficient in the set of fair allocations.

These results establish an operationally meaningful sense in which the two-person divide-and-choose method is fair, and show that it has some tendency

146

toward efficiency. However, when preferences are common knowledge, the role of divider is an advantage, in the sense that the divider always weakly prefers his allocation to what he would receive if he were chooser. This follows from the facts that the game always yields a fair allocation and the divider can divide so that any desired fair allocation is the result. Further, n-person versions of the divide-and-choose method need not even yield fair allocations.

Crawford (1979) and Crawford (1980) study schemes that improve upon the classical divide-and-choose method while preserving its good points. In the two-person scheme studied in Crawford (1980), D offers C a choice between a proposal of D's choosing and equal division, instead of making him choose between a proposal and its complement. The resulting perfect-equilibrium outcomes are both fair and efficient, under reasonable assumptions; the role of divider is still an advantage, but less so than in the classical divide-and-choose method. These results extend, in part, to the n-person case.

In the n-person scheme studied in Crawford (1979), the role of divider in the scheme of Crawford (1980) is auctioned off. This completely eliminates the asymmetry of roles, and yields perfect-equilibrium allocations that are both efficient and egalitarian-equivalent, in the sense of Pazner and Schmeidler (1978): an allocation is *egalitarian-equivalent* if and only if it is indifferent, for all people, to equal division of some (not necessarily feasible) bundle of goods. However, although egalitarian-equivalence shares many of fairness's advantages as an equity notion, egalitarian-equivalent allocations need not be fair.

Despite their flaws, the schemes just described share several advantages over the traditional approach of choosing an allocation that maximizes a neoclassical social welfare function.

First, they deal with notions of equity that (like efficiency) do not involve interpersonal comparisons and have an objective meaning.

Second, their prescriptions are implementable in a stronger sense than those of neoclassical welfare economics. The classical welfare theorems establish that a competitive equilibrium is efficient and that, under reasonable assumptions, any efficient allocation can be obtained as a competitive equilibrium for suitably chosen initial endowments. But finding the endowments that yield the allocation that maximizes social welfare is informationally virtually equivalent to computing the entire optimal allocation. By contrast, the fair-division approach often allows the specification of procedures that are independent of the details of the environment but still yield equitable and efficient allocations.

Finally, most of the procedures studied in the literature on fair division are self-administered, in the sense that they can be implemented without a referee. This is difficult to formalize, but clearly important in practice.

BIBLIOGRAPHY

Crawford, V. 1977. A game of fair division. *Review of Economic Studies* 44(2), June, 235–47.
Crawford, V. 1979. A procedure for generating Pareto-efficient egalitarian-equivalent allocations. *Econometrica* 47(1), January, 49–60.

Crawford, V. 1980. A self-administered solution of the bargaining problem. *Review of Economic Studies* 47(2), January, 385–92.

Crawford, V. and Heller, W. 1979. Fair division with indivisible commodities. *Journal of Economic Theory* 21(1), August, 10–27.

Dubins, L. and Spanier, E. 1961. How to cut a cake fairly. *American Mathematical Monthly* 68(1), January, 1–17.

Foley, D. 1967. Resource allocation and the public sector. *Yale Economic Essays* 7(1), Spring, 45–98.

Kolm, S. 1972. *Justice et équité*. Paris: Editions du Centre National de la Recherche Scientifique.

Kuhn, H. 1967. On games of fair division. Ch. 2 in *Essays in Honor of Oskar Morgenstern*, ed. M. Shubik, Princeton: Princeton University Press.

Luce, R. and Raiffa, H. 1957. *Games and Decisions: Introduction and Critical Survey*. New York: John Wiley.

Pazner, E. and Schmeidler, D. 1978. Egalitarian equivalent allocations: a new concept of economic equity. *Quarterly Journal of Economics* 92(4), November, 671–87.

Steinhaus, H. 1948. The problem of fair division. *Econometrica* 16(1), January, 101–4.

Steinhaus, H. 1950. *Mathematical Snapshots*. New York: Oxford University Press.

Games with Incomplete Information

ROBERT J. WEBER

Classical economic models almost universally assume that the resources and preferences of individuals (or firms) are known not only to the individuals themselves but also to their competitors. In practice, this assumption is rarely correct. Once the attempt is made to include uncertainty (not just about the environment but also about other strategic actors) within economic models, it becomes necessary to broaden those models substantially to include considerations about the beliefs of individuals concerning the status of their competitors, as well as about learning as it takes place over time. A standard approach for doing this is to model the situation under investigation as a game with incomplete information, and to study the (Bayesian) equilibrium points of that game.

This approach has been used in recent years to analyse such issues as negotiation, competitive bidding, social choice, limit pricing, the signalling roles of education and advertising, together with a variety of other phenomena which arise under the general heading of industrial organization.

GAMES IN STRATEGIC FORM. Consider first games in strategic form, wherein the competitors each must choose a single action. In principle, any game can be reduced to this form by letting the actions available to the players be sufficiently complex (e.g. poker can be modelled in this manner).

An n-player *game with incomplete information* consists of the following elements: (1) for each player i, a probability space T_i of that player's possible types, a set A_i of actions available to that player, and a pay-off function u_i defined for every combination $(t, a) = (t_1, \ldots, t_n, a_1, \ldots, a_n)$ of player types and actions; and (2) a probability measure μ on the space $T = T_1 \times \ldots \times T_n$. It is assumed that the elements of the game are commonly known to the players. At the start of the game, the n-tuple of player types is determined according to μ. Each player is privately informed of his own type, and then the players simultaneously announce

149

their chosen actions. Each player finally receives the pay-off corresponding to the combination (t, a) of types and announced actions.

For example, assume that each player in a game knows his own preferences but is uncertain about the preferences (and hence, about the strategic motivations) of his competitors. This situation may be modelled as a game in which the pay-off functions have the form $u_i(t_i, a)$. The realization of the random variable t_i is player i's type, known to him but unknown to the other players.

In contrast, assume that the preferences of the players are known to all, but that the pay-offs are affected by some chance event represented by the random variable t_0; that is, each pay-off function can be written in the form $v_i(t_0, a)$. The variable t_i represents a private signal received by player i prior to his choice of an action. Note that a player's signal may be informative about the signals of the others, as well as just about the chance event, through the joint distribution of $(t_0, t_1, \ldots, t_n)$. In this case, the expected pay-off of a player, given that the vector $t = (t_1, \ldots, t_n)$ of signals has arisen and the players have selected the actions $a = (a_1, \ldots, a_n)$, is $u_i(t, a) = E[v_i(t_0, a)|t_1, \ldots, t_n]$.

THE NOTION OF 'TYPE'. The type-based formulation of a game with incomplete information is due to Harsanyi (1967–8), who proposed it as a way of cutting through the complexities of modelling not only a player's information and preferences but who his beliefs about other players' information and preferences, and his beliefs about their beliefs, and so on.

Mertens and Zamir (1985) subsequently presented a formulation of games with incomplete information which unifies the type-based approach with the beliefs-about-beliefs (and so on) approach to settings of incomplete information. By specifically modelling the iterated sequence of beliefs which determines a player's state of knowledge at the beginning of the game, and then considering 'consistent beliefs-closed subspaces' of the general space of players' beliefs, they were able to show that the original Harsanyi formulation involves no essential loss of generality.

STRATEGIES AND EQUILIBRIA. A *strategy* for a player specifies the action (or randomized choice of action) to be taken by each potential type of that player. The action specified for his actual type can be thought of as his 'private strategy'. In practice, even when a player has already learned his type, in order to decide upon his own appropriate action he must form a hypothesis concerning the strategies to be used by the others. But to analyse their strategic problems, he must ask himself what strategy they will expect him to follow. Therefore, it is necessary for him to consider the strategic choices his other potential types would make, in order to select an appropriate action for his actual type.

A (Bayesian) *equilibrium point* of a game is an n-tuple of strategies, in which the private strategy of each type of each player is a best response for that type of the $(n-1)$-tuple of strategies specified for the other players. This definition directly generalizes that of a Nash equilibrium point for a game with complete information.

As an example, consider two individuals who jointly own a piece of land. They have decided to sever their relationship, and for one of the two to buy the land from the other. Each knows how valuable the land is to himself, but is unsure of its worth to the other. They agree that each will write down a bid; the high bidder will keep the land and will pay the amount of his bid to the other.

Assume that each is equally likely to value the land at any level between $0 and $1200, and that both know this. At the unique Bayesian equilibrium point of the bidding game, each bids one-third of his own valuation. If, for example, one of them values the land at $300 and believes the other to be following the indicated equilibrium strategy, then by bidding $100 he has an expected pay-off of $1/4 \cdot \$200 + 3/4 \cdot \$250$; that is, he expects to win with probability $1/4$, and when he loses, he expects the other's (winning) bid to be between $100 and $400. This private strategy is optimal for him, given his belief about the other's behaviour. More generally, given his belief that his partner will bid a third of the partner's valuation, his own expected pay-off, when his valuation is v and he bids b, is $(3b/1200) \cdot (v - b) + (1 - 3b/1200) \cdot (b + 400)/2$. This is maximized by taking $b = v/3$.

DISTRIBUTIONAL STRATEGIES. In order to study the sensitivity of equilibrium results to variations in the informational structure of a game, it is necessary to define topologies on both the spaces of player strategies and the space of games. The first may be done by recasting the definition of a strategy in distributional form:

A *distributional strategy* v for a player is a probability measure on the product of his type and action spaces, with the property that the marginal distribution of v on the player's type space coincides with the original marginal distribution induced by μ. Player i, knowing his type t_i, chooses his action according to the condition distribution $v(\cdot | t_i)$; an outside observer, seeing the player's action a_i, will revise his beliefs concerning the players type to $v(\cdot | a_i)$. A natural topology on a player's strategy space v is the topology of weak convergence of probability measures.

Taking this distributional perspective. Milgrom and Weber (1985) proved a general equilibrium existence theorem; in particular, it follows from this theorem that any game with compact action spaces, uniformly continuous pay-off functions, and for which the type distribution is absolutely continuous with respect to the product of the marginal type distributions (i.e. for which the joint distribution of types has a corresponding joint probability density function), has an equilibrium point in distributional strategies. They also showed that, with the appropriate topology defined on the space of games, any limit point of equilibria of a sequence of games is an equilibrium point of the limit game. One consequence of the distributional approach is that when the games in a sequence provide a player with private information which disappears in the limit game, a sequence of pure strategies for that player can converge to a randomized strategy in the limit game. This reinforces an observation first offered by Harsanyi (1973) to explain why, in practice, decision-makers are rarely observed to randomize their choices of actions: the existence of a slight amount of private information is sufficient, in most cases, to allow the decision-makers to follow pure strategies which present, to their competitors, the appearance of a randomized choice of actions. In essence, competitors observe the marginal distribution, induced by a player's distributional strategy, on his action space

INEFFICIENCIES CREATED BY INCENTIVE CONSTRAINTS. In many circumstances, parties holding private information can find it difficult, or even impossible, to arrange efficient trades. A simple example, drawn from a class of problems first discussed by Akerlof (1970), concerns the owner of a car, attempting to arrange the sale of that car to a prospective buyer. Assume that the value of the car to the seller is primarily based on the quality of the car, and that the seller knows this value. Further assume that, whatever the car is worth to the seller, it is worth 50 per cent more to the buyer. And finally, assume that the buyer's only knowledge about the seller's value is that it is uniformly distributed between $0 and $1000.

In this case, it is commonly known to the two parties that a mutually advantageous trade exists. Nevertheless, no sale can be expected to take place, since the seller's willingness to accept any price $x signals to the buyer that the seller's valuation lies between $; and $x, and therefore that the expected value of the car to the buyer is most likely no more than $3/2 \cdot (x/2) = 3/4 \cdot x$. As long as the initial uncertainty persists (i.e. as long as no pre-sale verification of the car's quality is possible), and as long as no contingent trade can be arranged (i.e. as long as no warranty can be written), trade is impossible – even if the parties agree to consult an intervenor.

Intervenors in settings of incomplete information typically act as game designers, influencing the flow of information between parties, enforcing agreements and in some cases actually specifying the final resolution of a dispute (e.g. binding arbitration). Essentially, an intervenor creates a game which the parties must play. Any theory of intervention must therefore be tied to the issue of designing games with desirable equilibrium outcomes.

The Akerlof example shows that if intervenors are restricted from playing an auditing role, and if the outcome of the game cannot be made contingent on the parties' true types, then ex-post inefficient outcomes are at times inevitable. This understanding has led to the development of the theory of 'incentive-efficient mechanism design'.

THE REVELATION PRINCIPLE. In the area of game design, a simple, yet conceptually deep, type of analysis has become standard. Consider any equilibrium pair of strategies in a particular two-person game. (The following analysis is equally valid for games involving more than two players.) Each party's strategy can be viewed as a book, with each chapter detailing the private strategy of one of that party's types. Given the two actual types, a pairing of the private strategies in the appropriate chapters of the two books will lead to an outcome of the game.

Now, step back from this setting and imagine the two parties in separate rooms, each instructing an agent on how to act on his behalf. Each agent holds in hand the strategy book of his side; all he must be told is which chapter to use. From this new perspective, the original two parties can be thought of as playing an 'agent-instruction' game, in which the strategy books are prespecified and each must merely tell his agent his type (or, equivalently, point to a chapter in his strategy book). An equilibrium point in this new 'type-revelation' game is for each to tell the truth to his agent. Otherwise, the original strategies could not have been in equilibrium in the original game. Consequently, anything which can be accomplished at equilibrium through the use of any particular dispute-resolution procedure can also be accomplished through the use of some other procedure in which the only actions available to the parties are to state their (respective) types, and in which it is in equilibrium for each to reveal his type truthfully.

This observation, known as the 'revelation principle', reduces the problem of game design to the problem of optimizing the designer's objective function, subject to a collection of 'incentive constraints', one for each type of each player. An early application of this approach was to the design of auction procedures which maximize the seller's expected revenue. Myerson (1984) subsequently applied the approach to the problem of bargaining under uncertainty, and provided a generalization of the classical complete-information Nash bargaining solution. A central feature of this generalization is the incorporation of intrapersonal (i.e. intertype) equity considerations.

GAMES IN EXTENSIVE FORM. A game with incomplete information in extensive form begins with a change move which determines the types of the players, and continues with an information structure which preserves the privacy of each player's information. Many multi-stage bargaining problems can be represented in this form; typically, such games have a large number of equilibria, including equilibria in which one party is completely intransigent and the other concedes immediately, as well as equilibria in which both parties make information-revealing concessions over the series of stages.

A classical approach to the identification of 'plausible' equilibria in games with complete information is to seek equilibria which are subgame-perfect; that is, which specify optimal actions for all parties in all subgames of the original game. For example, Rubinstein (1982) presented a repeated offer-counteroffer game with many equilibria, and demonstrated that the requirement of subgame perfection uniquely identified one of those equilibria. However, subgame perfection is a concept of little use in distinguishing between equilibria of a game with incomplete information, since the privacy of the players' information typically results in the original game having no proper subgames.

Selten (1975), with his notion of 'trembling-hand' perfection, and Kreps and Wilson (1982), with their closely related notion of sequential equilibrium, provided extensions of the concept of subgame perfection which require that players act optimally at positions off the equilibrium path of the game. Central to the Kreps–Wilson approach is the incorporation of players' interim beliefs (about the other players' types, and past and future actions) at all game positions in the specification of an equilibrium point. Subsequent work on equilibrium selection in games with incomplete information has relied heavily on the study of justifiable out-of-equilibrium beliefs.

REPEATED GAMES. A special kind of extensive-form game consists of an initial chance move which determines the players' types, followed by the repeated play of a single game with type-dependent pay-offs. Players are not allowed to observe the actual stage-to-stage pay-offs during play, but are allowed to monitor the stage-to-stage actions of their competitors. The study of such games provides insight into the way players learn about one another over time; that is, insights into the way reputations are developed and maintained or changed.

Beginning in 1965 with research sponsored by the US Arms Control and Disarmament Agency, substantial effort has been focused on the study of infinitely repeated games with incomplete information. A principal result in the two-person, zero-sum case is that optimal strategies typically involve a single initial reference to the information a party holds, followed by period-to-period moves which depend only on the outcome of that single reference. (In an infinitely repeated game, short-term pay-offs are unimportant. Whatever behaviour a player adopts, his opponent's beliefs will converge to some limit; the long-term pay-offs will depend only on the limiting beliefs of the players. Therefore, in a strictly competitive environment it is sufficient for a player to determine at the beginning of the game precisely how much information he will eventually reveal.) Hart (1985) extended this analysis to games with private information on one side, and gains available to the players through cooperative actions. His work demonstrates that, when mutual gains are available, equilibrium behaviour may involve a series of references by the informed player to his information, interspersed with joint randomizing actions between the players which determine what information will next be revealed.

For many years, the finitely repeated Prisoner's Dilemma posed a dilemma for game theorists. Set in the framework of complete information, this game has a unique equilibrium outcome: the players never cooperate with one another. However, experiments repeatedly showed that actual players frequently establish a pattern of cooperation which persists until the game approaches its final stage. Kreps, Milgrom, Roberts and Wilson (1982) finally offered an explanation for this discrepancy, by demonstrating that a slight change in the initial informational framework yields games with equilibrium outcomes similar to the observed experimental outcomes. For example, assume that each player initially assigns a small positive probability to his opponent being the type of individual who (irrationally) will always respond to cooperation in one stage with further cooperation in the next. Then there will be equilibria in which, even when both players are actually rational, they will (with high probability) cooperate until near the end of the game. An interpretation of such equilibrium behaviour is that each finds it to his benefit to build a reputation as the irrational, cooperative type. The incomplete information model is necessary to obtain this behaviour. If the initial uncertainty as to type did not exist in the mind of a player's opponent, such a reputation would be impossible to build. An emerging 'theory of reputation' has its roots in this analysis.

BIBLIOGRAPHY

Akerlof, G. 1970 The market for lemons: qualitative uncertainty and the market mechanism. *Quarterly Journal of Economics* 84, 488–500.

Harsanyi, J.C. 1967–8. Games with incomplete information played by Bayesian players. *Management Science* 14, 159–82, 320–34, 486–502.

Harsanyi, J.C. 1973. Games with randomly-distributed payoffs: a new rationale for mixed-strategy equilibrium points. *International Journal of Game Theory* 2, 1–23.

Hart, S. 1985. Nonzero-sum two-person repeated games with incomplete information. *Mathematics of Operations Research* 10, 117–53.

Kreps, D.M. and Wilson, R. 1982. Sequential equilibria. *Econometrica* 50, 863–94.

Kreps, D.M., Milgrom, P., Roberts, J. and Wilson, R. 1982. Rational cooperation in the finitely repeated Prisoner's Dilemma. *Journal of Economic Theory* 27, 245–52.

Mertens, J.-F. and Zamir, S. 1985. Formulation of Bayesian analysis for games with incomplete information. *International Journal of Game Theory* 14, 1–29.

Milgrom, P.R. and Weber, R.J. 1985. Distributional strategies for games with incomplete information. *Mathematics of Operations Research* 10, 619–32.

Myerson, R.B. 1984. Two-person bargaining problems with incomplete information. *Econometrica* 52, 461–87.

Rubinstein, A. 1982. Perfect equilibrium in a bargaining model. *Econometrica* 50, 97–109.

Selten, R. 1975. Reexamination of the perfectness concept for equilibrium points in extensive games. *International Journal of Game Theory* 4, 25–55.

Harold Hotelling

KENNETH J. ARROW

Harold Hotelling, a creative thinker in both mathematical statistics and economics, was born in Fulda, Minnesota, on 29 September 1895 and died in Chapel Hill, North Carolina, on 26 December 1973. His influence on the development of economic theory was deep, though it occupied a relatively small part of a highly productive scientific life devoted primarily to mathematical statistics; only ten of some 87 published papers were devoted to economics, but of these six are landmarks which continue to this day to lead to further developments. His major research, on mathematical statistics, had, further, a generally stimulating effect on the use of statistical methods in different specific fields of application, including econometrics.

His early interests were in journalism; he received his BA in that field from the University of Washington in 1919. Later in classes, he would illustrate the use of dummy variables in regression analysis by a study (apparently never published) of the effect of the opinions of different Seattle newspapers on the outcome of elections and referenda. The mathematician and biographer of mathematicians, Eric T. Bell, discerned talent in Hotelling and encouraged him to switch his field. He received an MA in mathematics at Washington in 1921 and a PhD in the same field from Princeton in 1924; he worked under the topologist, Oswald Veblen (Thorstein Veblen's nephew), and two of his early papers dealt with manifolds of states of motion.

The year of completing his PhD, he joined the staff of the Food Research Institute at Stanford University with the title of Junior Associate. In 1925 he published his first three papers, one on manifolds, one on a derivation of the F-distribution and one on the theory of depreciation. Here, apparently for the first time, he stated the now generally accepted definition of depreciation as the decrease in the discounted value of future returns. This paper was a turning-point both in capital theory proper and in the reorientation of accounting towards more economically meaningful magnitudes.

In subsequent years at Stanford he became Research Associate of the Food Research Institute and Associate Professor of Mathematics, teaching courses in mathematical statistics and probability (including an examination of Keynes's *Treatise on Probability*) along with others in differential geometry and topology. In 1927, he showed that trend projections of population were statistically inappropriate and introduced the estimation of differential equations subject to error; he returned to the statistical interpretation of trends in a notable joint paper (1929a) with Holbrook Working, largely under the inspiration of the needs of economic analysis.

The same year he published the famous paper on stability in competition (1929b), in which he introduced the notions of locational equilibrium in duopoly. This paper is still anthologized and familiar to every theoretical economist. As part of the paper, he noted that the model could be given a political interpretation, that competing parties will tend to have very similar programmes. Although it took a long time for subsequent models to arise, these few pages have become the source for a larger and fruitful literature.

The paper was in fact a study in game theory. In the first stage of the game, the two players each chose a location on a line. In the second, they each chose a price. Hotelling sought what would now be called a subgame perfect equilibrium point. However, there was a subtle error in his analysis of the second stage, as first shown by d'Aspremont, Gabszewicz and Thisse (1979). Hotelling indeed found a local equilibrium, but the payoff functions are not concave; if the locations are sufficiently close to each other, the Hotelling solution is not a global equilibrium. Unfortunately, this is the interesting case, since Hotelling concluded that the locations chosen in the first stage would be arbitrarily close in equilibrium. In fact the optimal strategies must be mixed (Dasgupta and Maskin, 1986, pp. 30–32).

His paper on the economics of exhaustible resources (1931a) applied the calculus of variations to the problem of allocation of a fixed stock over time. All of the recent literature, inspired by the growing sense of scarcity (natural and artificial), is essentially based on Hotelling's paper. Interestingly enough, according to his later accounts, the *Economic Journal* rejected the paper because its mathematics was too difficult (although it had published Ramsey's papers earlier); it was finally published in the *Journal of Political Economy*.

In 1931, he was appointed Professor of Economics at Columbia University, where he was to remain until 1946. There he began the organization of a systematic curriculum in theoretical statistics, which eventually attained the dignity of a separate listing in the catalogue, though not the desired end of a department or degree-granting entity. Toward the end of the 1930s, he attracted a legendary set of students who presented the bulk of the next generation of theoretical statisticians. His care for and encouragement of his students were extraordinary: the encouragement of the self-doubtful, the quick recognition of talent, the tactfully-made research suggestion at crucial moments created a rare human and scholarly community. He was as proud of his students as he was modest about his own work.

He also gave a course in mathematical economics. The general environment was not too fortunate. The predominant interests of the Columbia Department of Economics were actively anti-theoretical, to the point where no systematic course in neoclassical price theory was even offered, let alone prescribed for the general student. Nevertheless, several current leaders in economic theory had the benefit of his teaching. But his influence was spread more through his papers, particularly those (1932, 1935) on the full development of the second-order implications for optimization by firms and households (contemporaneous with Hicks and Allen) and above all by his classic presidential address (1938) before the Econometric Society on welfare economics. Here we have the first clear understanding of the basic propositions (Hotelling, as always, was meticulous in acknowledging earlier work back to Dupuit), as well as the introduction of extensions from the two-dimensional plane of the typical graphical presentation to the calculation of benefits with many related commodities. He argued that marginal-cost pricing was necessary for Pareto optimality even for decreasing-cost industries, used the concept of potential Pareto improvement, and showed that suitable line integrals were a generalization of consumers' and producers' surplus for many commodities. Here also we have the clearest expression in print of Hotelling's strong social interests which motivated his technical economics. His position was undogmatic but in general it was one of market socialism. He had no respect for acceptance of the *status quo* as such, and the legitimacy of altering property rights to benefit the deprived was axiomatic with him; but at the same time he was keenly aware of the limitations on resources and the importance in any human society of the avoidance of waste.

Important as was his contribution to economics, most of his effort and his influence were felt in the field of mathematical statistics, particularly in the development of multivariate analysis. In a fundamental paper (1931b), he generalized Student's test to the simultaneous test of hypotheses about the means of many variables with a joint normal distribution. In the course of this paper, he gave a correct statement of what were later termed 'confidence intervals'. In two subsequent papers (1933, 1936) he developed the analysis of many statistical variables into their principal components and developed a general approach to the analysis of relations between two sets of variates. The statistical methodologies of these papers and in particular the last contributed significantly to the later development of methods for estimating simultaneous equations in economics.

In 1946, he finally had the long-desired opportunity of creating a department of mathematical statistics, at the University of North Carolina, where he remained until retirement. He continued his active interest in economics there.

Space forbids more than the brief mention of his important work in the foundation of two learned societies, the Econometric Society and the Institute of Mathematical Statistics, both of which he served as President at a formative stage. He received many formal honours during his lifetime, including honorary degrees from Chicago and Rochester; he was the first Distinguished Fellow of the American Economic Association when that honour was created, as well as a member of the National Academy of Sciences and the Accademia Nazionale dei Lincei, Honorary Fellow of the Royal Statistical Society and Fellow of the Royal Economic Society.

SELECTED WORKS

1925. A general mathematical theory of depreciation. *Journal of the American Statistical Association* 20, 340–53.

1927. Differential equations subject to error. *Journal of the American Statistical Association* 22, 283–314.

1929a. (With H. Working). Applications of the theory of error to the interpretation of trends. *Journal of the American Statistical Association* 24, 73–85.

1929b. Stability in competition. *Economic Journal* 39, 41–57.

1931a. The economics of exhaustible resources. *Journal of Political Economy* 39, 137–75.

1931b. The generalization of Student's ratio. *Annals of Mathematical Statistics* 21, 360–78.

1932. Edgeworth's taxation paradox and the nature of supply and demand functions. *Journal of Political Economy* 40, 577–616.

1933. Analysis of a complex of statistical variables with principal components. *Journal of Educational Psychology* 24, 417–41, 498–520.

1935. Demand functions with limited budgets. *Econometrica* 3, 66–78.

1936. Relation between two sets of variates. *Biometrika* 28, 321–77.

1938. The general welfare in relation to problems of taxation and of railway and utility rates. *Econometrica* 6, 242–69.

BIBLIOGRAPHY

Dasgupta, P. and Maskin, E. 1986. The existence of equilibrium in discontinuous economic games, II: Applications. *Review of Economic Studies* 53, 27–41.

d'Aspremont, C., Gabszewicz, J.-J. and Thisse, J. 1979. On Hotelling's 'Stability in Competition'. *Econometrica* 47, 1145–50.

Large Economies

JOHN ROBERTS

Economists have often claimed that our theories were never intended to describe individual behaviour in all its idiosyncrasies. Instead, in this view, economic theory is supposed to explain only general patterns across large populations. The prime example is the theory of competitive markets, which is designed to deal with situations in which the influence of any individual agent on price formation is 'negligible'.

As in so many aspects of economics, Cournot (1838) was the first to make the role of large numbers explicit in his analysis. Cournot provided a theory of price and output which, as the number of competing suppliers increases without bound, asymptotically yields the competitive solution of price equals marginal and average cost. However, for any given finite number of competitors, an imperfectly competitive outcome results.

It took over a century for Cournot's insights on the role of large numbers to be fully appreciated. Edgeworth (1881) argued the convergence of his contract curve as the economy grew, and increasing numbers of authors assumed that the number of agents was 'sufficiently large' that each one's influence on quantity choices was negligible, but it was not until the contributions of Shubik (1959) and Debreu and Scarf (1963) to the study of the asymptotic properties of the core that the number of agents took a central role in economic analysis.

The crucial step in this line of analysis was taken by Aumann (1964). Arguing that, in terms of standard models of behaviour, an individual agent's actions could be considered to be negligible only if the individual were himself arbitrarily small relative to the collectivity. Aumann modelled the set of agents as being (indexed by) an atomless measure space. In this context, an individual agent corresponds to a set of measure zero, while aggregate quantities are represented as integrals (average, per capita amounts). Then changing the actions of a single individual (or any finite number) actually has no influence on aggregates.

The non-atomic measure space formulation beings three mathematical properties that have proven important. The first is that it provides a consistent modelling of the notion of individual negligibility: only in such a context is an individual truly able to exert no influence on prices. Thus, this model correctly represents the primary reason for appealing to 'large numbers': in it, competitive price-taking behaviour is rational. Moreover, this individual negligibility, when combined with an assumption that individual characteristics are sufficiently 'diffuse', means that discontinuities in individual demand disappear under aggregation (Sondermann, 1975).

The second property is that a (non-negligible) subset of agents drawn from an economy with a non-atomic continuum of agents is essentially sure to be a representative sample of the whole population. This property has proven crucial in the literature relating the core and competitive equilibrium. (See Hildenbrand (1974) for a broad-ranging treatment of these issues.) It is also used in showing equivalence of core and value allocations (Aumann, 1975).

The other important property of the non-atomic continuum model is the convexifying effect. Even though individual entities (demand correspondences, upper-contour sets, production sets) may not be convex, Richter's theorem implies that the aggregates of these are convex sets when the set of agents is a non-atomic continuum. This property yields existence of competitive equilibrium in large economies even when the individual entries are ill behaved and no 'diffuseness' is assumed.

In the non-atomic continuum modelling, the individual agent formally disappears. Instead, one has coalitions (measurable sets of agents), and an individual is formally indistinguishable from any set of measure zero. The irrelevance of individuals is made very clear in the model of Vind (1964), where only coalitions are defined and individual agents play no part. Debreu (1967) showed the equivalence of Vind's and Aumann's approaches. A further extension of this line is to consider economies in terms only of the distributions of individual characteristics and allocations in terms of distributions of commodities. The strengths of this approach are shown in Hildenbrand (1974).

This disappearance of the individual is intuitively bothersome: economists are used to thinking about individual agents being negligible, but not about individuals having no existence whatsoever. Brown and Robinson (1972) provided an escape from this dilemma by their modelling of a large set of agents via nonstandard analysis. This approach gives formal meaning to such notions as an infinitesimal that had been swept out of mathematics and replaced by 'epsilon-delta' arguments. In interpreting nonstandard models, one distinguishes between how things appear from 'inside the model' and what they look like from 'outside'. From outside, these models may have an infinity of (individually negligible, infinitesimal) agents, yet from inside each agent is a well-defined, identifiable entity. Using this mathematical modelling eases the interpretation of large economies and also allows formalization of some very intuitive arguments that otherwise could not be made. Unfortunately, the difficulties of mastering the mathematics of nonstandard analysis has limited the number of economists using this approach.

While these formal models capture the essential intuition about the nature of the economic behaviour of large economies, results obtained in this context should be of interest only to the extent that these models provide a good approximation to large but finite economies. This point was first emphasized by Kannai (1970), and its elaboration was the central issue confronting mathematical general equilibrium theory through the 1960s and early 1970s. The issue is one of continuity: in what sense are infinite economy models the limits of finite economies as the economy grows, and do the various constructs of interest (competitive or Lindahl allocations, cores, value allocations, etc.) of the finite economies approach those of the limit, infinite economies? These questions are extremely subtle. A good introduction to them is Hildenbrand (1974).

The study of the limiting, asymptotic properties of various economic concepts represents an alternative, more direct (but often less tractable) approach to large economy questions than does working with infinite economies. This line begins with Cournot's (1838) treatment of the convergence of oligopoly to perfect competition, the general equilibrium development of which has been a major focus of recent activity (see Mas-Colell, 1982 and the references there). The work growing out of Edgeworth (1881) and Debreu and Scarf (1963) on the core-competitive equilibrium equivalence noted above also follows this line.

Once such convergence is established, the crucial question becomes that of the rate of convergence because asymptotic results are of limited interest if convergence is too slow. This question was first addressed for the core by Debreu (1975), who showed convergence at a rate of at least one over the number of agents.

A more direct approach to this issue of how large a market must be for its outcomes to be approximately competitive is to employ a model in which price formation is explicitly modelled. (Note that this is not a property of the Cournot or Arrow–Debreu analyses.) In a partial equilibrium context the Bertrand (1883) model of price-setting homogeneous oligopoly indicates that 'two is large', in that duopoly can yield price equal to marginal cost. Recent striking results in the same line for the double auction are due to Gresik and Satterthwaite (1985), who show that, even with individual reservation prices being private information, equilibrium under this institution can yield essentially competitive, welfare-maximizing volumes of trade with as few as six sellers and buyers.

This work is very heartening, for it tends to justify the profession's traditional reliance on competitive models which make formal sense only with an infinite set of agents. Another basis for optimism on this count comes from experimental work which shows strong tendencies for essentially competitive outcomes to be attained with quite small numbers. The further study of such institutions is clearly indicated.

BIBLIOGRAPHY

Aumann, R.J. 1964. Markets with a continuum of traders. *Econometrica* 32, 39–50.

Aumann, R.J. 1975. Values of markets with a continuum of traders. *Econometrica* 43, 611–46.

Bertrand, J. 1883. (Review of) Théorie mathématique de la richesse sociale. *Journal des Savants* 48, 499–508.

Brown, D.J. and Robinson, A. 1972. A limit theorem on the cores of large standard exchange economies. *Proceedings of the National Academy of Sciences of the USA* 69, 1258–60.

Cournot, A. 1838. *Recherches sur les principes mathématiques de la théorie des richesses.* Paris: Hachette.

Debreu, G. 1967. Preference functions on measure spaces of economic agents. *Econometrica* 35, 111–22.

Debreu, G. 1975. The rate of convergence of the core of an economy. *Journal of Mathematical Economics* 2, 1–8.

Debreu, G. and Scarf, H. 1963. A limit theorem on the core of an economy. *International Economic Review* 4, 235–46.

Edgeworth, F.Y. 1881. *Mathematical Psychics.* London: Kegan Paul; New York: A.M. Kelley, 1967.

Gresik, T. and Satterthwaite, M. 1984. The rate at which a simple market becomes efficient as the number of traders increases: an asymptotic result for optimal trading mechanisms. Discussion Paper 641, Center for Mathematical Studies in Economics and Management Science, Northwestern University.

Hildenbrand, W. 1974. *Core and Equilibria of a Large Economy.* Princeton: Princeton University Press.

Kannai, Y. 1970. Continuity properties of the core of a market. *Econometrica* 38, 791–815.

Mas-Collel, A. (ed.) 1982. *Non-cooperative Approaches to the Theory of Perfect Competition.* New York: Academic Press.

Shubik, M. 1959. *Strategy and Market Structure; Competition, Oligopoly, and the Theory of Games.* New York: Wiley.

Sondermann, D. 1975. Smoothing demand by aggregation. *Journal of Mathematical Economics* 2, 201–24.

Vind, K. 1964. Edgeworth-allocations in an exchange economy with many traders. *International Economic Review* 5, 165–77.

Oskar Morgenstern

MARTIN SHUBIK

Morgenstern was born in Goerlitz, Silesia, on 24 January 1902. He died on 26 July 1977 at his home in Princeton, New Jersey. The two main intellectual centres of his life were Vienna and Princeton. In each case the source of his intellectual stimulation was not primarily the university but institutions such as the Wienerkreis of Moritz Schlick in Vienna, where he counted among his friends Karl Popper, Kurt Göddel and Karl Schlesinger, and the Institute for Advanced Study at Princeton. He obtained his doctorate in 1925 from the University of Vienna where he was greatly influenced by Karl Menger and the writings of Eugen Böhm-Bawerk.

Morgenstern's first major work, *Wirtschaftsprognose* (1928) which was published in Vienna, served as his Habilitation thesis leading to his appointment as a *Privatdozent* at the University of Vienna in 1929. In this book he began to consider the difficulties and paradoxes inherent in economic prediction, being particularly concerned with prediction where the action of a few powerful individuals could influence the outcome. He illustrated some of these difficulties with the example of Sherlock Holmes's pursuit of Professor Moriarty (an example repeated in the *Theory of Games*, 1944).

He became a professor at the University of Vienna in 1935, and in the same year published in the *Zeitschrift für Nationalökonomie* (of which he was managing editor) an article on fundamental difficulties with the assumption of perfect foresight in the study of economic equilibrium. It was then that the mathematician Edward Čech noted that the problems raised by Morgenstern were related to those treated by von Neumann in his article 'Zur Theorie der Gesellschaftspiele', published in 1928.

Morgenstern did not have the opportunity to meet von Neumann until somewhat later. They both recalled meeting at the Nassau Inn in Princeton on

1 February 1939, although each believed that they had met once before. They became close friends and remained so until von Neumann's death on 8 February 1957.

In Vienna, Morgenstern was also director of the Austrian Institute for Business Cycle Research (1931–8) where he employed Abraham Wald, whom he later helped go to the United States. In 1938, due to his opposition to the Nazis, Morgenstern was dismissed from the University of Vienna as 'politically unbearable' and he accepted an offer from Princeton, to some extent because of the presence of von Neumann at the Institute for Advanced Study. Their close collaboration resulted in the publication in 1944 of their book, *Theory of Games and Economic Behavior*. This major work contained a radical reconceptualization of the basic problems of competition and collaboration as a game of strategy among several agents, as well as an important novel approach to utility theory (presented in detail in the second edition, 1947).

Both Morgenstern and von Neumann were well aware of the limitations of their great work. They stressed that they were beginning by offering a sound basis for a static theory of conscious individually rational economic behaviour and that the history of science indicated that a dynamic theory might be considerably different. They warned against premature generalization.

In his years at Princeton from 1938 until his retirement in 1970, Morgenstern encouraged the work of a distinguished roster of younger scholars in game theory and combinatoric methods. This was feasible primarily through the strength of the Mathematics Department and its connections with the Institute. There was little interest in the subject in the Department of Economics at the time. The ideas of the *Theory of Games* were so radical that they have taken many years to permeate the social sciences. Even at the time of his death many in the economics profession were sceptical of or indifferent to its contributions.

Although his work on the theory of games was undoubtedly Morgenstern's greatest contribution and collaboration, his interest were wide-ranging. His two books, *On the Accuracy of Economic Observations* (1950), and *Predictability of Stock Market Prices* (1970), written jointly with Clive W. Granger, indicate these interests. He was also concerned with matters of national defence and in 1959 published *The Question of National Defense*.

In 1959 he was one of the founders of Mathematica, a highly successful and sophisticated consulting firm, and served as Chairman of the Board. After retiring from Princeton he was Distinguished Professor at New York University until his death.

SELECTED WORKS

1928. *Wirtschaftsprognose: Eine Untersuchung ihrer Voraussetzungen und Möglichkeiten.* Vienna: Julius Springer.

1935. Vollkommene Voraussicht und wirtschaftliches Gleichgewicht. *Zeitschrift für Nationalökonomie* 6(3), August, 337–57.

1944. (With J. von Neumann) *Theory of Games and Economic Behavior.* Princeton: Princeton University Press, 2nd edn, 1947.

1950. *On the Accuracy of Economic Observations.* Princeton: Princeton University Press.
1959. *The Question of National Defense.* New York: Random House.
1970. (With C.W.J. Granger) *Predictability of Stock Market Prices.* Lexington, Mass.: Heath Lexington Books.

Nash Equilibrium

DAVID M. KREPS

The concept of a *Nash equilibrium* plays a central role in noncooperative game theory. Due in its current formalization to John Nash (1950, 1951), it goes back at least to Cournot (1838). This entry begins with the formal definition of a Nash equilibrium and with some of the mathematical properties of equilibria. Then we ask: To what question is 'Nash equilibrium' the answer? The answer that we suggest motivates further questions of *equilibrium selection*, which we consider in two veins: the informal notions, such as Schelling's (1960) *focal points*; and the formal theories for *refining* or *perfecting* Nash equilibria, due largely to Selten (1965, 1975). We conclude with a brief discussion of two related issues: Harsanyi's (1967–8) notion of a *game of incomplete information* and Aumann's (1973) *correlated equilibria*.

I. DEFINITION AND SIMPLE MATHEMATICAL PROPERTIES. We give the definition in the simple setting of a finite player and action game in normal form. There are I players, indexed by $i = 1, \ldots, I$. Player i chooses from N_i (pure) strategies; we write S_i for this set of strategies, and s_i for a typical member of S_i. A *strategy profile*, written $s = (s_1, \ldots, s_I)$, is a vector of strategies for the individual players – we write S for $\Pi_{i=1}^I S_i$, the set of all strategy profiles. For a strategy profile $s = (s_1, \ldots, s_I) \in S$ and a strategy $s_i' \in S_i$ for player i, we write $s|s_i'$ for the strategy profile $(s_1, \ldots, s_{i-1}, s_i', s_{i+1}, \ldots, s_I)$ or s with the part of i changed from s_i to s_i'. For each player i and strategy profile s, $u_i(s)$ denotes i's expected utility or payoff if players employ strategy profile s.

Definition. A *Nash equilibrium* (in pure strategies) is a strategy profile s such that for each i and $s_i' \in S_i$, $u_i(s) \geqslant u_i(s|s_i')$. In words, no single player, by changing his own part of s, can obtain higher utility if the others stick to their parts.

This basic definition is often extended to independently mixed strategy profiles, as follows. Given S_i, write Σ_i for the set of mixed strategies for player i; that is,

167

all probability distributions over S_i. Write Σ for $\Pi^I_{i=1}\Sigma_i$, $\sigma = (\sigma_1, \ldots, \sigma_I)$, $\sigma|\sigma'_i$, and so on, as before. Extend the utility functions u_i from domain S to domain Σ by letting $u_i(\sigma)$ be player i's expected utility:

$$u_i(\sigma) = \sum_{S_1} \ldots \sum_{S_I} u_i(s_1, \ldots, s_I)\sigma_1(s_1) \ldots \sigma_I(s_I).$$

Then define a Nash equilibrium in mixed strategies just as above, with σ in place of s and σ_i in place of s_i. Equivalently, player i puts positive weight on pure strategy s_i only if s_i is among the pure strategies that give him the greatest expected utility.

This formal concept is due to John Nash (1950, 1951). Luce and Raiffa (1957) provided an important and influential early commentary. Nash also proved that in a finite player and finite action game, there always exist at least one Nash equilibrium, albeit existence can only be guaranteed if we look at mixed strategies – standard examples (such as matching pennies) show that there are games with no pure strategy equilibria. The proof that a Nash equilibrium always exists is an application of Brouwer's fixed point theorem. The concept of a Nash equilibrium is extended in natural fashion to games with infinitely many players and/or pure strategies, although in such cases existence can be problematic; we do not discuss these matters further here.

II. THE PHILOSOPHY OF NASH EQUILIBRIUM. To what question is 'Nash equilibrium' the answer? This has been and continues to be the subject of much discussion and debate. Most authors take a position that is a variation on the following.

Suppose that, in a particular game, players *by some means unspecified at the moment* arrive at an 'agreement' as to how each will play the game. This 'agreement' specifies a particular strategy choice by each player, and each player is aware of the strategies chosen by each of his fellow players, although players may not resort to enforcement mechanisms except for those given as part of the formal specification of the game. One would not consider this agreement *self-enforcing* (or strategically stable) if some one of the players, hypothesizing that others will keep to their parts of the agreement, would prefer to deviate and choose some strategy other than that specified in the agreement. Thus, to be self-enforcing in this sense, it is *necessary* that the agreement form a Nash equilibrium. (If players could perform a public randomization as part of the agreement, we would get convex combinations of Nash equilibria as candidate self-enforcing agreements. See section VI for what can be done with partially private randomizations.)

This does not say that every Nash equilibrium is a self-enforcing agreement. For example, in the context being modelled, it might be appropriate to consider multi-player defections (and the concept of a *strong equilibrium*, a strategy assignment in which no coalition can profitably deviate, then comes into play). It does not say how this agreement comes about, nor what will transpire if there is no agreement. Indeed, in the latter case the concept of a Nash equilbrium has no particular claim upon us.

We are moved to ask, then: What other necessary conditions might be added to the condition that the agreement forms a Nash equilibrium? Some (but certainly not all) answers are given in section IV. What does transpire if no agreement arises? We will not touch on this question here, except to send the reader to recent work by Bernheim (1984) and Pearce (1984). And how might an agreement arise? This we take up next.

III. REACHING AN 'AGREEMENT'. One means to an agreement on how to play the game might be explicit negotiation among the players, conducted prior to play of the game. (If this happens, it may be important that negotiations take place before any player possesses private information, as such information might become revealed during the course of the negotiations.) We cannot guarantee that the players will come to an agreement, nor can we say what agreement will be reached. But, if the agreement is to be self-enforcing as above, it must be an equilibrium. That is, the range of possible self-enforcing agreements, arrived at via preplay negotiation, is contained within the set of Nash equilibria.

Any story about preplay negotiation contains within it an opportunity to choose among Nash equilibria, depending on the mechanism one imagines for the preplay negotiation. For example, if we imagine that exactly one player is allowed to make a speech, after which play occurs, then it is natural to suppose that the player, if he proposes an equilibrium at all, would propose one that is advantageous to him (see Farrell, 1985). How the type of preplay negotiation affects the nature of any agreement that is reached is a relatively unexplored topic. (We return to preplay negotiation later, in our discussion of correlated equilibria.)

But what if there is no explicit, preplay negotiation? Even then, *in some contexts, for some particular games*, player may *know* what each will do (at least, with high probability). A very simple example is the two player bimatrix game in Table 1. The two players are called Row and Col, and each is asked, simultaneously and without consultation, to make a choice: Row must choose either the top row or the bottom, and Col must choose either the left column or the right. Given these choices, payoffs are as in the chosen cell with Row's payoff listed first; so, for example, in Table 1, if the choices are Top and Left, then Row gets 1 and Col gets 0. For the game in Table 1, players usually have very little problem deciding what to do: Row chooses Top, and Col chooses Right. Note that this is a Nash equilibrium. But Bottom and Left is another. Being Nash is only necessary, and not sufficient.

Table 1

	Left	Right
Top	1, 0	5, 5
Bottom	2, 2	0, 1

Another bimatrix illustrates the point that such implicit agreements do not always rise. Consider the game in Table 2, where Row picks between rows 1 and 2, and Col selects one of four columns. This game possesses three Nash equilibria, two in pure strategies and one in mixed strategies, and in none of the three equilibria is column 3 played with positive probability. None the less, in the majority of cases (in informal experiments with students, with payoffs in units such as nickels), Col selects column 3, and Row selects row 2. A nontrivial fraction of Row players pick row 1, enough so that column 3 is an optimal choice for Col. Because there is no clear 'agreement', Col may well optimize by choosing a column that appears in *no* equilibrium.

Table 2

	Column 1	Column 2	Column 3	Column 4
Row 1	20, 5	0, 4	1, 3	$2, -10^4$
Row 2	$0, -10^4$	$1, -10^3$	3, 3	5, 10

The game in Table 1 seems too simple to be of consequence, but a similar phenomenon can be found in much more complex games. Consider the following game. There are two players, both American college students. A list of eleven cities in the United States is given: Atlanta, Boston, Chicago, Dallas, Denver, Kansas City, Los Angeles, New York, Philadelphia, Phoenix, San Francisco. Each city has been assigned an 'index' reflecting its importance to commerce, the arts, etc. All that the students know about this index is that New York is highest, with index 100, and Kansas City is lowest, with index 1. Each student is asked to choose, independently and without consultation, a subset of the cities, with one told that he must list Boston, and the other told that he must list San Francisco. (All these rules are common knowledge among the players.) After the two lists have been prepared, they are compared. If a city appears on one list and not the other, the student listing that city wins as many dollars as the city's index. If a city appears on both lists, each loses twice as many dollars as the city's index. And if the students manage to partition the eleven cities between them, their total winnings are tripled.

In pure strategies, this game has 512 Nash equilibria. Yet when played, students achieve a quite striking level of coordination. The Boston list nearly always contains New York, and Philadelphia, with Chicago less likely (but still very likely), and Atlanta a bit less still; the San Francisco list almost invariably includes Los Angeles, Phoenix and Denver, with Dallas a bit less likely, and Kansas City less likely still. (When there is contention, it nearly always involves Atlanta and/or Kansas City.) The reader will, of course, recognize what is going on here: Students focus very quickly on a division based on geographical principles. They do this without consultation – something in the game seems to focus attention in this manner.

This is an example of a *focal point* Nash equilibrium, as proposed and discussed by Schelling (1960). Schelling discusses a number of properties that focal points tend to possess (or, rather, that in some cases become the focus of the focal point): symmetry, qualitative uniqueness, equity. Beyond these vague generalities, it is clear that the context and presentation of the game matter. If instead of eleven cities we had eleven letters: A, B, C, D, E, K, L, N, P, Q and S, then the B list would contain A, C, D, E and (perhaps) K, while the S list would contain L, N, P, Q and (perhaps) K. (In simulation, K tends to go to the B list, presumably on grounds that players know that N has the highest index, and some sort of equity consideration intrudes.) The identities of the participants matter: if the cities game is played by two foreign students (each of whom knows that the other is foreign), there is increased use of the alphabetical rule. And experience matters: Roth and Schoumaker (1983) examine a bargaining game that admits two natural focal points; they show experimentally that players are conditioned by experience to key on one or the other.

The theory of focal points, while clearly quite important (both with regard to the use of Nash equilibrium and by itself), remains undeveloped. Until formal development occurs, the application of Nash equilibrium in many contexts relies for justification on a very vague idea.

The experimental work of Roth and Schoumaker suggests another explanation that is sometimes given for how agreements arise; namely through a dynamic process of adaptive expectations. Imagine a population of players engaged in a particular game over and over, learning after each round of play how opponents have played, and adapting subsequent choices to what has been learned. We might imagine that, in this process, there is convergence to some stationary equilibrium, which then would be a Nash equilibrium. But an imagination this vivid should be tempered: If the players are engaged with the same (or a small and recognizable set of) opponents over and over, then in the large (super-)game that they play, there are many more equilibria than in the single-shot game. Even if opponents change, players may carry with them reputations from past play, which will enlarge the set of equilibria. To nullify these effects, the players must face changing opponents, with no record of anyone's past play brought to bear. This is far from realistic; and still one must be careful concerning the amount of information that is passed after each round, if a 'dynamic stationary equilibrium' of such a process is to be a Nash equilibrium. With all these caveats, some study has been made of such dynamic processes, providing a further way in which 'agreements' might arise.

Finally, and again in the spirit of focal points, 'agreements' would arise if there were a single, unanimously adopted theory as to how games (or the game in question) are played. An example of such a theory is the tracing procedure of Harsanyi (1975).

IV. FURTHER NECESSARY CONDITIONS: PERFECTION AND OTHER REFINEMENTS. Consider the bimatrix game depicted in Table 3. There are two Nash equilibria in pure strategies here: Top-Left and Bottom-Right. Suppose that, somehow, Bottom-

Right is agreed upon. (For example, imagine a process of pre-play negotiation in which only Col is allowed to speak, so that Col proposes the equilibrium that is most advantageous to him.) Would we consider this a self-enforcing agreement?

Table 3

	Left	Right
Top	2, 1	0, 0
Bottom	1, 2	1, 2

Note that Col, by picking Right, is picking a weakly dominated strategy. That is, no matter what Row does, Col does as well with Left, and Col does strictly better if Row picks Top. Bottom-Right is a Nash equilibrium because Col does just as well with Right as with Left if Row can be trusted to play Bottom, but we might think that Col, entertaining the slightest doubts about whether Row will indeed stick to the agreement, would move to Left. If we think this, then Bottom-Right would not seem to be a self-enforcing agreement.

Consider next the following *extensive game* (hereafter called game A). Here one player, named Row, begins the game by choosing one of two actions, called *T* and *B*. If Row chooses *B*, then the game is over, with Row receiving 1 and a second player, Col, receiving 2. If Row chooses *T*, then Col must select between two actions, called *L* and *R*. The choices of *T* and *L* net 2 for Row and 1 for Col, while the choices of *T* and *R* net 0 for each. Now if Row does choose *T*, then Col, it seems, would pick *L*; it is better to get 1 than 0. And if Col is going to pick *L*, then Row prefers *T* to *B*. Indeed, *T, L* is a Nash equilibrium for game A. But *B, R* is another Nash equilibrium. (Note that, although the choice of *B* by Row moots any choice by Col, we specify a choice, in this case *R*, so that Row can evaluate what will happen if he should choose *T* instead.) If Row thinks that Col will choose *R*, then Row responds with *B*. And if Row is to choose *B*, then Col's choice of *R* costs Col nothing. This second equilibrium, however, does not seem to be a self-enforcing agreement: If Row does choose *T*, then Col is put on the spot; will he really choose *R*, faced with the *fait accompli* of *T*?

The connection between these two games should be clear: Table 3 gives the normal form representation of game A. In each case, for (perhaps) slightly different reasons, we see that there can be Nash equilibria that do not seem viable candidates for self-enforcing agreements. These examples raise the general question: What further formal necessary criteria can be stated for self-enforcing agreements?

Game A is a finite game of complete and perfect information: there are finitely many moves and countermoves, and a player who is moving always knows what has transpired previously. It seems obvious how to solve (and play) games of this sort. Beginning at the end of the game tree, one finds how the last player to move will move. Then one can move back one step, and find the move of the penultimate player, and so on, using backwards induction to derive the solution. Going back to Kuhn (1953) (and perhaps earlier), it has been known that this procedure generates a Nash equilibrium. (And if there are never any ties at any stage of the backwards induction, it will generate a unique solution.) Correspondingly, in the normal form one sometimes comes across games that are *dominance solvable* – where the iterated elimination of dominated (weak or strict) strategies leads one to a single strategy combination. When such criteria apply, it seems sensible to use them. (Although in some applications the application of these criteria does lead to counter-intuitive results: see Selten (1978) and the literature that follows on the chain-store paradox.).

The intuition applied in game A can be generalized beyond the class of finite games with complete and perfect information. Beginning with the seminal work of Selten (1965, 1975), several authors have refined or 'perfected' the concept of a Nash equilibrium, to capture further necessary conditions for self-enforcing agreements. The first of these refinements is Selten's (1965) notion of subgame perfection: If at any point in an extensive game, all players agree as to what has transpired, then 'what remains' is, by itself, an extensive game. We might require that, in such circumstances, players expect that the agreement for this subgame constitutes a Nash equilibrium for the subgame. This applies to game A and, generally, to all finite games with complete and perfect information. But it applies fruitfully as well to games that are not finite (e.g. Rubinstein, 1982) or that do not have complete and perfect information. Selten (1975) proposes further conditions called *perfection* (or, sometimes in the literature, trembling hand perfection). This is somewhat harder to describe, but the basic idea is that each player's strategy should be a best response to the others' strategies, where the first player does not rule out the possibility that his opponents might (with very small probability) fail to keep to the agreement. So, for example, in Table 3, Col, fearing that Row might play Top 'by mistake' as it were, will select Left.

Following these ideas, a number of alternative refinements (both stronger and weaker) have been proposed. Three are mentioned here (with apoligies to those omitted): Myerson (1978) strengthens perfection to what is called *properness*, where (roughly) it is assumed that the chances of a 'mistake' made by some player are related to how severe that mistake is. Kreps and Wilson (1982) propose a weaker (than perfection) criterion for extensive games called sequential equilibrium: The basic idea is that behaviour in all parts of a game tree should be rationalized by some beliefs as to the play of the game that are not contradicted by what the player knows for sure. This bites wherever subgame perfection does; in game A, Col, asked to move, can no longer believe that Row will choose B; the fact that he is asked to move contradicts this. So his choice must be made optimally given the beliefs that, in this case, he must hold, once he is asked to move. But the notion is stronger than subgame perfection; indeed, it is 'almost equivalent' to perfection. Finally, Kohlberg and Mertens (1982), noting that the other criteria fail in certain applications and fail to possess natural properties such as invariance to alternative extensive form representations of the same normal form game, propose *stability*, a set-valued concept, which captures a number of very intuitive restrictions.

At the time of writing this entry, work on refinements is an active and ongoing subject. This brief description is probably outdated as it is written, and it will surely be outdated by the time it is read. Still, the programme of this work should be clear: Nash equilibrium gives a necessary condition for 'self-enforcing agreements' that is far from sufficient; there is much room for further formal criteria against which candidate agreements can be measured.

V. GAMES WITH INCOMPLETE INFORMATION. In a Nash equilibrium, it is (essentially) presumed that players are all aware of the strategies their opponents are selecting. This presumption would seem especially incredible in cases where some players initially possess knowledge that other players lack, concerning their own tastes, abilities and even the rules of the game. Imagine, for example, that Row and Col are playing the game A, but that Row is not certain what Col's payoffs are. In particular, Row entertains the possibility that Col might well prefer R to L if faced with the choice by Row of T. This is not so fanciful as it may seem; it might, perhaps, represent situations where Row is uncertain to what extent Col derives 'psychological utility' from seeing Row hurt. In economic applications, the uncertainty (if Row and Col are firms) might reflect one firm's initial uncertainty about the financial or human capital resources of its rivals, and so on. To apply Nash equilibrium analysis (and game theory generally) to such situations, therefore, seems a witless exercise.

There is, however, a standard technique to deal with such situations. This involves what is called a *game with incomplete information*, as developed by John Harsanyi (1967–8). The concept is subtle, but a brief description can be given. We imagine that the differences in players' initial information can be traced to a two-step preplay procedure. At the start, every player is on an equal informational footing. There is initial uncertainty as to what rules of the game, etc., will prevail when the game is played, and players have their prior assessments as to how that uncertainty will resolve. (It is almost always assumed that these prior assessments are identical; indeed, this assumption is held by many to be the only philosophically sensible assumptions to make, and it is called the *Harsanyi doctrine* in many places.) Nature resolves the uncertainty and *selectively* reveals to the players part of that resolution. That is, one player may learn (in this initial round of revelation) things not revealed to another. *Then* the game begins; the 'initial' differences in what players know about the rules of the game trace to differences in what the players were told by nature before the game 'begins'. So, for example, to model Row's uncertainty about Col's payoffs in game A, we imagine: There are several possible games that the players might play, distinguished by Col's payoff structure. There is an initial probability distribution over what Col's payoffs will be. Nature picks a payoff structure for Col, and nature reveals to Col *but not to Row* what that structure is. Hence the game begins with Row uncertain about Col's payoffs.

In this model, Col is aware of the nature of Row's uncertainty. And, in doing

Nash equilibrium analysis, Col will (if he can) take advantage of that uncertainty. In a Nash equilibrium, we specify the players' choices of actions, as before, for the particular 'rules' that nature has indeed selected. But we *also* specify how players would have acted had nature chosen (and informed them) differently. This is necessary because when one player is uncertain about part of nature's choice, it is important what his fellow players would have done had nature chosen differently.

The example we have given is too simple to let one see the full power of this construction, but the reader need not go far into the literature to find examples. This technique has been applied in many instances, to extend the reach of Nash (and game theoretic) analysis. Applied skillfully, it can be used to model all sorts of situations, and while (in order to retain tractability) one must be content with highly stylized models, qualitative insights that have considerable intuitive appeal have been derived.

VI. CORRELATED EQUILIBRIUM. One of the stories told to justify Nash equilibria holds that players meet prior to play, and they (perhaps) negotiate a self-enforcing agreement. It turns out that, in some cases, by being clever, players can do better than they can with any Nash equilibrium.

Consider the bimatrix game in Table 4, taken from Aumann (1987). There are three Nash equilibria here, Bottom-Left, Top-Right, and a mixed strategy equilibrium in which each player has an expected payoff of 14/3.

Table 4

	Left	Right
Top	6, 6	2, 7
Bottom	7, 2	0, 0

Now imagine that, in preplay negotiation, one player suggests to the other that they hire a referee to perform the following steps. The referee will roll a six-sided die. If the die comes up with one or two dots on top, the referree will privately instruct Row to pick Top and Col to pick Left. For three or four dots, the instructions will be Top to Row and Right to Col. For five or six the instructions will be Bottom to Row and Left to Col. And, what is crucial, the instructions to each will not include what is being told to the other side; each player is told by the referee *only* what that player should do.

Are these instructions self-enforcing, in the sense that each player, assuming the other will carry out his instructions, would do so as well? Consider Row. If told to play Bottom, Row knows that the die came up with five or six up, and so Col must have been told to play Left. Thus Bottom is indeed Row's best choice. If told to play Top, Row only knows that the die came up with between one and four spots. Hence Col may have been told to play Right, and may have

175

been told Left, each with probability 1/2. But if Row assesses that Col is choosing between Left and Right, each with probability 1/2, then Top is indeed better than Bottom. Symmetric reasoning shows that this arrangement is self-enforcing on Col.

With these instructions, the vector expected payoff to the players is (5, 5), which lies outside the set of Nash equilibria; indeed, it lies outside the convex hull of the set of Nash payoffs. Apparently (the convex hull of) the set of Nash equilibrium *is not* the entire set of potential self-enforcing agreements to the game, at least, if the players can hire and instruct referees that act to *correlate* the actions of the players.

The last sentence is the key. In a Nash equilibrium, the players are presumed to select their strategies independently of one another. Through the intervention of a referee, they can achieve correlation in their choices. This is the basic insight of Aumann (1973). It has been extended by Forges (1985) and Myerson (1984), who note that the possibilities for correlation may expand still further if the referee can send messages during the course of an extensive game, and further still if players can, during the course of play, communicate privately to the referee information that they possess or will come to possess.

The set of correlated equilibria, unlike the set of Nash equilibria, has a very simple mathematical structure; it is a convex polyhedron, which is easy to compute, using simple mathematical programming techniques (Computing Nash equilibria is much more difficult.) Perhaps most importantly, Aumann (1987) establishes a beautiful linkage between correlated equilibria, a particular class of games with incomplete information, and 'the common knowledge of Bayesian rationality by all papers'.

BIBLIOGRAPHY

Aumann, R. 1973. Subjectivity and correlation in randomized strategies. *Journal of Mathematical Economics* 1, 67–96.

Aumann, R. 1987. Correlated equilibrium as an expression of Bayesian rationality. *Econometrica* 55, 1–18.

Bernheim, D. 1984. Rationalizable strategic behaviour. *Econometrica* 52, 1007–28.

Cournot, A. 1838. *Recherches sur les principes mathématiques de la théorie des richesses.* Paris. Trans. as *Researches into the Mathematical Principles of the Theory of Wealth,* New York: Macmillan and Company, 1897.

Farrell, J. 1985. Communication equilibria in games. GTE Laboratories, Waltham.

Forges, F. 1985. An approach to communication equilibrium. *Econometrica* 54(6), November, 1375–85.

Harsanyi, J. 1967–8. Games with incomplete information played by Bayesian players. Parts I, II and III. *Management Science* 14, 159–82; 320–34; 486–502.

Harsanyi, J. 1975. The tracing procedure. *International Journal of Game Theory* 4, 61–94.

Kohlberg, E. and Mertens, J.-F. 1982. On the strategic stability of equilibrium. Working Paper, CORE, Catholic University of Louvain; forthcoming in *Econometrica.*

Kreps, D. and Wilson, R. 1982. Sequential equilibrium. *Econometrica* 50, 863–94.

Kuhn, H. 1953. Extensive games and the problem of information. In *Contributions to the Theory of Games,* Vol. 2, ed. H. Kuhn and A. Tucker, Princeton: Princeton University Press.

Luce D.R. and Raiffa, H. 1957. *Games and Decisions*. New York: John Wiley.

Myerson, R. 1978. Refinements of the Nash equilibrium concept. *International Journal of Game Theory* 7, 73–80.

Myerson, R. 1984. Sequential equilibria of multistage games. DMSEMS Discussion Paper No. 590, Northwestern University.

Nash, J.F. 1950. Equilibrium points in *n*-person games. *Proceedings of the National Academy of Sciences USA* 36, 48–9.

Nash, J.F. 1951. Non-cooperative games. *Annals of Mathematics* 54, 286–95.

Pearce, D. 1984. Rationalizable strategic behaviour and the problem of perfection. *Econometrica* 52, 1029–50.

Roth, A. and Schoumaker, F. 1983. Expectations and reputations in bargaining: an experimental study. *American Economic Review* 73, 362–72.

Rubinstein, A. 1982. Perfect equilibrium in a bargaining model. *Econometrica* 50, 97–109.

Schelling, T. 1960. *The Strategy of Conflict*. Cambridge, Mass.: Harvard Unitersity Press.

Selten, R. 1965. Spieltheoretische Behandlung eines Oligopolmodells mit Nachfrageträgheit. *Zeitschrift für die gesamte Staatswissenschaft* 121, 301–24.

Selten, R. 1975. Re-examination of the perfectness concept for equilibrium points in extensive games. *International Journal of Game Theory* 4, 25–55.

Selten, R. 1978. The chain-store paradox. *Theory and Decision* 9, 127–59.

Noncooperative Games

JOSEPH E. HARRINGTON, JR

Game theory analyses multi-agent situations in which the payoff to an agent is dependent not only upon his own actions but also on the actions of others. Zero-sum games assume that the payoffs to the players always sum to zero. In that case, the interests of the players are diametrically opposed. In non-zero-sum games, there is typically room for cooperation as well as conflict.

The normal or strategic form characterizes a game by three elements. First, the set of players, $N = \{1, 2, \ldots, n\}$, who will be making decisions. Second, the set of strategies, S_i, available to player $i \forall i \in N$ where a strategy is a rule which tells a player how to behave over the entire course of the game. A strategy often takes the form of a function which maps information sets (that is, a description of where a player is at each stage in the game) into the set of possible actions. Thus, an action is a realization of a strategy. Finally, the normal form specifies the payoff function, $V_i(\cdot)$, of player $i \forall i \in N$. A payoff function is a composition of a player's von Neumann–Morgenstern utility function over outcomes and the outcome function which determines the outcome of the game for a given set of strategies chosen. The normal form of a particular game is presented in Figure 1. The set N is $\{1, 2\}$ while $S_1 = \{\alpha, \beta, \gamma\}$ and $S_2 = \{a, b, c\}$. The payoff to player 1 (2), for a given pair of strategies, is the first (second) number in the box.

A game is classified as either cooperative or noncooperative, a distinction which rests not on the behaviour observed but rather on the institutional structure. A cooperative game assumes the existence of an institution which can make any agreement among players binding. In a noncooperative game, no such institution exists. The only agreements in a noncooperative game that are meaningful are those which are *self-enforcing*. That is, it is in the best interest of each player to go along with the agreement, given that the other players plan to do so. In analysing the pricing behaviour of firms in an oligopolistic industry, a non-cooperative game is generally appropriate since, in most countries, cartel agreements are prohibited by law. Therefore, firms do not have access to legal institutions for enforcing contracts and making agreements binding.

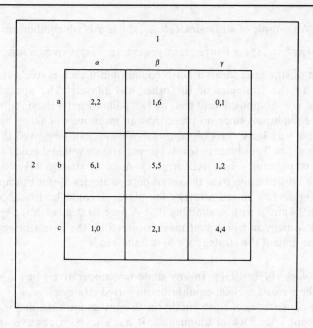

Figure 1

Let us examine the game in Figure 1 under the assumptions that it is noncooperative and that players are allowed preplay communications. After discussing how they each plan to behave, players 1 and 2 will simultaneously make a decision as to which strategy to play. After the strategies are chosen, the payoffs will be distributed. It is straightforward to show that the class of self-enforcing agreements for this game is $\{(\alpha, a), (\gamma, c)\}$. Consider the agreement that player 1 chooses α and player 2 chooses a. By choosing a, player 2 maximizes his payoff under the assumption that player 1 goes along and plays α. Similarly, player 1 finds it optimal to choose α if he believes player 2 will go along with the agreement. Thus, (α, a) is a self-enforcing agreement.

To understand the cost imposed by the restriction that an agreement must be self-enforcing, consider the agreement (β, b). Since it yields payoffs which are Pareto-superior to both (α, a) and (γ, c), the two players obviously have an incentive to try and achieve those strategy choices. However, even if they came to the agreement (β, b), it would be ineffectual. If player 1 truly believed that player 2 would honour the agreement and play b, player 1 would be better off reneging and choosing α instead. Because agreements cannot be made binding, the two players are then forced to settle on a Pareto-inferior outcome.

A solution concept for noncooperative games which encompasses the notion of self-enforcing agreements is *Nash equilibrium*. Originally formulated by Nash (1950, 1951), the concept finds its roots in the work of Cournot (1838).

179

Game Theory

Definition: An n-tuple of strategies, $(s_1^*, \ldots, s_n^*)$, is a Nash equilibrium if

$$V_i(s_1^*, \ldots, s_n^*) \geqslant V_i(s_1^*, \ldots, s_{i-1}^*, s_i, s_{i+1}^*, \ldots, s_n^*) \forall s_i \in S_i, \forall i \in N. \qquad (1)$$

A profile of strategies forms a Nash equilibrium if each player's strategy is a best reply to the strategies of the other $n-1$ players. The appeal of Nash equilibrium as a solution concept rests on two pillars. First is the stability inherent in a Nash equilibrium since no player has an incentive to change his strategy. Second is the very large class of games for which it can be proved that a Nash equilibrium exists. To substantiate this last remark, we will first need to introduce an additional concept – the mixed strategy. A mixed strategy takes the form of a probability distribution over the set of pure strategies S_i (for example, for the game in Figure 1, a mixed strategy for player 1 could be to choose α with probability 0.4 and β with probability 0.6). A pure strategy is thus a special case of a mixed strategy in which unit mass is placed on the pure strategy. A game is said to be finite if the strategy set S_i is finite $\forall i \in N$.

Theorem (Nash, 1950, 1951): In any finite noncooperative game $\langle N, \{S_i\}_{i \in N}, \{V_i\}_{i \in N} \rangle$, there exists a Nash equilibrium in mixed strategies.

The ease of existence of Nash equilibria also brings forth the major drawback to the concept – the lack of uniqueness. It has also been observed that when multiple Nash equilibria exist, some of them can be quite unreasonable. For the two-player game in Figure 2, there exist two pure-strategy Nash equilibria, $\{(\alpha, a), (\beta, c)\}$. However, (α, a) is rather unreasonable as it entails player 1 using

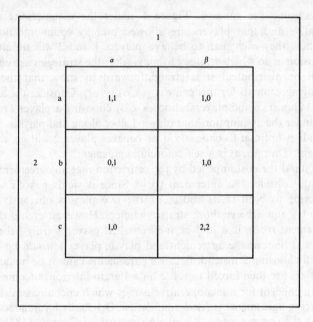

Figure 2

the strategy α which is weakly dominated by β. (That is, by choosing β instead of α, he would never be worse off and could end up better off.) In attempting to define what is meant by reasonable and to achieve a unique solution, work by Selten (1975), Myerson (1978), Kreps and Wilson (1982), Kalai and Samet (1984) and others has developed solution concepts that are more restrictive than Nash equilibrium.

Due to the difference in institutional structures, the issues analysed under a noncooperative game setting tend to be quite different from those dealt with in cooperative games. Since all agreements can be made binding in cooperative games, much of the analysis is concerned with determining which point in the Pareto-efficient set the players will settle on. Issues of importance are then coalition formation and the division of gains among coalition members. In contrast, in a noncooperative game, at issue is whether players can even reach the Pareto-efficient frontier; in the game in Figure 1, they do not. However, it has been observed in both experimental and real world situations (e.g., see Axelrod, 1984) that when the game is repeated players are indeed able to achieve Pareto efficiency in a noncooperative game like in Figure 1. An important issue in noncooperative games is then to understand the role of repetition in allowing players to overcome the inability to cooperate.

Let us suppose the one-shot game in Figure 1 is repeated T times, where $T \geqslant 2$, and the players are fully aware of the repetition. A strategy for player i now takes the form of a sequence of functions, $\{G_i^t\}_{t=1}^T$, where G_i^t maps the history of play over $\{1,\ldots,t-1\}$ into the set $\{\alpha,\beta,\gamma\}(\{a,b,c\})$ if $i = 1(2)$. Assume that the payoff to a player is the (undiscounted) sum of the single-period payoffs.

Let g_i^t denote the observed action of player i in period t. Consider the following pair of strategies:

$$G_1^1 = \beta$$

$$G_1^t = \begin{cases} \beta \text{ if } g_1^\tau = \beta \cdot g_2^\tau = b, \tau = 1,\ldots,t-1, 2 \leqslant t \leqslant T-1 \\ \gamma \text{ if } g_1^\tau = \beta, g_2^\tau = b, \tau = 1,\ldots,T-1, t = T \\ \alpha \text{ otherwise;} \end{cases} \tag{2}$$

$$G_2^1 = b$$

$$G_2^t = \begin{cases} b \text{ if } g_1^\tau = \beta, g_2^\tau = b, \tau = 1,\ldots,t-1, 2 \leqslant t \leqslant T-1 \\ c \text{ if } g_1^\tau = \beta, g_2^\tau = b, \tau = 1,\ldots,T-1, t = T \\ a \text{ otherwise.} \end{cases} \tag{3}$$

The strategy of player 1 says that he will start off by playing β and will continue to do so as long as (β, b) has been observed in all previous periods. If (β, b) was observed for all $t \in \{1,\ldots,T-1\}$, player 1 will choose γ in the final play. However, if the path ever deviates from (β, b) for any $t \leqslant T-1$, he will choose α for the remainder of the game. The strategy of player 2 is similarly defined.

If the two players pursue these strategies, the path of play will be (β, b) *for*

181

$t \in \{1, \ldots, T-1\}$ and (γ, c) for period T. Each player will earn a total payoff of $5T - 1$. The key issue, however, is whether these strategies form a Nash equilibrium. Given that player 1 pursues $\{G_1^t\}_{t=1}^T$, can player 2 earn a payoff higher than $5T - 1$ by choosing a strategy different from $\{G_2^t\}_{t=1}^T$? If not, then player 2's strategy in (3) is optimal. The strategy in (3) calls for player 2 to cooperate over $\{1, \ldots, T-1\}$ in the sense of not maximizing his single-period payoff. The alternative strategy is to choose a rather than b for some $t \leqslant T-1$ and earn 6 rather than 5 in that period. Since the gain from cheating is only in that period, it is best to cheat at the last moment so as to maximize the time of cooperation. The best alternative strategy for player 2 is then to choose b over $\{1, \ldots, T-2\}$ and cheat in period $T-1$ in playing a. The resulting payoff is $5(T-2) + 6 + 2 = 5T - 2$. Since this is less than $5T - 1$ then $\{G_2^t\}_{t=1}^T$ is the best reply to $\{G_1^t\}_{t=1}^T$. Similarly, one can show that this is true for player 1 as well and therefore the two strategies form a Nash equilibrium.

Repetition on the one-shot game has allowed players to earn an average payoff to $5 - (1/T)$ compared with 4 or 2 in the one-short game. Furthermore, as the horizon tends to infinity, the average payoff converges to the Pareto-efficient solution. Repetition expands the set of self-enforcing agreements by allowing players to be penalized in the future for cheating on an agreement. The penalty here is that the game moves to the Pareto-inferior single-period Nash equilibrium of (α, a). Because it is a Nash equilibrium, this threat is credible. Cooperation is rewarded by settling at the preferred solution (γ, c) in the final period. Note that cooperation cannot be maintained over the entire horizon since, in the final period, it is just like the one-shot game. Thus, the players must settle at either (α, a) or (γ, c). Development of cooperative behaviour in the finite horizon setting is due to work by Benoit and Krishna (1985), Friedman (1985) and Moreaux (1985). However, the original work for the infinite horizon game goes back to Friedman (1971).

When players are allowed preplay communication, there is a very strong basis for requiring a solution to be a Nash equilibrium because such equilibria are self-enforcing. However, when players cannot communicate, Nash equilibrium loses some of its appeal as a solution concept. (Actually, if there are multiple Nash equilibria, this is also true for games with preplay communication as players may fail to come to an agreement.) Work by Bernheim (1984) and Pearce (1984) suggests that there can be profiles of strategies which are reasonable for players to choose yet which do not constitute a Nash equilibrium.

Let us start with the basic premise that each player holds a subjective probability distribution over the strategies *and* beliefs of other players. Furthermore, impose the axiom that 'rationality is common knowledge'. That is, it is common knowledge that each player acts to maximize his payoff subject to his subjective beliefs. A set of beliefs is said to be *consistent* if it is not in violation of the 'rationality is common knowledge' axiom. In particular, you do not expect another player to pursue a non-optimal strategy. A strategy is *rationalizable* if there exists a set of consistent beliefs for which that strategy is optimal.

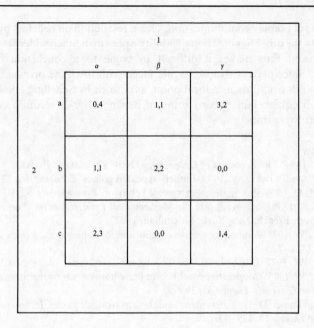

		α	β	γ
	a	0,4	1,1	3,2
2	b	1,1	2,2	0,0
	c	2,3	0,0	1,4

Figure 3

To understand rationalizability as a solution concept, consider the game in Figure 3. The unique pure-strategy Nash equilibrium is (β, b). It is easy to show that every Nash equilibrium strategy is rationalizable. β is optimal for player 1 if he believes player 2 will choose b. This belief is consistent if 1 believes that 2 believes that 1 will choose β so that b is a best reply for player 2. Similarly, the belief of player 1 that 2 believes that 1 will choose β is consistent if 1 believes that 2 believes that 1 believes that 2 will choose b and so forth. Thus, Nash equilibria are always rationalizable. However, one can show that γ is also a rationalizable strategy even though it is not part of a Nash equilibrium. γ is optimal for 1 if he believes 2 will choose a. That belief is consistent if 1 believes that 2 believes that 1 will play α so that a is a best reply. Now that belief is consistent if 1 believes that 2 believes that 1 believes that 2 will choose c so that α is a best reply. Finally, if 1 believes that 2 believes that 1 believes that 2 believes that 1 will play γ then c is a best reply and we have a cycle of $(\gamma - a - \alpha - c)$. By repeating this cycle we have a consistent set of beliefs which makes γ rationalizable. Actually, all the strategies in that cycle can be rationalized by a set of beliefs generated by that cycle. Thus, each strategy in this game is consistent with *some* basic premise concerning rational behaviour.

In this light, we gain a better idea of what the Nash equilibrium concept actually demands. It is not only a restriction on strategies but also on beliefs. It requires that strategies be best responses to some set of conjectures and that these conjectures about other players' strategies be fulfilled in equilibrium. In a game without preplay communication, such a restriction on beliefs is by no means natural. On the other hand, rationalizability opens up a much wider set of possible outcomes and thus makes it difficult to come to a conclusion concerning behaviour. Since players themselves are faced with the same problem, they may resort to Nash equilibria as a focal point, as defined by Schelling (1960). On this basis, Nash equilibrium regains some of its appeal as a solution concept for noncooperative games.

BIBLIOGRAPHY

Axelrod, R. 1984. *The Evolution of Cooperation.* New York: Basic Books.

Benoit, J.-P. and Krishna, V. 1985. Finitely repeated games. *Econometrica* 53, 905–22.

Bernheim, B.D. 1984. Rationalizable strategic behavior. *Econometrica* 52, 1007–28.

Cournot, A.A. 1838. *Researches into the Mathematical Principles of the Theory of Wealth.* Trans. from French, New York: Macmillan, 1897.

Friedman, J.W. 1971. A non-cooperative equilibrium for supergames. *Review of Economic Studies* 38, 1–12.

Friedman, J.W. 1977. *Oligopoly and the Theory of Games.* Amsterdam: North-Holland.

Friedman, J.W. 1985. Cooperative equilibria in finite horizon noncooperative supergames. *Journal of Economic Theory* 35, 390–8.

Kalai, E. and Samet, D. 1984. Persistent equilibria in strategic games. *International Journal of Game Theory* 13, 129–45.

Kreps, D.M. and Wilson, R. 1982. Sequential equilibria. *Econometrica* 50, 863–94.

Moreaux, M. 1985. Perfect Nash equilibrium in finite repeated games and uniqueness of Nash equilibrium in the constituent game. *Economics Letters* 17, 317–20.

Myerson, R.B. 1978. Refinements of the Nash equilibrium concept. *International Journal of Game Theory* 7, 73–80.

Nash, J.F., Jr. 1950. Equilibrium points in *n*-person games. *Proceedings of the National Academy of Sciences of the United States* 36, 48–9.

Nash, J.F., Jr. 1951. Non-cooperative games. *Annals of Mathematics* 54, 286–92.

Pearce, D.G. 1984. Rationalizable strategic behaviour and the problem of perfection. *Econometrica* 52, 1029–50.

Schelling, T.C. 1960. *The Strategy of Conflict.* Cambridge, Mass.: Harvard University Press.

Selten, R. 1975. Reexamination of the perfectness concept for equilibrium points in extensive games. *International Journal of Game Theory* 4, 25–55.

Vorob'ev, N.N. 1977. *Game Theory.* New York: Springer-Verlag.

Oligopoly and Game Theory

HUGO SONNENSCHEIN

Oligopoly theory is concerned with market structures in which the actions of individual firms affect and are affected by the actions of other firms. Unlike the polar cases of perfect competition and monopoly, strategic issues are fundamental to the study of such markets. In this entry we will explain some of the central themes of oligopoly theory, both modern and classical, and emphasize the connection between these themes and developments in the noncooperative theory of games.

Section 1 presents a simple static oligopoly model and uses it to discuss the classic solutions of Cournot (1838), Bertrand (1883) and Stackelberg (1934). Section 2 contains an introductory account of a modern line of research into a class of dynamic oligopoly models. In these models, firms and consumers meet repeatedly under identical circumstances. An example is presented to illustrate the important result that a firm's behaviour in such situations can drastically differ from that in the static model. Section 3 is concerned with a 'folk theorem' which states that with free entry, and when firms are small relative to the market, the market outcome approximates the result of perfect competition. Novshek's Theorem (1980) gives a price statement of this result, and in doing so provides an important bridge between oligopoly theory and the theory of perfect competition.

I. We consider a market in which n firms ($n > 1$) produce a single homogeneous product. The quantity of output produced by the ith firm is denoted by q_i and the cost associated with production of q_i by $C_i(q_i)$. Demand is specified by an inverse demand function $F(\cdot)$: $F(Q)$ is the price when $Q(= \Sigma_i q_i)$ is the aggregate output of firms. Let q and q_{-i} denote the vectors $(q_1, \ldots, q_n)$ and $(q_1, \ldots, q_{i-1}, q_{i+1}, \ldots, q_n)$ respectively. The profit of the ith firm is given by

$$\Pi_i(q) = F(Q)q_i - C_i(q_i).$$

185

The interdependence of firms' actions is reflected in the fact that the profits of the ith firm depend not only on its own quantity decision but also on the quantity decisions of all other firms.

A Cournot equilibrium is an output vector $\bar{q} = (\bar{q}_1, \ldots, \bar{q}_n)$ such that

$$\forall i, \quad \forall q_i, \quad \Pi_i(\bar{q}) \geqslant \Pi_i(q_i, \bar{q}_{i-1}),$$

where $(q_i, \bar{q}_{i-1})$ denotes the vector $(\bar{q}_1, \ldots, \bar{q}_{i-1}, q_i, \bar{q}_{i+1}, \ldots, \bar{q}_n)$. The equilibrium $\bar{q}$ is symmetric if $\bar{q}_1 = \cdots = \bar{q}_n$.

In the Cournot model, firms make quantity decisions. A single homogeneous good is produced, which all firms sell at the same price. At equilibrium, no firm can increase its profit by a unilateral decision to alter its action. A Cournot equilibrium is illustrated in the following example.

Example 1: Let n firms have identical linear cost functions: $C_i(q_i) = cq_i$ for all i. Assume that the inverse demand function is linear: $F(Q) = a - bQ$, where $a, b > 0$, and $a > c$. Thus,

$$\Pi_i(q) = (a - bQ)q_i - cq_i.$$

At Cournot equilibrium $\bar{q}$,

$$\frac{\partial \Pi_i(\bar{q})}{\partial q_i} = 0 \qquad \text{for all } i.$$

Therefore,

$$a - b \sum_i \bar{q}_i - b\bar{q}_i - c = 0 \qquad \text{for all } i.$$

It follows that equilibrium is unique and symmetric and

$$\bar{q}_i = \frac{a - c}{b(n + 1)} \qquad \text{for all } i.$$

Equilibrium aggregate output is $(a - c)/b(1 + 1/n)$; thus with two or more firms it is greater than monopoly output $(a - c)/2b$ but less than competitive output $(a - c)/b$. (The competitive output is defined by the condition that inverse demand price is equal to the constant per unit cost.).

It can be argued that Cournot incorrectly deduced from the fact that, in equilibrium, a homogeneous commodity can have only one price, the conclusion that an oligopolist cannot choose a different price from one charged by its competitors (see Simon, 1984). Bertrand observed that if firms choose prices rather than quantities, then the Cournot outcome is not an equilibrium. For the case in which prices rather than quantities are the strategic variable, the analysis proceeds as follows. Assume that all n firms ($n > 1$) have linear cost functions as described in Example 1 and that demand is continuous. Since the good being produced is homogeneous, a firm charging a price lower than that of other firms can capture the entire market. (To be specific we assume that all sales are shared equally among the firms that charge the lowest price.) Let $\bar{p}$ and $\bar{\Pi}$ denote price and individual profits respectively at the symmetric Cournot equilibrium. A firm can earn profits arbitrarily close to $n\bar{\Pi}$ (and hence, greater than Π) by lowering its price by a little from $\bar{p}$. The same argument can be used to show that in Bertrand equibrium there is only one price at which sales are made. This price equals marginal cost and aggregate output is the competitive output. In Bertrand equilibrium, no firm can make a higher profit by altering its price decision.

An alternative equilibrium concept, due to Stackelberg, will be applied to the case of duopoly. There are two firms, labelled 1 and 2. The function $H_2(\cdot)$, called the reaction function of firm 2 (see Friedman, 1977), is defined by

$$q_2 = H_2(q_1) \quad \text{if} \quad \forall \tilde{q}_2, \Pi_2(q_1, q_2) \geqslant \Pi_2(q_1, \tilde{q}_2).$$

The output vector $q = (\hat{q}_1, \hat{q}_2)$ is a Stackelberg equilibrium with firm 1 as the leader and firm 2 as the follower if firm 1 maximizes profit subject to the constraint that firm 2 chooses according to his reaction function; that is,

$$\forall q_1, \quad \Pi_1[\hat{q}_1, H_2(\hat{q}_1)] \geqslant \Pi_1[q_1, H_2(q_1)] \quad \text{and} \quad \hat{q}_2 = H_2(\hat{q}_1).$$

In the model of Example 1, the Stackelberg equilibrium is

$$(\hat{q}_1, \hat{q}_2) = \left(\frac{a-c}{2b}, \frac{a-c}{4b} \right) \quad \text{and} \quad \hat{p} = \frac{a+3c}{4}.$$

The Stackelberg equilibrium is interpreted as follows. The leader decides on a quantity to place on the market: this quantity is fixed. The follower decides how much to place on the market as a function of the quantity placed on the market by the leader. Again, equilibrium requires that neither firm can increase its profit by altering its decision.

Despite the fact that for the same model the Cournot, Bertrand and Stackelberg outcomes differ from each other, there is an important respect in which they are similar. In particular, they can all be viewed as the application of the Nash equilibrium solution concept (see the entry on NASH EQUILIBRIUM) to games which differ with respect to the choice of strategic variables and the timing of moves. Thus, Cournot and Bertrand equilibria are Nash equilibria of simultaneous move games where the strategic variables are quantities and prices respectively. The Stackelberg equilibrium is the subgame perfect equilibrium of a game where firms make quantity choices but where the leader moves before the follower. This observation points to a general characteristic of oligopoly theory; the results are very sensitive to the details of the model. Nash equilibrium is the dominant solution concept in the analysis of oligopolistic markets and because its application is so pervasive one might expect substantial unity in the predictions of oligopoly theory. Unfortunately, as the preceding analysis makes clear, this is not so.

II. It was observed in Example 1 that aggregate output in Cournot equilibrium exceeds monopoly output. This holds generally and it implies that aggregate profit in a Cournot equilibrium is less than monopoly profit. Thus, there exists a pair of (identical) quantity choices for firms such that with these choices each firm earns a higher profit than in Cournot equilibrium. Since such choices do not form a Cournot equilibrium, it would be in some firms' interest to deviate unilaterally from the choice assigned to it. In other words, without the possibility of binding contracts, the higher profit choices cannot be sustained, at least not in a static model. In this section, an extended example is presented to illustrate that if firms and consumers meet repeatedly, then it is possible for them to act more collusively than would be the case if they met only once. This result is very general and its importance for oligopoly theory was first pointed out by Friedman (see Friedman, 1971).

There are two firms labelled 1 and 2. Each firm has three pure strategies L, M and H which can be thought of as representing 'low', 'middle' and 'high' quantities of output respectively. The payoffs are indicated in the matrix shown in Figure 1, where (L, L), (M, M) and (H, H) may be thought of as the monopoly, Cournot and competitive outcomes respectively. In this game, (M, M) is the unique Nash equilibrium: given that one's opponent plays M, the best that he can do is play M himself.

Consider now the game which is an infinite repetition of the game described above. The point that we wish to develop is that with repeated play it is possible to sustain outcomes that are much more collusive than (M, M). Strategies in the repeated game are more complicated than in the single period game. Specifically, the play of firm i in period t is a function of the 'history' of the game; i.e., of the plays of both firms in all periods preceding t. This allows a firm to 'punish' or 'reward' other firms. An outcome of the infinitely repeated game is a pair of infinite streams of returns, one for each firm. These infinite streams can be evaluated according to various criteria: two examples are considered. The stream $\{x_t\}_{t=0}^{\infty}$ is preferred to the stream $\{y_t\}_{t=0}^{\infty}$ according to the limit of means criterion if

$$\lim_{T \to \infty} (1/T) \sum_{t=0}^{\infty} (x_t - y_t) > 0.$$

In the case where there is discounting, $\{x_t\}_{t=0}^{\infty}$ is preferred to $\{y_t\}_{t=0}^{\infty}$ if the

		2's output		
		L	M	H
	L	15, 15	5, 21	3, 10
1's output	M	21, 5	12, 12	2, 5
	H	10, 3	5, 2	0, 0

Figure 1

former has a higher present value; that is, if

$$\sum_{t=0}^{\infty} \frac{x_t - y_t}{(1+r)^t} > 0,$$

where r is the discount rate.

Consider first the case where outcomes are evaluated according to the limit of means criterion. The strategies in which both players choose M, no matter what the history, is easily seen to constitute an equilibrium. However, strategies in which both players choose L in every period (call this (L, L)) provided there has been no deviation also form a subgame perfect Nash equilibrium. If there is a deviation (L, L), then the equilibrium strategies call for players to play the subgame perfect Nash equilibrium (M, M). A firm contemplating a unilateral deviation from (L, L) at time t must weigh an immediate gain of 6 against a loss of at least 3 from $t + 1$ onwards. The deviation is unprofitable according to the limit of means criterion since a gain of 6 today becomes arbitrarily small when averaged over an increasingly large number of periods. The *mean* gain from the deviation is thus zero, while the mean loss from the deviation is 3. This argument can be used to demonstrate that any feasible payoff which dominates (M, M) can be realized by some equilibrium. (Strategies which involve reversion to Nash equilibrium forever cannot be used to characterize the entire set of subgame perfect Nash equilibria utility outcomes. In fact, the shaded area in Figure 2 can be obtained). These ideas are developed further in Aumann–Shapley (1976), Friedman (1971) and Rubinstein (1979). See also Axelrod (1984) and Fudenberg and Maskin (1986).

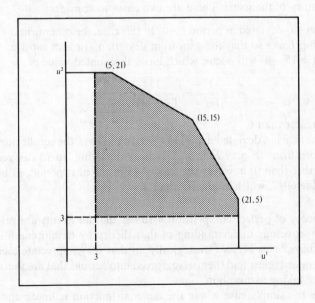

Figure 2

It is considerably more difficult to characterize the set of subgame perfect equilibria in the case where outcomes are evaluated according to their present value. However, Abreu (1986) provides results which help to determine the amount of collusion that is possible with various amounts of discounting. Of course this amount depends on the interest rate. It also depends on punishments that are a good deal more subtle than the threat to repeat the single period Nash equilibrium in the event of any deviation. To introduce you to this work we return to Figure 1 and consider first the case where $r = 1/4$. The threat of playing (M, M) forever, if there is a deviation from (L, L), sustains (L, L) as an equilibrium. To see this, note that a firm by deviating gains 6 immediately and loses 3 forever, thereafter. This loss has a present value of $3/r = [3/(1/4)] = 12$, so deviation is not profitable. On the other hand, if $r = 3/4$ the present value of the loss is $3/r = [3/(3/4)] = 4$, which is less than the gain from deviating. Therefore, deviation is profitable. But note that (L, L) can be sustained by a pair of subgame perfect Nash equilibrium strategies which are recursively defined as follows:

(a) The prescribed initial play is L for both players.

(b) If both players act according to the prescription in t, then they are both to play L in $t + 1$.

(c) If one or both do not play according to the prescription in t, then they are both to play H in $t + 1$.

To verify that this is a subgame perfect equilibrium, it has to be checked that no pattern of unilateral deviations is beneficial to a firm for any history of the game. The requirement argument is somewhat technical and is not given here (see Abreu, 1986); however, we will show that no one-period deviation is profitable for any history of the game. There are two cases to consider:

(a) No firm has deviated in period $t - 1$. In this case, the other firm is considered to be playing L at t so that the gain from deviation at t is at most 6. At $t + 1$, a loss of 15 $(= 15 - 0)$ will occur, which has a discounted value of

$$\frac{15}{1 + r} = \frac{15}{1 + (3/4)} = \frac{60}{7},$$

which is greater than 6.

(b) Some firm has deviated in period $t - 1$. In this case, the equilibrium strategy requires both firms to play H in t. A firm by deviating (to L) can receive 3 in period t rather than 0; however the loss of 15 in the next period, as before, has present value 60/7, which is greater than 3.

III. The theory of perfect competition assumes that all agents are price takers. We can improve our understanding of that theory by developing foundations for it that have firms behave strategically, in that they appreciate their market power, but nevertheless find themselves forced into actions that are well explained by the price taking assumption.

Consider the simple case where the demand function is linear and all firms have identical cost functions of the type $C = cq_i$. Recall from Example 1 that aggregate output in Cournot equilibrium is $(a - c)/b(1 + (1/n))$ and the equilibrium is therefore $a - (a - c)/1 + 1/n$. As the number of firms n increases, equilibrium price converges to c, which is the competitive price. This result does not generalize to the case of U-shaped average cost curves; furthermore, it has the defect that the number of firms in the market is fixed exogenously rather than being the result of a competitive process of free entry. These deficiencies are remedied in the work of Novshek.

Novshek's model. Novshek considers economies of the type described in Figure 3.

In the figure, F denotes an inverse demand function and AC an average cost curve associated with the employment of any one of an unlimited number of available units of an entrepreneurial factor. The price P^* and the output Y^* are the (perfectly) competitive price and the (perfectly) competitive output respectively. An intuitive argument for the convergence of equilibrium to P^* runs as follows. Suppose price $\bar{P}$ exceeds P^*. A firm can now enter the market and make a profit by producing at minimum average cost provided that it does not change prices by 'too much'. If the minimum efficient scale is small relative to the market, price will not change by 'too much' when the firm enters. Since there is an inexhaustible supply of potential entrants, $\bar{P}$ is not viable. Prices below P^* are not viable since firms are free to leave the market.

Novshek's theorm may be interpreted as a formalization of the intuitive argument presented above. The theorem states that there exists a quantity-setting Cournot equilibrium with entry when efficient scale is small relative to demand

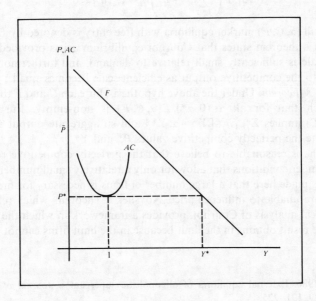

Figure 3

and that in this case the equilibrium output and price are approximately competitive. We conclude with a formal statement of the result. Assumptions: All firms have the same cost function C:

$$C(q_i) = 0 \quad \text{if} \quad q_i = 0,$$

and

$$C(q_i) = C_0 + v(q_i) \quad \text{if} \quad q_i > 0,$$

where $C_0 > 0$ and for all $q_i \geqslant 0$, $v' > 0$ and $v'' > 0$. Assume further that average cost is minimized uniquely at $q_i = 1$.

The inverse demand function $F(Q)$ is assumed to be twice continuously differentiable, with $F' < 0$ whenever $F > 0$, and there exists $Y^* > 0$ such that $F(Y^*) = C(1)$ (price equals minimum average cost). Definitions: An α ($\alpha > 0$) size firm corresponding to C is a firm with cost function $C_\alpha(q_i) = \alpha C(q_i/\alpha)$. Average cost for an α size firm is minimized at $q_i = \alpha$. For each α, C and F, one considers a pool of available firms, each with cost function C_α, facing inverse market demand F.

Given C, F and α, an (α, C, F) market equilibrium with free entry is an integer n and an output vector $\bar{q} = (\bar{q}_1, \ldots, \bar{q}_n)$ such that (a) $\bar{q}$ is an n firm Cournot equilibrium (without entry), that is,

$$\forall_i = 1, \ldots, n, \quad \forall q_i, \quad \Pi_i(\bar{q}) \geqslant \Pi_i(q_i, \bar{q}_{-i}),$$

where $\Pi_i(\cdot)$ is the profit function for firm i described in Section 1 and (b) entry is not profitable, that is,

$$\forall q_i, F\left(\sum_{j=1}^{n} q_j + q_i \right) q_i - C_\alpha(q_i) \leqslant 0.$$

The set of all (α, C, F) market equilibria with free entry is denoted by $E(\alpha, C, F)$.

Novshek's theorem states that Cournot equilibrium exists provided that the efficient scale is sufficiently small relative to demand, and furthermore, that it converges to the competitive output as efficient scale becomes small.

Novshek's theorem: Under the above hypothesis, for each C and F there exists $\alpha^* > 0$ such that for all $\alpha \in (0, \alpha^*)$, $E(\alpha, C, F)$ is non-empty. Furthermore, $\bar{q} \in E(\alpha, C, F)$ implies $\Sigma_{j=1}^{n} \bar{q}_j \in [Y^* - \alpha, Y^*]$ and so aggregate output and price approximate the perfectly competitive values P^* and Y^*.

It is perhaps reasonable to believe that the perfectly competitive result will also hold under conditions that allow for only a relatively small number of firms. No claim is made here that a large number of firms is necessary for firms to *act as if* they are unable to influence price. Novshek's Theorem, which relates well to th classical analysis of Cournot, provides a framework in which the perfectly competitive result obtains in the limit because in the limit firms cannot influence price.

BIBLIOGRAPHY

Abreu, D. 1986. External equilibria of oligopolistic supergames. *Journal of Economic Theory* 39, 191–225.

Aumann, R.J. and Shapley, L. 1976. Long term competition – a game theoretic analysis. Unpublished manuscript.

Axelrod, R.M. 1984. *The Evolution of Cooperation*. New York: Basic Books.

Bertrand, J. 1883. (Review of) Théorie mathématique de la richesse sociale. *Journal des Savants* 48, 499–508.

Cournot, A. 1838. *Recherches sur les principes mathématiques de la théorie des richesses*. Paris: Hachette. Trans. by N.T. Bacon as *Researches into the Mathematical Principles of the Theory of Wealth*, New York: Macmillan, 1927.

Friedman, J.W. 1971. A non-cooperative equilibrium of supergames. *Review of Economic Studies* 38, 1–12.

Friedman, J.W. 1977. *Oligopoly and the Theory of Games*. Amsterdam: North-Holland.

Fudenberg, D. and Maskin, E. 1986. The folk theorem in repeated games with discounting and with incomplete information. *Econometrica* 54, 533–54.

Novshek, W. 1980. Cournot equilibrium with free entry. *Review of Economic Studies* 47, 473–86.

Rubinstein, A. 1979. Equilibrium in supergames with the overtaking criterion. *Journal of Economic Theory* 21, 1–9.

Simon, L. 1984. Bertrand, the Cournot Paradigm and the theory of perfect competition. *Review of Economic Studies* 51, 209–30.

Stackelberg, H. von. 1934. *Marktform and Gleichgewicht*. Vienna: Springer.

Perfect Information

LEONARD J. MIRMAN

Perfect information is usually thought of as complete knowledge of a person's economic environment. It is clear that nobody in a real economy has perfect knowledge about every aspect of the economy. However, it has been argued that perfect knowledge is unnecessary since the price system summarizes all necessary information. Under this line of reasoning the only information that economic agents need are their own tastes and prices. This seems like a very naive argument. The real world is more complicated than this argument suggests. Even the prices system itself is not so simple: there are nonlinear prices, e.g. quantity discounts, as well as different prices for exactly the same commodity. Moreover the economy would function quite differently if the information structure was different, for example if all agents had more knowledge about economic variables. Hence the question arises: how are prices and information used in ideal models of the economy where many very complicated real world relationships have been simplified? In the following discussion the effect of information and the value of prices in conveying and summarizing this information in economic models is described. It appears that in economic models of the economy the 'information content' of prices is not as valuable as it appears on the surface. A well-functioning economy needs much more information than is contained in the price system.

In the quest for the effect of information on the economic environment two basic models come to mind. These are the general equilibrium and partial equilibrium models. The remarks in this essay will be aimed basically at the Walrasian general equilibrium model without production. However, many of the points dealing with equilibrating prices – and information – can be made about partial equilibrium models as well as general equilibrium models with production.

The Walrasian paradigm envisioned an economy consisting of a large number of agents trading many goods. Each person, at each point in time, knowing their own tastes and stock of resources (or endowments) decides how much of each good to buy or sell at each possible price, i.e. excess demands can be calculated on the basis of each person's environment (tastes and endowments) and the market price. Walras envisioned a steady state or stationary economy. Prices were thought to be generally in equilibrium, known to the consumers or economic agents but with perhaps slight, insignificant fluctuations. In this stable environment the price system regulates the supply to the market and dictates market clearing. In fact each individual agent reacts to the price system which summarizes all necessary information for this agent. Hence if any agent found himself confronted with an equilibrium price vector, then knowledge of only his own tastes and endowments would be sufficient to find the demands which equilibrate the market. However, to actually find the equilibrium price vector requires considerably more information. This difficulty also occurs in a partial equilibrium environment in which the price regulates the market clearing quantity and even the long run number of producers.

This perception of the Walrasian economy translates into the well-known modern general equilibrium model. In this model there are generally assumed to be a finite number of commodities and a finite number of agents. Each agent is assumed to be a price taker. Equilibrium is found from the market clearing condition on the basis of the aggregate excess demand functions. The price taking behaviour is somewhat unnatural with a finite number of agents, since each agent has some market power and therefore would naturally be expected to use strategic behaviour rather than passively taking prices as given. However, there is a very important extension of this model in which there is a continuum of agents. In this extension price taking behaviour is natural since no agent has any market power.

In this economy agents, in deriving their excess demands, need only information about their own tastes and endowments as well as prices. This model is analogous to the Walrasian paradigm described above. However, the analogy does not hold exactly since in the mathematical model there is no historical equilibrium price vector. Hence it is necessary to use an agent outside of the model, e.g. an auctioneer, to set equilibrium prices. In order to do this, aggregate excess demands must be known to the auctioneer. As a result although each agent needs to know prices only, any equilibrating mechanism can work only if it has information about all the agents. If no auctioneer is used then it is necessary to design some sort of *tâtonnement* or groping mechanism to find equilibrating prices. However for such a mechanism to work and to converge to equilibrium prices, it must take account of all agents. In particular, information about excess demands must be available to make the mechanism work.

In order to make clear exactly how information is used in an economic environment, consider a simple economy consisting of two goods and two individuals. Each agent is assumed to take prices as given. For each of these agents only the price is required to describe excess demands while knowledge of both consumers is needed for an equilibrium. Suppose now that agent 2 can have two possible endowments. The first possibility corresponds to a good year while the second corresponds to a lean year. The good year results in high endowments and the lean year results in low endowments. The process of determining the excess demand function for agent 1 remains the same as before: no knowledge of agent 2 is necessary. Agent 2 on the other hand has two possible excess demand functions – one corresponding to the good year, the other to the lean year. These two excess demand functions will in general be quite different, leading to two quite different equilibria. Since he is a price taker, no knowledge of agent 1 is needed by agent 2. To find equilibrium prices and allocations, however, the exact characteristics of each agent must be known, no matter what means is chosen to find an equilibrium.

The ideas discussed above can be illuminated by studying various equilibrium concepts and their informational requirements from the theory of games. In particular the information requirements in the general equilibrium model can be highlighted using the core concept of a cooperative game.

First consider the various notions of information in the game context. A distinction is made between games with perfect information and games with complete information. Perfect information in the game theoretic sense pertains to knowledge of the previous history of the game; that is, for perfect information all previous actions of the agents and equilibrium outcomes of the game are known. The notion of complete information in a game theoretic setting pertains to knowledge about the environment. In the general equilibrium context, complete information means that each agent knows his own taste and endowments as well as the tastes and endowments of all other agents. An even sharper notion of information is used in game theoretic models. This is the notion of common knowledge. Common knowledge implies not only that each agent knows his own environment – complete information – but each agent knows that the other agents know that the first agent has complete information and so on *ad infinitum*.

To see the importance of the common knowledge requirement in a noncooperative game consider a duopolistic market structure using the Cournot–Nash equilibrium concept. In this model each firm maximizes profits given the behaviour of the other firm. An equilibrium is a pair of outputs which is optimal for each firm given that the other firm is playing its equilibrium strategy (or output). In this model, each firm must know its own and its opponents' payoff function but each firm must also know that the opponent knows this information. This is clearly the case since the opponent's strategy will dependend upon whom he thinks he is playing against. Moreover the opponent should know that the first firm knows that the opponent has this information. This chain must be continued indefinitely in order to achieve a Cournot–Nash equilibrium. Clearly for a Cournot–Nash equilibrium to obtain, i.e. for the common knowledge requirement to be valid, a great deal of information is required.

Another game theoretic equilibrium concept is the core of an economy. The general equilibrium model is a very natural setting for the cooperative notion of the core. The relationship between the purely game theoretic idea of the core and the general equilibrium concept using prices again illustrates the importance and role of information in a Walrasian general equilibrium model. The core of a general equilibrium economy is defined as the set of outcomes or allocations which cannot be improved upon by any coalition or group of agents. This means that, for any allocation in the core, no subset of agents can band together, trade among themselves using their own endowments and make each agent as well off and at least one agent better off than with the allocation in the core. The core is a cooperative game with complete information. Since the idea of a core involves coalitional or cooperative behaviour the core and competitive equilibrium are quite different. In particular the price taking assumption is incompatible with cooperative behaviour. Hence it is not surprising that more information seems to be needed to find the set of core allocations. The surprising result is that for economies with a continuum of players the set of core allocations coincide with the set of competitive allocations. The use of a continuum of agents is a natural way to model price taking behaviour since no individual agent has power to affect prices. The notion of a core for large economies involves the use, by each agent, of considerably more information than the competitive economy, and yet for large economies the informational content of both notions is exactly the same. Moreover even for finite economies a similar, although not identical, statement can be made. This result is surprising since the core does not contain any explicit reference to prices. However, the relationship between competitive equilibrium and the core does show that prices are implicitly contained in the idea of a core. The relationship also underlines the fact that more information than is contained in prices is needed to find a general competitive equilibrium.

The discussion thus far has centred on perfect information in a general equilibrium model without uncertainty. Putting uncertainty into the model involves changing the specification of the market structure and the informational flow of the model. It is now necessary to know when the uncertainty is resolved to specify how the market reacts. Moreover it is also necessary to specify the agent's subjective beliefs about the likelihood of the various states of nature. Although the advent of uncertainty raises many interesting questions about imperfect or incomplete information – for example, moral hazard problems when actions are unobservable or adverse selection problems when information is unobservable – questions remain about perfect information in models with uncertainty. In particular consider an Arrow–Debreu world under uncertainty. In this model the information requirements are analogous to the requirements in a general equilibrium model under certainty with perfect information. In this economy trading takes place for contingent claims or Arrow–Debreu commodities. More precisely, since each state of the world can be distinguished, trading for commodities occurs for each commodity for each state of the world. This increases considerably the number of markets and the number of trades. However except for information about which state of the world has occurred, there are no extra informational requirements in this model. Each agent, knowing his own tastes and endowments in each state of the world, must know only prices. To actually find equilibrium prices, however, excess demands must be known in each possible state of the world.

Perhaps a more reasonable economy under uncertainty is to allow trading to take place on the basis of expectations or beliefs about the likelihood of the states of the world and not to assume that the state of the world is known after trading

197

occurs, i.e. not to allow contingent trades. The informational requirement in this model is quite different than in the Arrow–Debreu model. In this model there is only one market clearing price for each commodity rather, as in the Arrow–Debreu world, than a price for each commodity in each state of the world. The agents (or auctioneer) need not know which state of the world actually occurred. However they must know which states are possible. Finally the equilibrium in this model depends crucially on the subjective beliefs of the agents, whereas in the Arrow–Debreu model subjective beliefs do not affect the equilibrium outcomes.

This difference in market structure and information requirement in these two models leads to a loss in efficiency. In the Arrow–Debreu model equilibrium is always Pareto optimal but in the noncontingent claims model it will, in general, not be Pareto optimal. Noncontingent claims equilibrium will in general be *ex ante* but not *ex post* Pareto optimal. In fact if the market were to reopen after the realization of the state of the world and trading were allowed to take place, a Pareto optimal Arrow–Debreu equilibrium would result.

Prisoner's Dilemma

ANATOL RAPOPORT

The game nicknamed 'Prisoner's Dilemma' by A.W. Tucker has attracted wide attention, doubtless because it has raised doubts about the universal applicability of the so called Sure-thing Principle as a principle of rational decision.

The game is illustrated by the following anecdote. Two men, caught with stolen goods, are suspected of burglary, but there is not enough evidence to convict them of that crime, unless one or both confess. They could, however, be convicted of possession of stolen goods, a lesser offence.

The prisoners are not permitted to communicate. The situation is explained to each separately. If both confess, both will be convicted of burglary and sentenced to two years in prison. If neither confesses, they will be convicted of possession of stolen goods and given a six-month prison sentence. If only one confesses, he will go scot-free, while the other, convicted on the strength of his partner's testimony, will get the maximum sentence of five years.

It is in the interest of each prisoner to confess. For if the other confesses, confession results in a two-year sentence, while holding out results in a five-year sentence. If the other does not confess, holding out results in a six-month sentence, while confession leads to freedom. Thus, 'to confess' is a *dominating strategy*, one that results in a preferred outcome regardless of the strategy used by the partner. A dominating strategy can be said to be dictated by the Sure-thing Principle. Nevertheless, if both, guided by the Sure-thing Principle, confess, both are worse off (with a two-year sentence) than if they had not confessed and had got a six-month sentence.

In this way, Prisoner's Dilemma is seen as an illustration of the divergence between individual and collective rationality. Decisions that are rational from the point of view of each individual may be defective from the point of view of both or, more generally, all individuals in decision situations where each participant's decision affects all participants.

Generalized to more than two participants (players), Prisoner's Dilemma becomes a version of the so-called Tragedy of the Commons (Hardin, 1968). It is in each farmer's interest to add a cow to his herd grazing on a communal pasture. But if each farmer follows his individual interest, the land may be overgrazed to everyone's disadvantage. Over-harvesting in pursuit of profit by each nation engaged in commercial fishing is essentially Tragedy of the Commons in modern garb.

Many social situations are characterized by a similar bifurcation between decisions prescribed by individual and collective rationality. Price wars and arms races are conspicuous examples. In the context of Prisoner's Dilemma, holding out would be regarded as an act of cooperation (with the partner, of course, not with the authorities); confession with noncooperation or defection.

Because the prescriptions of individual and collective rationality are contradictory, a normative theory of decision in situations of this sort becomes ambivalent. Attention naturally turns to the problem of developing a *descriptive* theory, one which would purport to describe (or to predict, if possible) how people, faced with dilemmas of this sort, actually decide under a variety of conditions.

As experimental social psychology was going through a rapid development in the 1950s, Prisoner's Dilemma became a favourite experimental tool. It enabled investigators to gather large masses of data with relatively little effort. Moreover, the data were all 'hard', since the dichotomy between a cooperative choice in a Prisoner's Dilemma game (C) and a defecting one (D) is unambiguous. Frequencies of these choices became the principal dependent variables in experiments on decision-making involving choices between acting in individual or collective interest. As for the independent variables, these ranged over the personal characteristics of the players (sex, occupation, nationality, personality profile), conditions under which the decisions were made (previous experience, opportunities for communication), characteristics of behaviour of partner, the payoffs associated with the outcomes of the game, etc. (cf. Rapoport, Guyer and Gordon, 1976, chs 9, 15, 18, 19).

Prisoner's Dilemma is usually presented to experimental subjects in the form of a 2×2 matrix, whose rows, C_1 and D_1, represent one player's choices, while the columns, C_2 and D_2 represent the choices of the other. The choices are usually made independently. Thus, the four cells of the matrix correspond to the four possible outcomes of the game: $C_1 C_2, C_1 D_2, D_1 C_2$ and $D_1 D_2$. Each cell displays two numbers, the first being the payoff to Row, the player choosing between C_1 and D_1, the second the payoff to Column, who chooses between C_2 and D_2. The magnitudes of the payoffs are such that strategy (choice) D of each player dominates strategy C. The decision problem is seen as a dilemma, because both players prefer outcome $C_1 C_2$ to $D_1 D_2$; yet to choose C entails forgoing taking advantage of the other player, should he choose C, or getting the worst of the four payoffs, should he choose D.

The experiments are usually conducted in one of three formats: (1) single play, where each player makes only one decision; (2) iterated play, in which several simultaneous sequential decisions are made by a pair of players; (3) iterated play against a programmed player, where the subject's co-player's choices are determined in a prescribed way, usually dependent on the subject's choices.

The purpose of a single play is to see how different subjects will choose when there is no opportunity of interacting with the other player. The purpose of iterated play with two bona fide subjects is to study the effects of interaction between the successive choices. The purpose of play against a programmed player is to see how different (controlled) strategies of iterated plays influence the behaviour of the subject, whether, for example, cooperation is reciprocated or exploited, whether punishing defections has 'deterrent' effect, etc. For an extensive review of experiments with a programmed player, see Oskamp (1971).

The findings generated by experiments with Prisoner's Dilemma are of various degrees of interest. Some are little more than confirmations of common sense expectations. For example, frequencies of cooperative choices in iterated plays vary as expected with the payoffs associated with the outcomes. The larger the rewards associated with reciprocated cooperation or the larger the punishments associated with double defection, the more frequent are the cooperative choices. The larger the punishment associated with unreciprocated cooperation, the more frequent are the defecting choices, and so on. As expected, opportunities to communicate with the partner enhance cooperation; inducing a competitive orientation in the subjects inhibits it.

Of greater interest are the dynamics of iterated play. Typically, the frequency of cooperative choices averaged over large numbers of subjects at first decreases, suggesting disappointment with unsuccessful attempts to establish cooperation. If the play continues long enough, average frequency of cooperation eventually increases, suggesting establishment of a tacit agreement between the players. The asymptotically approached frequency of cooperation represents only the mean and not the mode. Typically, the players 'lock in' either on the $C_1 C_2$ or on the $D_1 D_2$ outcome (Rapoport and Chammah, 1965).

Bimodality is observed also in iterated plays against a programmed player who cooperates unconditionally. Roughly one half of the subjects have been observed to reciprocate this cooperation fully, while one half have been observed to exploit it throughout, obtaining the largest payoff.

Comparison of the effects of various programmed strategies in iterated play showed that the so-called Tit-for-tat strategy was the most effective in eliciting cooperation from the subjects. This strategy starts with C and thereafter duplicates the co-player's choice on the previous play. Of some psychological interest is the finding that the subjects are almost never aware that they are actually playing against their own mirror image one play removed. In a way, this finding is a demonstration of the difficulty of recognizing that others' behaviour towards one may be largely a reflection of one's behaviour towards them. Escalation of mutual hostility in various situations may well be a consequence of this deficiency.

Perhaps the most interesting result of Prisoner's Dilemma experiments with iterated play is that even if the number of iterations to be played is known to both subjects, nevertheless a tacit agreement to cooperate is often achieved. This finding is interesting because it illustrates dramatically the deficiency of prescriptions based on fully rigorous strategic reasoning.

At first thought, it seems that a tacit agreement to cooperate is rational in

201

iterated play, because a defection can be expected to be followed by a retaliatory defection in 'self defence', so to say, by the other player with the view of avoiding the worst payoff associated with unreciprocated cooperation. However, this argument does not apply to the play known to be the last, because no retaliation can follow. Thus, D dominates C on the last play, and according to the Sure-thing Principle, $D_1 D_2$ is a foregone conclusion. This turns attention to the next-to-the-last play, which now is in effect, the 'last play', to which the same reasoning applies. And so on. Thus, rigorous strategic analysis shows that the strategy consisting of D's throughout the iterated play is the only 'rational one', regardless of the length of the series.

The backward induction cannot be made if the number of iterations is infinite or unknown or determined probabilistically. In those cases, provided the probability of termination is not too large, the 100 per cent D strategy is not necessarily dictated by individual rationality. The question naturally arises about the relative merit of various strategies in iterated play of Prisoner's Dilemma. This question was approached empirically by Axelrod (1984).

Persons interested in this problem were invited to submit programmes for playing iterated Prisoner's Dilemma 200 times. Each programme was to be matched with every other programme submitted, including itself. The programme with the largest cumulated payoff was to be declared the winner of the contest.

Fifteen programmes were submitted, Tit-for-tat among them. It obtained the highest score. A second contest was announced, this time with probabilistic termination, 200 iterations being the expected number. The results of the first contest together with complete descriptions of the programmes submitted were publicized with the invitation to the second contest. This time 63 programmes were submitted from six countries. Tit-for-tat was again among them (submitted by the same contestant and by no other) and again obtained the highest score.

The interesting feature of this result was the fact that Tit-for-tat did not 'beat' a single programme against which it was pitted. In fact, it cannot beat any programme, since the only way to get a higher score than the co-player is to play more D's than he, and this, by definition, Tit-for-tat cannot do. It can only either tie or lose, to be sure by no more than one play. It follows that Tit-for-tat obtained the highest score, because other programmes, presumably designed to beat their opponents, reduced each other's scores when pitted against each other, including themselves. The results of these contests can be interpreted as further evidence of the deficiency of strategies based on attempts to maximize one's individual gains in situations where both cooperative and competitive strategies are possible. Moreover, the superiority of cooperative strategies does not necessarily depend on opportunities for explicit agreements.

Support for the latter conjecture came from a somewhat unexpected source, namely, applications of game-theoretic concepts in the theory of evolution (Maynard Smith, 1982; Rapoport, 1985). Until recently, game-theoretic models used in theoretical biology were so-called games against nature (e.g. Lewontin, 1961). A 'choice of strategy' was represented by the appearance of a particular genotype in a population immersed in a stochastic environment. Degree of adaptation to the environment was reflected in relative reproductive success of the genotype, i.e. statistically expected numbers of progeny surviving the reproductive age. In this way, the population evolved towards the best adapted genotype.

In this model, adaptation depends only on the probability distribution of the states of nature occurring in the environment (e.g. wet or dry seasons) but not on the fraction of the population that has adopted a given strategy. When this dependence is introduced, the model becomes a genuine game-theoretic model with more than one bona fide player.

The model suggested by Prisoner's Dilemma appeared in theoretical biology in connection with combats between members of the same species, for example over mates or territories. Assuming for simplicity two modes of fiting, fierce and mild, we can see the connection to Prisoner's Dilemma by examining the likely result of evolution. In an encounter between a fierce and a mild fighter, the former wins, the latter loses. However, an encounter between two fierce fighters may impose more severe losses on both than an encounter between two mild fighters. With proper rank ordering of payoffs (relative reproductive success), the model becomes a Prisoner's Dilemma. Development of non-lethal weapons, such as backward curved horns or behavioural inhibitions may have been results of natural selection which made lethal combats between members of the same species rare.

Iterated combats suggest comparison of the effectiveness of strategies in iterated play. Maynard Smith and Price (1973) observed a computer-simulated population of iterated Prisoner's Dilemma players, using different strategies, whereby the payoffs were translated into differential reproduction rates of the players using the respective strategies. In this way, the 'evolution' of the population could be observed. Eventually, the 'Retaliators', essentially Tit-for-tat players, replaced all others.

A central concept in game-theoretic models of evolution is that of the evolutionarily stable strategy (ESS). It is stable in the sense that a population consisting of genotypes representing that strategy cannot be 'invaded' by isolated mutants or immigrants, since such invaders will be disadvantaged with respect to their reproductive success. It has been shown by computer simulation that a population represented by programmes submitted to the above-mentioned contests evolved towards Tit-for-tat as an evolutionarily stable strategy. It was, however, shown subsequently that it is not the only such strategy.

In sum, the lively interest among behavioural scientists and lately many biologists in Prisoner's Dilemma can be attributed to the new ideas generated by the analysis of that game and by results of experiments with it. The different prescriptions of decisions based on individual and collective rationality in some conflict situations cast doubt on the very meaningfulness of the facile definition of 'rationality' as effective maximization of one's own expected gains, a definition implicit in all manner of strategic thinking, specifically in economic, political and military milieus. Models derived from Prisoner's Dilemma point to a clear refutation of a basic assumption of classical economics, according to which pursuit of self-interest under free competition results in collectively optimal equilibria. These models also expose the fallacies inherent in assuming the 'worst case' in conflict situations. The assumption is fully justified in the context of two-person zero sum games but not in more general forms of conflict, where interests of participants partly conflict and partly coincide. Most conflicts outside the purely military sphere are of this sort.

Finally, Prisoner's Dilemma and its generalization, the Tragedy of the Commons, provide a rigorous rationale for Kant's Categorical Imperative: act in the way you wish others to act. Acting on this principle reflects more than altruism. It reflects a form of rationality, which takes into account the circumstance that the effectiveness of a strategy may depend crucially on how many others adopt it and the fact that a strategy initially successful may become self-defeating *because* its success leads others to imitate it. Thus, defectors in Prisoner's Dilemma may be initially successful in a population of cooperators. But if this success leads to an increase of defectors and a decrease of cooperators, success turns to failure. Insights of this sort are of obvious relevance to many forms of human conflict.

BIBLIOGRAPHY

Axelrod, R. 1984. *The Evolution of Cooperation.* New York: Basic Books.

Hardin, G. 1968. The Tragedy of the Commons. *Science* 162, 1243–8.

Lewontin, R.C. 1961. Evolution and the theory of games. *Journal of Theoretical Biology* 1, 382–403.

Maynard Smith, J. 1982. *Evolution and the Theory of Games.* Cambridge: Cambridge University Press.

Maynard Smith, J. and Price, G.R. 1973. The logic of animal conflict. *Nature* 246, 15–18.

Oskamp, S. 1971. Effects of programmed strategies on cooperation in the Prisoner's Dilemma and other mixed-motive games. *Journal of Conflict Resolution* 15, 225–59.

Rapoport, A. 1985. Applications of game-theoretic concepts in biology. *Bulletin of Mathematical Biology* 47, 161–92.

Rapoport, A. and Chammah, A.M. 1965. *Prisoner's Dilemma.* Ann Arbor: University of Michigan Press.

Rapoport, A., Guyer, M. and Gordon, D. 1976. *The 2 × 2 Game.* Ann Arbor: University of Michigan Press.

Repeated Games

JEAN-FRANÇOIS MERTENS

Repeated game is a generic name for any model where players take simultaneous actions alternately and then a lottery, depending on those actions and the current state of nature, selects jointly a new state of nature, and a private signal and current payoff for each player. Players are interested in some long-term average of the payoffs.

The 'repetitive' aspect will typically stem from an assumption of finiteness (or compactness...) of the set of states of nature. The particular case where there is only one state of nature, and hence the same game is repeated over and over again, was originally named a supergame. We propose to keep that name, for the sake of precision in the vocabulary, and to reserve 'repeated game' for the above general model. Accordingly, we refer the reader to the article on SUPERGAMES for that particular case, and will not treat it here.

To complete the above model, an initial state has to be specified, and the stipulation made that players remember all past information. The model is particularly flexible. For example, uncertainty about the initial state of nature (incomplete information) is modelled just by adding an initial state, in which the players' actions are immaterial, payoffs zero, and an appropriate lottery selects the true initial state and initial information of the players. Information lags can be accommodated just by enlarging the state space, so as to keep in the current state all information about the past that still has to be transmitted. Similarly, all single state games may in fact be extensive form games of varying duration – this too can be reduced to the above, etc. For the game to be well defined, the model must be such that, at every stage, players are at least informed of their current action set – but, by duplicating some actions, one can always assume each player has a single action set, independent of the state of nature.

Now the model is well defined. The long term average could be a limiting average, or a discounted average, or even an average over a fixed, large number of stages – note that the latter two can be reduced to the former, again by appropriately enlarging the state space. The signals may, but do not have to, inform players of their current payoffs.

Such models apply to an enormous variety of situations – even outside economics: the original study of repeated games with incomplete information by Aumann and Maschler (1968) was (at least in part) motivated by arms control and disarmament negotiations. The first applications of information lags were to bomber–battleship duels; one could also consider, for example, negotiations over the release of hostages. Within economic theory the central importance of Harsanyi's model of games with incomplete information cannot be overstated (1967–8); it now pervades most subfields – insurance, finance, labour economics, agency theory, industrial organization, and poses major questions for general equilibrium theory. 'Moral hazard' is the counterpart in the insurance literature of the fact that only some signals are observed, not the actions themselves (e.g. effort level) – just as in the same literature incomplete information is called adverse selection, because of its frequent effect of turning a market into a 'market for lemons' (Akerlof, 1970). More generally, this unobservability is referred to as 'imperfect monitoring' in the agency literature. The much more drastic unobservability of the actual outcome, and of the player's own payoff as dependent on this outcome, constitutes the explanation for the enormous quality control literature and activity (and also probably in part for industrial standards, to make 'quality' more monitorable as well as more contractable).

Many situations require most features of the model at the same time, and in an essential way. Consider for instance a typical principal–agent relationship, such as that between a firm and a subcontractor. Initially, the firm may have a high degree of uncertainty about the capabilities of the subcontractor – and this explains a lot of signalling activity at the stage, as in Spence's (1974) analysis of the labour market, or in Milgrom and Roberts's (1984) analysis of advertising. But the potentially long term nature of the relationship cannot be ignored, even at this stage: it will allow the firm to monitor at least to some extent, if not capabilities, at least the final quality; and is the basic explanation for the signalling activity in Milgrom and Roberts: it is worthwhile for good-quality firms to engage in advertising in order to discriminate themselves from the others, since they may hope for a longer term, and so more profitable, relationship. During the repetition of the game, this initial uncertainty will continue to play a major strategic role, the high-capability subcontractor trying, for instance, to hide from the firm how low his costs in fact are. And not only can the actual costs or effort level of the subcontractor not be monitored, even the actual quality of output, which determines the firm's utility or objective function (e.g. some function of quality minus costs) will not be observable – except statistically, if the firm decides to take specific quality control steps; but those are costly, and part of the firm's strategic decision problem. In fact, in many such relationships those are one of the most essential parts of the relation. Furthermore, in many such situations there are essential state variables changing as a function of the players' actions. Think for instance of the subcontractor as a portfolio manager; the current value of the portfolio is the essential variable of the problem, and cannot be treated except as a state variable. It might be objected that, in this case at least, the state variable is monitorable through regular statements, but this leads us to the problem of information lags, which are of crucial importance in this business.

Analysis of repeated games has proceeded up to now in two main directions: (1) stochastic games, where the signals inform each player of at least the next state of nature and the last payoff vector; and (2) repeated games with incomplete information, where all states but the initial state remain fixed forever. In (2), actions in the initial state are immaterial and the initial state is left immediately, in which case it is more convenient to remove the initial state from the model, to include the signals to the players which may arise from the initial lottery in the description of the states (thus expanding the state space), and to say that each player has a partition of the set of states, determined by his initial signals. An initial state is then selected with some probability distribution p on the set of states S, each player is informed of his corresponding partition element, and then players forever play the chosen game.

There is no room here to go into the history of (1) and (2), and we will briefly describe the current state of the art. A recent and much more thorough survey of the subject was given in a lecture by the present author at the International Congress of Mathematicians (1986) in Berkeley, and will appear in the *Proceedings* of that Congress. It also contains a fairly complete bibliography.

On stochastic games, fairly complete results are available by now. A recent result of Mertens and Parthasarathy (1986) shows the existence of equilibria (and a characterization) in the discounted case – or more generally, e.g. whenever there is a uniform (in initial state and in strategies) bound on the expected number of stages before the game stops (the discounted case can be interpreted as a uniform, fixed stopping probability). This allows for general state and actions sets, with the usual measurability assumption in the state variables and continuity as a function of strategies. As for the infinite game, in the two-person zero-sum case, a value is known to exist (Mertens and Neyman, 1981) under essentially a somewhat strengthened convergence assumption on the values of the discounted games (those typically exist by the previously mentioned result – continuity assumptions can even be weakened). This assumption is always satisfied for finite state and action sets, by a previous result of Bewley and Kohlberg (1976b). It is also known (Mertens, 1982) that with finite state and action sets there exist stationary equilibria which are a semi-algebraic function of the discount factor, hence converge; but a result of Sorin (1986) shows that the ε-equilibria of the infinite game (for which no existence theorem is yet available) may be far away in payoff space from those limits. It is not clear in his example which of the two solutions is more appropriate as a model for long games, and the result raises serious questions about any meaningful 'folk theorem' for stochastic games.

Games with incomplete information are systematically studied under finiteness assumptions on all sets (states and signals), which entails no conceptual loss of generality. We refer to the entry on supergames for the motivation of the study of the two-person zero-sum case. Under the assumption, three main cases are solved. The first is when one player is initially informed of everything, i.e. the true state of nature and the initial signal of the other players. In that case, Aumann, Maschler and Stearns proved the existence of the value and of optimal strategies (with easier strategies later by Kohlberg, 1975). The second is when the signals which the players receive after each state are independent of the state of nature. In this case, the limit v of V_n and of v was obtained by the author; later, Mertens and Zamir (1980) obtained maxmin and minmax of the infinite game, which are typically different, since the incentive to use one's information only after having obtained all possible information the opponent may reveal turns the game into a game like 'picking the largest integer'. The third is when both players always have the same information; here Forges (1982) proved existence of a value.

The non-zero sum case was studied only when one player is initially informed of everything, and the signals received by the players after each stage are the last pair of actions. A characterization of the set of Nash equilibria was obtained by Hart (1985), and further by Aumann and Hart (1986). A (generic) example by Forges (1984a) shows that the unbounded number of signalling stages required by the characterization is indeed necessary. This is even an example of a pure signalling game, where after the informed player has received his private information the players may exchange simultaneous messages in an arbitrarily large language for as long as they wish before the uninformed player takes a single action. Even in this case an unbounded (but finite) number of signalling stages – and in particular, of messages of the uninformed player – may be required to achieve payoffs far superior to anything that can be achieved without.

Aumann's correlated equilibria (1974) and their extensive form relatives ('extensive form correlated equilibria' and 'communication equilibria') introduced in Forges (1986) were ($\pm$) characterized for the same model by Forges (1984b).

This body of work on incomplete information already provides many fundamental insights into the proper use of information in repetitive economic situations.

BIBLIOGRAPHY

Akerlof, G. 1970. The market for 'lemons', qualitative uncertainty and the market mechanism. *Quarterly Journal of Economics* 84, 488–500.

Aumann, R.J. 1974. Subjectivity and correlation in randomized strategies. *Journal of Mathematical Economics* 1, 67–95.

Aumann, R.J. 1985. Repeated games. In *Issues in Contemporary Microeconomics and Welfare*, ed. G.R. Feiwel, London: Macmillan.

Aumann, R.J. and Hart, S. 1986. Bi-convexity and bi-martingales. *Israel Journal of Mathematics* 54, 159–80.

Aumann, R.J. and Maschler, M. 1968. Repeated games of incomplete information: the zero-sum extensive case. In *Mathematica* (Report to the US Arms Control and Disarmament Agency), ST–143, ch. III, 37–116 (prepared by Mathematica Inc., Princeton).

Bewley, T. and Kohlberg, E. 1976a. The asymptotic theory of stochastic games. *Mathematics of Operations Research* 1, 197–208.

Bewley, T. and Kohlberg, E. 1976b. The asymptotic solution of a recursion equation occurring in the stochastic games. *Mathematics of Operations Research* 1, 321–36.

Bewley, T. and Kohlberg, E. 1978. On stochastic games with stationary optimal strategies. *Mathematics of Operations Research* 3, 104–25.

Forges, F. 1982. Infinitely repeated games of incomplete information: symmetric case with random signals. *International Journal of Game Theory* 11, 203–13.

Forges, F. 1984a. A note on Nash equilibria in repeated games with incomplete information. *International Journal of Game Theory* 13, 179–87.

Forges, F. 1984b. Communication equilibria in repeated games with incomplete information. CORE Discussion Papers 8406, 8411, 8412, Louvain-la-Neuve, Belgium.

Forges, F. 1986. An approach to communication equlibria. *Econometrica* 54(6), 1375–86.

Harsanyi, J.C. 1967–8. Games of incomplete information played by Bayesian players. *Management Science* 14, Pt I, 159–82; Pt II, 320–34; Pt III, 486–502.

Hart, S. 1985. Nonzero-sum two-person repeated games with incomplete information. *Mathematics of Operations Research* 10, 117–53.

Kohlberg, E. 1975. Optimal strategies in repeated games with incomplete information. *International Journal of Game Theory* 4, 7–24.

Mertens, J.-F. 1972. The value of two-person zero-sum repeated games: the extensive-case. *International Journal of Game Theory* 1, 217–25.

Mertens, J.-F. 1982. Repeated games: an overview of the zero-sum case. In *Advances in Economic Theory*, ed. W. Hildenbrand, Cambridge: Cambridge University Press.

Mertens, J.-F. and Neyman, A. 1981. Stochastic games. *International Journal of Game Theory* 10(2), 53–6.

Mertens, J.-F. and Parthasarathy, T. 1986. Existence and characterization of Nash equilibria for discounted stochastic games. CORE Discussion Paper, Louvain-la-Neuve, Belgium.

Mertens, J.-F. and Zamir, S. 1980. Minmax and maxmin of repeated games with incomplete information. *International Journal of Game Theory* 9, 201–15.

Milgrom, P. and Roberts, J. 1984. Price and advertising signals of product quality. Mimeo, Stanford University.

Sorin, S. 1986. Asymptotic properties of a non-zero sum stochastic game. *International Journal of Game Theory* 15, 101–7.

Spence, M. 1974. *Market Signalling*. Cambridge, Mass.: Harvard University Press.

Shapley Value

SERGIU HART

The *value* of an uncertain outcome (a 'gamble', 'lottery', etc.) to a participant is an evaluation, in the participant's utility scale, of the prospective outcomes: It is an *a priori* measure of what he expects to obtain (this is the subject of 'utility theory'). In a similar way, one is interested in evaluating a *game*; that is, measuring the *value* of each player in the game.

Such an approach was originally developed by Lloyd S. Shapley (1951, 1953a). The framework was that of *n-person games in coalitional form with side-payments*. Such a game is given by a finite set N together with a function v that associates to every subset S of N a real number $v(S)$. Here, N is the set of 'players', v is the 'characteristic function' and $v(S)$ is the 'worth' of the 'coalition' S: the maximal total payoff the members of S can obtain. This model presumes the following: (i) There are finitely many players. (ii) Agreements between players are possible and enforceable (the game is 'cooperative'). (iii) There exists a medium of exchange ('money') that is freely transferable in unlimited amounts between the players, and moreover every player's utility is additive with respect to it (i.e. a transfer of x units from one player to another decreases the first one's utility by x units and increases the second one's utility by x units; the total payoff of a coalition can thus be meaningfully defined as the sum of the payoffs of its members). This assumption is known as existence of 'side-payments' or 'transferable utility'. (iv) The game is adequately described by its characteristic function (i.e. the worth $v(S)$ of each coalition S is well defined, and the abstraction from the extensive structure of the game to its characteristic function leads to no essential loss; the game is then called a 'c-game'). It should be noted that these underlying assumptions may be interpreted in a broader and more abstract sense. For example, in a voting situation, a 'winning coalition' is assigned worth 1, and a 'losing' coalition – worth 0. The important feature is that, for each coalition, its prospects may well be summarized by one real number.

The *Shapley value* of such a game is a unique payoff vector for the game (i.e. a payoff to each player). It is determined by the following four axioms (this differs from Shapley's original approach only unessentially). (1) *Symmetry* or *equal treatment*: If two players in a game are substitutes (i.e. the worth of no coalition changes when replacing one of the two players by the other one), then their values are equal. (2) *Null* or *dummy player*: If a player in a game is such that the worth of a coalition never changes when he joins it, then his value is zero. (3) *Efficiency* or *Pareto optimality*: The sum of the values of all players equals $v(N)$, the worth of the grand coalition of all players (in a superadditive game $v(N)$ is the maximal amount that the players can jointly get; note that this axiom actually combines feasibility with efficiency). (4) *Additivity*: The value of the sum of two games is the sum of the values of the two games (an equivalent requirement is that the value of a probabilistic combination of two games is the same as the probabilistic combination of the values of the two games; this is analogous to the 'expected utility' postulate). The result of Shapley is that these axioms uniquely determine one payoff vector for each game.

Remarkably, the Shapley value of a player i in a game v turns out to be exactly the *expected marginal contribution of player i to a random coalition S*. For a coalition S not containing i, the marginal contribution to i to S is the change in the worth when i joins S, i.e. $v(S \cup \{i\}) - v(S)$. A random coalition S not containing i is obtained by arranging all n players in line (e.g. $1, 2, \ldots, n$), and then putting in S all those that precede i; it is assumed that all $n!$ orders are equally likely. This formula is remarkable, first, since it is a consequence of the very simple and basic axioms above and, second, since the idea of marginal contribution is so fundamental in much of economic analysis.

It should be emphasized that the value of a game is an *a priori* measure – before the game is actually played. Unlike other solution concepts (e.g. the core, von Neumann–Morgenstern solutions, bargaining sets, etc.), it need not yield a 'stable' outcome (the probable final result when the game is played). These final stable outcomes are in general not well determined; the value – which is uniquely specified – may be thought of as their *expectation* or average. Another interpretation of the value axioms regards them as rules for 'fair' division, guiding an impartial 'referee' or 'arbitrator'. Moreover, as suggested above, the Shapley value may be understood as the utility of playing the game (Shapley, 1953a; for a formalization, see Roth, 1977).

In view of both its strong intuitive appeal and its mathematical tractability, the Shapley value has been the focus of much research and applications. Some of these will be briefly mentioned here (an excellent survey is Aumann, 1978).

CHANGING THE DOMAIN. Following Shapley's pioneering approach, the concept of *value* has been extended to additional classes of games, dispensing with (part of) the assumptions (i)–(iv) above.

'Large games' – where the number of players is infinite – have been extensively studied. This includes games with countably many players (Shapley, 1962; Artstein, 1971; Berbee, 1981); non-atomic games (a continuum of small players who are individually insignificant; the monumental book of Aumann and Shapley,

1974; Kannai, 1966; Neyman and Taumann, 1976; Hart, 1977a; Neyman, 1977, 1981; Tauman, 1977; Mertens, 1980); 'oceanic games' (a continuum of small players together with finitely many larger players; Shapiro and Shapley, 1960; Milnor and Shapley, 1961; Hart, 1973; Fogelman and Quinzii, 1980; Neyman, 1986). The study of large games, which involves the solution of deep mathematical problems, has led to very valuable insights. One example is the so-called 'diagonal principle'; the value is determined by those coalitions S which are close in composition to the whole population (i.e. the proportion of each type of player in S is almost the same as in the grand coalition N of all players).

When the game is not necessarily a 'c-game' (see (iv) above; this is the case when, for example, threats by the complement $T = N - S$ of the coalition S are costly to T), Harsanyi (1959) has suggested using a 'modified characteristic function' and applying to it the Shapley value (see also Selten, 1964).

Another class of much interest consists of games 'without side-payments', or 'with non-transferable utility' ('NTU-games', for short); here, assumption (ii) on the existence of a medium of utility exchange is not necessarily satisfied. The simplest such games – two-person pure bargaining – were originally studied by Nash (1950): a unique solution is determined by a set of simple axioms. A value for general NTU-games, which coincides with the Shapley value in the side-payments case, and with the Nash solution in the two-person case, was proposed by Harsanyi (1959, 1963). Another value (with the same properties) was introduced by Shapley (1969). The latter has been widely studied, in particular in large economic models (see below).

Other extensions include games with communication graphs (Myerson, 1977), coalition structures (Aumann and Drèze, 1974; Owen, 1977; Hart and Kurz, 1983), and so on.

CHANGING THE AXIOMS. The four axioms (1) to (4) have been in turn replaced by alternative axioms or even completely dropped. This has led to new foundations for the Shapley value, as well as to the introduction of various generalizations.

If, in addition to the characteristic function, the data of the game include (relative) weights between the players, then a *weighted Shapley value* may be defined (Shapley, 1953b). In the unanimity game, for example, the values of the players are no longer equal but, rather, proportional to the weights; the usual (symmetric) Shapley value results if all the weights are equal. This model is useful when players are of unequal 'size' (e.g. a player may represent a 'group', a 'department', and so on).

Abandoning the efficiency axiom leads to the class of *semi-values* (Dubey, Neyman and Weber, 1981). An interesting semi-value is the *Banzhaf–Coleman index* (Banzhaf, 1965; Dubey and Shapley, 1979); it has been proposed originally as a measure of power in voting games. It can be computed in the same way as the Shapley value: expected marginal contribution, but assuming that all coalitions not containing player i are equally likely.

Another approach to the value uses the following 'consistency' or 'reduced game' property: Given a solution concept (that associates payoff vectors to games), assume that a group of players in a game has already agreed to it, and they are paid off accordingly; consider the reduced game among the remaining players. If the solution of the reduced game is always the same as that of the original game, then the solution is said to be *consistent*. It turns out that consistency, together with some simple requirements for two-player games, characterizes the Shapley value (Hart and Mas-Colell, 1989).

ECONOMIC APPLICATIONS. The model of an *exchange economy* has been the focus of much study in economic theory. The main solution concept there is the *competitive equilibrium*, where prices are determined in such a way that total supply equals total demand. The cooperative game obtained by allowing each coalition to exchange freely the commodities they own among themselves, is called a *market game*. One can then find the value of the corresponding market game. The following result (known as the 'value equivalence principle') has been obtained in various models of this kind (in particular, both when utility is transferable and when it is not): In a *large* exchange economy (where traders are individually insignificant), all value allocations are competitive; moreover, if the utilities are smooth, then all competitive allocations are also value allocations. (It should be noted that in the NTU case there may be more than one value allocation.) This remarkable result joints together two very different approaches; on the one hand, competitive prices which arise from supply and demand; on the other hand, marginal contributions of the economic agents (Shapley, 1964; Shapley and Shubik, 1969; Aumann and Shapley, 1974; Aumann, 1975; Champsaur, 1975; Hart, 1977b; Mas-Colell, 1977; note moreover that for large markets, the set of competitive equilibria coincides with the core).

Other applications of the value to economic theory include models of taxation, where a political power structure is superimposed on the exchange or production economy (Aumann and Kurz, 1977). Further references on economic applications can be found in Aumann (1985).

Next, consider the problem of allocating joint costs in a 'fair' manner. It turns out that the axioms determining the Shapley value are easily translated into postulates suitable for this kind of problem (e.g. the efficiency axiom becomes total cost sharing). The various 'tasks' (or 'projects', 'departments', etc.) become the players, and $v(S)$ is the total cost of the set S of tasks (Shubik, 1962). Two notable applications are airport landing fees (a task here is an aircraft landing; Littlechild and Owen, 1973) and telephone billing (each time unit of a phone call is a player; the resulting cost allocation scheme is in actual use at Cornell University; Billera, Heath and Raanan, 1978). Further research in this direction can be found in Shapley (1981a; the use of weighted Shapley values is proposed there); Billera and Heath (1982); Mirman and Tauman (1982); and the book edited by Young (1985).

POLITICAL APPLICATIONS. The Shapley value has been widely applied to the study of power in voting and other political systems. A trivial observation – although

213

not always remembered in practice – is that the political power need not be proportional to the number of votes (the Board of Supervisors in the Nassau County, N. Y. is a good example; Shapley, 1981b). It is therefore important to find an objective method of measuring power in such situations. The Shapley value (known in this setup as the *Shapley–Shubik index*; Shapley and Shubik, 1954) is, by its definition, a very good candidate. Indeed, consider a simple political game; it is described by specifying for each coalition whether it is 'winning' or 'losing'. The Shapley value of a player i is then the probability that i is a 'pivot'; namely, that in a random order of all players, those preceding i are losing, whereas together with i they are winning. For example, in a simple majority voting situation (half of the votes are needed to win), assume there is one large party having $\frac{1}{3}$ of the votes, and the rest of the votes are divided among many small parties; the value of the large party is then approximately $\frac{1}{2}$ – much higher than its share of the votes. In comparison, when there are two large parties each having $\frac{1}{3}$ of the votes (the rest being again divided among a large number of small parties), the value of each large party is close to $\frac{1}{4}$ – less than its voting weight (this phenomenon may be explained by the competition – or lack of it – for the 'favours' of the small parties).

The Shapley value has also been used in more complex models, where 'ideologies' and 'issues' are taken into account (thus, not all arrangements of the voters are equally likely; an 'extremist' party, for example, is less likely to be the pivot than a 'middle-of-the road' one; Owen, 1971; Shapley, 1977). References on political applications of the Shapley value may be found in Shapley (1981b); these include various parliaments (USA, France, Israel), United Nations Security Council and others.

BIBLIOGRAPHY
The following list is by no means complete; it contains some of the original contributions to the study of value as well as surveys and pointers to further references.

Artstein, Z. 1971. Values of games with denumerably many players. *International Journal of Game Theory* 1, 27–37.

Aumann, R.J. 1975. Values of markets with a continuum of traders. *Econometrica* 43, 611–46.

Aumann, R.J. 1978. Recent developments in the theory of the Shapley Value. *Proceedings of the International Congress of Mathematicians*, Helsinki, 995–1003.

Aumann, R.J. 1985. On the non-transferable utility value: a comment on the Roth–Shafer examples. *Econometrica* 53, 667–78.

Aumann, R.J. and Drèze, J.H. 1974. Cooperative games with coalition structures. *International Journal of Game Theory* 3, 217–37.

Aumann, R.J. and Kurz, M. 1977. Power and taxes. *Econometrica* 45, 1137–61.

Aumann, R.J. and Shapley, L.S. 1974. *Values of Non-atomic Games*, Princeton: Princeton University Press.

Banzhaf, J.F. 1965. Weighted voting doesn't work: a mathematical analysis. *Rutgers Law Review* 19, 317–43.

Berbee, H. 1981. On covering single points by randomly ordered intervals. *Annals of Probability* 9, 520–28.

Billera, L.J. and Heath, D.C. 1982. Allocation of shared costs: a set of axioms yielding a unique procedure. *Mathematics of Operations Research* 7, 32–9.

Billera, L.J., Heath, D.C. and Raanan, J. 1978. Internal telephone billing rates: a novel application of non-atomic game theory. *Operations Research* 26, 956–65.

Champsaur, P. 1975. Cooperation versus competition. *Journal of Economic Theory* 11, 393–417.

Dubey, P. and Shapley, L.S. 1979. Mathematical properties of the Banzhaf Power Index. *Mathematics of Operations Research* 4, 99–131.

Dubey, P., Neyman, A. and Weber, R.J. 1981. Value theory without efficiency. *Mathematics of Operations Research* 6, 122–8.

Fogelman, F. and Quinzii, M. 1980. Asymptotic value of mixed games. *Mathematics of Operations Research* 5, 86–93.

Harsanyi, J.C. 1959. A bargaining model for the cooperative *n*-person game. In *Contributions to the Theory of Games*, Vol. 4, ed. A.W. Tucker and D.R. Luce, Princeton: Princeton University Press, 324–56.

Harsanyi, J.C. 1963. A simplified bargaining model for the n-person cooperative game. *International Economic Review* 4, 194–220.

Hart, S. 1973. Values of mixed games. *International Journal of Game Theory* 2, 69–85.

Hart, S. 1977a. Asymptotic value of games with a continuum of players. *Journal of Mathematical Economics* 4, 57–80.

Hart, S. 1977b. Values of non-differentiable markets with a continuum of traders. *Journal of Mathematical Economics* 4, 103–16.

Hart, S. and Kurz, M. 1983. Endogenous formation of coalitions. *Econometrica* 51, 1047–64.

Hart, S. and Mas-Colell, A. 1989. Potential, value and consistency. *Econometrica* 57 (forthcoming).

Kannai, Y. 1966. Values of games with a continuum of players. *Israel Journal of Mathematics* 4, 54–8.

Littlechild, S.C. and Owen, G. 1973. A simple expression for the Shapley value in a special case. *Management Science* 20, 370–72.

Mas-Colell, A. 1977. Competitive and value allocations of large exchange economies. *Journal of Economic Theory* 14, 419–38.

Mertens, J.-F. 1980. Values and derivatives. *Mathematics of Operations Research* 5, 523–52.

Milnor, J.W. and Shapley, L.S. 1961. Values of large games II: oceanic games. RAND RM 2649. Also in *Mathematics of Operations Research* 3, 1978, 290–307.

Mirman, L.J. and Tauman, Y. 1982. Demand compatible equitable cost-sharing prices. *Mathematics of Operations Research* 7, 40–56.

Myerson, R.B. 1977. Graphs and cooperation in games. *Mathematics of Operations Research* 2, 225–9.

Nash, J.F. 1950. The bargaining problem. *Econometrica* 18, 155–62.

Neyman, A. 1977. Continuous values are diagonal. *Mathematics of Operations Research* 2, 338–42.

Neyman, A. 1981. Singular games have asymptotic values. *Mathematics of Operations Research* 6, 205–12.

Neyman, A. 1986. Weighted majority games have asymptotic values. The Hebrew University, Jerusalem, RM 69.

Neyman, A. and Tauman, Y. 1976. The existence of non-diagonal axiomatic values. *Mathematics of Operations Research* 1, 246–50.

Owen, G. 1971. Political games. *Naval Research Logistics Quarterly* 18, 345–55.

Owen, G. 1977. Values of games with a priori unions. In *Essays in Mathematical Economics and Game Theory*, ed. R. Henn and O. Moeschlin, New York: Springer-Verlag, 76–88.

Roth, A.E. 1977. The Shapley value as a von Neumann–Morgenstern utility. *Econometrica* 45, 657–64.

Selten, R. 1964. Valuation of n-person games. In *Advances in Game Theory*, ed. M. Dresher, L.S. Shapley and A.W. Tucker, Princeton: Princeton University Press, 577–626.

Shapiro, N.Z. and Shapley, L.S. 1960. Values of large games I: a limit theorem. RAND RM 2648. Also in *Mathematics of Operations Research* 3, 1978, 1–9.

Shapley, L.S. 1951. Notes on the n-person game II: the value of an n-person game. RAND RM 670.

Shapley, L.S. 1953a. A value for n-person games. In *Contributions to the Theory of Games*, Vol. II, ed. H.W. Kuhn and A.W. Tucker, Princeton: Princeton University Press, 307–17.

Shapley, L.S. 1953b. Additive and non-additive set functions. PhD thesis, Princeton University.

Shapley, L.S. 1962. Values of games with infinitely many players. In *Recent Advances in Game Theory*, Princeton University Conferences, 113–18.

Shapley, L.S. 1964. Values of large games VII: a general exchange economy with money. RAND RM 4248-PR.

Shapley, L.S. 1969. Utility comparison and the theory of games. In *La Décision*: *agrégation et dynamique des ordres de préférence*, Paris: Editions du CNRS, 251–63.

Shapley, L.S. 1977. A comparison of power indices and a nonsymmetric generalization. RAND P-5872.

Shapley, L.S. 1981a. Comments on R.D. Banker's 'Equity considerations in traditional full cost allocation practices: an axiomatic perspective'. In *Joint Cost Allocations*, ed. S. Moriarity: University of Oklahoma, 131–6.

Shapley, L.S. 1981b. Measurement of power in political systems. *Game Theory and its Applications*, Proceedings of Symposia in Applied Mathematics, Vol. 24, American Mathematical Society, 69–81.

Shapley, L.S. and Shubik, M. 1954. A method for evaluating the distribution of power in a committee system. *American Political Science Review* 48, 787–92.

Shapley, L.S. and Shubik, M. 1969. Pure competition, coalitional power, and fair division. *International Economic Review* 10, 337–62.

Shubik, M. 1962. Incentives, decentralized control, the assignment of joint costs and internal pricing. *Management Science* 8, 325–43.

Tauman, Y. 1977. A non-diagonal value on a reproducing space. *Mathematics of Operations Research* 2, 331–7.

Young, H.P. (ed.) 1985. *Cost Allocation: Methods, Principles, Applications*. New York: Elsevier Science.

Statistical Decision Theory

JAMES O. BERGER

Decision theory is the science of making optimal decisions in the face of uncertainty. Statistical decision theory is concerned with the making of decisions when in the presence of statistical knowledge (data) which sheds light on some of the uncertainties involved in the decision problem. The generality of these definitions is such that decision theory (dropping the qualifier 'statistical' for convenience) formally encompasses an enormous range of problems and disciplines. Any attempt at a general review of decision theory is thus doomed; all that can be done is to present a description of some of the underlying ideas.

Decision theory operates by breaking a problem down into specific components, which can be mathematically or probabilistically modelled and combined with a suitable optimality principle to determine the best decision. Section 1 describes the most useful breakdown of a decision problem – that into actions, a utility function, prior information and data. Section 2 considers the most important optimality principle for reaching a decision – the Bayes Principle. The frequentist approach to decision theory is discussed in section 3, with the Minimax Principle mentioned as a special case. Section 4 compares the various approaches.

The history of decision theory is difficult to pin down, because virtually any historical mathematically formulated decision problem could be called an example of decision theory. Also, it can be difficult to distinguish between true decision theory and formally related mathematical devices such as least squares estimation. The person who was mainly responsible for establishing decision theory as a clearly formulated science was Abraham Wald, whose work in the 1940s, culminating in his book *Statistical Decision Functions* (1950), provided the foundation of the subject. (The book does discuss some of the earlier history of decision theory.) General introductions to decision theory can be found, at an advanced level, in Blackwell and Girshick (1954) and Savage (1954); at an intermediate level in Raiffa and Schlaifer (1961), Ferguson (1967), De Groot (1970) and Berger (1985); and at a basic level in Raiffa (1968) and Winkler (1972).

217

1 ELEMENTS OF A DECISION PROBLEM

In a decision problem, the most basic concept is that of an action a. The set of all possible actions that can be taken will be denoted by A. Any decision problem will typically involve an unknown quantity or quantities; this unknown element will be denoted by θ.

Example 1. A company receives a shipment of parts from a supplier, and must decide whether to accept the shipment or to reject the shipment (and return it to the supplier as unsatisfactory). The two possible actions being contemplated are:

$$a_1: \text{accept the shipment,} \qquad a_2: \text{reject the shipment.}$$

Thus $A = \{a_1, a_2\}$. The uncertain quantity which is crucial to a correct decision is:

$$\theta = \text{the proportion of defective parts in the shipment.}$$

Clearly action a_1 is desirable when θ is small enough, while a_2 is desirable otherwise.

The key idea in decision theory is to attempt a quantification of the gain or loss in taking possible actions. Since the gain or loss will usually depend upon θ as well as the action a taken, it is typically represented as a function of both variables. In economics this function is generally called the *utility function* and is denoted by $U(\theta, a)$. It is to be understood as the gain achieved if action a is taken and θ obtains. (The scale for measuring 'gain' will be discussed later.) In the statistical literature it is customary to talk in terms of loss instead of gain, with typical notation $L(\theta, a)$ for the loss function. Loss is just negative gain, so defining $L(\theta, a) = - U(\theta, a)$ results in effective equivalence between the two formulations (whatever maximizes utility will minimize loss).

Example 1 (cont.). The company determines its utility function to be given by:

$$U(\theta, a_1) = 1 - 10\theta, \qquad U(\theta, a_2) = - 0.1.$$

To understand how these might be developed, note that if a_2 is chosen the shipment will be returned to the supplier and a new shipment sent out. This new shipment must then be processed, all of which takes time and money. The overall cost of this eventuality is determined to be 0.1 (on the scale being used). The associated utility is -0.1 (a loss is a negative gain). Note that this cost is fixed: that is, it does not depend on θ.

When a_1 is chosen, quite different considerations arise. The parts will be utilized with, say, gain of 1 if none are defective. Each defective part will cause a reduction in income by a certain amount, however, so that the true overall gain will be 1 reduced by a linear function of the proportion of defectives. $U(\theta, a_1)$ is precisely of this form. The various constants in $U(\theta, a_1)$ and $U(\theta, a_2)$ are chosen to reflect the various importance of the associated costs.

The scale chosen for a utility function turns out to be essentially unimportant, so that any convenient choice can be made. If the gain or loss is monetary, a suitable monetary unit often can provide a natural scale. Note, however, that utility functions can be defined for any type of gain or loss, not just monetary. Thus, in example 1, the use of defective parts could lead to faulty final products from the company, and affect the overall quality image or prestige of the company. Such considerations are not easily stated in monetary terms, yet can be important enough to include in the overall construction of the utility function. (For more general discussion of the construction of utility functions, see Berger, 1985.)

The other important component of a decision problem is the information available about θ. This information will often arise from several sources, substantially complicating the job of mathematical modelling. We content ourselves here with consideration of the standard statistical scenario where there are available (i) *data*, X, from a statistical experiment relating to θ; and (ii) background or *prior* information about θ, to be denoted by $\pi(\theta)$. Note that either of these components could be absent.

The data, X, is typically modelled as arising from some *probability density* $p_\theta(X)$. This, of course, is to be interpreted as the probability of the particular data value when θ obtains.

Example 1 (cont.). It is typically too expensive (or impossible) to test all parts in a shipment for defects, so that a statistical sampling plan is employed instead. This generally consists of selecting, say, n random parts from the shipment, and testing only these for defects. If X is used to denote the number of defective parts found in the tested sample, and if n is fairly small compared with the total shipment size, then it is well known that $p_\theta(X)$ is approximately the binomial density:

$$p_\theta(X) = \frac{n!}{X!(n-X)!}\theta^X(1-\theta)^{n-X}.$$

The *prior* information about θ is typically also described by a probability density $\pi(\theta)$. This density is the probability (or mass) given to each possible value of θ in the light of beliefs as to which values of θ are most likely.

Example 1 (cont.). The company has been receiving a steady stream of shipments from this supplier and has recorded estimates of the proportion of defectives for each shipment. The records show that 30 per cent of the shipments had θ between 0.0 and 0.025, 22 per cent of the shipments had θ between 0.025 and 0.05, 15 per cent had θ between 0.05 and 0.075, 11 per cent had θ between 0.075 and 0.10, 13 per cent had θ between 0.10 and 0.15, and the remaining 9 per cent had θ bigger than 0.15. Treating the varying θ as random, a probability density which provides a good fit to these percentages is the beta (1,14) density given (for $0 \leqslant \theta \leqslant 1$) by:

$$\pi(\theta) = 14(1-\theta)^{13}.$$

(E.g. the probability that a random θ from this density is between 0.0 and 0.025 can be calculated to be 0.30, agreeing exactly with the observed 30 per cent.) It is very reasonable to treat θ for the current shipment as a random variable from this density, which we will thus take as the prior density.

2 BAYESIAN DECISION THEORY

When θ is known, it is a trivial matter to find the optimal action; simply maximize the gain by maximizing $U(\theta, a)$ over a. When θ is unknown, the natural generalization is to first 'average' $U(\theta, a)$ over θ, and then maximize over a. The correct method of 'averaging over θ' is to determine the overall probability density of θ, to be denoted $\pi^*(\theta)$ (and to be described shortly), and then consider the *Bayesian expected* utility:

$$U^*(a) = E^{\pi^*}[U(\theta, a)] = \int U(\theta, a)\pi^*(\theta)\, d\theta.$$

(This last expression assumes that θ is a continuous variable taking values in an interval of numbers. If it can assume only one of a discrete set of values, then this integral should be replaced by a sum over the possible values.) Maximizing $U^*(a)$ over a will yield the optimal *Bayes action*, to be denoted by a^*.

Example 1 (cont.). Initially, assume that no data, X, are available from a sampling inspection of the current shipment. Then the only information about θ is that contained in the prior $\pi(\theta)$; $\pi^*(\theta)$ will thus be identified with $\pi(\theta) = 14(1 - \theta)^{13}$. Calculation yields:

$$U^*(a_1) = \int_0^1 (1 - 10\theta)14(1 - \theta)^{13}\, d\theta = 0.33,$$

$$U^*(a_2) = \int_0^1 (-0.1)14(1 - \theta)^{13}\, d\theta = -0.1.$$

Since $U^*(a_1) > U^*(a_2)$, the Bayes action is a_1, to accept the shipment.

When data, X, are available, in addition to the prior information, the overall probability density π^* for θ must combine the two sources of information. This is done by *Bayes' Theorem* (from Bayes, 1763), which gives the overall density, usually called the *posterior density*, as:

$$\pi^*(\theta) = p_\theta(X) \cdot \pi(\theta)/m(X),$$

where:

$$m(X) = \int p_\theta(X)\pi(\theta)\, d\theta$$

(or a summation over θ if θ assumes only a discrete set of values), and $p_\theta(X)$ is the probability density for the experiment with the observed values of the data X inserted.

Example 1 (cont.). Suppose a sample of $n = 20$ items is tested, out of which $X = 3$ defectives are observed. Calculation gives that the posterior density of θ is:

$$\pi^*(\theta) = p_\theta(3) \cdot \pi(\theta)/m(3) = \left[\frac{20!}{3!\,17!}\theta^3(1 - \theta)^{17}\right] \cdot [14(1 - \theta)^{13}]/m(3)$$

$$= (185{,}504)\theta^3(1 - \theta)^{30},$$

which can be recognized as the beta $(4, 31)$ density. This density describes the location of θ in the light of all available information. The Bayesian expected utilities of a_1 and a_2 are thus:

$$U^*(a_1) = \int_0^1 (1 - 10\theta)\pi^*(\theta)\,d\theta = \int_0^1 (1 - 10\theta)(185{,}504)\theta^3(1 - \theta)^{30}\,d\theta = -0.14,$$

and

$$U^*(a_2) = \int_0^1 (-0.1)\pi^*(\theta)\,d\theta = -0.1.$$

Clearly a_2 has the largest expected utility, and should be the action chosen.

3 FREQUENTIST DECISION THEORY

An alternative approach to statistical decision theory arises from taking a 'long run' perspective. The idea is to imagine repeating the decision problem a large number of times, and to develop a decision strategy which will be optimal in terms of some long-run criterion. This is called the *frequentist* approach, and is essentially due to Neyman, Pearson and Wald (see Neyman and Pearson, 1933; Neyman, 1977; Wald, 1950).

To formalize the above idea, let $d(X)$ denote a *decision strategy* or *decision rule*. The notation reflects the fact that we are imagining repetitions of the decision problem which will yield possibly different data X, and must therefore specify the action to be taken for any possible X. The utility of using $d(X)$ when θ obtains is thus $U[\theta, d(X)]$. The statistical literature almost exclusively works with loss functions instead of utility functions; for consistency with this literature we will thus use the loss function $L(\theta, d) = -U(\theta, d)$. (Of course, we want to minimize loss.)

The first step in a frequentist evaluation is to compute the *risk function* (expected loss over X) of d, given by:

$$R(\theta, d) = E_\theta\{L[\theta, d(X)]\} = \int L[\theta, d(X)]p_\theta(X)\,dX.$$

(Again, this integral should be a summation if X is discrete valued.) For a fixed θ this risk indicates how well $d(X)$ would perform if utilized repeatedly for data arising from the probability density $p_\theta(X)$. For various common choices of L this yields familiar statistical quantities. For instance, when L is 0 or 1, according to whether or not a correct decision is made in a two-action hypothesis-testing problem, the risk becomes the 'probabilities of type I or type II error'. When L is 0 or 1, according to whether or not an interval $d(X)$ contains θ, the risk is 1 minus the 'coverage probability function' for the confidence procedure $d(X)$. When $d(X)$ is an estimate of θ and $L(\theta, d) = (\theta - d)^2$, the risk is the 'mean squared error' commonly considered in many econometric studies. (If the estimator $d(X)$ is unbiased, then this mean squared error is also the variance function for d.)

Example 2. Example 1, involving acceptance or rejection of the shipment, is somewhat too complicated to handle here from the frequentist perspective; we thus consider the simpler problem of merely estimating θ (the proportion of defective parts in the shipment). Assume that loss in estimation is measured by *squared error*; that is:

$$L[\theta, d(X)] = [\theta - d(X)]^2.$$

A natural estimate of θ, based on X (the number of defectives from a sample of size n), is the sample proportion of defectives $d_1(X) = X/n$. For this decision rule (or *estimator*), the risk function when X has the binomial distribution discussed earlier (so that X takes only the discrete values $0, 1, 2, \ldots, n$) is given by:

$$R(\theta, d) = \sum_{X=0}^{n} \left(\theta - \frac{X}{n} \right)^2 p_\theta(X) = \theta(1 - \theta)/n.$$

The second step of a frequentist analysis is to select some criterion for defining optimal risk functions (and hence optimal decision rules). One of the most common criteria is the *Minimax Principle*, which is based on consideration of the maximum possible risk:

$$R^*(d) = \max_\theta R(\theta, d).$$

This indicates the worst possible performance of $d(X)$ in repeated use, and hence has some appeal as a criterion based on a cautious attitude. Using this criterion, an optimal decision rule is, of course, defined to be one which minimizes $R^*(d)$, and is called a *minimax decision rule*.

Example 2 (cont.). It is easy to see that:

$$R^*(d_1) = \max_\theta R(\theta, d_1) = \max_\theta \frac{\theta(1 - \theta)}{n} = \frac{1}{4n}.$$

However, d_1 is not the minimax decision rule. Indeed, the minimax desicion rule turns out to be:

$$d_2(X) = (X + \sqrt{n}/2)/(n + \sqrt{n}),$$

which has $R^*(d_2) = 1/[4(1 + \sqrt{n})^2]$ (cf. Berger, 1985, p. 354). The minimax criterion here is essentially the same as the minimax criterion in game theory. Indeed, the frequentist decision problem can be considered to be a zero-sum two-person game with the statistician as player II (choosing $d(X)$), an inimical 'nature' as player I (choosing θ), and payoff (to player I) of $R(\theta, d)$. (Of course, it is rather unnatural to assume that nature is inimical in its choice of θ.) (For further discussion of this relationship, see Berger, 1985, ch. 5.)

Minimax optimality is but one of several criteria that are used in frequentist decision theory. Another common criterion is the Invariance Principle, which calls for finding the best decision rule in the class of rules which are 'invariant' under certain mathematical transformations of the decision problem. (See Berger, 1985, ch. 6, for discussion).

There also exist very general and elegant theorems which characterize the class of acceptable decision rules. The formal term used is 'admissible'; a decision rule, d, is *admissible* if there is no decision rule, d^*, with $R(\theta, d^*) \leq R(\theta, d)$, the inequality being strict for some θ. If such a d^* exists, then d is said to be *inadmissible*, and one has obvious cause to question its use. Very common decision rules, such as the least squares estimator in three or more dimensional normal estimation problems (with sum of squares error loss), can turn out rather astonishingly to be inadmissible, so this avenue of investigation has had a substantial impact on decision theory. A general discussion, with references, can be found in Berger (1985).

4 COMPARISON OF APPROACHES

For solving a real decision problem, there is little doubt that the Bayesian approach is best. It incorporates all the available information (including the prior information, $\pi(\theta)$, which the frequentist approach ignores), and it tends to be easier than the frequentist approach by an order of magnitude. Maximizing $U^*(a)$ over all actions is generally much easier than minimizing something like $R^*(d)$ over all decision rules; the point is that, in some sense, the frequentist approach needlessly complicates the issue by forcing consideration of the right thing to do for each possible X, while the Bayesian worries only about what to do for the actual data X that are observed. There are also fundamental axiomatic developments (see, Ramsey, 1931; Savage, 1954; and Fishburn, 1981, for a general review) which show that only the Bayesian approach is consistent with plausible axioms of rational behaviour. Basically, the arguments are that situations can be constructed in which the follower of any non-Bayesian approach, say the minimax analyst, will be assured or inferior results.

Sometimes, however, decision theory is used as a formal framework for investigating the performance of statistical procedures, and then the situation is less clear. In Example 2, for instance, we used decision theory mainly as a method to formulate rigorously the problem of estimating a binomial proportion θ. If one is developing a statistical rule, $d(X)$, to be used for binomial estimation problems in general, then its repeated performance for varying X is certainly of interest. Furthermore, so the argument goes, prior information may be unavailable or inaccessible in problems where routine statistical analyses (such as estimating a binomial proportion θ) are to be performed, precluding use of the Bayesian approach.

The Bayesian reply to these arguments is that (i) optimal performance for each X alone will guarantee good performance in repeated use, negating the need to consider frequentist measures explicitly; and (ii) even when prior information is unavailable or cannot be used, a Bayesian analysis can still be performed with what are called 'non-informative' prior densities.

Example 2 (cont.). If no prior information about θ is available, one might well say that choosing $\pi(\theta) = 1$ reflects this lack of knowledge about θ. A Bayesian analysis (calculating the posterior density and choosing the action with smallest Bayesian expected squared error loss) yields, as the optimal estimate for θ when X is observed:

$$d_3(X) = (X + 1)/(n + 2).$$

This estimate is considerably more attractive than, say, the minimax rule $d_2(X)$ (see Berger, 1985, p. 375).

In practical applications of decision theory, it is the Bayesian approach which is dominant, yet the frequentist approach retains considerable appeal among theoreticians. A general consensus on the controversy appears quite remote at this time. This author sides with the Bayesian approach in the above debate, while recognizing that there are some situations in which the frequentist approach might be useful. For an extensive discussion of these issues, see Berger (1985).

BIBLIOGRAPHY

Bayes, T. 1763. An essay towards solving a problem in the doctrine of chances. *Philosophical Transactions of the Royal Society*, London 53, 370–418.

Berger, J. 1985. *Statistical Decision Theory and Bayesian Analysis*. New York: Springer-Verlag.

Blackwell, D. and Girshick, M.A. 1954. *Theory of Games and Statistical Decisions*. New York: Wiley.

De Groot, M.H. 1970. *Optimal Statistical Decisions*. New York: McGraw-Hill.

Ferguson, T.S. 1967. *Mathematical Statistics: A Decision Theoretic Approach*. New York: Academic Press.

Fishburn, P.C. 1981. Subjective expected utility: a review of normative theories. *Theory and Decision* 13, 139–99.

Neyman, J. 1977. Frequentist probability and frequentist statistics. *Synthese* 36, 97–131.

Neyman, J. and Pearson, E.S. 1933. On the problem of the most efficient tests of statistical hypotheses. *Philosophical Transactions of the Royal Society*, London, 231–289–337.

Raiffa, H. 1968. *Decision Analysis: Introductory Lectures on Choices under Uncertainty*. Reading, Mass.: Addison-Wesley.

Raiffa, H. and Schlaifer, R. 1961. *Applied Statistical Decision Theory*. Boston: Division of Research, Graduate School of Business Administration, Harvard University.

Ramsey, F.P. 1931. Truth and probability. In *The Foundations of Mathematics and Other Logical Essays*, London: Kegan, Paul, Trench and Trubner. Reprinted in *Studies in Subjective Probability*, ed. H. Kyburg and H. Smokler, New York: Wiley, 1964, 61–92.

Savage, L.J. 1954. *The Foundations of Statistics*. New York: Wiley.

Wald, A. 1950. *Statistical Decision Functions*. New York: Wiley.

Winkler, R.L. 1972. *An Introduction to Bayesian Inference and Decision*. New York: Holt, Rinehart & Winston.

Strategic Reallocation of Endowments

ZVI SAFRA

In the framework of pure exchange economies it might well happen that economic agents will find it advantageous to change their endowment holdings and by this increase their utility. Such an increase is achieved by acting competitively with the new endowments and comparing the new equilibrium allocation with the one that would have been achieved without the change.

When such a phenomenon happens we say that a *strategic reallocation of endowments* has occurred. Examples of such strategic behaviour can easily be found in reality. For example, farmers sometimes destroy part of their crops in order to raise their selling price; oil companies give false reports on their reserves for the same reason and insured agents, partially for that reason, report to the insurer on less levels of wealth than they really have.

Such strategic behaviour by single economic agents contradicts the fundamental competitive assumption that agents cannot influence market prices. Mathematically, this assumption is equivalent to single agents being negligible relative to the whole economy. For that reason strategic behaviour of single economic agents is strongly connected to the finiteness of the economy. Strategic behaviour of groups of agents, however, can very well be effective in continuum economies. Thus the phenomenon of strategic reallocation of endowments, although more probable in finite economies, is surely not limited to the finite cases.

Strategic change in endowments, sometimes called *manipulation via endowments*, is closely related to the subject called manipulation of preferences, which deals with strategic behaviour that concerns the second parameter of economic agents – their preferences (utility functions). In fact, it can be shown that every manipulation via endowments can be considered as a manipulation of preferences. This relation however, does not prove to be very valuable in answering questions concerning the existence of strategic reallocation of endowments or the existence of Nash equilibrium in the resulting game (see below). For that reason, results from manipulation of preferences cannot be directly applied here.

225

We now turn to definitions of pure exchange economies and to the notions that are needed for the definition of strategic reallocation of endowments. Then we define four kinds of manipulation via endowments. Finally, we give some important results concerning this phenomenon. In stating the results we choose to put more emphasis on group manipulations and to explain the other results more briefly.

DEFINITIONS

Assume a pure exchange economy with $l \geqslant 2$ commodoties that consists of $m \geqslant 2$ consumers (the economic agents). All consumers have the same consumption set X, which is a subset of the l-dimensional Euclidean space R^l. Consumer i has a vector of initial endowment ω_i in X and a quasi-concave surjective and smooth utility function $u_i: R^i \to R$ such that (i) u_i has a strictly positive gradient; (ii) $u_i^{-1}(t)$ has a non-zero Gaussian curvature and (iii) $u_i^{-1}(t, \infty)$ is bounded from below, for all t in R. These assumptions ensure that consumer i has a smooth demand function $f_i: S \times R \to X$ where

$$S = \{ p \in R^l_{++} \,|\, |p^l| = 1 \}$$

is the set of price vectors (where the lth commodity serves as the numeraire) and R represents the possible range for ω_i – consumer i's income (which, in this case, is equal to $p\omega_i$, the scalar product of the price and the initial endowment vectors). The function $Z_i: S \times R \to R^l$ defined by $Z_i = f_i - \omega_i$ is consumer i's excess demand function.

A vector p in S is an *equilibrium price vector* for the initial allocation $\omega = (\omega_1, \ldots, \omega_m)$ in X^m if

$$Z(p, \omega) = \sum_{i=1}^{m} Z_i(p, p\omega_i) = 0,$$

that is, if total demand is equal to total supply. The pair (p, ω) is called an *equilibrium* and the allocation $f(p, \omega) = [f_1(p, p\omega_1), \ldots, f_m(p, p\omega_m)]$ is called an *equilibrium allocation*. We denote by E the set of all possible equilibrium pairs (p, ω) in $S \times X^m$.

It is known that, generically, every initial allocation has an odd number of isolated equilibrium price vectors. Since this number can be greater than one we define for every equilibrium (p, ω) a function $P: X^m \to S$ by

$$P(\omega'; p, \omega) = \arg \min \| p' - p \| \qquad \text{s.t. } Z(p', \omega') = 0.$$

The function P gives the equilibrium price vector p' of ω' which is closest to the equilibrium price vector p (of ω). If (p, ω) is regular (which means that the Jacobian matrix of Z at (p, ω) is of full rank, and generically this is the situation) then P is really a function that describes the smooth selection of E that passes through (p, ω).

We can now formally define the concepts of strategic reallocations of endowments. For this let (p, ω) be in E and assume that ω' in the following definition is close enough to ω so that P is well defined.

Definition: (i) A coalition D of consumers can *C-manipulate* in (p, ω) if there exist ω' in X^m and $p' = P(\omega'; p, \omega)$ such that

$$\omega_i' = \omega_i \quad \text{for } i \notin D, \qquad \sum_{i \in D} \omega_i' = \sum_{i \in D} \omega_i$$

and

$$u_i[f_i(p', p'\omega_i')] > u_i[f_i(p, \omega_i)], \qquad \text{for all } i \in D.$$

(ii) Consumer i can *W-manipulate* in (p, ω) if there exist w$'$ in X^m and $p' = P(\omega'; p, \omega)$ such that

$$\omega_i' < \omega_i, \quad \omega_j' = \omega_j, \qquad \text{for } j \neq i$$

and

$$u_i[f_i(p', p'\omega_i') + \omega_i - \omega_i'] > u_i[f_i(p, p\omega_i)].$$

(iii) Consumer i can *G-manipulate* in (p, ω) if there exist $j \neq i$, ω' in X^m and $p' = P(\omega'; p, \omega)$ such that

$$(t > 0 \text{ is in } R^l) \quad \omega_i' = \omega_i - t, \quad \omega_j' = \omega_j + t, \quad \omega_h' = \omega_h \qquad \text{for } h \neq i, j$$

and

$$u_i[f_i(p', p'\omega_i')] > u_i[f_i(p, p\omega_i)].$$

(iv) Consumer i can *D-manipulate* in (p, ω) if there exist ω' in X^m and $p' = P(\omega'; p, \omega)$ such that

$$\omega_i' < \omega_i, \quad \omega_j' = \omega_j, \qquad \text{for } j \neq i$$

and

$$u_i[f_i(p', p'\omega_i')] > u_i[f_i(p, p\omega_i)].$$

The definition of C-manipulation (C for coalition) captures the main idea of strategic reallocations of endowments. The coalition C-manipulates in (p, ω) if its participants can reallocate their resources (this is the change from ω to ω') and by this achieve a new equilibrium allocation $[f(p', w')]$ which gives each one of them a higher utility level than in the original equilibrium allocation $f(p, \omega)$. By doing so, the coalition D exploits its ability to influence the equilibrium prices and does it to its advantage.

The definition of W-manipulation (W for withholding) is also a kind of strategic reallocation of endowments, except that here the reallocation is done by a unique consumer (i in the definition) and it deals with the partition of his initial endowment vector ω_i into two parts: the first is the part that is declared as his new endowment (ω_i') and enters the market; the second is the part of the endowment that is withheld from the market. At the end of the trade the W-manipulating consumer adds the withheld part ($\omega_i - \omega_i'$) to his new equilibrium vector $f_i(p', p'\omega_i')$ and his utility is thus computed at the vector that is the sum of these two vectors. To summarize, by changing the allocation of his initial

Game Theory

endowment ω_i from 'ω_i to the market and 0 to withholding' to 'ω_i' to the market and $\omega_i - \omega_i'$ to withholding' the final utility of consumer i may increase. If this is the case then we say that consumer i can W-manipulate in (p, ω).

The third part of the definition refers to G-manipulation (G for gift). In such a manipulation a gift (the vector t) is given by consumer i to consumer j such that in the new resulting equilibrium allocation $f(p', \omega')$ the utility level of i is higher than his utility level in the original equilibrium allocation. In this case the reallocation is made among consumers i and j. Note that a conceptual shortcoming of this reallocation is that consumer j has to agree to accept this gift, and he would do so only if his utility will also rise. In such a case we are back in the C-manipulation situation. However, since this kind of manipulation attracted a lot of interest in the theory of international trade (under the name of *the transfer paradox*) we decided to define it separately.

The last part of the definition deals with manipulation of endowments that is done by destroying part of them (D is for destroying). In this case a consumer might find it advantageous simply to destroy part of his endowments and by this achieve a better equilibrium allocation. Again, some kind of reallocation of consumer i's endowments is done here: part of his endowments is taken away from the market and transferred to the 'non-existing' phase.

RESULTS

C-manipulation. The first example of an economy where C-manipulation exists was given by Gabszewicz and Drèze (1971). In that example the economy had a continuum of consumers. Examples of finite exchange economies were given by Gale (1974) for non-smooth utilities and then by Aumann and Peleg (1974) for the smooth case. The existence of those examples was very nicely generalized by Guesnerie and Laffont (1978) who proved that any set of consumers in which at least two have different vectors of income effects can be embedded in an infinite number of economies where it can C-manipulate.

The vector of income effects of consumer i is simply the vector of the partial derivatives of the demand function f_i with respect to i's income; that is, the vector $(\partial f_i^1/\partial w_i, \ldots, \partial f_i^1/\partial w_i)$. Their result thus implies not only that examples exist where C-manipulation occurs, but that indeed there is an infinite number of such examples. Moreover, almost every set of consumers (the condition of their result is generic) can be that coalition which can C-manipulate, and again, in an infinite number of economies.

Guesnerie and Laffont's result, although saying that many examples of C-manipulation exist, says nothing about the size of the set of economies where this phenomenon happens. It might still be the case that such economies are very exceptional. Some results that shed more light on the structure of the set of C-manipulable economies (and that of its complement) were given by Safra (1983). In that work the number of consumers, their utilities and the sum of the economy's resources are given; the main results are the following.

First, if every initial allocation has a unique (and fixed) price equilibrium, then no equilibrium is C-manipulable. This case is very exceptional. Secondly, in all other cases the set of C-manipulable equilibria has a non-empty interior, it 'spreads' over all the equilibrium set E and, generically, it contains every non-regular equilibrium. This result clearly implies that C-manipulation is very common. The last part of the result is very intuitive since a necessary condition for C-manipulation is that the change in prices will be large enough to compensate each coalition's members for possible losses of wealth. Thirdly, the complement of the set of C-manipulable equilibrium contains an open set which includes the equilibria of the Pareto-optimal allocations, and finally, a given coalition can C-manipulate if, and only if, a condition similar to that of Guesnerie and Laffont is satisfied.

Another result concerning C-manipulation (as well as G-manipulation and D-manipulation) is that of Polterovich and Spivak (1983). They have shown that if the demand correspondence (it need not be a function) satisfies gross substitutability and responds positively to changes in income, then no coalition of consumers can C-manipulate.

Postlewaite (1979) was concerned with manipulating more general resource allocating mechanisms. His result concerning C-manipulation states that *every* individually rational and Pareto optimal mechanism (including the competitive mechanism) can be C-manipulated in the sense that there exists at least one economy where such a mechanism can be C-manipulated.

W-manipulation. An example for the occurrence of W-manipulation was given by Postlewaite (1979) who also showed (as mentioned above) that a whole class of mechanisms are W-manipulable. In fact, the occurrence of W-manipulation for the competitive mechanism is much more common than one might surmise from the above example; as claimed by Thomson (1979), almost every economy is W-manipulable.

In view of these negative results interest has shifted to questions of second-best type, concerning the degree of W-manipulability of the competitive mechanism. For measurement of that degree one looks at the Nash equilibria of the W-manipulation game (where the strategies of the consumers are the W-manipulations available to them), and measures the distance between these Nash equilibria and the equilibrium allocation. An important work was that of Thomson (1979) who defined and characterized those Nash-equilibria (although no proof of their existence was given) and gave specific examples showing that no specific relation exists between those equilibria and the equilibrium allocation. The existence question was addressed by Safra (1985) for (finite) large enough economies, which also showed that under some regularity conditions every sequence of such Nash equilibria converges (as the economy becomes large) to an equilibrium allocation.

G-manipulation. As mentioned above, this kind of strategic reallocation of endowments is closely related to what is called the *transfer paradox* in the theory of international trade. The first example of this phenomenon was given by Leontief (1936) and the main interest in that literature has been the relation between that phenomenon and (Walrasian) instability of the price equilibrium. Many researchers have been working on this and it is now known that with more than three consumers G-manipulability can very well occur at stable equilibria.

Other results concerning G-manipulability can easily be deduced from results concerning C-manipulability.

D-manipulation. The last kind of strategic reallocation of endowments is also related to the theory of international trade where its mirror image was discussed under the name of *immiserizing growth.* The phenomenon of immiserizing growth occurs when a consumer's resources increase and his utility in the new resulting equilibrium decreases. It can be seen that under very mild conditions D-manipulation occurs if and only if immiserizing growth occurs.

The first discussion of this phenomenon is that of Bhagwati (1958), while an example can also be found in Aumann and Peleg's paper (1974). Bhagwati, and later Mas-Colell (1976) and Mantel (1982) gave conditions which preclude this phenomenon, and Hatta (1983) showed some similarities among these various conditions; those relating to gross substitutability and normality also appear in Polterovich and Spivak (1983).

The last result to be mentioned is that of Postlewaite (1979) and concerns general mechanisms. This time, contrary to the above cases, there exist mechanisms that are immune to D-manipulability and which yield Pareto optimal and individually rational allocations.

BIBLIOGRAPHY

Aumann, R. and Peleg, B. 1974. A note on Gale's example. *Journal of Mathematical Economics* 1, 209–11.

Bhagwati, J.N. 1958. Immiserizing growth: a geometrical note. *Review of Economic Studies* 25, June, 201–5.

Gabszewicz, J.J. and Drèze, J.H. 1971. Syndicates of traders in an economy. In *Differential Games and Related Topics*, ed. H.W. Kuhn and G. Szego, Amsterdam: North-Holland.

Gale, D. 1974. Exchange equilibrium and coalitions: an example. *Journal of Mathematical Economics* 1, 63–6.

Guesnerie, R. and Laffont, J.J. 1978. Advantageous reallocation of initial resources. *Econometrica* 46(4), July, 835–41.

Hatta, T. 1983. Immiserizing growth in a many commodity setting. Working Paper, The Johns Hopkins University, September.

Leontief, W. 1936. Note on the pure theory of capital transfer. In *Explorations in Economics*, Taussig Festschrift, New York: McGraw-Hill.

Mantel, R. 1982. Substitutability and the welfare effects of endowment increases. Paper presented at the Econometric Society Meeting in Mexico.

Mas-Collel, A. 1976. En torno a una propiedad poco atractiva del equilibrio competitivo. *Moneda y Credito* [Madrid], no. 136, 11–27.

Polterovich, V.M. and Spivak, V.A. 1983. Gross substitutability of point-to-set correspondences. *Journal of Mathematical Economics* 11(2), April, 117–40.

Postlewaite, A. 1979. Manipulation via endowments. *Review of Economic Studies* 46(2), April, 255–62.

Safra, Z. 1983. Manipulation by reallocating initial endowments. *Journal of Mathematical Economics* 12(1), September, 1–17.

Safra, Z. 1985. Existence of equilibrium for Walrasian endowment games. *Journal of Economic Theory* 37(2), December, 366–78.

Thomson, W. 1979. The equilibrium allocations of Walras and Lindahl manipulation games. Discussion Paper, University of Minnesota, Center of Economic Research, No. 111.

Strategy-Proof Allocation Mechanisms

MARK A. SATTERTHWAITE

In abstract form an allocation mechanism may be thought of as a function
mapping agents' preferences into final allocations. For example, the competitive
allocation mechanism calculates market-clearing prices to select a feasible, Pareto
optimal, final allocation that varies with agents' preferences. This simple view,
however, of the mechanism being only a map from preferences to final allocation
is inadequate because it fails to satisfy the basic tenet of microeconomic theory:
agents, within the rules of the mechanism, maximize their utility subject to
technological and informational constraints.

The problem is this. An agent's preferences may be private to himself and
unverifiable except through circumstantial interference. Therefore, whenever
they are private, the competitive mechanism must in fact depend on each agent's
report of what his preferences are, not on his actual preferences. That is, agents
can lie about their preferences. Provided that the number of agents in the economy
is finite, then each individual agent can affect the market-clearing prices by
strategically misreporting his preferences.

If he knows what other agents are likely to report as their preferences, then
through misrepresentation he can affect prices so that he secures a final allocation
that he prefers over the final allocation that he would have received if he had
reported his preferences truthfully. Consequently, the competitive mechanism,
for finite collections of agents, is in fact a mapping from preferences and each
agent's information about other agents' preferences and information. Inclusion
of agents' information about other agents enormously complicates the analysis
of allocation mechanisms. Game theoretic methods become necessary.

These observations are now new. Black (1958, p. 182) reports that J.-C. Borda,
18th-century French inventor of the 'Borda count' rule for making committee
decisions, exclaimed that 'My scheme is only intended for honest men' when he

was contronted with the possibilities of strategic misrepresentation. Careful analyses of the competitive mechanism have generally skirted the problem by proceeding under cover of the assumption that the numbers of buyers and sellers in each market are so large that no individual agent can affect price strategically. Arrow (1951, p. 7), in his classic study of social welfare functions, recognized that agents may have an incentive to misrepresent. Vickrey (1960) evaluated several committee voting procedures using vulnerability to strategic misrepresentation as one of his criteria.

The study of strategy-proof allocation mechanisms is an effort to circumvent the complications that strategic misrepresentation creates. Roughly speaking, an allocation mechanism is strategy-proof if every agent's utility-maximizing choice of what preferences to report depends only on his own preferences and not on his expectations concerning the preferences that other agents will report. If the mechanism is strategy-proof, then each agent can disregard his expectations concerning other agents' reports and straightforwardly report the preference ordering that uniformly maximizes his utility. That is, each agent always has a dominant strategy if the mechanism is strategy-proof. Understanding the strategic choices of agents when the allocation mechanism is strategy-proof is trivial; they always play their dominant strategies. Thus, for example, if the Borda count were a strategy-proof mechanism, Borda would not have needed to wish for honest men only to utilize his mechanism. He could have settled for maximizing men, an easier order to fill.

Strategy-proof mechanisms are desirable, but do they exist? This is the central question of this essay and has been the central question in the study of strategy-proof allocation mechanisms. That some voting procedures and the competitive mechanism fail strategy-proofness suggests the conjecture that all other attractive allocation mechanisms also fail strategy-proofness. This conjecture, which Dummett and Farquharson (1961) first made, turns out to be true. An impossibility theorem due to Gibbard (1973) and Satterthwaite (1975) shows that no strategy-proof allocation mechanism exists that satisfies minimal requirements of responsiveness to individual agents' preferences.

Precise statement of this fundamental result requires the introduction of some notation. Let $I = \{1, 2, \ldots, n\}$ be a fixed set of n agents who must select a single alternative from a set $X = \{x, y, z, \ldots\}$ of $|X|$ distinct, conceivable final allocations. Each agent $i \in I$ has asymmetric, transitive preferences P_i over the allocations X. Let P_i represent strict preference. Thus for each $x, y \in X$ and each $i \in I$, only three possibilities exist: xP_iy (agent i strictly prefers x over y), yP_ix (agent i strictly prefers y over x), or neither xP_iy nor yP_ix (agent i is indifferent between x and y). Not every asymmetric, transitive ordering X is necessarily admissible as a preference ordering P_i. For example, for a particular $x, y \in X$, xP_iy might be the only admissible ordering because allocation x dominates allocation y in terms of the usual non-satiation axiom of consumer demand theory. Therefore let Σ represent all possible asymmetric, transitive preference orderings over X and let $\Omega \subset \Sigma$ represent the set of all asymmetric, transitive preference orderings over X that are admissible. Thus P_i is an admissible ordering for agent i only if $P_i \in \Omega$.

Let $\Omega^n = \Omega \times \Omega \times \cdots \times \Omega$ be the n-fold Cartesian product of Ω. If every asymmetric, transitive ordering is admissible, then preferences are said to be unrestricted and $\Omega = \Sigma$. Let the triple $\langle I, X, \Omega \rangle$ be called the environment.

An n-tuple $P = (P_1, \ldots, P_n) \in \Omega^n$ is called a preference profile, and a subset $W \subset X$ is called a feasible set. Let Δ be the set of subsets of X. An allocation mechanism is then a function $f: \Omega^n \times \Delta \to X$. That is, an allocation function maps a preference profile and feasible set into the feasible set: $f(P|W) \in W$. Agent i can manipulate allocation function f at profile $P \in \Omega^n$ and feasible set $W \subset X$ if an admissible ordering $P_i' \in \Omega$ exists such that:

$$f(P_1, \ldots, P_{i-1}, P_i', P_{i+1}, \ldots, P_n | W) P_i f(P|W). \tag{1}$$

The interpretation of (1) is this. Preference ordering P_i is agent i's true preferences. The other agents report preference orderings $P_{-i} = (P_1, \ldots, P_{i-1}, P_{i+1}, \ldots, P_n)$. If agent i reports his preferences truthfully, then the outcome is $f(P_i, P_{-i}|W) \equiv f(P|W)$. If he misrepresents his preferences to be P_i', then the outcome is $f(P_i', P_{-i}|W) \equiv f(P_1, \ldots, P_{i-1}, P_i', P_{i+1}, \ldots, P_n|W)$. Relation (1) states that agent i prefers $f(P_i', P_{-i}|W)$ to $f(P_i, P_{-i}|W)$. Therefore agent i has an incentive to manipulate f at profile P by misrepresenting his preferences to be P_i' rather than P_i.

An allocation mechanism f is strategy-proof if no admissible profile $P \in \Omega^n$ and subset $W \subset X$ exists at which f is manipulable. This means that even if, for example, agent i has perfect foresight about the preferences the other $n - 1$ agents will report, agent i can never do better than to report his true preferences P_i. Truth is always every agent's dominant strategy. Presumably this is sufficient to induce every agent always to report his preferences truthfully. Gibbard (1973) and Satterthwaite (1975) showed that strategy-proof allocation mechanisms generally do not exist.

> *Theorem.* If admissible preferences are unrestricted ($\Omega^n = \Sigma^n$) and at least three possible allocations exist ($|X| \geqslant 3$), then no strategy-proof allocation mechanism f exists that is non-dictatorial and Pareto optimal.

An allocation mechanism is dictatorial if, for some feasible set $W \subset X (|W| \geqslant 2)$ and all profiles $P \in \Omega^n$, an agent i exists such that $f(P|W) \in \max_W P_i$ where $\max_W P_i = \{x : x \in W$ and, for all $y \in W$, not $y P_i x\}$. That is, dictatorial mechanism always gives the dictator one of the feasible alternatives that he most prefers. A non-dictatorial mechanism is a mechanism that is not dictatorial. A mechanism satisfies Pareto optimality if and only if, for any profile $P \in \Omega^n$, any feasible set $W \subset X$, and any $x, y \in W$, $x P_i y$ for all $i \in I$ implies $f(P|W) \neq y$. Pareto optimality in this context means that if unanimity exists among the agents that an allocation x is the most preferred feasible allocation, then the mechanism picks x.

The theorem can be proved either by appeal to Arrow's impossibility theorem for social welfare functions (Gibbard, 1973) or through a self-contained, constructive argument (Satterthwaite, 1975). Schmeidler and Sonnenschein (1978) present short proofs of both types.

Gibbard and Satterthwaite's theorem is a non-existence theorem for strategy-proof allocation mechanisms because mechanisms that violate either non-dictatorship or Pareto optimality are unattractive. If the environment is $\langle I, X, \Sigma \rangle$ where $|X| = 2$, then majority rule is an attractive, non-dictatorial, Pareto optimal and strategy-proof mechanism. But as soon as $|X|$ increases beyond two, if $\Omega = \Sigma$, then non-dictatorship, Pareto optimality and strategy-proofness become incompatible. Normally $|X| > 2$ for economic environments. Therefore the theorem implies that existence can be obtained (if at all) only for environments $\langle I, X, \Omega \rangle$ where admissible preferences Ω are restricted to a strict subset of Σ.

Strategy-proof allocation mechanisms are – almost – formally equivalent to social welfare functions of the type Arrow (1951) analysed. A social welfare function, for a given environment $\langle I, X, \Omega \rangle$ is a mapping $g : \Omega^n \to \Omega$. Thus a social welfare function g has as its argument an admissible preference profile and as its image an admissible ordering of X. The ordering $g(P)$ is interpreted to be the social ordering of X given that individual preferences $P = (P_1, \ldots, P_n)$. Arrow's impossibility theorem states that if $|X| \geqslant 3$ and admissible preferences are unrestricted, then no non-dictatorial social welfare function exists that satisfies the conditions of Pareto optimality, independence of irrelevant alternatives and monotonicity.

An allocation mechanism f is called rational if and only if a social welfare function g exists such that, for all $P \in \Omega^n$ and all $W \subset X, f(P|W) \in \max_W g(P)$. That is $f(P|W)$ is rational if a social ordering $g(P)$ exists that rationalizes its choices. Kalai and Muller (1977) showed that, for a given environment $\langle I, X, \Omega \rangle$, a non-dictatorial, rational, strategy-proof allocation mechanism f satisfying Pareto optimality can be constructed if and only if a non-dictatorial social welfare function satisfying Pareto optimality, monotonicity and independence of irrelevant alternatives can be constructed. In other words, if one limits consideration to rational allocation mechanisms, reasonable strategy-proof mechanisms exist for an environment if and only if reasonable (in Arrow's sense) social welfare functions exist for the environment.

A great deal of research has been done to identify environments on which non-dictatorial, Pareto optimal, strategy-proof allocation mechanisms exist. Two main approaches have been taken. First, authors have characterized sets of admissible preferences Ω for which rational, Pareto optimal, non-dictatorial, strategy-proof allocation mechanisms exist on $\langle I, X, \Omega \rangle$ for $|X| > 2$. Second, for specific sets of restricted preferences Ω authors have investigated if reasonable strategy-proof allocation mechanisms exist on $\langle I, X, \Omega \rangle$ for $|x| > 2$. The results of both approaches have been uniformly discouraging. Generally, in order to get existence, Ω must be restricted to an extent that is greater than can be justified within economic contexts. Gibbard and Satterthwaite's theorem seems to apply to a much wider class of environments than just $\langle I, X, \Sigma \rangle$ with its unrestricted preferences. Muller and Satterthwaite (1985) review this literature.

There appear to be only two exceptions to this generalization that Gibbard and Satterthwaite's impossibility result is robust to restrictions on Ω. First, if Ω has the property that all admissible preferences are linear in money, then Groves mechanisms are strategy-proof in an attractive way. Groves mechanisms do, however, violate Pareto optimality (see Groves and Loeb, 1975; Green and Laffont, 1979). Second, if Ω has the property that all admissible preferences are single-peaked, then generalizations of majority rule are strategy-proof and Pareto optimal (see Blin and Satterthwaite, 1976; Border and Jordan, 1983).

This discussion, as is the case for most of the literature on strategy-proofness, uses the social-choice-theory model of requiring agents to report their preference orderings as the allocation rule's input. This seems restrictive because most economic allocation mechanisms do not require agents to report their full preference orderings. Gibbard (1973), however, showed that in fact this model is not restrictive at all. The insight is this. The essence of strategy-proofness is that each agent's optimal strategy depends only on his own preferences and is invariant with other agents' choices of strategies. That is, if an allocation mechanism is strategy-proof, then each agent always has a dominant strategy. Gibbard called such allocation mechanisms, for which each agent always has a dominant strategy, straightforward game forms. Gibbard showed that if a straightforward game form requires agents to select among an arbitrary set of admissible strategies that are not necessarily orderings of X, then the game form is equivalent to a strategy-proof allocation mechanism. Thus, if a non-dictatorial, Pareto optimal, strategy-proof allocation mechanism does not exist for an environment $\langle I, X, \Omega \rangle$, then neither does a non-dictatorial, Pareto optimal, straightforward game form.

The implication of Gibbard's observation concerning straightforward game forms is that if an economic situation is such that agents' preferences are not *a priori* known with certainty, then the situation is not strategy-proof (or, equivalently, straightforward). That is, each agent's optimal strategy depends on his own preferences, his expectations concerning other agents' strategies and, by backward induction, his expectations concerning the other agents' preferences and their expectations concerning agents' strategies and preferences, etc. The resulting game is formally a game of incomplete information and should be analysed using techniques appropriate for such games. Thus, to summarize, for economic theory the main implication of Gibbard and Satterthwaite's impossibility theorem for strategy-proof allocation mechanisms is that whenever agents' preferences are *a priori* uncertain to other agents, then the agents are engaged in a game of incomplete information.

BIBLIOGRAPHY

Arrow, K. 1951. *Social Choice and Individual Values*. New York: Wiley.

Black, D. 1958. *The Theory of Committees and Elections*. Cambridge: Cambridge University Press.

Blin, J.-M. and Satterthwaite, M. 1976. Strategy-proofness and single-peakedness. *Public Choice* 26, 51–8.

Border, K. and Jordan, J. 1983. Straightforward elections, unanimity and phantom voters. *Review of Economic Studies* 50, 153–70.

Dummett, M. and Farquharson, R. 1961. Stability in voting. *Econometrica* 29, 33–44.

Gibbard, A. 1973. Manipulation of voting schemes: a general result. *Econometrica* 41, 587–602.

Green, J. and Laffont, J.-J. 1979. *Incentives in Public Decision-making*. Studies in Public Economics, vol. I. Amsterdam: North-Holland.

Groves, T. and Loeb, M. 1975. Incentives and public inputs. *Journal of Public Economics* 4, 211–26.

Kalai, E. and Muller, E. 1977. Characterization of domains admitting non-dictatorial social welfare functions and non-manipulable voting procedures. *Journal of Economic Theory* 16, 457–69.

Muller, E. and Satterthwaite, M. 1985. Strategy-proofness: the existence of dominant-strategy mechanisms. In *Social Goals and Social Organization*: *Essays in Memory of Elisha Pazner*, ed. L. Hurwicz, D. Schmeidler and H. Sonnenschein, Cambridge: Cambridge University Press, 131–71.

Satterthwaite, M. 1975. Strategy-proofness and Arrow's conditions: existence and correspondence theorems for voting procedures and social welfare functions. *Journal of Economic Theory* 10, 187–217.

Schmeidler, D. and Sonnenschein, H. 1978. Two proofs of the Gibbard–Satterthwaite theorem on the possibility of a strategy-proof social choice function. In *Decision Theory and Social Ethics*: *Issues in Social Choice*, ed. H. Gottinger and W. Leinfellner, Dordrecht, Holland: Reidel, 227–34.

Vickrey, W. 1960. Utility, strategy and social decision rules. *Quarterly Journal of Economics* 74, 507–35.

Supergames

JEAN-FRANÇOIS MERTENS

'Supergame' is the original name for situations where the same game is played repetitively, and players are interested in their long run average payoff. Repeated game is used for more general models, and we refer the reader to that article for those. For the supergame to be well defined, one has to specify the information players receive after each stage: it is assumed that a lottery, depending on the pure strategy choices of all players in the last stage, will select for each player his payoff and a signal. The lottery stands for the compound effect of all moves of nature in the extensive form of the game, while the signals stand for a new datum – an information partition for each player on the terminal nodes of this extensive form. It is assumed that this information partition describes all information available to the player at the end of the game – in particular, he is not informed (except possibly through the signal) of his own payoff. The motivation for this degree of generality in the model is discussed in the entry on REPEATED GAMES. The present article is quite brief; a more thorough survey may be found in a lecture by the author at the International Congress of Mathematicians (1986) in Berkeley, which will appear in the *Proceedings* of that Congress, under the title 'Repeated Games', together with a bibliography.

For the supergame to be completely defined, a payoff function still has to be specified. The 'long run average' could be the limiting average, or the average over a fixed number of periods, or a discounted average – and in the latter two cases, one is basically interested in the asymptotic behaviour of the solutions, as the number of periods grows to infinity or the discount factor tends to zero. In the former case, additional care is needed in the definitions. Everything in the literature concerns the non-zero-sum case: in the zero-sum case, players just repeat period after period their optimal strategies in the single period game.

The study of supergames was initially – and still is to a large extent – motivated by the theme that 'repetition enables cooperation'. This theme has far-reaching implications in economic theory, far exceeding its obvious implications in

238

industrial organization and anti-trust policy. It is best illustrated by the Prisoner's Dilemma. This is the game where, simultaneously, each of both players can ask the referee *either* to give $2 to his opponent, *or* to give $1 to himself. Clearly, in equilibrium, each will ask for the latter. But in the supergame, they can reach, in equilibrium, the payoff (2,2), by always asking the referee to give 2 to the opponent (until the other no longer does – from that time on, always take 1 for yourself). Clearly, this is an equilibrium; nobody has any advantage in deviating from his strategy if the opponent adheres to his. This argument proves more generally that, when the signals are the opponents' last actions, the equilibrium payoffs of the supergame are the feasible, individually rational points of the game: this is the 'folk theorem' of game theory. Feasible payoffs are those in the convex hull of the payoff vectors appearing in the normal form – they are achieved in the supergame by alternating in a fixed, prescribed order between pure strategy choices, such that the limiting frequency yields the appropriate point in the convex hull. Individual rationality of a player's payoff means that he can be prevented by his opponents from achieving more in the game. The 'folk theorem' can thus be interpreted as saying that any cooperatively feasible point of the game can be achieved in equilibrium in the supergame (and vice versa). Experimental evidence is amply documented in Axelrod (1984).

Starting from this paradigm, interest has fanned out in a number of directions. The first, by Aumann, consisted in showing that other cooperative solution concepts of the game, like the core, could also be 'justified' as a set of appropriate equilibrium points ('strong equilibrium points') of the supergame.

The equilibrium of the supergame we exhibited for the folk theorem has the obvious defect in relying on threats which are suboptimal when carried out. A modified equilibrium concept, like perfect equilibrium, would not have this defect. Aumann, Rubinstein and Shapley showed that the folk theorem still holds even with perfect equilibria. The investigation of finite and discounted games brought another surprise: in any finite repetition of the Prisoner's Dilemma, there is still a unique equilibrium, (1,1): we have a discontinuity in the limit. It was shown, however, by Benoit and Krishna (1985), that (generically), as soon as the game had, for any player, a (perfect) equilibrium giving him more than his individually rational level, then the set of (perfect) equilibria of the finitely repeated games would converge to that of the infinite game. For the equilibria of the discounted games, convergence does hold generically (Sorin, 1986), but not always (Forges, Mertens and Neyman, 1986).

Even for the Prisoner's Dilemma, Kreps, Milgrom, Roberts and Wilson (1982) showed that, if only one player assigned initially an ε-probability to his opponent being in fact a 'tit-for-tat' player (start with '2', next repeat always your opponent's previous move), then the perfect equilibria of the finitely repeated games would converge to (2,2): repetition even forces cooperation. The high expectations generated by this conclusion were, however, soon quashed by Fudenberg and Maskin (1986), who showed that in a generic class of games, if one assigned for each player an ε-probability to his having a different payoff function, then the limits of perfect equilibria of the finite games would cover the whole equilibrium set of the supergame when the different payoff functions vary: the 'folk theorem' was restored. The four authors' work had, however, a major impact in the recognition of reputation effects (as related to signalling): a very small number of deviations of a player from a hypothetical equilibrium strategy towards the tit-for-tat strategy will be sufficient to change his opponent's probability of his being the tit-for-tat player from ε to a very substantial number; his reputation as a tit-for-tat player thus established, the opponent will follow suit, with result (2,2). The same authors have amply documented the importance of such reputation effects in a number of economic situations – like potential entry in a monopolistic market. Despite this result of Fudenberg and Maskin, Aumann and Sorin succeeded recently in restoring some plausibility to the theme that repetition forces cooperation.

Finally, in the last few years, there has been considerable interest in extending the analysis to the more general information pattern described in the beginning of this article, in order to allow the study of economic phenomena like long term insurance relationships or principal–agent relationships, where imperfect monitoring is essential. Radner, Rubinstein, Yaari and others have studied a number of examples. Lehrer has recently obtained a characterization of the equilibrium payoffs of the supergame in the two-player case, where the signals inform each player of his own utility. This is a very significant extension of the folk theorem, in that it shows in particular that all efficient individually rational points can be achieved as equilibria of the supergame.

BIBLIOGRAPHY

Aumann, R.J. 1959. Acceptable points in general cooperative n-person games. In *Contributions to the Theory of Games*, Vol. IV, ed. A.W. Tucker and R.D. Luce, Annals of Mathematics Studies 40, Princeton: Princeton University Press, 287–324.

Aumann, R.J. 1960. Acceptable points in games of perfect information. *Pacific Journal of Mathematics* 10, 381–7.

Aumann, R.J. 1961. The core of a cooperative game without side payments. *Transactions of the American Mathematical Society* 98, 539–52.

Axelrod, R. 1984. *The Evolution of Cooperation*. New York: Basic Books.

Benoit, J.-P. and Krishna, V. 1985. Finitely repeated games. *Econometrica* 53, 905–22.

Forges, F., Mertens, J.-F. and Neyman, A. 1986. A counterexample to the folk-theorem with discounting. *Economic Letters* 20, 7.

Fudenberg, D. and Maskin, E. 1986. The folk theorem in repeated games with non-observable actions. The Hebrew University, Jerusalem, CRIME and GT, RM 72.

Kreps, D., Milgrom, F., Roberts, J. and Wilson, R. 1982. Rational cooperation in the finitely-repeated prisoner's dilemma. *Journal of Economic Theory* 27, 245–52.

Kreps, D. and Wilson, R. 1982a. Reputation and imperfect information. *Journal of Economic Theory* 27, 253–79.

Lehrer, E. 1986. Lower equilibrium payoffs in two-players repeated games with non-observable actions. The Hebrew University, Jerusalem, CRIME and GT, RM 72.

Mertens, J.-F. 1980. A note on the characteristic function of supergames. *International Journal of Game Theory* 9, 189–90.

Milgrom, P. and Roberts, J. 1982. Predation, reputation and entry deterrence. *Journal of Economic Theory* 27, 280–312.

Radner, R. 1980. Collusive behavior in non-cooperative epsilon-equilibria in oligopolies with long but finite lives. *Journal of Economic Theory* 22, 136–54.

Radner, R. 1986. Optimal equilibria in a class of repeated partnership games with imperfect monitoring. *Review of Economic Studies* 53, 43–58.

Rubinstein, A. 1977. Equilibrium in supergames. The Hebrew University, Jerusalem, CRIME and GT, RM 25.

Rubinstein, A. 1980. Strong perfect equilibrium in supergames. *International Journal of Game Theory* 9, 1–12.

Rubinstein, A. and Yaari, M. 1983. Repeated insurance contracts and moral hazard. *Journal of Economic Theory* 30, 74–97.

Sorin, S. 1986. On repeated games with complete information. *Mathematics of Operations Research* 11, 147–60.

John von Neumann

GERALD L. THOMPSON

HIS LIFE. Jansci (John) von Neumann was born to Max and Margaret Neumann on 28 December 1903 in Budapest, Hungary. He showed an early talent for mental calculation, reading and languages. In 1914, at the age of ten, he entered the Lutheran Gymnasium for boys. Although his great intellectual (especially mathematical) abilities were recognized early, he never skipped a grade and instead stayed with his peers. An early teacher, Laslo Ratz, recommended that he be given advanced mathematics tutoring, and a young mathematician Michael Fekete was employed for this purpose. One of the results of these lessons was von Neumann's first mathematical publication (joint with Fekete) when he was 18.

Besides his native Hungarian, Jansci (or Johnny, as he was universally known in his later life) spoke German with his parents and a nurse and learned Latin and Greek as well as French and English in school. In 1921 he enrolled in mathematics at the University of Budapest but promptly left for Berlin, where he studied with Erhard Schmidt. Each semester he returned to Budapest to take examinations without ever having attended classes. While in Berlin he frequently took a three-hour train trip to Göttingen, where he spent considerable time talking to David Hilbert, who was then the most outstanding mathematician of Germany. One of Hilbert's main goals at that time was the axiomatization of all of mathematics so that it could be mechanized and solved in a routine manner. This interested Johnny and led to his famous 1928 paper on the axiomatization of set theory. The goal of Hilbert was later shown to be impossible by Kurt Gödel's work, based on an axiom system similar to von Neumann's, which resulted in a theorem, published in 1930, to the effect that every axiomatic system sufficiently rich to contain the positive integers must necessarily contain undecidable propositions.

After leaving Berlin in 1923 at the age of 20, von Neumann studied at the Eidgenossische Technische Hochschüle in Zurich, Switzerland, while continuing to maintain his enrolment at the University of Budapest. In Zurich he came into contact with the famous German mathematician, Hermann Weyl, and also the equally famous Hungarian mathematician, George Polya. He obtained a degree in Chemical Engineering from the Hochschüle in Zurich in 1925, and completed his doctorate in mathematics from the University of Budapest in 1926. In 1927 he became a privatdozent at the University of Berlin and in 1929 transferred to the same position at the University of Hamburg. His first trip to America was in 1930 to visit as a lecturer at Princeton University, which turned into a visiting professorship, and in 1931 a professorship. In 1933 he was invited to join the Institute for Advanced Study in Princeton as a professor, the youngest permanent member of that institution, at which Albert Einstein was also a permanent professor. Von Neumann held this position until he took a leave of absence in 1954 to become a member of the Atomic Energy Commission.

Von Neumann was married in 1930 to Marietta Kovesi, and his daughter Marina (now a vice-president of General Motors) was born in 1935. The marriage ended in a divorce in 1937. Johnny's second marriage in 1938 was to Klara Dan, whom he met on a trip to Hungary. They maintained a very hospitable home in Princeton and entertained, on an almost weekly basis, numerous local and visiting scientists. Klara later became one of the first programmers of mathematical problems for electronic computers, during the time that von Neumann was its principal designer.

In 1938 Oskar Morgenstern came to Princeton University. His previous work had included books and papers on economic forecasting and competition. He had heared of von Neumann's 1928 paper on the theory of games and was eager to talk to him about connections between game theory and economics. In 1940 they started work on a joint paper which grew into their monumental book, *Theory of Games and Economic Behavior* published in 1944. Their collaboration is described in Morgenstern (1976).

Von Neumann became heavily involved in defence-related consulting activities for the United States and Britain during World War II. In 1944 he became a consultant to the group developing the first electronic computer, the ENIAC, at the University of Pennsylvania. Here he was associated with John Eckert, John Mauchly, Arthur Burks and Herman Goldstine. These five were instrumental in making the logical design decisions for the computer, for example, that it be a binary machine, that it have only a limited set of instructions that are performed by the hardware, and most important of all, that it run an internally stored program. It was acknowledged by the others in the group that the most important design ideas came from von Neumann. The best account of these years is Goldstine (1972). After the war von Neumann and Goldstine worked at the Institute for Advanced Study where they developed (with others) the JONIAC computer, a successor to the ENIAC, which used principles some of which are still being used in current computer designs.

In 1943 von Neumann became a consultant to the Manhattan Project which was developing the atomic bomb in Los Alamos, New Mexico. This work is still classified but it is known that Johnny performed superbly as a mathematician, an applied physicist and an expert in computations. His work continued after

243

the war on the hydrogen bomb, with Edward Teller and others. Because of this work he received a presidential appointment to the Atomic Energy Commission in 1955. He took leave from the Institute for Advanced Study and moved to Washington. In the summer of 1955 he fell and hurt his left shoulder. Examination of that injury led to a diagnosis of bone cancer which was already very advanced. He continued to work very hard at his AEC job, and prepared the Silliman lectures (von Neumann, 1958), but was unable to deliver them. He died on 8 February 1957 at the age of 53 in the Walter Reed Hospital, Washington, DC.

THE THEORY OF GAMES. Without question one of von Neumann's most original contributions was the theory of games, with which it is possible for formulate and solve complex situations involving psychological, economic, strategic and mathematical questions. Before his great paper on this subject in 1928 there had been only a handful of predecessors: a paper by Zermelo in 1912 on the solution in pure strategies of chess; and three short notes by the famous French mathematician E. Borel. Borel had formulated some simple symmetric two-person games in these notes, but was not able to provide a method of solution for the general case, and in fact conjectured that there was no solution concept applicable to the general case. For a commentary on the priorities involved in these two men's work see the notes by Maurice Frechet, translations (by L.J. Savage) of the three Borel papers and a commentary by von Neumann, all of which appeared with von Neumann (1953a).

The three main results of von Neumann's 1928 paper were: the formulation of a restricted version of the extensive form of a game in which each player either knows nothing or everything about previous moves of other players; the proof of the minimax theorem for two-person zero-sum games; and the definition of the characteristic function for and the solution of three-person zero-sum games in normal form. Von Neumann also carried out an extensive study of simplified versions of poker during this time, but they were not published until later.

The *extensive* form of a game is the definition of a game by stating its rules, that is, listing all of the possible legal moves that a player can make for each possible situation he can find himself in during a play of the game. A *pure strategy* in a game is a much more complicated idea; it is a listing of a complete set of decisions for each possible situation the player can find himself. A complete enumeration of all possible strategies shows that the number of such strategies is equal to the product of the number of legal moves for each situation, which implies that there is an astronomical number of possible strategies for any non-trivial game such as chess. Most of these are bad, and would never be used by a skilful player, but they must be considered to find its solution. The *normalized* form of a game is obtained by replacing the definition of a game as a statement of its rules, as is done in its extensive form, by a listing of all of the possible pure strategies for each player. To complete the normalized form of the game, imagine that each player has made a choice of one of his pure strategies. When pitted against another a unique (expected) outcome of the game will result. For the moment we will imagine that the outcome of the game is monetary, and therefore each player gets a 'payoff' at the end of the game which is actually money. (Later we will replace money by 'utility'.) If the sum of the payments to all players is zero the game is said to be *zero-sum*; otherwise it is a *non-zero-sum* game.

The normalized form of a game is also called a *matrix game*, and any real $m \times n$ matrix can be considered a two-person zero-sum game. The row player has m pure strategies, $i = 1, \ldots, m$, and the column player has n pure strategies, $j = 1, \ldots, n$. If the row player chooses i and the column player chooses j then the payoff $a(i,j)$ is exchanged between them, where $a(i,j) > 0$ means that the row player receives $a(i,j)$ from the column player, while a negative payoff means that the column player receives the absolute value of that amount from the row player.

The importance of the careful analysis of the extensive and normalized forms of a game is that it separates out the concept of strategy and psychology in any discussion of a game. As an example, in poker bidding high when having a weak hand is commonly called 'bluffing', and considered an aggressive form of play. As a result of this formulation, and the solution of simplified versions of the game, von Neumann showed that in order to play poker 'optimally' it is necessary to bluff part of the time, i.e., it is a required part of the strategy of any good poker player. A similar analysis for simplified bridge shows that a required part of an optimal bridge strategy is to signal, via the way one discards low cards in a suit, whether the player holds higher cars in that suit.

The analysis of special kinds of games shows that some of them can be solved by using pure strategies. This class includes the games of 'perfect information' such as the board games of chess and checkers. However, even such a simple game as matching pennies shows that an additional strategic concept is needed, namely, that of a 'mixed strategy'. This concept appeared first in the context of symmetric two-person games in Borel's 1921 paper. Briefly, a mixed strategy for either player is a finite probability function on his set of pure strategies. For matching pennies the common strategy of flipping the penny to choose whether to play heads or tails is a mixed strategy that chooses both alternatives with equal probability ($1/2$), and is, in fact, an optimal strategy for that game.

We now discuss the way that von Neumann made precise the definition of a solution to a matrix game. Let A be an arbitrary $m \times n$ matrix with real number entires. Let x be an m-component row vector, and let f be an m-component column vector all of whose components are ones. Then x is a *mixed strategy* vector for the row player in the matrix game A if it satisfies: $xf = 1$ and $x \geqslant 0$. Similarly, let y be an n-component column vector, and let e be an n-component row vector all of whose components are ones. Then y is a *mixed strategy* vector for the column player in the matrix game A if it satisfies: $ey = 1$ and $y \geqslant 0$. Mixed strategy vectors are also called *probability* vectors because they have non-negative components that sum to one, and hence could be used to make a random choice of a pure strategy by spinning a pointer, choosing a random number, etc. To complete the definition of the solution to a game, we need a real number v, called the *value of the game*. The solution to the matrix game A is now a triple, a mixed strategy x for the row player, a mixed strategy y for the column player and a value v for the game: these quantities must solve the following pair of (vector) inequalities:

$$xA \geqslant ve \quad \text{and} \quad Ay \leqslant vf.$$

Because these are linear inequalities, one might suspect (and would be correct) that the optimal x, y and v can be found by using a linear programming code and a computer.

However, in the 1920s it was not clear that such a solution existed. In fact, Borel conjectured that it did not. The most decisive result of von Neumann's 1928 paper was to establish, using an argument involving a fixed point theorem, his famous *minimax theorem* to the effect that for an arbitrary real matrix A there exists a real number v and probability vectors x and y such that

$$Maximum \quad Minimum \quad xAy = Minimum \quad Maximum \quad xAy$$
$$\quad\; x \qquad\quad y \qquad\qquad\qquad y \qquad\quad x$$

This theorem became the keystone not only for the theory of two-person matrix games, but also for n-persons games via the characteristic function (to be discussed later).

We now discuss the major differences between von Neumann and Morgenstern (1944) and von Neumann's 1928 paper. The information available to each player was assumed, in the 1928 paper, to be the following: when required to move, each player knows either everything about the previous moves of his opponents (as in chess), or nothing (as in matching pennies). By using information trees, and partitioning the nodes of such trees into information sets, in 1944 this concept was extended to games in which players have only partial information about previous moves when they are required to make a move. This was a difficult but major extension, which has not been substantially improved upon since its exposition in the 1944 treatise.

A second major change in the basic theory of games was in the treatment of payoff functions. In the 1928 paper payoffs were treated as if they were monetary, and it was implicitly assumed that money was regarded as equally important by each of the players. In order to take into account the well-known objections, such as those of Daniel Bernoulli, to the assumption that a dollar is equally important to a poor man as a rich man, a monetary outcome to a player was replaced by the *utility* of the outcome. Although Bernoulli had suggested that the utility of x dollars should be the natural logarithm of x, so that the addition of a dollar to a rich man's fortune would be valued less than the addition of a dollar to a poor man's fortune, this specific utility concept was never universally accepted by economists. So utility remained a fuzzy, intuitive concept. Von Neumann and Morgenstern made the absolutely decisive step of axiomatizing utility theory, making it unambiguous and they can properly be said to have started the modern theory of utility, not only for game theory, but for all of economics and the social sciences.

Almost two-thirds of the 1944 treatise consists of the theory of n-person constant-sum games, of which only a small part, the three person zero-sum case, appears in the 1928 paper. When $n > 2$, there are opportunities for cooperation and collusion as well as competition among the players, so that there arises the problem of finding a way to evaluate numerically the position of each player in the game. In 1928 von Neumann handled his problem for the zero-sum case by introducing the idea of the *characteristic* function of a game defined as follows: For each *coalition*, that is, subset S of players, let $v(S)$ be the minimax value that S is assured in a zero-sum two-person game played between S and its complementary set of players.

To describe the possible division of the total gain available among the players the concept of an imputation, which is a vector $(x(1), \ldots, x(n))$ where $x(i)$ represents the amount the player i obtains, was introduced. For a coalition C in a constant-sum game $v(C)$ is the minimum amount that the coalition C should be willing to accept in any imputation, since by playing alone against all the other players, C can achieve that amount for itself. Except for this restriction there is no other constraint on the possible imputations that can become part of a solution. An imputation vector x is said to *dominate* imputation vector y if there exists a coalition C such that (1) $x(i) \geqslant y(i)$ for all i in C, and (2) the sum of $x(i)$ for i in C does not exceed $v(C)$. The idea is that the coalition C can 'enforce' the imputation x by simply threatening to 'go it alone', since it can do no worse by itself.

One might think, or hope, that a single imputation could be taken as the definition of a solution to an n-person constant-sum game. However, a more complicated concept is needed. By a von Neumann–Morgenstern solution to an n-person game is meant a set S of imputations such that (1) if x and y are two imputations in S then neither dominates the other; and (2) if z is an imputation not in S, then there exists an imputation x in S that dominates z. Von Neumann and Morgenstern were unable (for good reasons, see below) to prove that every n-person game had a solution, even though they were able to solve every specific game they considered, frequently finding a huge number of solutions.

At the very end of the 1944 book there appears a chapter of about 80 pages on general non-zero-sum games. These were formally reduced to the zero-sum case by the technique of introducing a fictitious player, who was entirely neutral in terms of the game's strategic play, but who either consumed any excess, or supplied any deficiency so that the resulting $n + 1$ person game was zero-sum. This artifice helped but did not suffice for a completely adequate treatment of the non-zero-sum case. This is unfortunate because such games are the most likely to be found useful in practice.

About 25 years after the treatise appeared, William Lucas (1969) provided as a counter-example, a general sum game that did not have a von Neumann–Morgenstern solution. Other solution concepts have been considered since, such as the Shapley value, and the core of a game.

One of the most interesting non zero-sum games considered in that chapter was the so-called *market game*. The first example of a market game (though it was not called that) was the famous horse auction of Böhm-Bawerk, published in 1881. The horses had identical characteristics, each of 10 buyers had a maximum price he was willing to bid, and each of 8 sellers had a minimum price he was willing to accept. Böhm-Bawerk's solution was to find the 'marginal pairs' of prices, which turned out to be included in the von Neumann–Morgenstern solution to this kind of game. Later work on this problem was done by Shapley and Shubik (1972) and Thompson (1980, 1981).

THE EXPANDING ECONOMY MODEL. Another of von Neumann's original contributions to economics was von Neumann (1937), which contained an expanding economy model unlike any other economic model that preceded it. When von Neumann gave a seminar to the Princeton economics department in 1932 on the model, which was stated in terms of linear inequalities not equations, and whose existence proof depended upon a fixed point theorem more sophisticated than any published in the mathematics literature of the time, it is little wonder that he made no impression on that group. He repeated his talk on the subject at Karl Menger's mathematical seminar in Vienna in 1936, and published his paper in German in 1937 in the seminar proceedings. The paper became more widely known after it was translated into English and published in *The Review of Economic Studies* in 1945 together with a commentary by Champernowne.

Von Neumann's model consists of a closed production economy in which there are m processes and n goods. In order to describe it we use the vectors e and f previously defined together with the following notation:

x is the $m \times 1$ intensity vector with $xf = 1$ and $x \geqslant 0$.

y is the $1 \times n$ price vector with $ey = 1$ and $y \geqslant 0$.

$\alpha = 1 + a/100$ is the expansion factor, where a is the expansion rate.

$\beta = 1 + b/100$ is the interest factor, where b is the interest rate. The model satisfies the following axioms:

Axiom 1. $xB \geqslant \alpha xA$ or $x(B - \alpha A) \geqslant 0$.
Axiom 2. $By \leqslant \beta Ay$ or $(B - \beta A)y \leqslant 0$.
Axiom 3. $x(B - \alpha A)y = 0$.
Axiom 4. $x(B - \beta A)y = 0$.
Axiom 5. $xBy > 0$.

Axiom 1 makes the model closed, i.e., the inputs for a given period are the outputs of the previous. Axiom 2 makes the interest rate be such that the economy is *profitless*. Axiom 3 requires that overproduced goods be *free*. Axiom 4 forces inefficient processes not to be used. And Axiom 5 requires the total value of all goods produced to be positive.

In order to demonstrate that for any pair of nonnegative matrices A and B, solutions consisting of vectors x and y and numbers α and β exist, an additional assumption was needed:

$$\text{Assumption V. } A + B > 0.$$

This assumption means that every process requires as an input or produces as an output some amount, no matter how small, of every good. With this assumption, and the assumption that natural resources needed for expansion were available in unlimited quantities, von Neumann showed that necessarily $\alpha = \beta$, that is, that the expansion and interest factors were equal. In his paper, von Neumann proved a sophisticated fixed point theorem and used it to prove the existence theorem for the EEM.

D.G. Champernowne (1945) provided the first acknowledgement that the economics profession had seen the article, and also provided its first criticisms. We mention three:

(1) Assumption V which requires that every process must have positive inputs or outputs of every other good was economically unrealistic.

(2) The fact that the model has no consumption, so that labour could receive only subsistence amounts of good as necessary inputs for production processes also seems unrealistic.

(3) The consequence of Axiom 3 that over produced goods should be free is too unrealistic.

Criticisms 1 and 2 were removed by Kemeny, Morgenstern and Thompson (1956), who replaced Assumption V by:

Assumption KMT-1. Every row of A has at least one positive entry.

Assumption KMT-2. Every column of B has at least one positive entry.

The interpretation of KMT-1 is that every process must use at least one good as an input. And the interpretation of KMT-2 is that every good must be produced by some process. With these assumptions they were able to show that there were a finite number of possible expansion factors for which intensity and price vectors existed satisfying the axioms. They also showed how consumption could be added into the model, which responded to criticism 2.

An alternative way of handling these criticisms appears in Gale (1956).

In Morgenstern and Thompson (1969, 1976), the third criticism above was answered by generalizing the model to become an 'open economy'. In such an economy the price of an overproduced good cannot fall below its export price, and it cannot rise above its import price. Generalizations of the open model have been made by Los (1974) and Moeschlin (1974).

VON NEUMANN'S INFLUENCE ON ECONOMICS. Although von Neumann has only three publications that can directly be called contributions to economics, namely, his 1928 paper on the theory of games, his 1937 paper (translated in 1945) on the expanding economy model and his 1944 treatise (with Morgenstern) on the theory of games, he had enormous influence on the subject. The small *number* of contributions is deceptive because each one consists of several different topics, each being important. We discuss these separately.

The expanding economy model, von Neumann (1937) consisted of two parts: the first, the input–output equilibrium model that permits expansion; and the second, the fixed-point theorem. The linear input–output model is a precursor of the Leontief model of linear programming as developed by Kantorovich and Dantzig, and of Koopman's activity analysis. This paper, together with A. Wald (1935) raised the level of mathematical sophistication used in economics enormously. Many current younger economists are high-powered applied mathematicians, in part, because of the stimulus of von Neumann's work.

The theory of games, von Neumann (1928) and von Neumann and Morgenstern (1944), was an enormous contribution consisting of several different parts: (1) the axiomatic theory of utility; (2) the careful treatment of the extensive form of games; (3) the minimax theorem; (4) the concept of a solution to a constant-sum n-person game; (5) the foundations of non-zero-sum games; (6) market games. Each of these topics could have been broken into a series of papers, had von Neumann taken the time to do so. And he could have forged a brilliant career in economics by publishing them. However, he found that making an exposition of the results that he had worked out in notes or in his head was less interesting to him than investigating still other new ideas.

Von Neumann's indirect contributions, such as the theory of duality in linear programming, computational methods for matrix games and linear programming, combinatorial solution methods for the assignment problem, the logical design of electronic computers, contributions to statistical theory, etc., are equally important to the future of economics. Each of his contributions, direct or indirect, was monumental and decisive. We should be grateful that he was able to do so much in his short life. His influence will persist for decades and even centuries in economics.

SELECTED WORKS

1928. Zur Theorie der Gesellschaftsspiele. *Mathematische Annalen* 100, 295–320.

1937. Über ein ökonomisches Gleichungssystem und eine Verallgemeinerung des Brouwerschen Fixpunktsatzes. *Ergebnisse eines Mathematische Kolloquiums* 8, ed. Karl Menger. Trans. as 'A model of general equilibrium', *Review of Economic Studies* 13, (1945–6), 1–9.

1944. (With O. Morgenstern.) *Theory of Games and Economic Behavior*. Princeton: Princeton University Press. 2nd edn, 1947; 3rd edn, 1953.

1947. Discussion of a maximum problem. Unpublished working paper, Princeton, November, 9 pp.

1948. A numerical method for determining the value and the best strategies of a zero-sum two-person game with large numbers of strategies. Mimeographed, May, 23 pp.

1953a. Communications on the Borel notes. *Econometrica* 21, 124–5.

1953b. (With G.W. Brown.) Solutions of games by differential equations. In *Contributions to the Theory of Games*, Vol. 1, ed. H.W. Kuhn and A.W. Tucker, Annals of Mathematics Studies No. 28, Princeton: Princeton University Press.

1953c. (With D.B. Gillies and J.P. Mayberry.) Two variants of poker. In *Contributions to the Theory of Games*, Vol. 1, ed. H.W. Kuhn and A.W. Tucker, Annals of Mathematics Studies No. 28, Princeton: Princeton University Press.

1954. A numerical method to determine optimum strategy. *Naval Research Logistics Quarterly* 1, 109–15.

1958. *The Computer and the Brain*. New Haven: Yale University Press.

1963. *Collected Works*, Vols I–VI. New York: Macmillan.

BIBLIOGRAPHY

Champernowne, D.G. 1945–6. A note on J. von Neumann's article. *Review of Economic Studies* 13, 10–18.

Debreu, G. 1959. *Theory of Value: an axiomatic analysis of economic equilibrium*. Cowles Foundation Monograph No. 17, New York: Wiley.

Gale, D. 1956. The closed linear model of production. In *Linear Inequalities and Related Systems*, ed. H.W. Kuhn and A.W. Tucker, Princeton: Princeton University Press. A counter-example showing that optimal prices need not exist in Gale's original model was published by J. Hulsman and V. Steinmitz in *Econometrica* 40, (1972), 387–90. Proof of the existence of optimal prices in a modified Gale model was given by A. Soyster in *Econometrica* 42, (1974), 199–205.

Goldstine, H.H. 1972. *The Computer from Pascal to von Neumann*. Cambridge, Mass.: MIT Press.

Heims, S.J. 1980. *John von Neumann and Norbet Wiener*. Cambridge, Mass.: MIT Press.

Kemeny, J.G., Morgenstern, O. and Thompson, G.L. 1956. A generalization of von Neumann's model of an expanding economy. *Econometrica* 24, 115–35.

Los, J. 1974. The existence of equilibrium in an open expanding economy model (generalization of the Morgenstern–Thompson model). In *Mathematical Models in Economics*, ed. J. and M.W. Los, Amsterdam and New York: North-Holland Publishing Co.

Lucas, W. 1969. The proof that a game may not have a solution. *Transactions of the American Mathematical Society* 137, 219–29.

Luce, R.D. and Raiffa, H. 1957. *Games and Decisions: Introduction and Critical Survey*. New York: John Wiley & Sons.

Moeschlin, O. 1974. A generalization of the open expanding economy model. *Econometrica* 45, 1767–76.

Morgenstern, O. 1958. Obituary, John von Neumann, 1903–57. *Economic Journal* 68, 170–74.

Morgenstern, O. 1976. The collaboration between Oskar Morgenstern and John von Neumann on the theory of games. *Journal of Economic Literature* 14, 805–16.

Morgenstern, O. and Thompson, G.L. 1969. An open expanding economy model. *Naval Research Logistics Quarterly* 16, 443–57.

Morgenstern, O. and Thompson, G.L. 1976. *Mathematical Theory of Expanding and Contracting Economies*. Boston: Heath–Lexington.

Oxtoby, J.C., Pettis, B.J. and Price, G.B. (eds) 1958. John von Neumann 1903–1957. *Bulletin of the American Mathematical Society* 64(3), Part 2.

Shapley, L.S. 1953. A value for n-person games. In *Contributions to the Theory of Games* II, ed. H.W. Kuhn and A.W. Tucker, Princeton: Princeton University Press.

Shapley, L.S. and Shubik, M. 1972. The assignment game. I: the core. *International Journal of Game Theory* 1, 111–30.

Shubik, M. 1982. *Game Theory in the Social Sciences: Concepts and Solutions*. Cambridge, Mass.: MIT Press.

Shubik, M. 1985. *A Game Theoretic Approach to Political Economy*. Cambridge, Mass.: MIT Press.

Thompson, G.L. 1956. On the solution of a game-theoretic problem. In *Linear Inequalities and Related Systems*, ed. H.W. Kuhn and A.W. Tucker, Princeton: Princeton University Press.

Thompson, G.L. 1980. Computing the core of a market game. In *External Methods and Systems Analysis*, ed. A.V. Fiacco and K.O. Kortanek, Berlin: Springer-Verlag.

Thompson, G.J. 1981. Auctions and market games. In *Essays in Game Theory and Mathematical Economics in Honor of Oskar Morgenstern*, ed. R.J. Aumann et al., Mannheim: Bibliographisches Institut Mannheim.

Wald, A. 1935. Über die eindeutige positive Lösbarkeit der neuen Produktionsgleichungen. *Ergebnisse eines mathematischen Kolloquiums*, ed. K. Menger 6, 12–20.

Zero-sum Games

MICHAEL BACHARACH

Zero-sum games are to the theory of games what the twelve-bar blues is to jazz: a polar case, and a historical point of departure. A *game* is a situation in which (i) each of a number of agents (*players*) has a set of alternative courses of action (*strategies*) at his disposal; (ii) there are outcomes which depend on the *combination* of the players' actions and give rise to preferences by the players over these combinations; (iii) the players know, and know that each other knows, these preferences. (Strictly, such a situation is a game of *complete information* in *normal form*: these qualifications should henceforth be understood.) In the case which dominates the literature of zero-sum games there are two players, A and B say, each with a finite set of strategies, and their preferences can be represented by von Neumann–Morgenstern utilities. The preference structure can then be displayed in a *payoff matrix*, whose (i, j)th entry (u_{ij}, v_{ij}) gives the expected utilities or *payoffs* of A and B respectively for A using his ith strategy and B using his jth. A game of this type in which $u_{ij} + v_{ij} = 0$ for all i, j is known as a *zero-sum matrix game* (henceforth simply *zero-sum game*). In a zero-sum game the players have exactly opposed preferences over strategy-pairs. Hence there is no scope for the pair of them to act *as* a pair – there is nothing for them to cooperate about. The theory of cooperative zero-sum games is thus an empty box; zero-sum games are noncooperative games, and each player must choose in uncertainty of the other's choice.

Figure 1 shows the payoff matrix of a zero-sum game ('The Battle of the Bismarck Sea'). As is conventional with zero-sum games, only the 'row-chooser's' payoff is shown. General Kenney (A) must decide whether to reconnoitre to the north, where visibility is poor (α_1) or to the south (α_2); the Japanese commander (B) whether to sail north (β_1) or south (β_2). Kenney's payoff is the expected number of days for which he will bomb the enemy fleet.

The theory of games was introduced by von Neumann and Morgenstern (1944) as part of the theory of rational action. It was to be the part that dealt with

253

B's strategies		
A's strategies	β_1	β_2
α_1	2	2
α_2	1	3

Figure 1

social contexts, in which the outcomes of concern to agents are radically dependent on each other's decisions. In such contexts characterizing the rational is problematical, as von Neumann and Morgenstern were acutely aware. The central theoretical problem is to say what A and B will do if each does what is best for him. But what is best for A depends on what B *will* do, and so, in any answer, on what is best for B. We are entrammelled in regress. To this deep problem von Neumann and Morgenstern believed they had discovered a satisfactory answer in the special case of zero-sum games. It is this answer which has made zero-sum games famous.

The power of von Neumann and Morgenstern's proposal lies in their demonstration that over a wide class of zero-sum games each of two quite independent principles of rational action gives the same answer to the question of what the players should do – and an essentially determinate one. This high degree of coherence in the theory, the reciprocal support of its postulates, may perhaps have led to too charitable a view of their individual merits. The two principles of rational action are the Equilibrium Principle and the Maximin Principle. The Equilibrium Principle says that the strategies α^* and β^* are rational only if each is a *best reply* to the other, that is, α^* maximizes $u(\alpha, \beta^*)$ and β^* maximizes $v(\alpha^*, \beta)$, where $u(\alpha, \beta)$, $v(\alpha, \beta)$ denote the payoffs of A and B respectively for the strategy-pair (α, β). 'Reply' here is metaphorical, for there is no communication. Such a pair is called a *noncooperative* or *Nash equilibrium* in game theory. Here, since $v(\alpha, \beta) = -u(\alpha, \beta)$, it is often called a *saddle-point*, for it locates a maximum of u over α and a minimum of u over β. The Equilibrium Principle has often been too casually accepted, but it has also been carefully defended (see e.g. Johansen, 1981). Von Neumann and Morgenstern saw with clarity that it can be no more than a necessary condition on rational choices by the players: *if* such choices exist they must, arguably, satisfy it, but some independent argument for this existence is needed (von Neumann and Morgenstern, 1944, section 17.3).

The Maximin Principle says that A should maximize over α the minimum over β of $u(\alpha, \beta)$ – he should 'maximin' u; and B should maximin v, or, what is equivalent, 'minimax' u. In other words, A should maximize his *security level*, where the security level of a strategy α is defined as $\min_\beta u(\alpha, \beta)$, the worst that α can bring him; and B should minimize his *hazard level* $\max_\alpha u(\alpha, \beta)$, the best that β can bring his adversary. This principle has been much criticized, and the qualified acceptance it has enjoyed owes something to its protective alliance with other elements of von Neumann and Morgenstern's theory. Their own arguments for it were suggestive rather than apodictic. It is claimed to express a rational caution in a situation in which a player has no valid basis for assigning probabilities to his opponent's decision. A second argument is also advanced, unworthy of them and justly attacked by Ellsberg (1956), according to which it is rational for A to choose by supposing he is playing the 'minorant game' associated with the payoff matrix: in this game A chooses first and B second in knowledge of A's choice (so that A is a Stackelberg 'leader'). In *this* situation rock-hard principles of decision under certainty make it rational for A to maximin. But convincing reasons for A to assume that it obtains are missing.

In the Bismarck Sea game it is readily seen that the set of maximin strategy-pairs and the set of saddle-points are the same. This fact instantiates a general fact (Theorem 1): In a zero-sum game which has a saddle-point, a strategy-pair is a saddle-point if and only if it is a maximin pair. Theorem 1 expresses the agreement of the two principles of choice. They are also effectively determinate, for we also have (Theorem 2): In a zero-sum game with a saddle-point, all maximin strategies of one player yield the same payoffs when paired with a given maximin strategy of the other player.

The significance of these results is impaired by their limitation to games which have saddle-points. Plenty do not. Von Neumann and Morgenstern's response was to seek a modest enlargement of the strategy-sets of the players of an arbitrary zero-sum game which would ensure a saddle-point. The ingenious mode of enlargement they propose is to provide the players with roulette wheels. More formally, if a player has strategies $\alpha_1, \ldots, \alpha_m$ at his disposal, it is supposed that he also has the strategy 'with probability p_1 do α_1 and ... and with probability p_m do α_m', where $p_1 + \ldots + p_m = 1$. The original strategies $\alpha_1, \ldots, \alpha_m$ are called *pure* strategies and the new ones *mixed* strategies. Now it may be shown that (Theorem 3): In any zero-sum game, $\max_\alpha \min_\beta u(\alpha, \beta) \leqslant \min_\beta \max_\alpha u(\alpha, \beta)$, with equality if and only if the game has a saddle-point. So a strategy-set enlargement which raises A's highest security level is a move towards ensuring a saddle-point. Allowing A to 'mix' his strategies is a hedging device which has just this effect. The security level of a strategy α is what A would get from it against a prescient opponent. But even such a being can only adopt one strategy. Generally, mixing raises A's security levels since, whatever that strategy is, with some probability it fails to inflict maximal damage.

The success of von Neumann and Morgenstern's manoeuvre is recorded in what is the most celebrated theorem in game theory, the so-called Minimax Theorem: Every zero-sum (matrix) game with mixed strategies has a saddle-point. The Minimax Theorem duly yields, as desired, counterparts of Theorems 1 and 2 for the class of all 'mixed' zero-sum games. The early proofs of the Minimax Theorem employed fixed-point theorems, but it may also be proved by a constructive method based on the properties of convex sets (see e.g. Gale, 1951). The main lines of this method may be gleaned from Figure 2 for the case in which A has two pure strategies.

255

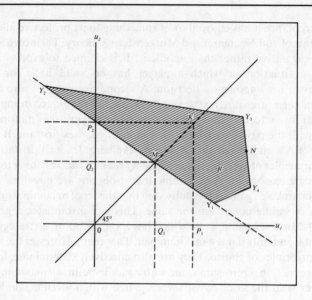

Figure 2

Let A's pure strategies be α_1, α_2 and B's be $\beta_1, \ldots, \beta_n$. Let $\mathbf{q} = (q_1, \ldots, q_n)$ denote the mixed strategy in which B does β_j with probability $q_j (j = 1, \ldots, n)$. Figure 2 shows a case in which $n = 4$. The axes measure A's payoffs to α_1, α_2 respectively. A vertex Y_j of the region R shows A's two payoffs if B chooses the pure strategy β_j, the other points of R his two payoffs against mixed strategies of B (e.g. the abscissa of the point N is $u(\alpha_1, \mathbf{q})$ for $\mathbf{q} = (0, 0, \frac{1}{2}, \frac{1}{2})$. At any point on a line like $P_1 K P_2$, B's hazard level is constant; hence B minimizes his hazard level at M (in other cases, not illustrated, the minimum-hazard point is along a side of a line of type $P_1 K P_2$ and at a *vertex* of R). At M, B is using the mixed strategy $\mathbf{q}^*(q^*, 1 - q^*, 0, 0)$, where $q^* = M Y_2 / Y_1 Y_2$; and A receives the payoff u^* say ($= O Q_1$) whatever pure (or mixed) strategy he uses. The region whose north-east border is $Q_1 M Q_2$ and the region R are both convex. Consider their separating line ℓ – the extension of $Y_1 Y_2$. It may be written $p^* u_1 + (1 - p^*) u_2 = u^*$, where $0 \leqslant p^* \leqslant 1$. Then if $\mathbf{p}^*$ is the mixed strategy in which A does α_1 with probability p^*, $(\mathbf{p}^*, \mathbf{q}^*)$ is the claimed saddle-point. For on one hand since all A's strategies give the same payoff against $\mathbf{q}^*$, $\mathbf{p}^*$ maximizes it. On the other hand, since ℓ is the specified separating line, $p^* u_1 + (1 - p^*) u_2 \geqslant u^*$ for all (u_1, u_2) in R, that is, A's payoff from $\mathbf{p}^*$ is at least u^* for all the strategies available to B.

The Minimax Theorem establishes that the agreement of von Neumann and Morgenstern's two principles of rational choice holds in all zero-sum games provided players may mix their strategies. The mixability assumption, unfortunately, is far from innocuous. Not only may randomization be excluded by the rules of a game or by physical constraint, but the idea that rational players employ it threatens downright contradiction. For the pure strategy picked out

256

by the wheel may have a lower security level than its alternatives, so that a maximinning agent has a motive to go back on his decision. This, moreover, he is in a position to anticipate.

It is worth considering briefly the empirical evidence about whether people play zero-sum games in the von Neumann–Morgenstern manner. The most important evidence is from laboratory experiments. Typically, the game situation is presented to the subjects in words, and they are invited to play a series of trials of the game for points or for small or fictitious reward: in some experiments subjects play against each other, in others against a programme. A fundamental difficulty is to make sure that subjects are solely motivated by the payoffs of the presented game, and do not 'import utilities', for example deriving utility from their opponents' payoffs. In most experiments subjects clearly have failed to choose in accordance with the theory, though sometimes a tendency has been noted for them to do so more nearly as trials progress. It should be noted that departure from saddle-point behaviour may be rational if it is rational to think that one's opponent is deviating from it. However, subjects have also typically failed to exploit programmed non-saddle-point play. They have declined, too, to avail themselves of randomizing facilities.

These experiments addressed an empirical question rather than the question to which von Neumann and Morgenstern claimed to have found an answer, that of how it is *rational* to act in zero-sum games. To the solution of the latter problem these authors made a revolutionary contribution which, however, did not dispose of it. Against the elegance, the formal satisfyingness and the pregnant originality of the von Neumann–Morgenstern theory must be set as yet unresolved doubts as to the adequacy of the pure theory of rational decision which it embodies.

BIBLIOGRAPHY

Colman, A. 1982. *Game Theory and Experimental Games*. Oxford: Pergamon.
Ellsberg, D. 1956. Theory of the reluctant duelist. *American Economic Review* 46, December, 909–23.
Gale, D. 1951. Convex polyhedral cones and linear inequalities. In *Activity Analysis of Production and Allocation*, ed. T.C. Koopmans, New York: Wiley.
Johansen, L. 1981. Interaction in economic theory. *Economie appliquée* 34(2–3), 229–67.
Von Neumann, J. and Morgenstern, O. 1944. *Theory of Games and Economic Behavior*. Princeton: Princeton University Press.

Contributors

Kenneth J. Arrow Joan Kenney Professor of Economics and Professor of Operations Research, Stanford University. Nobel Memorial Prize in Economic Science, 1972; John Bates Clark Medal, American Economic Association, 1957; Von Neumann Prize, Operations Research Society of America and The Institute of Management Sciences, 1986; various honorary degress. 'Le rôle des valeurs boursières pour la répartition meilleure des risques', *Econométrie*, Colloques Internationaux du Centre National de la Recherche Scientifique, 11 (1953); 'Existence of equilibrium for a competitive economy', (with G. Debreu) *Econometrica* 22 (1954); 'Uncertainty and the welfare economics of medical care', *American Economic Review* 53 (1963); *Social Choice and Individual Values* (1963); *Essays in the Theory of Risk-Bearing* (1971).

Robert J. Aumann Professor of Economics, The Hebrew University, Jerusalem. Fellow, Econometric Society; Member, American Academy of Arts and Sciences; Member, National Academy of Sciences (USA). 'Markets with a continuum of traders', *Econometrica* 32 (1964); 'Subjectivity and correlation in randomized strategies', *Journal of Mathematical Economics* 1 (1974); 'Agreeing to disagree', *Annals of Statistics* 4 (1963); 'Power and taxes', (with M. Kurz) *Econometrica* 45 (1977); 'Game theoretic analysis of a bankruptcy problem from the Talmud', (with M. Maschler) *Journal of Economic Theory* 36 (1985); 'What is Game Theory trying to accomplish?', in *Frontiers of Economics* (ed. K. Arrow and S. Honkapohja, 1985).

Michael Bacharach Tutor in Economics, Christ Church, Oxford. 'Estimating nonnegative matrices from marginal data', *International Economic Review* 6 (1965); 'Group decisions in the face of differences of opinion', *Management Science* 22 (1975); *Economics and the Theory of Games* (1976); 'Normal Bayesian dialogues', *Journal of the American Statistical Association* 74 (1979); 'Some extensions of a claim of Aumann in an axiomatic model of knowledge', *Journal of Economic Theory* 37 (1985); 'A theory of rational decision in games', *Erkenntnis* 27 (1987).

James O. Berger Richard M. Brumfield Distinguished Professor of Economics, Purdue University. Guggenheim Fellow, 1977–8; Sloan Fellow, 1979–81; Committee of Presidents, Statistical Societies 'President's' Award, 1985. 'Testing of a point null hypothesis: the irreconcilability of significance levels and evidence', *Journal of the American Statistic Association* (1982); 'The robust Bayesian viewpoint' in *Robustness in Bayesian Statistics* (ed. J. Kadane, 1984); *Statistical Decision Theory and Bayesian Analysis* (1985); *The Likelihood Principle: a review and generalizations* (1988); 'Analyzing data: is objectivity possible?' *American Scientist* (1988).

Simone Clemhout Professor of Economics, Cornell University. 'The class of homothetic isoquant production function', *Review of Economics Studies* (1968); 'Learning-by-doing and infant industry protection', (with Henry Wan, Jr.) *Review of Economic Studies* (1970); 'Assessment of consumer research for a valuation of a quality-of-life policy', *International Journal of Social Indicators Research* (1974); 'Policy evaluation of housing cyclicality: a spectral analysis', *Review of Economics and Statistics* (1981); 'The impact of housing cyclicality on the construction of residual units and housing costs', *Land Economics* (1981); 'A dynamic analysis of common property problems: resource exploitation and environmental degradation', (with Henry Wan, Jr.) *Journal of Optimization Theory and Applications* (1985).

Vincent P. Crawford Professor of Economics, University of California, San Diego. 'On compulsory-arbitration schemes', *Journal of Political Economy* (1979); 'Job matching with heterogeneous firms and workers', (with Elsie M. Knoer) *Econometrica* (1981); 'A theory of disagreement in bargaining', *Econometrica* (1982); 'Strategic information transmission', (with Joel Sobel) *Econometrica* (1982); 'Long-term relationships governed by short-term contracts', *American Economic Review* (1988).

Eric van Damme Professor of Economics, Center for Economic Research, Tilburg University (The Netherlands); SFB 303, University of Bonn. *Refinements of the Nash Equilibrium Concept* (1983); 'A relation between perfect equilibria in extensive form games and proper equilibria in normal form games', *International Journal of Game Theory* 13 (1984); 'Auctions and distributional conflicts with incomplete information', (with Werner Guth) *Social Choice and Welfare* 3 (1986); 'The Nash bargaining solution is optimal', *Journal of Economic Theory* 38 (1986); *Stability and Perfection of Nash Equilibria* (1987); 'Renegotiation-proof equilibria in repeated prisoner's dilemma', *Journal of Economic Theory* 46 (1989).

259

James W. Friedman Professor of Economics, University of North Carolina at Chapel Hill. Fellow, Econometric Society. 'A noncooperative equilibrium for supergames', *Review of Economic Studies* (1971); 'Noncooperative equilibria in time dependent supergames', *Econometrica* 1974; *Oligopoly and the Theory of Games* (1977); *Oligopoly Theory* (1983); 'Cooperative equilibria in finite horizon noncooperative supergames', *Journal of Economic Theory* (1985); *Game Theory with Application to Economics* (1986).

Joseph E. Harrington, Jr. Assistant Professor of Economics, Johns Hopkins University, 'Limit pricing when the potential entrant is uncertain of its cost function', *Econometrica* 54 (1986); 'Collusion in multiproduct oligopoly games under a finite horizon', *International Economic Review* 28 (1987); 'Finite rationalizability and cooperation in the finitely repeated prisoners' dilemma', *Economics Letters* 23 (1987); 'Oligopolistic entry deterrence under incomplete information', *Rand Journal of Economics* 18 (1987); 'A re-evaluation of perfect competition as the solution to the Bertrand price game', *Mathematical Social Sciences*, (forthcoming); 'Collusion and predation under (almost) free entry', *International Journal of Industrial Organization* (forthcoming).

John C. Harsanyi Flood Research Professor in Business Administration and Professor of Economics, University of California, Berkeley. Fellow, Econometric Society; Fellow, American Academy of Arts and Sciences. *Essays on Ethics, Social Behaviour and Scientific Explanation* (1976); *Rational Behaviour and Bargaining Equilibrium in Games and Social Situations* (1977); *Papers in Game Theory* (1982); *A General Theory of Equilibrium Selection in Games* (with Reinhard Selten, 1988).

Sergiu Hart Professor, Dept of Statistics, Tel-Aviv University. Fellow, Econometric Society. 'Formation of cartels in large markets', *Journal of Economic Theory* 7 (1974); On equilibrium allocations as distributions on the space of commodities', (with W. Hildenbrand and E. Kohlberg) *Journal of Mathematical Economics* 1 (1974); 'Values of non-differentiable markets with a continuum of traders', *Journal of Mathematical Economics* 4 (1977); 'Non-zero-sum two-person repeated games with incomplete information', *Mathematics of Operations Research* 10 (1985); 'An axiomatization of Harsanyi's non-transferable utility solution', *Econometrica* 53 (1985); 'Potential, value and consistency', (with A. Mas-Collel) *Econometrica* 57 (1989).

Werner Hildenbrand Professor of Economics, University of Bonn. Fellow, Econometric Society; Member, Akademie der Wissenschaften (Dusseldorf); Leibniz Prize, Deutsche Forschungsgemeinschaft, 1987. *Core and Equilibrium of a Large Economy* (1974); *Introduction to Equilibrium Analysis* (with A. Kirman, 1976); 'Short-run production functions based on microdata', *Econometrica* (1981); 'Core of an economy', *Handbook of Mathematical Economics* (1982); 'On the law of demand', *Econometrica* (1983).

Jack Hirshleifer Professor of Economics, UCLA. Fellow, American Academy of Arts and Sciences; Fellow, Econometric Society; Vice-President, American Economic Association, 1979. *Water supply: Economics, Technology and Policy* (with J.C. DeHaven and J.W. Milliman, 1969); *Investment, Interest and Capital* (1970); *Economic Behaviour in Adversity* (1987); *Price Theory and Applications* (1988).

David M. Kreps Paul E. Holden Professor of Economics, Graduate School of Business, Stanford University. Fellow, Econometric Society; Sloan Foundation Fellow, 1983–5; Guggenheim Foundation Fellow, 1988–9. 'A representation theorem for 'Preference for flexibility'', *Econometrica* 47 (1979); 'Martingales and arbitrage in multiperiod securities markets', (with J. Michael Harrison) *Journal of Economic Theory* 20 (1979); 'Sequential equilibria', (with Robert Wilson) *Econometrica* 50 (1982); 'Corporate culture and economic theory', in *Technological Innovation and Business Strategy* (ed. M. Tsuchiya, 1986, in Japanese, English version to be reprinted in *Rational Perspectives on Political Economy* ed. Alt and Shepsle, forthcoming); 'Signalling games and stable equilibria', (with In-Koo Cho) *Quarterly Journal of Economics* 102 (1987); *Notes on the Theory of Choice* (1988).

A. Mas-Collel Professor of Economics, Harvard University. Fellow, Econometric Society; Fellow, American Academy of Arts and Sciences. *The Theory of General Economic Equilibrium: A Different Approach* (1985); 'The price existence equilibrium problem in topological vector latices', *Econometrica* (1986); 'Capital theory paradoxes: anything goes', in *The Economics of John Robinson* (ed. G. Feiwel, 1988); 'An equivalence theorem for a bargaining set', *Journal of Mathematical Economics* (1989); 'Potential, value and consistency', (with S. Hart) *Econometrica* (forthcoming).

Jean-François Mertens Professor of Economics, Catholic University of Louvain. 'The value of two-person zero-sum repeated games; the extensive case', *International Journal of Game Theory* 1(4), (1971/2); 'A note on the characteristic function of supergames', *International Journal of Game Theory* 9(4), (1980); 'Stochastic games', (with A. Neyman) *International Journal of Game Theory* 10(2), (1981); 'The strategic stability of equilibria', (with E. Kohlberg) *Econometrica* 54(5), (1986); 'The Shapley value in the non-differentiable case', *International Journal of Game Theory* 17(1), (1987).

Leonard J. Mirman Professor of Economics, University of Virginia. 'Economic growth and success: the discounted case', (with William Brock) *Journal of Economic Theory* (1972); 'Risk aversion with many commodities', (with Richard Kihlstrom) *Journal of Economic Theory* (1974); 'The great fish war: an example using a Cournot-Nash solution', (with David Levhari) *Bell Journal of Economics* (1980); 'Demand compatible, equitable, cost-sharing prices', (with Yair Tauman) *Mathematics of Operations Research* (1982); 'Equilibrium limit pricing: the

261

effects of private information and stochastic demand', (with Steve Matthews) *Econometrica* (1983); 'Supportability, sustainability, and subsidy-free prices', (with Yair Tauman and Israel Zang) *Rand Journal of Economics* (1985).

Anatol Rapaport Professor of Peace and Conflict Studies, University of Toronto. Lenz International Peace Research Award, 1975; Comprehensive Achievement Award, Society for General Systems Research, 1983; Harold D. Lasswell Award for Distinguished Scientific Contribution to Political Psychology, 1986. *Operational Philosophy* (1953); *Fights, Games and Debates* (1960); *Strategy and Conscience* (1964); *Conflict in Man-made Environments* (1974); *Mathematical Methods in the Social and Behavioural Sciences* (1983); *General System Theory* (1986).

John Roberts Jonathan B. Lovelace Professor of Economics, Associate Dean, Graduate School of Business, Stanford University. Fellow, Econometric Society. 'Existence of Lindahl equilibrium with a measure space of consumers', *Journal of Economic Theory* 6 (1973); 'On the foundations of the theory of monopolistic competition', (with Hugo Sonnenschein) *Econometrica* 45 (1977); 'Limit pricing and entry under incomplete analysis', (with Paul Milgrom) *Econometrica* 50 (1982); 'Predation, reputation and entry deterrence', (with Paul Milgrom) *Journal of Economic Theory* 27 (1982); 'An equilibrium model with involuntary unemployment at flexible, competitive prices and wages', *American Economic Review* 77 (1987); 'An economic approach to influence activities in organizations', (with Paul Milgrom) *American Journal of Sociology* 94 (1988).

Zvi Safra Professor of Economics, Tel-Aviv University. 'Manipulation by reallocating initial endowments', *Journal of Mathematical Economics* 12 (1983); 'Existence of equilibrium for Walrasian endowment games', *Journal of Economic Theory* 12 (1985); 'Risk aversion in the theory of expected utility with rank-dependent probabilities', (with Chew Soo Hong and Edi Karni) *Journal of Economic Theory* 42 (1987); "Preference Reversal' and the observability of preferences by experimental methods', (with Edi Karni) *Econometrica* 55 (1987); 'On the structure of non-manipulative equilibria', *Journal of Mathematical Economics* 17 (1988); 'Efficient sets with and without the expected utility hypothesis', (with Itzhaj Zilcha) *Journal of Mathematical Economics* (1988).

Mark A. Satterthwaite Earl Dean Howard Professor of Managerial Economics, Kellogg Graduate School of Management, Northwestern University. Fellow, Econometric Society. 'Strategy-proofness and Arrow's conditions: existence and correspondence theorems for voting procedures and social welfare functions', *Journal of Economic Theory* 10 (1975); 'Consumer information, equilibrium industry price and the number of sellers', *Bell Journal of Economics* 10 (1979); 'Strategy-proof allocation mechanisms at differential points', (with Hugo Sonnenschein) *Review of Economic Studies* 48 (1981); 'Efficient mechanisms for bilateral trading', (with R. Myerson) *Journal of Economic Theory* 29 (1983); 'The rate at which a simple market becomes efficient as the number of traders increases: an asymptotic result for optimal trading mechanisms', (with Thomas A. Gresik) *Journal of Economic Theory* (forthcoming); 'Bilateral trade with the sealed bid double auction: existence and efficiency', (with Steven R. Williams) *Journal of Economic Theory* (forthcoming).

Martin Shubik Seymour Knox Professor of Mathematical Institutional Economics, Yale University. Lanchester Prize; Honorary Professor, University of Vienna. 'Edgeworth market games', in *Contributions to the Theory of Games* (ed. A.W. Tucker and R.D. Luce, 1959); 'Incentives, decentralized control and the assignment of joint costs and internal pricing', *Management Science* 8 (1962); 'On market games', (with L.S. Shapley) *Journal of Economic Theory* 1 (1969); 'Commodity money, credit and bankruptcy in a general equilibrium model', *Western Economic Journal* 2 (1973); *Game Theory in the Social Sciences* Vol. 1 (1982), Vol. 2 (1984).

Hugo F. Sonnenschein Dean and Thomas S. Gates Professor, School of Arts and Sciences, University of Pennsylvania. President, Econometric Society; Fellow, American Academy of Arts and Sciences. 'Market excess demand functions', *Econometrica* (1972); 'Do Walras' Law and continuity characterize the class of community excess demand functions?', *Journal of Economic Theory* (1978); 'Equilibrium in abstract economics without ordered preferences', (with Wayne Shafer) *Journal of Mathematical Economics* (1975); 'Cournot and Walras equilibrium', (with William Novshek) *Journal of Economic Theory* (1978); 'Price dynamics based on the adjustment of firms', *American Economic Review* (1982); 'Foundations of dynamic monopoly', (with Faruk Gul and Bob Wilson) *Journal of Economic Theory* (1986).

Gerald L. Thompson IBM Professor of Systems and Operations Research, Carnegie Mellon University. *Introduction to Finite Mathematics* (with J.G. Kemeny and J.L. Snell, 1974); *Mathematical Theory of Expanding and Contracting Economies* (with Oskar Morgenstern, 1976); *Optimal Control Theory: Applications to Management Science* (with Suresh P. Sethi, 1981); 'The pivot and probe algorithm for solving a linear program', (with Awanti P. Sethi) *Mathematical Programming* 29 (1984); 'A forward simplex method for staircase linear programs', (with J.E. Aronson and T.E. Morton) *Management Science* 31 (1985); 'A heuristic method for the multi-storey layout problem', (with B.K. Kabu and I. Baybars) *European Journal of Operational Research* 37 (1988).

Henry Wan, Jr. Professor of Economics, Cornell University. Louis Levy Medal, Franklin Institute of Philadelphia, 1981, (shared with Dr George Leitmann). With Simone Clemhout: 'Interactive economics and dynamic games', *Journal of Optimization, Theory and Applications* (1979); 'Resource exploitation and ecological degradations as differential games', *Journal of Optimization, Theory and Applications* (1985); 'Common-property exploitations under risks of resource

263

extinctions' in *Dynamic Games and Applications in Economics* (ed. T. Basar, 1986); 'A general dynamic model of bargaining: the perfect information case', in *Advances in Optimization and Control* (ed. H.A. Eiselt and G. Pederzoli, 1988); 'On games of cake-eating', in *Dynamic Policy Games in Economics* (ed. Rick van der Ploeg and Aart de Zeeuw, forthcoming); 'Differential games: the applications', in *The Handbook in Game Theory* (ed. Robert Aumann and Sergiu Hart, forthcoming).

Robert J. Weber Professor of Managerial Economics and Decision Sciences, J.L. Kellogg Graduate School of Management, Northwestern University. 'Attainable sets of markets: an overview', in *Generalized Concavity in Optimization and Economics* (ed. S. Schaible and W.T. Ziemba, 1981); 'A theory of auctions and competitive bidding', (with P.R. Milgrom) *Econometrica* 50 (1982); 'The value of information in a sealed-bid auction', (with P.R. Milgrom) *Journal of Mathematical Economics* 10 (1982); 'Distributional strategies for games with incomplete information', (with P.R. Milgrom) *Mathematics of Operations Research* 10 (1985); 'Auctions and comparative bidding', *Fair Allocation, Proceedings of Symposia in Applied Mathematics*, 33 (1985); 'Probabilistic values for games' in *The Shapley Value: Essays in Honor of Lloyd S. Shapley* (ed. A.E. Roth, 1988).

Sergio Ribeiro da Costa Werlang Getulio Vargas Foundation Postgraduate School of Economics. 'Support restrictions and sequential equilibria', (with V. Madrigal and T.C.-C. Tan) *Journal of Economic Theory* 43(2), (1987); 'The consistency of welfare judgements with a representative consumer', (with J. Dow) *Journal of Economic Theory* 44(2), (1988); 'The Bayesian foundations of solution concepts of games', (with T.C.-C. Tan) *Journal of Economic Theory* 45 (1988).